W9-CID-461

Safety Nets,
Politics,
and the
Poor

Carol Graham

Safety Nets, Politics, *and the* Poor

TRANSITIONS TO MARKET ECONOMIES

The Brookings Institution
Washington, D.C.

Library of Congress Cataloging-in-Publication data:

Graham, Carol, 1962–
    Safety nets, politics, and the poor : transitions to market
    economies / Carol Graham.
       p. cm.
    Includes bibliographical references and index.
    ISBN 0-8157-3228-7
    1. Public welfare—Developing countries—Case studies.
    2. Developing countries—Social policy—Case studies.
    3. Developing countries—Economic policy—Case studies.
    I. Title.
HV525.G73   1994
362.5′8′09172′4—dc20   94-2782
                                          CIP

9 8 7 6 5 4 3 2 1

This paper used in this publication meets the minimum requirements of the
American National Standard for Information Sciences—Permanence of paper
for Printed Library Materials, ANSI Z39.48-1984

Typeset in Times Roman

Composition by Harlowe Typography
Cottage City, Maryland

Printed by R.R. Donnelley and Sons Co.
Harrisonburg, Virginia

ⓑ THE BROOKINGS INSTITUTION

Foreword

GOVERNMENTS—and ultimately societies—must make difficult choices as they allocate scarce public resources during the painful transition from state-run to market-oriented economies. A host of countries in regions as diverse as Latin America, Africa, and Eastern Europe are attempting such transitions, most of them under fragile democratic regimes. The high social and political costs of the transition process are understandably a major concern for such regimes, particularly since many reform programs are derailed or stalled by popular opposition before their completion.

Concern over the social costs of reform has led to a variety of programs to provide short-term compensation—safety nets—for sectors of society that bear the brunt of transitional costs. But there is often an absence of consensus on who these groups actually are, as well as on what kind of safety net might best be provided for them. Indeed, concern about those opposing reform often overrides concern for the poor and vulnerable, and more vocal and organized groups monopolize the benefits of compensation at the expense of the poor. The conventional wisdom and usual practice is that trade-offs must be made between political and poverty-reduction objectives: because the poor have a weak political voice, efforts to give them a safety net will not provide governments with the political capital necessary to sustain reforms.

Carol Graham disagrees. In this book she examines these trade-offs in detail and concludes that at times they can be overcome. In reaching this conclusion, the author examines experiences with safety nets in six different countries: Chile, Bolivia, Peru, Senegal, Zambia, and Poland. The lessons that emerge should prove useful to policymakers involved in implementing economic reform as well as to scholars who are examining the process.

Carol Graham, a guest scholar in the Brookings Foreign Policy Studies program at the time of writing, is now a visiting fellow in the Vice Presidency for Human Resources at the World Bank. This project would not have been possible without the helpful comments and support of a number of people. These include Vittorio Corbo, Richard Feinberg, Stephan Haggard, Peter Hakim, Ian Hopwood, Maritza Izaguirre, Steen Jorgensen, Alexandre Marc, Branco Milanovic, Moises Naim, Joan Nelson, Dagmar Raczynski, Helena Ribe, Frances Stewart, and Stephen Webb. Special thanks are due to Alan Angell for extensive comments and moral support at several stages of the project. The author also thanks Hilary Creed Kanashiro, George Graham, Claudio Lanatta, Guillermo Lopez de Romana, and Mary Penny of the Nutrition Research Institute in Lima, Peru, for their constant willingness to share and explain valuable data from field studies in the peri-urban areas of Lima and for making the author's studies possible. Many other people, too numerous to mention, made her field studies possible in Bolivia, Chile, Senegal, Zambia, and Poland, and merit deep appreciation.

At Brookings, John Steinbruner supported the project from its inception. Charlotte Baldwin gave invaluable logistical support; Mark Lundy, Michelle Kendall, Thierry Van Bastelaer, Jennifer Boone, and Jacqueline Nolan provided excellent research assistance. Venka Macintyre edited the manuscript; Andrew Solomon and Mary Ann Noyer verified its factual content; and Stacey Seaman provided staff assistance. Robert Elwood prepared the index. Finally, the author's appreciation goes especially to her husband, John Mann, who patiently awaited her return from numerous field trips.

The author and Brookings are grateful to the John D. and Catherine T. MacArthur Foundation, the Swiss Trust Fund of the World Bank, and the Inter-American Development Bank for generous support for this project.

The views expressed in this book are solely those of the author and should not be attributed to the persons and organizations whose assistance is acknowledged, or to the trustees, officers, or staff members of the Brookings Institution.

BRUCE K. MACLAURY
President

July 1994
Washington, D.C.

For John,
to read to
Alexander

Contents

xi

Tables

Figure

CHAPTER ONE

Market Transitions and the Poor:
New Coalitions for Economic Reform?

THIS BOOK is about the many difficult choices confronting societies in transition as they attempt to allocate scarce public resources while struggling to build market economies. In particular it focuses on the role of compensation, in the form of safety nets, for needy or vulnerable groups that may be at risk during the transition. The threat to their welfare, along with the other social costs of market-oriented reforms, is now of widespread concern.

The new or newly restored democracies that are trying to implement economic reform are often overwhelmed by the demands of diverse interest groups, many of them vocal and well organized, and some eager to maintain the pre-reform system. The demands of such groups usually outweigh those of the poor and vulnerable, especially under a democratic regime, which inherently responds to the loudest and best-organized members of the public. Governments in transition do have alternatives, however: at times it *is* possible to break with common practice and focus compensatory efforts on the poor. Yet doing so means departing from another convention: instead of concentrating only on the political obstacles to economic reform, governments must recognize that such reform can create unique political opportunities for redirecting public resources to the poor.

To date little effort has been made to study the impact of safety nets implemented during economic reform—either their political impact or their contribution to poverty reduction. Broadly defined, safety nets are

1

interventions specifically designed to sustain or enhance the welfare of poor or vulnerable groups at a time of economic transition. This analysis examines the effects of such interventions in six countries: Chile, Bolivia, Peru, Senegal, Zambia, and Poland. The lessons of their experience are many. Above all, they suggest that safety nets can successfully reach the poor as well as the vocal and organized, and that wherever they have not succeeded, it is usually because of political obstacles rather than insurmountable economic constraints.

Another vital lesson is that market reform tends to challenge the position of powerful organized interest groups by removing special privileges or opportunities for profit within the public sector. This process may provide governments with opportunities to redirect public sector resources to less privileged groups. Yet market reform also usually includes measures that hurt the poor, such as the removal of universal consumer subsidies. Although these measures may free resources for programs for the poor, they tend to be viewed with suspicion by poor and nonpoor groups alike. And, as already mentioned, most democratic governments are more responsive to the demands of vocal and organized groups for compensation than to the demands of the poor.

A dilemma for governments in this situation is that on the one hand they must remain in power long enough for reforms to take hold and yield tangible benefits. At the same time, they must try to protect the groups that can least afford the negative effects of economic change. The politics of adjustment are indeed complex, for these two "imperatives" may, and often do, conflict.[1] Few governments, unless they are in unusually strong positions, are likely to ignore the demands of politically influential groups who make demands on scarce public resources. Yet allocating all such resources to vocal rather than needy groups poses a moral dilemma and is also economically inefficient. Moreover, it is unlikely that their actions will have the desired political effect of obtaining the support of organized interest groups opposed to reform. What most governments fail to recognize is that they can and should direct compensation to poorer and more vulnerable groups, and by doing so can, at times, simultaneously achieve political and poverty reduction objectives.

This book breaks with conventional thinking and posits that rapid economic reform can open up unique political opportunities for redirecting resources to traditionally marginalized groups. It also asserts that these opportunities should be used to precipitate broad social sector reforms that can be implemented *in conjunction* with the economic reform program, rather than as an afterthought, as is usually the case.[2] To build a base of popular support for such an approach, the government must make a major effort to communicate with the public, and it must attempt to incorporate the participation of the poor in safety net programs, so as to enhance their capacity to solicit and sustain resource shifts in their direction in the future. The particular balance that is achieved in compensating the vocal, the poor in general, and the very poor in particular will depend on the political context in which economic reform and safety nets are implemented, the size and relative strength of each of these groups, and the specific strategies adopted by the government.

These conclusions emerge from the case studies presented in the following chapters, which include failures (Peru, Senegal, Poland), as well as success stories (Chile, Bolivia, Zambia). Each of the studies is framed around three propositions. The first is that the political and institutional environment plays a major role in determining what kind of safety nets are implemented and who benefits from them. An open political system, for example, provides greater opportunities for building coalitions in support of new resource allocations to the poor than do highly partisan or authoritarian ones. Democratic regimes, at least in theory, are more amenable to the demands of broad sectors of society and thus are more likely to respond to the poor or vulnerable if their political voice is strong. At the same time, it may be easier for an authoritarian government to target the poorest groups because it is less vulnerable to pressure from organized interest groups (as in the case of the Pinochet regime in Chile) than a democratic regime would be. Of course, there is no guarantee that such a regime will even be concerned with the poorer sectors of society (Chile is more than likely an exception rather than the rule).

The second, which is evident from the case studies, is that safety nets can serve to enhance the political sustainability of economic reform. By demonstrating the government's commitment to addressing social welfare concerns during the often difficult and uncertain period of adjustment, safety net programs can generate popular support for the government implementing the reforms, if not for reform per se, at a critical time.[3] How and to whom benefits are allocated—if they permit the participation of previously marginalized groups, for example—will determine how widespread and sustainable that support will be.

The third proposition—that safety nets can, although they do not always, contribute to the reduction of poverty over the long term—depends, as does political sustainability, on the kinds of programs implemented. Programs in which the beneficiaries have a say are likely to be more effective in reducing poverty over the long term. A great deal also depends on who benefits from the safety nets: if vocal and organized groups benefit at the expense of the poor, there is likely to be little if any impact on poverty. However, if programs are directed only to the poorest of the poor, they are unlikely to lift many people above the poverty line and certainly are unlikely to be adopted by governments that need to respond to broader social sectors. Before safety nets can make a permanent dent in poverty, they must be linked to longer-term macroeconomic and social reform.

Safety Nets Broadly Defined

Few people doubt that the poor, or particular groups of the poor, are adversely affected by certain adjustment measures.[4] The most severe increases in poverty, however, are caused by the prolonged economic crises that necessitate adjustment; that is, extensive macroeconomic distortions, such as inflation-causing fiscal deficits and regressively distributed subsidization of consumer goods and social services, which tend to hurt the poor more than other social groups. Those countries that postpone or avoid corrective policies experience more severe economic declines, which also cause the poorest sectors to suffer disproportionately.[5] In addition, such declines can have immediate and harmful effects on distribution.[6] Thus the question for policymakers is not *whether* to adjust, but *how* to adjust in a manner that minimizes the negative impact on poverty, or, even better, that transforms plans for alleviating poverty into a strategy for attaining sustainable economic growth. Some of the safety net efforts examined in this volume provide examples of how this can be done.

Before the role of safety nets can be fully understood, it is important to note that the philosophy and objectives of market-oriented reform programs are manifested at three policy levels: macro, meso, and compensatory.[7] These policy levels may not always be distinguished in practice, however, particularly in countries with less developed institutional structures.

At the macro level, reform policy is concerned with eliminating macroeconomic distortions and with establishing sustainable growth. At the meso level, it is concerned with improving the capacity of the state to provide essential services such as primary health care and education. This does not mean that the functions of the state are being expanded, but rather that the state is getting out of the production business and into that of providing basic social welfare services. The state cannot perform these services without a certain administrative capacity and efficiency. At the compensatory level, the policy concern is to safeguard the human capital of the poor during the transition by increasing their income and other assets through targeted transfers. Such transfers are usually more politically acceptable, and probably more efficient economically, than general income redistribution.[8] Moreover, in the short term they may be easier to carry out than institutional reforms in the social sector. Nonetheless, they will still entail difficult choices about how to allocate scarce public resources at a time when economic crisis or uncertainty is affecting many others in society besides the poor.[9]

In the short term, these allocations can be made through safety nets: new and temporary programs or agencies, such as social investment funds, public works employment programs, or other income maintenance activities. In developing countries, where administrative systems are weak, safety nets rarely provide direct transfer payments. Instead, they provide services (such as employment and basic infrastructure) or targeted subsidies (such as food coupons or stamps).

Safety nets should not be confused with what the market or the state is expected to deliver; namely, economic growth and production in the first case and basic social services in the second.[10] Safety nets *cannot* substitute for coherent macroeconomic management or the effective provision of basic services.[11] These are the responsibility of the state; its capacity to deliver on these fronts will be enhanced by the elimination of distortions in order to promote economic growth and by the reform of basic state services. Both are time-consuming processes, and neither capital nor labor is as flexible as it is theoretically presumed to be.[12] Thus safety net measures are often necessary to compensate for this lack of flexibility during the transition period. Indeed, the majority of successful cases of adjustment, whether under democratic or authoritarian regimes, have included some sort of safety net program.[13]

The case studies in this volume demonstrate the use of two kinds of safety nets implemented in several countries around the world in the past two decades. The first are centrally implemented schemes for public works employment. Such schemes can be effective at targeting the very poor through self-selection, but their speed, scale, and targeting advantages hinge on whether the public sector is capable of administering the programs.[14] The second kind are demand-based social funds, which are temporary programs with some autonomy from the public sector that are often run by managers from the private sector. The funds respond to proposals from local governments, nongovernmental organizations (NGOs), and community organizations and then subcontract them to the local private sector or NGOs for implementation. By avoiding partisan politics and the state bureaucracy and by accepting proposals from the bottom up, these funds not only respond to the demand for essential services but enable the poor to participate in the formulation of proposals and thereby increase their potential political influence.

In other words, demand-based social funds establish links between the poor and the state by providing a new mechanism through which the poor can solicit services from the state. By requiring the poor to participate in and contribute to the schemes, funds avoid a host of unrealistic demands on the one hand and centrally imposed solutions on the other. One drawback to such schemes, however, is that the poorest of the poor—who are at the margins of society because of poor health, low education, or remote locations—are the least likely to present viable proposals.

Political Sustainability and Poverty Reduction Objectives during Economic Reform

The ability of governments to implement effective safety nets during economic reform depends on a variety of political factors. Some of these factors are tied in with the political dynamics underlying reform, some with the prevailing theories on the politics of adjustment, and some with the lessons of past experience. All have an impact on the political sustainability of reform and on the degree of poverty reduction.

A determining factor in sustaining economic reform appears to be the capacity of citizens to build coalitions of support that can outlast elections or other regime changes.[15] There is ample empirical evidence to suggest that authoritarian regimes are no more successful at implementing economic reforms than are established democratic ones.[16] Thus the sustainability of reform programs may hinge more on the commitment of leaders and capacity of governments to implement the programs, on the political response from influential groups in the state, and on the government's response to opposition from such groups.[17] If people are confident in the government at the time they are suffering a serious crisis, they are usually willing to accept radical and painful adjustment measures, at least temporarily.[18] All of these factors affect not only the sustainability of the reforms but also the way in which compensatory resources are allocated, as the diverse cases in this study demonstrate.

Although current theories on the politics of adjustment emphasize the role of compensation,[19] no quantitative measures are yet available to judge its impact. What is clear, however, is that compensation—usually in the form of a safety net program—is an ingredient of a majority of the adjustment programs that have succeeded, under both democratic and authoritarian auspices.[20] There is also some suggestion that the allocation of compensatory benefits is closely linked to how reforms are "packaged" and "sold" to the public. *Who* they benefit, however, will depend a great deal on the political context, a notion that is central to this volume.

That context is defined in part by the power or weight of privileged interest groups in relation to the poor. The pace and character of economic and political change greatly affect this power relationship in that they determine whether the government will be able to respond to the more vocal or the more needy groups during reform. If it implements reform measures while it has political momentum—for example, immediately after an election—it can avoid the opposition that tends to grow when reforms are introduced piecemeal. Similarly, rapid and dramatic economic or political change often provides an opportunity to redirect resources to the poor, as it temporarily undermines the positions of organized interest groups that previously had privileged access to state resources.

As mentioned, compensation also depends on the extent to which the government can communicate with and sell its reforms to the public— and also explain the benefits of new private service delivery systems to nonpoor groups.[21] Many leaders who are effective communicators have demonstrated that it is possible to implement drastic reforms in contexts where far less severe measures have caused riots or public protests.

A case in point is Zambia. The Kaunda government, on the one hand, incited public protests and even a coup attempt (in 1990) when it declared a sudden hike in the price of maize meal without any public explanation. The Chiluba government, on the other hand, campaigned on a pro-adjustment platform and before raising the price of maize took great pains to explain its reform program to the public. In December 1991 it was able to free the price of maize—and thereby allow it to quadruple—with virtually no public protest. Similarly, when Peru's finance minister, Juan Carlos Hurtado Miller, a brilliant public communicator, gave the public detailed information on the shock stabilization program implemented in August 1990 and the price of gasoline subsequently rose 3,000 percent and most basic goods 500 percent overnight, there was no public protest. In fact, Hurtado Miller remained a popular politician until his resignation a year later. In contrast, in neighboring Venezuela, when gas prices were raised by only 50 percent in February 1989 with no explanation, there were widespread riots, and more than 300 people were killed.

If leaders can convey the idea that the social costs of reform are being shared equitably, this, too, can help ensure sustainability: "while real or apparent equity is no guarantee of acceptance of austerity, obvious inequity has fueled public bitterness in many countries."[22] At the same time, the absence of social insurance or any other safety net in the face of the increasing economic uncertainty that reform initially brings may increase the public's general opposition to further economic change, while a visible mechanism to alleviate the risk of dislocation can ameliorate that opposition.[23] In Poland in late 1993 the reformist government was voted out of office in favor of an opposition group led by former communists clearly because of the public's concern over inadequate safety nets, and this reaction threatened to jeopardize the entire transition (see chapter 7).[24]

Of course, the existence of a safety net is by no means a guarantee that it will benefit the poor, as the case of Senegal (chapter 5) demonstrates. Few governments have immediate political incentives for helping the economically poor, who also tend to be poor with respect to political voice.[25] Institutions that in theory should represent the poor, such as parties and unions, rarely reach them.[26] Common sense dictates that a precarious government implementing economic reform will be more concerned with the political sustainability of its program—and ultimately with its ability to remain in power—than with finding the optimal poverty policy. Another important point to consider is that economic reform may bring previously nonpoor groups, such as displaced workers, close to or below the poverty line. These "new" poor tend to be more vocal and organized than the "old" poor and thus are the primary beneficiaries of safety net efforts during reform, even though they are less needy.

At times the most politically viable means of reaching the poor may be with programs that simultaneously benefit the "popular" or middle groups of society, who may be losing more during adjustment than the poor, although the poor have less margin for loss.[27] In some cases, such as Peru and Zambia (chapters 4 and 6), the crisis preceding adjustment as well as the necessary corrective measures are so severe that the majority of the middle groups fall below the poverty line, even though they are still at higher income levels than the old poor. Governments worry about these groups—the public sector unions, citizens' groups, and students and teachers—because they are the ones most likely to protest against adjustment policies.[28] Thus there is a strong political incentive to focus compensation on groups other than the poor during economic reform, and most governments fall right into this trap, even though the resulting programs have had an extremely bad record to date.[29]

As this study demonstrates, governments do have alternatives, however, that may be even more cost-effective than the typical strategies of compensation. From an efficiency standpoint, it makes little sense to concentrate all the government's efforts on placating those who may be losing out under the reform measures. They are unlikely to support reform in the short term regardless of the level of compensation provided, particularly when they are among the large, loosely defined group that cannot easily be compensated. Where they are concentrated in small, well-organized, and politically powerful groups, some form of compensation may be a political necessity. Yet governments can still take advantage of the political and economic dynamics created by economic reform to redirect resources to the parts of society that are excluded from state benefits. Any strategy for reaching these groups with government services is likely to have greater impact than more expensive "buy-off" schemes directed at the vocal opponents of reform, who, in any case, have probably been the primary beneficiaries of state services for some time.

Furthermore, if the economic adjustment includes the provision of needed services for the poor, they may perceive that they have a stake in the reforms, as was true in Zambia and Bolivia during their adjustments. Such a perception is far less likely to develop among groups that are receiving short-term compensation for permanent drops in income or the loss of employment. With a stake in reform, the poor can increase their political influence as well as their economic potential. The poor can vote and are numerically important, if not organized.[30] Safety net programs that give them a political voice provide new channels of access to the state. By inviting new actors to help implement the programs, such as NGOs, the government can create a new political space for the poor, garner their political support, and thereby increase their chances of sustaining the redirection of public resources. This does not imply that hard-hit middle sectors of society do not merit some form of compensation or that they will not be the focus of government attention in the future. Rather, the point is that there are compelling efficiency, political, and social welfare reasons for not focusing solely on those groups.

The feasibility of this new strategy for helping the poor becomes greater, of course, if the programs can be insulated from partisan politics. In the past, clientelism and patronage have played a large role in the allocation of government resources to the poor. But recent experience with safety net programs indicates that private sector managers, coupled with some degree of institutional autonomy, tend to implement programs in a more efficient and nonpartisan manner than these earlier programs did, and that resources are allocated according to need and project merit rather than patronage or clientelist criteria, which tend to benefit better-off groups.

The politics of who benefits from safety nets is also greatly affected by foreign financing. Foreign funds are often essential to ease the resource constraints that accompany economic reform, particularly to provide the extra investment needed to establish safety nets.[31] However, if donors alone fund social welfare programs without a prior commitment from the implementing government to indicate that it intends to sustain these programs, pressures are bound to arise to allocate resources in other directions. Once an independent political commitment is made to allocate resources to the poor, foreign funds will then be a critical factor in making the programs for the poor sustainable.[32] In the absence of such a commitment, safety net efforts are unlikely to succeed, regardless of the level of foreign financing, as the cases of Peru, Senegal, and Zambia demonstrate (see chapters 4–6).

In sum, policymakers face a great many political constraints in deciding how to allocate compensatory resources. At times these constraints may force them to allocate all the available resources to vocal opponents of reform, even if it is at the expense of needier groups. At other times they may have more room in which to maneuver. Whatever the circumstances, they must be willing to challenge conventional practice and to make major efforts to communicate with the public if their safety net efforts are to create new coalitions of support for reform *and* reduce poverty.

Getting Beyond the Trade-offs between the Old Poor and the New

The zero-sum conflict between the competing demands of the vocal and organized opponents of reform and the less often heard demands of the very poor can be resolved in several ways without having to compensate those in the middle who are affected by economic reform.[33] One way is to incorporate market principles into the delivery of safety net measures; that is, treat beneficiaries as active participants in the market for services. As in other market-oriented schemes, this strategy lets the market take care of production while enhancing the state's capacity to deliver essential services. It has been applied in Bolivia, Senegal, Zambia, and Chile (after the transition to democracy). Program participants "cease to be beneficiaries passively receiving largesse from the government, but more like customers who must be enabled to pay the costs, with their time, labor and capital, for what they see will bring about their own betterment."[34] Poverty reduction efforts that rely on beneficiary participation are more likely to be sustainable than are traditional compensation measures, such as one-shot severance pay for state workers.[35] And incorporating the participation of the poor in the design and implementation of safety net programs can give them a perceived stake in the ongoing process of economic reform.

A participatory approach also increases the political voice of the poor and enhances their capacity to solicit services and contribute to their implementation in the future. This can result in new coalitions for economic reform, which, because the poor are so numerous, can provide a counterweight to the opponents of reform. Such a strategy not only encourages the poor to speak out but also provides them with a means of self-expression and the opportunity to influence outcomes. Participating in demand-based programs usually strengthens the ties among the poor, NGOs, local governments, and the state, establishing new channels of representation. Underlying this approach to poverty alleviation is the idea that "it is not enough for the poor to act in the economic market;

they must also be able to act in the *political* market by increasing their organizational ability to influence public policies."[36]

Ideally, a competitive system with disciplined parties tends to better represent the interests of the poor and provide them with links to the state than do noncompetitive or weak party systems.[37] Yet it is difficult, if not impossible, for policymakers to create such systems, at least in the short term. Traditional political parties, many of which operate on a patronage basis, may be ill-suited to the task and have weak links to the poor. NGOs, often the groups most closely connected to the poor, are a good channel but tend to have weak links to the central state and to be limited by diseconomies of scale.[38] Decentralization of the government, a strategy that is often proposed in the context of reform, is also helpful, but on its own is not enough. Unless local power structures are also reformed, decentralization may merely allow the local elites to become more powerful.[39] In the short term, a demand-based safety net program is probably the most effective way to provide the poor or previously marginalized groups with effective channels of representation to the state.

Resource constraints and changing political views worldwide are resulting in new approaches to social welfare spending that reinforce the prospects for a strategy of targeting the poor rather than the more vocal groups in society. The focus of government spending is shifting from a wide range of subsidies for all income groups to the universal provision of only basic health and education services, combined with targeted interventions—safety nets—for the neediest groups. This shift, at least in theory, should make it easier to direct public expenditure to the neediest rather than to the more privileged groups such as organized interest groups or unionized workers. Safety nets cannot, however, substitute for broader institutional reforms in the social sectors. Yet in some cases the political changes accompanying economic reform and the related safety net programs may actually provide the impetus for such longer-term changes.

Poverty and Safety Nets during Economic Reform

The effects of economic reform on the poor have been studied at length, and one of the conclusions emerging from this body of work is that because initial economic, political, and institutional conditions differ from one state to another, economic reform—and therefore safety nets—

will have considerably different short-term effects on poverty. Those countries with severe macroeconomic distortions (such as fiscal deficits, bloated public sectors, unviable price and exchange controls, and regressive universal subsidy systems), an unequal distribution of income, and inadequate social welfare systems can be described as "inefficient inegalitarian."[40] In such cases the mere elimination of macroeconomic distortions will have immediate benefits for all sectors of society, including the poorest. For example, hyperinflation may be brought under control.[41] In "inefficient egalitarian" countries, such as those of the former socialist republics, macropolicy distortions coexist with comprehensive (but often unsustainable) social welfare systems. There, any effort to eliminate economic distortions (for example, by removing universal subsidies or trimming unnecessary public sector employment) may increase inequality and poverty in the short term, although it will lay the basis for sustained growth in the longer term.

Although the poor are rarely the most affected by adjustment, they do suffer some negative consequences and, as already mentioned, cannot afford to absorb sharp deteriorations in their standard of living. Furthermore, they have fewer options for coping with economic crisis.[42] Changes in relative prices and reductions in public expenditure on basic services probably hurt the poor more than other groups, who may be able to afford alternatives such as private health care or education.[43] The style of adjustment and ultimately growth, as well as the specific safety net measures taken, can make a great deal of difference. Costa Rica and Colombia, for example, have consistently reduced poverty with much lower overall growth rates than Brazil or Mexico have.[44] This underscores the underlying theme of the study; namely, that governments do have alternatives during economic reform—at least in the realm of compensation—and that the alternatives chosen make a noticeable difference in the final outcomes.

Another important factor to remember is that the poor do not constitute a homogeneous group. The differences between the poorest of the poor and the poor may actually be greater than the differences between the nonpoor and the poor, a distinction that was introduced into the measurement of poverty by Amartya Sen.[45] These methods combine the headcount ratio with the average income shortfall of the poor and the measure of income inequality among them (the Gini coefficient as applied to the poor rather than to society as a whole).[46] The question for all policymakers attempting to reduce poverty is whether it is better to lift the largest possible number of people at the margin of the poverty line above it, using a straight headcount measure, or to focus on improving the lot of the poorest, even if the number of people below the poverty line remains the same. This question becomes particularly complex during economic reform when displaced workers or "new poor" enter the ranks of the poor and compete with the old or structural poor (usually defined as the poorest income decile or quintile) for limited government resources.

There may be an inherent value in raising a person above the poverty line, particularly if he or she is able to sustain that position and have a positive effect on family or relatives and thereby raise the standard of living of substantial numbers of poor indirectly. The same policies that help raise the marginal poor above the poverty line—such as extra income from short-term employment provided by safety nets, or increased access to education as a result of broader policy reform—may be less effective when directed at the poorest, who may face debilitating constraints in their ability to take advantage of safety nets. If the poorest are malnourished, for example, they may not be able to take advantage of increased expenditure on education. The poorest, or structural poor, may require welfare services before they are able to take advantage of the productivity-enhancing policies that can help raise the higher-income deciles of the poor above the poverty line, policies that range from improved primary health and education services to short-term employment or credit extension. It also often costs more—in terms of resources and administrative time—to reach the poorest and to raise them above the poverty line. For policymakers implementing safety nets, political urgency increases the opportunity costs of spending disproportionate amounts of time and resources on the very poor.

This does not imply that governments should neglect the very poor. They are an easily identifiable group, and the kinds of services that they require are distinct from those of the rest of the poor. This group is usually fairly small and can be reached with small, specialized programs that are politically difficult for any group to oppose.[47] Governments should also be aware, however, that efforts to protect the poorest or most vulnerable will not raise many people above the poverty line and are likely to have marginal, if any, impact on the political sustainability of adjustment.[48] Yet the rest of the poor, whether they are new or old poor, can clearly benefit from policies linked to economic reform at the macro, meso, and compensatory levels. Safety nets can therefore have a significant impact on poverty reduction, particularly if they reach large numbers of poor, both new and old, even if they are not the very poorest, or "ultra" poor. In most cases, political realities, as well as limitations in administrative and financial resources, will probably dictate that the most effective safety net programs, at least in the short term, are those that are targeted at poor (rather than vocal and organized) sections of the population, but not necessarily at the poorest among them.

A Note about Method

The choice of countries for this study depended on whether they had introduced both market-oriented reforms and safety net programs and on the viability of conducting field research. Although dozens of countries throughout the world have attempted market reforms and most of them included some kind of compensatory element, the number with continuing reform processes *and* coherent safety net programs (as opposed to piecemeal compensatory measures) is far fewer (approximately ten to fifteen). For the purposes of this study, countries had to have at least a stable government, ongoing reform programs, and some kind of safety net program. Since regional balance was also sought, cases were selected more on the basis of what was possible than on complex or quantifiable criteria.

In addition, an effort was made to select various regime types. Not all the countries are democracies; Chile, for example, was under an authoritarian regime for much of the period covered in the case study. Senegal, meanwhile, is not a fully free democracy. Interestingly, Chile had the best record of all the countries in targeting the poorest, because the government was more insulated from the demands of organized pressure groups than a democratic regime would have been. But without beneficiary participation there was less hope of generating self-sustaining poverty reduction efforts. In addition, where regime legitimacy was in question, as in Chile and Senegal, safety nets were less likely to contribute to political sustainability. This occurred either because the programs failed to reach parts of society that did not already support the government or because in the absence of participation it was impossible to create new coalitions of support, for either the government or for reform more generally.

In cases where electoral results were available at the time safety net programs were implemented (that is, in Peru, Bolivia, Senegal, and Zambia), the results were used to gauge a program's effect on political sustainability. A correlation between per capita resource allocation or program enrollments and support for the government by a district or municipality was taken to indicate that the programs contributed to support for the government and, conversely, that program resources were being allocated according to political rather than poverty criteria. In cases where political protest was significant, as in Chile, program resources or allocation were at times affected by the location of protests.

In determining whether a correlation existed between electoral outcomes and support for economic reform programs, the results did not have to favor specific parties or governments implementing the reform, but rather the continuation of the reform policies more generally. In Chile in 1989, for example, the opposition ran on a more moderate and pro-adjustment platform than did the Pinochet government itself. In Bolivia the Nationalist Revolutionary Movement won a plurality in the 1989 election, but then lost to an opposition alliance in the congressional runoff. Regardless, pro-reform candidates garnered more than 60 percent of the popular vote.

Not all safety net programs in the study were initiated during adjustment, and thus the sequencing of programs is not always comparable. The programs in Peru and Zambia were launched before adjustment and then continued in a similar form with a change of government and the implementation of economic reform. Cases that were less than perfect had to be accepted because few comparative references exist, and because the lessons and contrasts that emerge from the "failures" are often as useful as the success stories.

The countries also vary in their levels of poverty, even within the same regions (see table 1-1). Poverty in Peru and Chile, for example, is far less similar than poverty in Peru and Senegal. Yet the cases are presented in their regional contexts because of political and cultural similarities and shared constraints in implementing reform. These shared traits are particularly significant in Africa.

The six case studies are presented in a similar format. First, the political context for adjustment is examined, then the extent and nature of poverty there. The specific safety net programs and their effects are discussed next. Finally, an effort is made to determine the impact of the local government and nongovernment institutions on both politics and poverty reduction efforts.

Table 1-1. *Basic Economic Indicators across Six Countries*

Item	Chile	Bolivia	Peru	Senegal	Zambia	Poland
GNP per capita						
1991 (U.S. dollars)	2,160	650	1,070	720	n.a.	1,790
Growth rate, 1980–91 (percent)	1.6	−2.0	2.4	0.1	n.a.	0.6
Population						
Mid-1991 (millions)	13.4	7.3	21.9	7.6	8.3	38.2
Annual growth, 1980–91						
(percent)	1.7	2.5	2.2	3.0	3.6	0.7
Infant mortality, 1991						
(per 1,000 live births)	17	83	53	81	106	15
Adult illiteracy, 1990 (percent)	7	23	15	62	27	n.a.
Population below poverty						
level (percent)[a]	41.2[b]	80.0[c]	54.7[d]	n.a.	70.0[e]	22.7[f]

Sources: World Bank, *World Development Report, 1993* (Oxford University Press, 1993); and World Bank, *Bolivia Poverty Report 1990*. The numbers for 1952–65 and 1980 are author's estimates

n.a. Not available.

a. Poverty lines are very difficult to compare across countries as they tend to be nationally rather than internationally determined.

b. Of this 1989 figure, 14.9 percent were considered indigent, and 26.3 percent were classified as poor. Indigent is defined as family income insufficient to meet basic food needs. Poor means insufficient income to meet other basic needs: a level of income less than twice that of indigence.

c. This is a rather rough estimate, since data were based in part on the 1976 census reports, which are not considered altogether reliable. Also, the 80 percent is for all those in Bolivia who are considered poor, meaning their income covers 70 percent or less of a basic needs basket. Of those who are poor, 40 percent of the total population is very poor, while another 20 percent is extremely poor. Very poor is defined as income that covers 80 percent or less of the basic needs *food* basket. Extremely poor means income covers only 30 percent or less of the basic food basket.

d. Based on monthly real adjusted food expenditures per adult "equivalent." This 1990 percentage employs a poverty line that defines as poor all households in which per capita food expenditures are below this amount. Data are for Lima only.

e. This figure can vary greatly depending on how the poverty line is defined. Using the Price and Incomes Commission's rather controversial poverty line, 42 percent of urban households were below the poverty line in 1990, and 24 percent were below the abject poverty line. Percentages of rural households below the poverty line vary from 20 percent of all households to 80 percent of the population (1989).

f. This percentage is based on 1987 data, as more recent figures are not yet available. Poverty increased after the 1989 stabilization plan.

The case studies are followed by a discussion of their lessons for policymakers implementing safety nets during economic reform. An appendix provides brief summaries of country experiences that are relevant to this study but in which field research was not conducted.

Regions of the Case Studies

The cases cover three regions: Latin America, Africa, and eastern Europe. The countries examined in the first region are Chile, Bolivia, and Peru (chapters 2–4). The African cases are Senegal and Zambia (chapters 5 and 6). Poland is the representative eastern European case (chapter 7).

Latin America

Economic adjustment and redemocratization first occurred on a wide scale in Latin America. The number of experiences—both successes and failures—and their relatively advanced stages, make the region an ideal starting point for comparing political sustainability and poverty issues during economic reform. The discussion opens with Chile, one of the first Latin American countries to undergo major structural reform and now considered an economic success. During this process, the government introduced a comprehensive, centrally implemented public employment scheme and targeted subsidies in health and education to protect the poor. Chile's social welfare indicators continued to improve throughout the adjustment period, despite the extreme nature of its economic crisis. The scale, duration, and scope of the programs suggest that they had a significant impact on the political sustainability of reform. With the initiation of sustained economic growth and the transfer to a democratic regime, the system of targeted programs has remained in place, although the employment programs were phased out. The new government is putting more emphasis on participation, as is evidenced by the implementation of a demand-based social fund, among other programs.

Bolivia implemented a shock stabilization and adjustment program in the mid-1980s under fragile democratic auspices. An integral part of the program was the Emergency Social Fund, the first multisectoral demand-based social fund to be implemented in Bolivia on a national scale. This demand-based approach to the delivery of social services has been tried throughout Latin America and in Africa, as well. Bolivia's program benefited more than a million poor in a total population of less than 7 million and contributed to the political sustainability of the adjustment process. It also fostered the development of democratic social institutions and NGOs and helped them establish a collaborative relationship with the state. Unfortunately, the program did not reach those most negatively affected by the adjustment—the tin miners—or the poorest deciles to the extent that it assisted others.

The third case, Peru, illustrates dramatic stabilization and adjustment without a safety net. Despite the draconian nature of the reform program and the marked increase in already severe poverty levels, it has drawn little if any public protest. The reason is that the political dynamic in Peru is unusual—having grown out of the severe economic crisis preceding adjustment, the exceptional communication abilities of the finance minister, and most important, the challenge from a radical guerrilla group, Sendero Luminoso. This group has provided an issue on which to evaluate the government that is of far more concern to most Peruvians than the economic reform program. As a result, the public is tolerating the social costs of reform—without a safety net—which would probably not be tolerated in other countries.

Africa

Political sustainability and poverty reduction are slightly different issues in Africa owing to the presence of poverty throughout the continent and to the limited scope of democracy. This dynamic may change, however, because of the recent political events in some countries there, coupled with frustration over the slow or stalled economic reform efforts in others. Senegal is a case in which stalled economic change and a semi-open political system have allowed privileged groups to become entrenched in positions that are opposed to economic reform and that dominate most government efforts at compensation. Participation in a demand-based social fund introduced in 1990 was severely constrained by the governing party's virtual monopoly on local government, which, coupled with the effects of constant economic policy reversals, has limited the fund's ability to reach the poor and to enhance their political voice or economic potential. Without a change in the political context in Senegal, as well as progress on the reform front, there will be little chance for safety net policies to become anything other than short-term buy-off schemes for privileged groups.

The case of Zambia is quite different. The landslide election of Frederick Chiluba overthrew the thirty-year monopoly of Kenneth Kaunda and his United National Independence Party and provided a unique opportunity to implement dramatic economic change and to redirect resources to the poor. Zambia has combined a demand-based social fund with public works employment by requiring community solicitation for projects and contributions in the form of labor. The newly open political context, as well as the government's commitment to free-market reforms, provides an ideal context for such programs. Yet because the majority of the population became impoverished during the last decade of the Kaunda regime, demand far outpaces the size and scope of the programs. At the same time, local institutions are severely underdeveloped owing to the legacy of the one-party state. Thus although dramatic political changes have provided an opportunity for economic reform and for re-directing resources to the poor, the extent of the economic decline before the change of government, the severity of poverty, and the underdeveloped nature of local institutions raise serious obstacles to sustainable reform and safety nets in Zambia.

Eastern Europe

The safety net issue is particularly complex in eastern Europe, because of the long domination of Marxist economic policies there, the absence of markets, the new and fragile nature of democracy, the fact that poverty is a new phenomenon, and the tradition of universal service provision. However, eastern Europe has the advantage of a relatively skilled work force and well-developed academic community and has received more Western attention than either Latin America or Africa. Although the inherited economic crises and poverty problems in eastern Europe are less severe than those in Latin America, the underlying structures require more far-reaching reform. The barriers to implementing adequate safety nets in the region are as much rooted in political problems as in resource constraints. Redistributive measures, for example, tend to be easier to implement in countries with unequal distribution than in those with less severe income differentials, as is typical of most countries in eastern Europe.[49]

Poland is a good representative case because of the pace of economic reform there, the recent establishment of democratic government, the initiation of decentralization, and the increase in poverty, which in the 1980s outpaced that in any of the neighboring countries with comparable economies. Widespread labor unrest and concern about the social costs of economic change have caused a strong political backlash against reform. The public's anxiety has been heightened by the lack of progress on the safety net front, coupled with the failure of successive governments to communicate proposed changes to the public. The resulting lack of consensus on how to compensate those hard hit by reform threatens to jeopardize the entire process. This case lends insight into the complexities of the safety net issue in eastern Europe and also demonstrates areas in which the social welfare lessons of Latin America might be usefully applied. Indeed, all the cases yield relevant lessons for policymakers and for academic research, as the following chapters show.

CHAPTER TWO

From Emergency Employment to Social Investment:

Politics, Adjustment, and Poverty in Chile

ONE OF THE first countries in Latin America to undergo extensive macroeconomic adjustment was Chile.[1] It emerged from that experience with strong growth rates, low inflation, and a liberal trade regime, and thus is now looked upon as a model for other countries of the region. Equally important, Chile succeeded in protecting its poor population from the extreme hardships that accompanied the adjustment. Despite the worsening income distribution and unprecedented levels of unemployment of that period, well-being—as measured by infant mortality, life expectancy, school enrollment, and literacy—continued to improve thanks to Chile's public employment and poverty programs, and to its extensive preexisting social welfare structure.

Paradoxically, the country's far-reaching economic reforms were implemented by an authoritarian regime. Free of the political constraints that would have arisen in a democratic environment, the government was able to reallocate resources from more organized sectors to poorer groups at will. Moreover, when it turned out that the initial benefits of reform fell on the wealthy and the burden on the poor and working classes, Pinochet's repressive regime was able to keep the latter at bay without some form of compensation.

Regardless, the reforms clearly could not have been sustained without Chile's extensive safety nets, which played a major role in preventing widespread social protest in the face of skyrocketing unemployment. Not only did the safety nets sustain the welfare of the poor in Chile during severe economic crisis, but they paved the way for poverty reduction once sustained growth was established in the mid-1980s.

Indeed, poverty and the appropriate government response became a central issue in the country's recent transition to democracy.[2] The debate focused on the extent of poverty, the proper methods to measure it, and the fundamental principles underlying the design of social welfare policy in general. The neoliberal view was that poverty occurs wherever individuals are unable to participate in the market economy and that it can be alleviated by meeting the basic needs of society. Others took a broader view and blamed poverty on a host of socioeconomic and cultural factors. Although these concepts are not necessarily at odds, they tended to lead to conflicting policy prescriptions. This problem can be traced in part to the political legacy of the regime that implemented Chile's dramatic structural reforms.

The Political Context

On September 11, 1973, the Chilean armed forces, led by General Augusto Pinochet, broke with a long tradition of democratic government in Chile by ousting Marxist president Salvador Allende in a bloody coup. At the time, Chile was in chaos: inflation was in the triple digits, strikes were rampant, basic goods were in short supply, and the government was at an impasse, crippled by economic mismanagement, the lack of cohesion within the governing socialist coalition, and increasingly violent behavior by extremists of both the left and the right. The Pinochet regime, which was staunchly anticommunist, became increasingly committed to the neoliberal economic philosophy of Milton Friedman and the Chicago school.[3] The regime freed itself of political constraints by brutally repressing all forces of organized opposition, such as political parties and labor unions, and pushed through a series of sweeping market-oriented reforms. The adjustment measures drastically increased unemployment, cut back social welfare benefits for all but the poorest groups, and triggered a severe recession as well as unrestricted competition from foreign

Table 2-1. *Infant Mortality in Chile, Selected Years, 1920–89*
Deaths per 1,000 live births

Year	Number	Year	Number
1920	>250.0	1972	72.7
1952	104.0	1974	65.2
1955	116.0	1976	56.6
1960	120.3	1978	40.1
1962	109.2	1980	33.0
1965	101.0	1988	20.0
1970	82.2	1989	19.0

Sources: Dagmar Raczynski and Cesar Oyarzo, "Porque Cae la Tasa de Mortalidad Infantile en Chile en Los Años 70?" Documento de Trabajo (Santiago: CIEPLAN, August 1981); and World Bank, *World Development Report, 1990* (Oxford University Press, 1990).

trade. Although the long-term economic results have been extremely positive, many Chileans focus on the costs of this progress: seventeen years of repressive dictatorship and unconstrained human rights abuses, and the dismantling of one of the most progressive and comprehensive social welfare structures on the continent.

In a national plebiscite held in October 1988, voters rejected Pinochet, who surprisingly accepted the results, as well as accepted the open presidential election that was to be held in the event of an opposition victory. In December 1989 Chileans elected Patricio Aylwin, who headed a coalition of Christian Democrats, socialists, and a number of minor parties. With the return of democratic politics, the debate on poverty and on the need for social welfare reform intensified.

Social welfare has been a policy concern in Chile since at least the 1920s. The state's involvement expanded substantially during the governments of Christian Democrat Eduardo Frei (1964–70) and Allende (1970–73). Under Pinochet, the state drastically reduced this involvement and concentrated instead on increasing basic services for the poorest members of society. Despite the reductions in per capita social welfare expenditures—which took a particularly heavy toll on those at the margins of poverty and in the middle and working classes—total spending for the poorest decile increased and, as mentioned earlier, indicators such as infant mortality continued to improve (see table 2-1).[4] In addition, benefits began reaching many of the lower deciles of the poor, who had been excluded under the previous system, with the result that in 1985, for example, 3.1 million people (or 38 percent of the population) were receiving some sort of benefit—with these benefits concentrated among the lowest income deciles—which was a particularly notable achievement in view of the record of most of the surrounding countries, where benefits were not as extensive or well focused on the poor.[5]

As social services became less of a citizen's right and flowed only to those who could not provide for themselves, the regime's policies came under fire for their *asistentialist* (paternalistic) and palliative approach. It seemed that the large-scale emergency employment programs of 1975 were as much concerned with preventing potential political destabilization as they were with meeting basic needs. Thus the lessons of this period, like its achievements, are limited by the extent to which the objectives of political control accompanied those of alleviating poverty. Nevertheless, these lessons are of interest to other countries seeking to protect their poor at a time of economic crisis or structural change. It is important to note not only how Chile made efficient use of its limited resources for social welfare, but also how the authoritarian preclusion of autonomous political initiative alienated the poor, made them dependent on the state, and often led to inappropriate policies.

The democratic regime that followed maintained the targeted policies of the Pinochet regime but also sought to improve social welfare more broadly defined, while still within a context of macroeconomic equilibrium, integrating Chile into the international economy, and fostering investment and long-term growth.[6] To ensure macroeconomic equilibrium, the Aylwin government passed a tax reform in its first few months in office that was to finance its social program. Among the early initiatives were a program to improve the quality of education in the thousand or so most disadvantaged primary schools in the country and an extensive training program for unskilled youth run out of the labor ministry.[7] In addition, the demand-based Fund for Solidarity and Social Investment was introduced to respond to proposals presented by local governments and community organizations.

Although Pinochet's efforts to alleviate extreme poverty had provided the Aylwin government with a firm basis for more comprehensive social welfare reform, the authoritarian regime had also left behind substantial barriers to demand-based, decentralized reform at the local level. Numerous questions have therefore arisen about the proper role of the government in the implementation of policies for the poor. These issues are particularly difficult to resolve in a country where openness and local participation have been absent from the political process for almost two decades: many actors are participating for the first time and are particularly vulnerable to partisan manipulation. Yet the decentralized, demand-based design of FOSIS gives it an inherent advantage in coping with political issues, as it both builds local participation into its operations and limits the potential for centralized political control. Furthermore, the program's reliance on beneficiary participation and contribution makes it more likely that poverty reduction initiatives will be sustained. Chile's present and past experience thus provides many useful lessons for future efforts to alleviate poverty.

The Extent of Poverty in Chile

Because the exact numbers are difficult to measure, the extent of poverty in Chile at the end of the Pinochet regime has been estimated at anywhere from 15 to 45 percent of the population. The Aylwin campaign referred to 5 million poor (which is equal to about 40 percent of the population), but some independent sources cite lower figures. The combined results of several studies and figures for government subsidies suggest that in 1985 the extreme poor numbered upward of 3 million, or 31 percent of the population.[8] What does seem clear is that levels of poverty correlate with employment, and that indigence, or extreme poverty, is concentrated among the unemployed or those employed in the informal sector.[9] Moreover, poverty remains a prevalent issue (see tables 2-2 and 2-3), although extreme poverty—defined as the inability to meet basic needs and measured by factors such as infant mortality—improved dramatically between 1975 and 1989, particularly when compared with the situation in the surrounding countries (see table 2-4).[10]

Despite the progress over that period in meeting basic needs such as nutrition, preventive health care (particularly for mothers and their children), and primary education, little attention had been given to such

Table 2-2. *Percent Share of Indigent, Poor, and Nonpoor Households in Santiago, Selected Years, 1969–89*

Status	1969	1979	1988	1989
Indigent[a]	8.4	11.7	22.9	14.9
Poor[b]	20.1	24.3	26.8	26.3
Nonpoor	71.5	64.0	50.3	58.8

Source: Mariana Schkolnik and Berta Teitelbolm, Programa de Economia del Trabajo, *Encuestas de Empleo: Santiago* (Santiago, 1989), p. 79.

a. Family income insufficient to meet basic food needs.

b. Insufficient income to meet other basic needs: a level of income less than twice that of indigence.

Table 2-3. *Percent Share of Indigent, Poor, and Nonpoor Workers in Chilean Work Force, 1990*

Status	Total	Employed	Unemployed
Indigent	9.3	7.3	30.8
Poor	21.7	20.8	31.3
Nonpoor	69.0	71.9	37.9

Source: Encuesta Casen, *Mideplan: Situacion Caracteristicas del Empleo en Chile en 1990* (Santiago: Mideplan, 1991), p. 45.

Table 2-4. *Infant Mortality in Five Latin American Countries, Selected Years, 1960–89*
Deaths per 1,000 live births

Year	Chile	Peru	Bolivia	Brazil	Mexico
1960	114	163	167	118	91
1965	103	131	160	104	82
1975	79	65	n.a.	n.a.	50
1980	43	88	131	77	56
1985	22	94	117	67	50
1989	19	79	106	59	40

Sources: World Bank. *World Development Report*, various years.
n.a. Not available.

Table 2-5. *Income Distribution in Chile, 1968, 1978, 1988*
Percent

Year	Quintile					Gini
	1	2	3	4	5	
1968	4.4	9.0	13.8	21.4	51.4	.426
1978	4.6	9.6	14.1	19.9	51.9	.448
1988	4.2	7.5	10.8	16.9	60.5	.525

Source: Ronald Fischer, "Efectos de una Apertura Comercial Sobre la Distribucion del Ingreso: Teoria y Evidencia," Coleccion Estudios CIEPLAN 33 (December 1991), p. 96.

other social needs as housing, curative health care, and advanced education. Per capita spending in these areas in 1986 was only 40 percent of the 1970 level, and the distribution of income in 1988 was far less equitable than it had been in 1968 (see table 2-5).[11] Since most of the new spending was targeted to the extreme poor and to the financing of the government's special employment programs, a large number of beneficiaries of the pre-1973 social welfare system either lost access or had their benefits cut substantially. Thus by 1987 as many as 2.1 million workers (more than half the labor force) lacked access to social security.[12]

Chile's labor code dates back to 1931, and its preventive health care system for workers' families to 1938. The Junta Nacional de Auxilio

Table 2-6. *Public Expenditure on Social Welfare, Selected Countries in Latin America and Organization for Economic Cooperation and Development, 1980*
Percent of GNP

Country	Social expenditure	Country	Social expenditure
Latin America		*OECD*	
Costa Rica	18.0	Germany	26.9
Chile	17.3	Canada	22.4
Brazil	11.5	Spain	14.3
Mexico	10.1	United States	16.3
Panama	13.6	France	25.7
Uruguay	13.9	Greece	14.7
Venezuela	10.2	Holland	34.8
Bolivia	6.0	Italy	29.9
Ecuador	6.1	Japan	13.2
El Salvador	6.3	United Kingdom	25.3
Guatemala	4.2	Sweden	22.0

Source: José Pablo Arrellano, *Politicas Sociales y Desarrollo: Chile 1924–1984* (Santiago: CIEPLAN, 1985), pp. 289–90.

Escolar (National Junta for Student Aid) was set up in 1952 to provide food and other essentials for low-income students, while the redistribution of income and increased expenditure on all aspects of social welfare, particularly on social security and education, became the focus in 1964–70 under the Christian Democratic Frei government. The Allende government of 1970–73 also emphasized redistribution but focused on labor rather than the middle class. Under both administrations, improvements were made in housing, curative medicine, and high school and university education. From 1920 to 1972, social welfare spending grew ten times faster than national income, providing vast coverage by the state's health, education, and social security systems. As a result, even after the Pinochet government made substantial reductions, average social welfare expenditure as a percentage of the gross national product (GNP) was comparable to that of several nations of the Organization for Economic Cooperation and Development (OECD) (see table 2-6).[13]

There was still a great deal of room for improvement in Chile's social welfare system, however. To begin with, the system was established in a rather uncoordinated fashion after decades of bargaining between certain groups of organized workers and the state. Workers in the most vital sectors of the economy, notably copper mining and the railroads, made the earliest strides and attained the most benefits. Pension and health

insurance schemes varied from industry to industry, as did the social
security benefits.

In this environment, Chile's poorer unorganized workers had little
access to social welfare benefits.[14] Either they had no way of joining the
system, or their employers failed to pay their share of the contribution,
or they were discriminated against in the granting of benefits. Only the
well-organized workers experienced any redistributive effects of the system.[15] Pinochet's military government set out to restructure the system
with two principal purposes in mind: to curb the power of organized
labor and to make the poorest groups the primary beneficiaries of the
state's social welfare programs.

Policies for the Poor under Military Rule

The neoliberal philosophy behind the restructuring was a marked departure from the traditional Chilean belief that the state should play a
progressive role in income distribution and welfare. Since the military
regime blamed poverty on rigidities in the social structure and distortions
in the functioning of the market, it saw no need to change the existing
economic and social order or to intervene in the economy. All the state
had to do was identify those groups existing below a basic standard of
living and provide them with the goods and services they needed to meet
that standard. Believing that the state's role was to provide assistance—
in the form of subsidies—for those unable to take care of themselves and
that subsidies were not designed to guarantee or enhance equity, the
regime reduced all expenditure on social welfare, both as a percentage
of GNP and per capita. Although the percentage of GNP going to social
expenditure returned to its former level by the early 1980s, in per capita
terms it continued to remain below traditional levels (see table 2-7), in
large part because of the regime's regressive wage and tax policy.[16] At
the same time, social spending on the poorest sectors increased in both
relative and absolute terms.

The regime's main objective was not only to increase the efficiency of
the social welfare system (through effective targeting of the poorest members of society) but also to decentralize it. By focusing on the poorest
groups, it hoped to correct the system's bias toward labor in the formal
sector. The targeting was directed by the National Planning Office (ODE-
PLAN). Under the decentralization plan, the government created thir-

Table 2-7. *Public Social Expenditure in Chile, Selected Years, 1969–85*
Millions of 1978 pesos

Year	Total	Per capita	Percent of GNP
1969	41,551	4,517	18.7
1970	45,330	4,853	19.8
1974	53,592	5,345	16.5
1976	40,293	3,885	16.7
1978	45,137	4,205	16.7
1980	41,968	3,779	16.6
1982	49,031	4,268	22.8
1984	n.a.	n.a.	20.7
1985	n.a.	n.a.	19.5

Sources: Alejandro Foxley and Dagmar Raczynski."Vulnerable Groups in Recessionary Situations: The Case of Children and the Young in Chile," *World Development*, vol. 12 (March 1984), p. 228; and Haindl and others, *Gasto Social Efectivo*, p. 33.
n.a. Not available.

teen administrative regions—set up by the Regional Secretariat for Co-ordination and Planning (SERPLAC) within ODEPLAN—and gradually devolved financial and programmatic responsibilities to municipal governments.[17] As a result, municipalities began administering a wide array of subsidies targeted at the extreme poor, along with the government's employment programs (discussed in the next section). Although in theory this process was supposed to achieve decentralization, municipalities were not allowed to hold democratic elections during the military years or to grant direct participation to local groups, and thus remained a link in a highly centralized chain of command.[18]

Some of the subsidies for those in extreme poverty were continuations or variations of preexisting programs, whose coverage was reduced, however, to include only the poorest deciles. Eligibility for these and the new programs was determined by a poverty index called the Ficha CAS (social stratification measurement system), which was based on household surveys conducted by municipalities. Five poverty deciles were identified under this system and a variety of criteria used to determine a person's position in them. These ranged from ownership of household appliances to education and employment, but income levels were conspicuously absent. Benefits, which were supposed to cover deciles 1–3, thus in reality usually reached only the first two. And during the economic crises of the 1970s and 1980s benefits were denied to many homeowners who were now below the poverty line or to owners of household appliances such as refrigerators and gas stoves that had ceased to function.[19]

One particularly noteworthy scheme already in existence when the military took over was the national complementary feeding program (PNAC), which was created in 1954 but had roots going back to the 1930s. PNAC benefits were available to all those covered by the national health system—namely, 80 percent of pregnant and nursing mothers, infants, and preschool children. In 1974 the program was restricted to children under the age of six and to pregnant and nursing mothers, and the caloric content of free milk was increased. This revamping of the feeding program was part of a broader policy designed to replace general food subsidies with targeted nutrition programs, such as the new Corporacion de Nutricion Infantil (CONIN). By 1985, 49.5 percent of PNAC benefits were flowing to the poorest 30 percent of the population and only 11 percent to the 30 percent at the top of the income scale. Credit also goes to the PNAC for the continued improvement in infant mortality and malnutrition during Chile's severe economic crisis, although it was but one step toward integrating nutrition and health programs, and the growth in maternal education also contributed to this improvement.[20]

Among the preschool care and education programs initiated in 1973 was the National Association of Child Care Centers (JUNJI). It provided food, day care, and a monthly subsidy of 4,000 pesos for each child in CAS level 1. Although this subsidy was a substantial amount for poor families (it equaled 60 percent of the minimum wage), JUNJI were not always well attended, one reason being cultural. Many people were unwilling to recognize publicly that someone else was taking care of their children. Another drawback was that certain JUNJIs went only to children at risk of malnutrition, with the result that a large number of poor mothers with healthy babies could not get access to subsidized day care if they wanted to work. In other cases, ironically, the material support requirements, such as certain items of clothing or minimal payment, precluded the poorest. Local participation in program implementation could have easily resolved these problems, but such an approach was anathema to the authoritarian regime.[21]

The school lunch program, created in 1964, was another one to be revamped. It covered all children from ages six to fourteen yet cost only 5 percent of the state's education budget. Nevertheless, the military regime made several attempts to reduce eligibility for the program, thereby reducing the number of beneficiaries and the amount of rations (see table 2-8). Because coverage was no longer universal, the recipients of school lunches were forced to declare their poverty publicly. Despite these cut-

Table 2-8. *School Feeding Programs in Chile, Selected Years, 1970–82*
Thousands of meals

Year	Breakfasts	Lunches or dinners
1970	1,301.2	619.2
1973	1,445.6	674.3
1976	769.8	361.0
1979	759.4	294.5
1982	759.0	295.3

Source: Foxley and Raczynski. "Vulnerable Groups in Recessionary Situations," p. 239.

backs, the program continued to function reasonably well and maintained equally good coverage in both rural and urban regions, which is a rare achievement in antipoverty programs.[22] It was able to do so because of its long history, experienced personnel, and well-established distribution network.

Housing programs underwent some of the same changes as other programs for the poor. For example, the state provision of low-cost housing was abandoned in favor of subsidies for the poorest. Lots with basic services were provided once homes were constructed by the recipients. Because the minimum required savings ratio precluded the poorest groups, at least half the subsidies leaked to the middle-income population. In addition, housing subsidies did not cover the total cost of home acquisition or construction, and the extreme poor usually lacked the credit or technical skills needed to complete a project. Furthermore, when low-cost homes were constructed by private firms, they tended to be in remote regions where it was cheaper to build, but where the inhabitants had to spend more time and money on travel and had less access to community services. With the growing concentration of poor in certain municipalities, it became more difficult for those areas to generate resources.[23] As these housing policies illustrate, the military government did as much to stigmatize and alienate the poor as it did to bring them into mainstream society.

The health care and social security systems were also revamped and tilted toward private provision for those who could afford it and state provision for those who could not. Primary health care programs focused on pregnant women, infants, and children; expenditures on secondary and tertiary care and on hospital services declined. Eligibility for free care was determined by an arbitrary income level, which left many people in the lower-middle-income groups without access to secondary and tertiary care. Preventive care was free. Pregnant women and children under the age of six received free coverage for all care. Previously, 90 percent of the population had received free care. Under the military regime, the quality of public services declined, as the bulk of resources flowed to the new private system, and more time was spent in queues in the public system. At the same time, the poorest groups—those without insurance and previously on the margins of the system—were able to attain access. The decentralization of health care administration may also have been a positive change, although at first there were problems in its implementation.[24]

Among the social security measures introduced was a network of pensions to provide minimum benefits for those without any such assistance. The disabled and the elderly whose incomes were less than 50 percent of the minimum pension also were eligible. With its partial privatization, the system became more solvent and offered access to all, not just to specific sectors. Under the previous system, benefits had little to do with contributions, which thus failed to accumulate value. Under the private system, pensions increased markedly, and payments to widows and orphans were more than twice their previous levels.[25]

Even many harsh critics of the military regime recognize its achievements in combating extreme poverty, although its authoritarian approach prevented its policies from reaching their full potential. By providing subsidies rather than investing in human capital, the government furnished merely a short-term remedy that encouraged dependence. Its programs for the poor also left much to be desired from the standpoint of incentives, as illustrated by its decision to restrict certain JUNJIs to malnourished children. At the same time, the targeting policy unquestionably "elevated the technical handling of social policies, propagating elements like the importance of diagnosing poverty situations."[26]

Emergency Employment Programs

Few programs implemented by the military regime created as much controversy as the emergency employment programs, the minimum employment program (PEM), and the occupational program for heads of households (POJH). Almost all observers agree that the special employment programs were necessary to alleviate the effects of the economic crisis, which pushed the open unemployment rate to an average 18.1

Table 2-9. *Labor Participation in Chile, by Employment Category, 1982, 1987*

Employment category	October–December 1982		March–May 1987	
	Number	Percent	Number	Percent
Employed	2,539,485	69.4	3,757,840	87.0
Unemployed	717,600	19.6	420,200	9.0
Special employment programs	403,615	11.0	164,960	4.0
Total labor force	3,660,700	100.0	4,343,000	100.0

Source: PREALC, *Empleos de Emergencia* (Santiago, 1988), p. 188.

percent between 1974 and 1982.[27] Yet they have also criticized the authoritarian manner in which the programs were implemented, which was particularly evident in PEM and POJH projects.[28] The emergency employment programs consumed a large share of the central government's social spending and of municipal resources. In 1983, at the height of the economic crisis, PEM and POJH employed close to 500,000 people, or 11 percent of the country's labor force (see table 2-9).[29]

Program History

As already mentioned, the military regime initiated the minimum employment program in March 1975 in the hope of staving off political destabilization during the economic crisis. Thus it was willing to waive its usual fiscal caution and allot a substantial amount to alleviating the rising unemployment.[30] PEM began as an improvisational response to the situation, providing extremely low-skilled work, such as street and park cleaning. As the crisis dragged on and unemployment increased, the government decided in September 1982 to set up a program for heads of households that would provide higher-skilled workers with better salaries and produce more sophisticated public works. By the mid-1980s the employment "crisis" had become less pressing and the government appeared to recognize the limited long-term benefits of its employment programs, as well as some of their negative aspects. As a result, it decided to try out a few more innovative programs, notably PIMO, which subsidized private sector hiring in labor-intensive projects; PEP, an expansion program for professionals; and a national training program for youth. As the economy recovered and unemployment gradually fell (to approximately 6 percent in 1989), the programs were phased out, PEM

Table 2-10. *Average Monthly Enrollment in Special Employment Programs in Chile, 1975–88*[a]
Thousands

Year	PEM	POJH	PIMO	Other	Total
1975	72.7	. . .	. . .	. . .	72.7
1976	157.8	. . .	. . .	. . .	157.8
1977	173.2	. . .	. . .	. . .	173.2
1978	117.6	. . .	. . .	. . .	117.6
1979	161.5	. . .	. . .	. . .	161.5
1980	203.1	. . .	. . .	. . .	203.1
1981	168.1	. . .	. . .	. . .	168.1
1982	336.5	102.8	. . .	. . .	439.2
1983	263.8	221.9	6.8	4.1	496.7
1984	170.9	207.6	13.6	19.1	411.2
1985	105.6	171.4	4.8	48.3	330.1
1986	61.4	122.8	1.0	42.9	228.1
1987	22.2	64.2	12.8[b]	5.1[b]	104.4
1988	3.5	5.3	11.4[b]	1.2[b]	21.4

Sources: Data from SERPLAC Metropolitan, Intendencia de Santiago; and PREALC, *Empleos de Emergencia*.
a. PEM: minimum employment program; POJH: occupational program for heads of households; PIMO: program that subsidized private sector hiring in labor-intensive projects.
b. Santiago metropolitan region only.

and POJH by the end of 1988 and PIMO at the end of 1989 (see table 2-10).

PEM was the largest and longest lasting of the three programs. In 1982 it employed more than 336,000 workers, or 9.2 percent of Chile's labor force. To date, it has been the largest employment program of its kind in Latin America. Its purpose was to provide temporary compensation for workers laid off in a severe recession. The program paid the equivalent of one-fourth of the minimum wage, usually for a partial day of labor. The minimum monthly wage in Chile in 1987 was approximately 12,500 pesos, or US$56, and a monthly minimum family basket in 1986 was about 8,000 pesos.[31]

To be eligible to join PEM, workers had to be eighteen or older and not receiving any other form of government compensation. They worked seven hours or less a day, five days a week. They were engaged in creating public parks, street cleaning, painting public buildings, building sanitation facilities in poor areas, and other such works. The percentage of female workers in PEM grew with time, particularly after the introduction of POJH. Fifty-seven percent of PEM workers had completed a basic education, 33 percent had a high school degree, and 5 percent had a higher technical or university degree.[32]

PEM and POJH provided the bulk of employment relief during the crisis years. POJH, which was intended specifically for heads of households, was more sophisticated in design than PEM. To be eligible for POJH, workers had to be the unemployed head of a household (not a student) between the age of eighteen and sixty-five and were to have had some stable job or profession before. Although POJH and PEM works were similar, the former differed in scale and salary was based on skill. POJH workers were also paid more than PEM workers, earning approximately 40 percent of the official minimum monthly wage (5,000 pesos, or US$36) for full-time work.[33]

The composition of the POJH work force reflects the different populations targeted. Seventy percent of POJH workers were men; 44 percent were between twenty-six and thirty-five; and 77 percent were married, widowed, or separated. Education levels in the two programs were similar, however. Fifty-five percent of the POJH workers had a primary education; 37 percent had a high school degree; and 5 percent had a university or higher technical degree. The majority (56 percent) had previously been blue-collar workers.[34] Neither PEM nor POJH workers had any sort of guarantee of job stability or social security; they were, however, eligible for the free state health care services designated for persons below a certain income level.

PIMO was initiated at the end of 1983 and, as mentioned, was designed to encourage private sector involvement in labor-intensive projects. Private firms were allowed to bid for projects selected by the central government in conjunction with the municipalities, and the successful firms became eligible for a subsidy for each post created. The subsidy could not exceed 20,500 pesos, or US$91 monthly, per post. PIMO workers came from various levels but in general were more skilled than those in the other programs and were salaried rather than subsidized. The disadvantage of PIMO was that it did not always reach out to poor groups, in part because most of the work took place in the city and usually required a certain level of skill. PIMO cost the government slightly more than 28,000 pesos a month per post; POJH averaged slightly more than 6,679 pesos per post created. PIMO generated 25,000 posts at its height, in 1987.[35]

PEP was created in March 1985 for unemployed professionals (those employed at a salary of 34,483 pesos, or US$157, a month) to fill open posts in state ministries or municipalities. Although the scale of the program was small—approximately 250 people a year—it did provide unemployed professionals the opportunity to use their skills and earn a salary more appropriate to their capacity than could have been offered by either PEM or POJH. PEP ran through the end of 1987.[36]

The national training program was established in November 1986 to train or prepare workers between the ages of eighteen and twenty-eight in special programs for entry into other jobs. From November 1986 through March 1987, when the program was phased out, 11,000 workers, primarily from PEM and POJH, completed training programs. The average cost of enrolling a worker in a ninety-day training program was 6,670 pesos. By the end of 1987 twenty-five percent of all trainees had found jobs in the private sector.[37] Given the duration and extensive nature of the special employment programs, the training programs seem to have been an afterthought of limited scale.[38] The reason for this difference is unclear, although the Pinochet regime was notably adept at responding to changing social and political circumstances.

Administration and Implementation

All the special employment programs were under the jurisdiction of the *intendencias* (regional administrations) and administered by the municipalities, which chose the works to be implemented through committees composed of the mayor, an urban adviser, the head of communal services for the municipality, three representatives from the communal union of the municipality, and two representatives from other communal groups. Although this arrangement appeared to include local participation and thus to depart from the typical centralized and patronage-based implementation of aid programs in much of Latin America, in practice it was merely a vertical extension of central authority. Mayors were appointed rather than elected, as were the representatives of neighborhood organizations. Implementation in the municipalities differed primarily in the degree of commitment among the mayors to both their municipalities and programs.[39]

In theory and in design, the special employment programs in Chile were superior to many of those in other Latin countries.[40] Nevertheless, like Chile's other social programs, they were severely limited by the authoritarian approach of the Pinochet government and in the early stages were run in an ad hoc manner by inexperienced staff, as program officials themselves admitted. Furthermore, they paid low wages, and offered little opportunity for advancement. Even at the height of the employment crisis, when the government was spending vast amounts on bailing out the failing banking sector and was providing subsidies totaling 3 percent of gross domestic product to fewer than 2,000 dollar debtors, only 1.5 percent of GDP was being earmarked for an unemployment subsidy for about 600,000 workers, while another 600,000 unemployed received nothing.[41] As a result, many saw PEM as an attempt to create a permanent worker underclass and to exercise control. People complained that negotiations for the right to work and a fair salary were "dominated by the threat of hunger and repression."[42]

At times, PEM labor was also misused. On one occasion, several hundred workers were assigned to sweep a downtown Santiago street. On other occasions, program workers were used to build projects for the military (such as an aerodrome) or for the wealthy (such as an access road to the airport for the northern suburbs of Santiago). Even so-called community improvements were often enjoyed by only a select few. In the municipality of La Cisterna, for example, the huge amphitheater built by POJH workers is now closed to the public and the football stadium they constructed is leased to a private company most of the time. The same resources could have been used to provide infrastructure such as schools, parks, and small cultural centers that would have benefited the entire community, including the workers in the program. It is little wonder that workers resented the heavy labor that went into clearing rocks from the amphitheater site. A few were even driven to try to burn the structure down.[43]

Program Effects

These negative aspects of the work programs were extremely demoralizing. Workers preferred "to do anything other than to enroll in the famous PEM . . . because it [was] the worst that there could be, like the ultimate humiliation of the worker."[44] When POJH workers were assigned to productive infrastructure works or projects that they deemed worthwhile, morale picked up, even if wages were still a quarter to half the minimum paid in other jobs.[45]

Workers also found that their association with the programs caused "irreparable damage" long after they left for other jobs. Private businesses were reluctant to hire former PEM and POJH workers, because of the poor working habits and discipline in the programs. Some even said the programs had a corrupting influence on workers.[46] In response to the growing criticism, the government introduced payment scales in POJH, PIMO, and the national training program, but the programs were still unable to shed the negative image that had been created from the start.

Despite their bad reputation, the programs helped reduce social unrest, especially since the government included emergency employment program workers as employed persons in its statistics, which made a significant difference in reported unemployment levels. This difference amounted to more than 10 percent in urban areas and was even greater in poor areas, where unemployment was much higher, as was participation in the special employment programs. In some Santiago *poblaciones* (shantytowns) up to 30 percent of the labor force was employed by PEM and POJH. Yet critics agreed that the very opportunity to work, even for an inadequate wage, had some inherent value.[47]

The employment programs also had unforeseen side effects on communities, especially on women. PEM in particular drew large numbers of women—they accounted for 75 percent of PEM participants in 1986—because the work was less physically demanding than that of POJH. More important, PEM provided women with their first opportunity to earn an income, no matter how minimal, and thus helped them escape the discrimination against female participation that pervaded the formal labor market. For female heads of households, the opportunity to earn desperately needed income in close proximity to home was invaluable. For women who were second-income earners, PEM offered financial independence for the first time. In PEM's later stages, workers were often organized into productive workshops that gave women a new avenue of social interaction in an environment where participating in autonomous organizations was often dangerous. In some communities this new-found independence created tension between men and women and caused an increase in divorces and marital problems.[48]

A Flawed Approach

These various problems stemmed not so much from the programs themselves but from the military government's approach to poverty. Because the regime defined poverty as the result of market failure and dismissed broader structural definitions, it made little attempt to link its employment efforts with its social policies. It seemed oblivious to the idea that the programs could be used to invest in human capital or to increase the capacity of the poor to generate income. Only in 1986, with the formation of the national training program, was a broader vision of the employment programs proposed. By then it was clearly too little, too late. In view of the vast resources invested in these programs and their proportionate share of social welfare spending, a valuable opportunity was lost for a long-term investment in human capital.

As the employment rate improved, the programs were phased out. Although to some extent they were thus no longer necessary, they had served another important purpose besides providing immediate relief. They had offered an alternative source of employment for the structurally unemployed, those workers (largely youths and women) who have difficulty entering the formal job market regardless of the state of the economy. There was a correlation between the programs and the level of unemployment in the mid-1980s (table 2-9). The stigma they created for program workers made it even more difficult for many of them to enter the formal sector. Consequently, underemployment rates and the size of the informal sector remained the same or grew in the decade the programs were in place.[49]

The extent to which short-term relief for the poor gives them the capacity to help themselves is one of the key measures of the success of antipoverty interventions. This was clearly not a government concern in the case of PEM and POJH. Rather, the military used these programs to exercise political control as well as alleviate poverty. Through the work programs, a segment of the poor became dependent on the state for survival and were publicly stigmatized as the sole users of state-provided employment, health services, and benefits such as school lunches. PEM and POJH, the government's most visible and far-reaching programs to subsidize income, were a central part of this strategy. By joining PEM and POJH, a worker became eligible for a group of subsidies that, if fully utilized, added up to more than a minimum wage income. Yet this net of subsidies entailed no participation, training, or communal participation in service provision.[50]

The government had little interest in sponsoring traditional community organizations, which it regarded as suspect, and indeed used PEM and POJH to discourage them. Thus those who were most active in such organizations were the least likely to participate in PEM or POJH. Many were also deterred by the government's authoritarian and deprecating treatment of workers. To make matters worse, women often suffered sexual abuse by the *capataces* (field supervisors), and workers were sometimes forced to go to Pinochet marches. And in response to PEM and POJH labor protests, such as in 1983 during a period of antigovernment unrest, the sizes of the program and enrollment levels in the communities with the highest level of protests were cut. Although this sort of manipulation of emergency employment workers has occurred in other countries, such as Peru, it created a great deal more resentment in Chile, where workers were more educated, had a history of strong organization, and were more politically conscious than most of their Latin American counterparts.[51]

The authoritarian nature of the PEM and POJH programs alarmed beneficiaries and nonparticipants alike, not to mention observers and critics in the opposition camp. Some said that "the POJH was the greatest misery that the dictatorship could have done for this country" and that all PEM did was "take a few steps, sweep the street" but did nothing positive. Many informal sector workers, who may have been earning the same as or even less than POJH income, took pride in *not* being in PEM or POJH and were happy to be their own *patrones* (bosses). That the programs left a negative impression on much of society is confirmed by former program officials themselves. In other countries, state-sponsored employment has drawn more mixed reactions, particularly among beneficiaries, at least some of whom have had a more positive view.[52]

Because of this widespread negative reaction and the fact that the regime and its municipalities were not too concerned with electoral politics, the programs were rarely used for political proselytizing, as has happened in many other countries. This view changed somewhat in the period before the 1988 plebiscite, however. Unlike the traditional party of the right (National Renovation), the pro-Pinochet party (the Independent Democratic Union) attempted to politicize the administration of the employment programs at the grass-roots level, making it virtually impossible for the regime's nonsympathizers to have any administrative role in them.[53] But their political ploy had little chance of paying off, since the employment programs were viewed in such a negative light, especially after failing earlier to encourage the political participation of the poor.

To be fair, Pinochet's emergency employment programs must be evaluated in their economic and political context, especially when comparing them with the policies implemented by Aylwin. The Pinochet programs were able to reach a great number of people and mobilize vast resources quickly in the face of a severe economic crisis. Even extreme critics of the programs admit that they provided necessary—if insufficient—income support at a time of high unemployment and social pressure.[54] Had it been a short-term crisis, the programs might have been better suited to meeting popular needs. As semipermanent institutions that drew increasing investment but lacked a basis in a longer-term strategy for social development, they instead became something of a liability.

Nevertheless, the programs did have some strong points, one being that they required work—although not always productive work—in exchange for the subsidy they provided. In the early stages, when productivity was not demanded, some argued that workers were being denied their right to make a productive contribution to society. Despite subsequent improvements, the programs remained suspect and participants were still considered lazy, unreliable, or likely to have poor work habits. Therefore it is not surprising that many former program workers remained on the margins of formal sector employment. It is important to remember the value of productivity, whatever employment or compensation programs are being contemplated. The Aylwin government has clearly kept this lesson in mind in designing its primary policy for the poor. Unlike its predecessor, the Aylwin administration has also recognized that however well designed a program may be in technical terms, its potential will be jeopardized if it is implemented in a top-down manner with no input from the beneficiaries.

Policies for the Poor after the Transition

The Aylwin government has not made any major changes in the structure of the social safety net since it was elected in March 1990. It did take immediate steps to make the tax system more progressive by slightly increasing taxes on the wealthiest sectors and directed all the revenue generated therefrom at social sector spending, which then increased by 10 percent. This move has had positive distributional effects. During the Pinochet period the income share of the bottom 40 percent declined, on average, by 1.5 percentage points in relation to the 1960–73 period, a drop of nearly 14 percent in the income share of that group. During its first two years the Aylwin government has reversed that trend: the share of the bottom 40 percent has increased by 1 percentage point in comparison with the Pinochet period.[55] The Aylwin government has also maintained its focus on the very poor: the two poorest quintiles received 65 percent of new social expenditure in 1990.[56] In addition, the government introduced a reform of the labor code, raised the minimum wage, and announced its intention to improve the quality of public education and to provide vocational training for unskilled youth.[57] The government also raised family allowances and subsidies for the poorest sectors.[58] This, coupled with relatively high growth rates, resulted in a decrease in the percentage of the population below the poverty line, from 45 percent in 1988 to 33–35 percent in 1992.[59]

A major innovation for the poor under the Aylwin government is, as mentioned earlier, the Fund for Solidarity and Social Investment (FOSIS). Although the program is still too new to evaluate, FOSIS is a clearly marked departure from the previous government's policy toward the poor. At the same time, it builds upon the existing social safety net, which continues to be administered through the relevant ministries, as well as on the relatively strong economic base inherited from the military regime. In addition, it builds on the experience of the military government with a centrally run employment scheme and on the recent experiences of other countries, such as Bolivia, with decentralized social investment funds.

FOSIS is an autonomous fund set up within the planning ministry (MIDEPLAN, successor to ODEPLAN) to respond to low-income communities' proposals for social welfare infrastructure and credit and technical support for productive activities, such as microenterprises. The proposals, which come from local governments and nongovernmental organizations, must meet specific technical criteria, and usually the projects also entail some sort of voluntary community participation. The demand-based design of the program not only encourages but depends on community participation. Such participation is vital because it ensures that projects are appropriate to local needs and thus increases their sustainability. And, by legitimizing the participation of the poor in bettering their communities and generating employment, it enhances their capacity to make the difficult progression from poverty to integration into the productive economy.

From the beginning, the creators of FOSIS decided to adopt a far different approach to poverty than the military regime had taken. Most of them were specialists in either poverty alleviation or employment and had years of experience in either international organizations or respected research institutes in Chile. They were just as aware of the need for fiscal constraint and long-term economic viability as their military predecessors, but they were also concerned with helping the poor overcome the many barriers that exclude them from the productive economy: notably the lack of access to credit, technology, and training; and the lack of projects that would improve the quality of life in poor communities, such as community centers, continuing support for preventive health care, recreational and cultural activities, training courses for community workers, and access to information about rights, resources, and services.[60]

The structure of FOSIS resembles that of social investment funds in other countries. It is an independent entity in the state planning ministry, and the executive director is appointed by and is directly accountable to the president of the republic. Although FOSIS is committed to cooperative work with the sector ministries, this independent status gives it a flexible and heterogeneous character that sectoral ministries do not have. Ironically, because ministries are efficient in Chile and have clearly delineated responsibilities, FOSIS had some initial difficulties establishing its relationship to them, with the result that there were some delays in launching the program. The budget for 1991 was US$19.5 million, with more than half the funds coming from foreign donors (who gave less than initially expected) and the rest from the tax reform. The staff is small (thirty-seven people), highly trained, and deeply committed to the cause of alleviating poverty. Such a combination proved to be highly effective in the case of Bolivia's Emergency Social Fund (ESF), but it is too early to say how FOSIS staff will perform. For now, they appear to be operating in an efficient and transparent manner. By the end of 1991, FOSIS had implemented 1,500 projects countrywide and had held several public "concursos," or meetings, to promote participation in its projects in shantytowns throughout Chile.[61]

FOSIS operates on three basic assumptions. First, state action is needed to ameliorate the effects of several years of economic adjustment. Second, this action should take place outside the traditional social welfare activities of the state, in view of the obvious limits of the authoritarian state and the need to incorporate local participation. Third, the state's approach to alleviating poverty has been limited and inflexible.

The design of FOSIS was heavily influenced by recent international experience with multisectoral development funds. Such funds are a response to the decline in state resources, the new emphasis on the role of the market in Latin America, and the need for local input in the design of aid or antipoverty programs. They are "a sort of synthesis of the participatory thesis of the more progressive sectors of society with the thesis of the subsidizing nature of the state, propounded by the neoliberals."[62] The funds act as complements to mainstream sectoral services—which have established institutions, infrastructure, and income-enhancing goals—but their ability to contribute to poverty alleviation over the long term hinges on the renewal of growth after adjustment. Proposed social welfare projects must not only provide for community or individual participation and support but also demonstrate post-FOSIS viability. FOSIS can react to the heterogeneous and decentralized nature of poverty in a way that is not possible for the state, which has to provide a certain basic and standard level of social welfare. Both areas of FOSIS activity, social development and support for productive enterprises, can be considered an investment in society: the former in health and welfare and the latter in people's capacity to generate their own income and means of support.

FOSIS has an advantage over similar funds in other countries. Its mission is to establish a new state role in social assistance, whereas many of its counterparts, such as Bolivia's Emergency Social Fund, are trying to establish an effective state role where none existed. Such funds are therefore forced to operate outside the sectoral ministries. In this sense, FOSIS has a unique flexibility to support innovation in productive and social welfare activities, because basic health, education, and other social services for the poor are already available.

FOSIS also has a strong base of nongovernmental organizations to rely on. Unlike Bolivia, where NGOs are relatively new and have yet to develop a cooperative relationship with state programs, Chile has many NGOs with a long tradition of involvement in social welfare policy. Church groups, too, are active in social welfare projects. Decentralization created some opportunities for these groups to participate in health, education, and housing, although these opportunities were, of course, limited by political considerations.[63] With the transition to democracy and the introduction of FOSIS, Chile's NGOs entered a new stage of collaboration with the government.

This is not to say that FOSIS will not face some of the same problems that plague other funds and antipoverty programs in developing countries. One major problem is that the very poor are the least organized and least able to solicit a demand-based aid program. Although FOSIS design has already taken this aspect of poverty into account, programs will still depend on local demand. Since Chile has ample information on the very poor and where they live, FOSIS will also operate with a "poverty map"; it will focus on both rural and urban poverty, and will direct its activities to regions as well as population groups. It will sponsor locally presented projects but will also have a bank of its own projects. And it will try to help some of the poorest communities present and execute projects. Thus while the most destitute may not be direct beneficiaries, some of the poorest communities will probably be reached, with the resulting projects likely to benefit most members of the communities.

Another problem, which is a legacy of the authoritarian regime, is that local government is extremely underdeveloped. For the first two years of the Aylwin government, mayors were not directly elected; and municipal elections were not held until June 30, 1992.[64] This means it will be difficult to incorporate the local participation that FOSIS requires.

At the same time, by their very nature democratic government and party politics create a constant pressure to allow partisan or political criteria to enter into program operation at both the local and central government levels. In the multiparty structure of the current government, an appointment such as the FOSIS directorship can create intraparty competition and may have played a role in the delay to appoint a successor to the fund's first executive director, Nicolas Flaño, when he resigned in December 1990.[65] Of course, the Fund has also had to take time to define its role in a highly structured, well-defined ministerial system.

Although its budget is no more than 1 percent of public social expenditure, FOSIS is becoming known among the *pobladores* (shantytown dwellers) and thereby increasing its political salience. Even so, its operations criteria remain technical rather than political. The extent to which partisan politics will affect FOSIS will depend to a large extent on local actors and organizations, but for the moment the autonomous pobladores' organizations are usually formed for functional rather than partisan reasons, which still play only a small role. NGOs, the main focus of FOSIS activity, are usually oriented to the left, and that certainly puts political pressure on FOSIS from critics on the right.[66] In any case, party politics at the poblador level are extremely complex and their full effect on FOSIS is as yet unclear.

Municipalities in Transition

To a large extent, municipal governments in Chile, as in most Latin American nations, have traditionally depended on the central government, both financially and administratively.[67] In theory, the military government's municipal reform laws opened the door to decentralized government by allowing municipalities to generate their own resources and hire additional technical and professional personnel. These laws also guaranteed certain fiscal transfers to the municipalities and established the common municipal fund (Fundo Comun Municipal), through which wealthier municipalities transferred resources to poorer ones.[68]

The military government's policies for the poor relied on municipalities to identify beneficiaries—through social action committees and criteria based on the Ficha CAS—and then to distribute the subsidies and provide the services. Although most of these resources were tied to specific tasks, municipalities also received lump sums for the implementation of the special employment programs and were given quite a bit of freedom to design and implement projects, as long as they adhered to certain standards regarding wage levels and the allocation of expenditures. These resources were by no means insignificant: at times they accounted for 30 to 90 percent of the total budgets of poor municipalities. Moreover, PEM and POJH workers were often used to make up for shortfalls in municipal personnel. As a result, many feared that municipal services would deteriorate after the special programs ended.[69]

Despite these efforts, complete decentralization never occurred: "Political participation, expression of demand, and local participation in investment decision-making . . . atrophied in Chile whereas in other countries, consultative process and negotiation formed part of . . . the evolution of decentralization strategies."[70]

During most of the Pinochet regime, all mayors were appointed by the central government. Although a new municipal law passed in 1988 transferred the right to the Community Development Council (CODECO) of each municipality, the mayors of the fifteen most populous cities still had to be directly appointed by the central government. The CODECO system, with its centrally appointed members, had been introduced by the military regime (before the coup "regidores," or local officials, were elected). Approximately half of these members were private sector representatives and half were Junta Vecinal (neighborhood organization) leaders and other neighborhood representatives. Functional organizations such as unions and political parties were denied access. Thus in 1988 more than 300 mayors in some of the poorest communities were appointed by the state for a term of office that went well beyond the 1990 transition to the Aylwin regime. Critics justifiably saw the 1988 municipal "reform" law as an attempt by the Pinochet regime to control the transition to democracy at the local level.[71]

Within the municipalities, the mayors had ultimate authority: they were "mini-Pinochets" who had complete control over the allocation of employment program resources. Indeed, the implementation of the programs varied with the personal goals or traits of the mayor.[72] However, community development was not among these goals. In general, mayors favored large infrastructural activities with high visibility, such as the amphitheater and football stadium in La Cisterna, rather than those with a training or social component.

The relationship between municipalities and communities as they carried out social policy was one of *asistentialism* and dependency. Their role was to identify the people who were in extreme poverty and to channel government subsidies to them. Municipal workers themselves were frustrated with the situation, which they described as being "of an emergency and 'window dressing' nature" and "pure giving and giving" without "training or development," in a word, without participation from below.[73]

Although FOSIS is guided by a different social policy, which emphasizes community participation, until recently its personnel had to contend with the remnants of the old structure. The new Junta Vecinales directors, most of whom were participating in politics for the first time in sixteen years, if not the first time ever, had to deal with mayors appointed by authoritarian bodies that were hardly accustomed to listening to demands from below, and the relationship between them was often antagonistic, at times even violent.[74] Thus it was by no means easy to introduce community participation. Even after the municipal elections of 1992 and the departure of the Pinochet-appointed officials, some community organizations that were not of the same political leaning as their mayors were more marginalized than ever.[75] If these circumstances continue, FOSIS may have to bypass or operate outside the municipal realm, but such a move could jeopardize Chile's coordinated efforts to alleviate poverty, as well as to carry through longer-term decentralization.

The transition has been slow in part because Aylwin had to delay municipal elections until his new government could reform the municipal law. A great deal of debate ensued as political parties vied for the formula that best suited their electoral chances. Under the law approved by the Senate in January 1992, Chile is required to hold direct elections for municipal councils. The size of the councils depends on the local population, and council members are required to elect the mayor if one candidate does not receive a sufficient proportion of total votes.

The main actors in the parliamentary debate over reform were the Party for Democracy (PPD) and the socialists on the left and the Independent Democratic Union (UDI) on the right. The same parties were competing at the municipal level. The left has long been active at the grass-roots level, but the UDI also ran a strong grass-roots campaign during the 1988 plebiscite and the 1989 elections in the hope of keeping its candidates in office, many of whom had received their appointments in exchange for garnering support for Pinochet in the plebiscite. The majority of the mayors appointed by Pinochet who were still in office under Aylwin were UDI members. They charged that the Aylwin government was denying them resources for political reasons. The fact that UDI managed to retain 10 percent of the municipal posts in the 1992 elections indicated the continuing political and local-center competition in the allocation of benefits for the poor. It also suggests that the local political system is still in transition.[76]

Pobladores' Organizations and Intermediary Institutions

The political impasse at the municipal level has greatly affected the pobladores and their neighborhood and functional associations. Pobladores' organizations are supposed to be the foundation of Chile's democratic municipal government and the driving force of FOSIS. Yet they remain by and large on the fringe of municipal government and have no strong ties with the country's political parties. Attempts to reach the disorganized pobladores have created considerable tension because the diverse and locally oriented interests of the pobladores do not necessarily coincide with the "corporatist" goals of the organizers. Not surprisingly, heterogeneous NGOs have been more successful in reaching the disorganized pobladores than have formal institutions such as the political parties and municipal governments.

Most pobladores are directly involved with municipal governments through the Juntas Vecinales. Although not all pobladores are organized, and indeed most are not, virtually every neighborhood has a Junta Vecinal.[77] These and other groups such as Centros de Madres were first given legal status by the Frei government.[78] In addition, organizations such as Promocion Popular were set up to encourage and support their activities. These groups multiplied and became increasingly political under the Allende government, in some cases to the detriment of their functional roles. Yet in general they took an increasingly active and co-operative role in promoting the delivery of or improvements in services such as health care and housing in conjunction with political parties and state agencies. These efforts gradually enabled the poor to "begin to tackle their own social needs in a collective fashion in such fields as literacy programs, public health, construction, vocational training, etc."[79]

The Pinochet government changed the juntas substantially, by dispensing with elections for junta directors and appointing them to office. Directors (*dirigentes*) were usually Pinochet loyalists or were paid as PEM and POJH workers to take on neighborhood leadership responsibilities. Also, neighborhoods interested in independent community development had to work through either NGOs or popular economic organizations rather than the juntas.

With the 1990 transition to democracy, juntas were again elected to office, after a lapse of seventeen years. Many of the "known" dirigentes—those appointed under Pinochet—were reelected because their communities were not used to making choices or participating in politics. Independent dirigentes—who were often in direct political opposition to previously appointed ones—were also elected. The former appointees had an obvious advantage in working with the mayor—also appointed—in most municipalities. The elected dirigentes ranged from those who were militant in their demands to those who knew little about their municipal rights and thus were easily manipulated by the authorities. Since they were less likely to know about FOSIS, they were more dependent on the municipalities for access to FOSIS projects. In addition, some juntas still in the control of the appointed dirigentes insisted that proposals to FOSIS from the community go through them. The appointed dirigentes were used to operating in a top-down manner and were uncomfortable with independent community activity.[80]

FOSIS activities clearly need to focus on the disorganized pobladores, which have few intermediary organizations to represent them. Their participation in FOSIS projects will depend on the efforts of the juntas and ultimately the municipal governments. Although municipal reform and the direct election of mayors helped promote the democratic process, it will take some time before there is a full transition to democracy at the Junta Vecinale level. That can only be achieved through civic education and experience in participatory politics. Yet low-income youth, for example, appear to have little interest in politics, after seventeen years of dictatorship.[81] In the short term, those communities with active popular organizations outside official local government channels will probably be best positioned to take advantage of the FOSIS mechanism.

Although Chile has many such organizations—two common examples are soup kitchens and popular economic organizations—most of them are concerned with day-to-day survival. Only 2 percent of all organized pobladores in the Santiago metropolitan region belong to territorial or coordinating committees with broader political goals.[82] Their reluctance to become involved with larger intermediary organizations is a reflection of the gap that exists between the concerns of the poor and politics at the national level, which is true in many other Latin American nations as well. In Chile prolonged authoritarian rule only made matters worse. Since 1990 these groups have been gradually growing in size and importance and in the long term may play a role in repairing the broken ties between private life and public action.

Nowhere is this gap more evident than in the attitude of pobladores' organizations toward political parties, which they see more as a threat to their autonomy than as a useful upward link to the state.[83] Their fears were fueled during the Pinochet years, when parties were no longer able to provide such links and political involvement could be penalized by repression.

In contrast to the popular economic organizations, organized interest groups are concerned with achieving certain rights—to work, housing, or health care—from the state. Consequently, their efforts are directed toward creating a vertical structure that can transmit their demands on the state to its leaders. Political parties often play a central role in organizing and directing the actions of such groups and mediating with the state. By contrast, groups with fundamental economic concerns are organized horizontally, since they have little to gain beyond the level of the neighborhood. For them, social networks hold out more hope than unions or confederations, and functional support organizations, not political parties, are the kinds of intermediaries they need.[84] Thus it is not surprising that the communal self-help organizations are less political than the parties, or that the parties play only a small role in the poblaciones.[85]

The relationship between grass-roots movements and parties is equally complex in other Latin American countries. In Peru, for example, grass-roots movements helped the unknown Alberto Fujimori win the presidency. At the same time, these groups have nothing like the organized base of support that a political party represents.[86] In Bolivia, parties are extremely out of touch with grass-roots movements, as can be seen in the growth of the antisystem populists with no party base, such as "Compadre" Palenque, who became the largest political force in La Paz virtually overnight, and in beer king Max Fernandez's rise to political prominence in the early 1990s.[87]

Chile's pobladores have traditionally been excluded from national politics because the country's political parties are based in unions rather than in grass-roots movements. Even the political parties of the left have no poblador in their central committees.[88] Some observers believe that pobladores reject parties because partisan competition and directives from the top serve to create divisions within their organizations rather than to represent their needs.[89]

Moreover, partisan competition at the national level has little bearing on the day-to-day concerns of pobladores. Even if reforms at the central level benefit pobladores in the long run, they do not bring immediate solutions to employment, security, unemployed youth, and the pobladores' many other problems.[90] When the parties moved to organize opposition to the Pinochet regime, they represented a cause with which pobladores could identify. Now that the parties are involved in more mundane political bargaining, this link has been weakened. One poblador dirigente who decided to run as an independent because she "wanted to do something for the community" observed that the party politicians "are all focused on getting posts at the municipal level."[91]

To be effective, at least in the near future, FOSIS will have to encourage the direct participation of pobladores and their functional organizations, since neither municipal governments nor political parties are well positioned to represent their concerns. As in other countries, social funds can provide an important new channel to the state for the poor, thereby strengthening their political voice as well as their economic potential. The success of FOSIS will also depend on whether the government continues to pursue its current policies, which are crucial to the state's ability to respond to the new demands of the poor. And in the longer term, political parties must adapt their strategies to include local organizations and concerns. Otherwise, a significant majority will remain at the margin of Chilean politics.

Conclusion

The Pinochet government's policies for alleviating poverty had mixed results. On the one hand, they provided for the basic needs of Chile's poorest people during a severe economic crisis, which was no small achievement in comparison with the record of other countries in the region. On the other hand, they placed a stigma on the poor because of the government's narrow vision of social welfare and its disdain for participatory institutions. Those who entered the government's programs became an underclass of sorts, since they grew heavily dependent on government subsidies. Yet the programs gave them no opportunity to improve their capacity to meet their own basic needs, while the authoritarian political system denied them a say in solving their own problems.

Under such a system, it was impossible for Chile's safety net programs to help sustain reform. Despite their impressive scale, scope, and rapid implementation of relief measures for the very poor, the Pinochet government's efforts involved political choices that were not too difficult, and the lessons for other countries are limited.

Although the new focus is on participation under the Aylwin regime, most poor people—except a small number who are highly organized—are ill equipped to take advantage of it. In the words of a neighborhood dirigente in Villa El Cobre, "People are used to being told what to do."[92] Nevertheless, FOSIS is showing considerable promise as a resource for helping the poor to help themselves. That such a goal is attainable has been shown by Bolivia's ESF. Indeed, this is one of the most important contributions that social funds can make.

Because local government in Chile is a complex combination of newly introduced democratic practices (such as direct elections for neighborhood juntas) and remnants of the authoritarian regime (such as previously appointed mayors), the poor and inexperienced find it difficult to participate in formulating the policies and projects that affect them. Their links to the intermediary institutions, such as political parties, that could help them to formulate their demands more effectively remain very weak. Although this situation is in part the result of an extended period of authoritarian rule, it is also typical of the politics of the poor in most countries: they tend to lack a political voice as well as economic resources.

As the country's political parties gradually consolidate their position at the national level and as municipal elections and municipal reform take root, this situation is likely to change. The parties and independent local organizations will both play an increasingly important role in the affairs of the poor and, it is hoped, will help them find their own solutions. Since a primary goal of FOSIS is to encourage the poor to formulate and implement their own solutions as well as to solicit state resources, it will have a vital role in this endeavor, particularly over the short term.

Although FOSIS is in a good position to help build an institutional base that is suited both to present-day economic and political realities and to the needs of the poor, it must be prepared for some tough challenges. At the central level, avoiding partisan pressure will be a constant concern. At the local level, it will have to foster genuine participation among an inexperienced and largely unorganized population surrounded by the remnants of authoritarian forces and deep divisions between left and right. This will clearly be no easy task.

Poverty indeed exists in Chile. In absolute terms, however, it is much less severe than in most countries on the continent. Despite the severity of the economic crises of the late 1970s and early 1980s, progress was made in lowering the incidence of extreme poverty (although the progress is less notable when extreme poverty is measured by indicators other than the official Ficha CAS).[93] The advances can be attributed to the preexisting social network, to the state's experience with social welfare programs, and to the effective and focused policies of the military regime. The regime's emphasis on targeting, meanwhile, introduced a valuable technical element into the management of social policies. Although people at the margin of the poverty line lost access to a host of extremely valuable state services, they will gradually regain that ground under the new democratic regime. By making inroads on extreme poverty as well as implementing a far-reaching program of economic reform, the military government left its democratic successors a firm base on which to implement diverse and innovative antipoverty efforts like FOSIS. Indeed, without sustained economic reform and renewed growth, programs like FOSIS would have a marginal, if any, impact. The multipartisan support for macroeconomic stability and fiscal responsibility that was evident throughout the democratic transition will need to continue, however, if Chile is to sustain reform and continue to reduce poverty.

The military performed more poorly on the political institutional front. Because it sought to alleviate poverty under the auspices of an authoritarian state, it failed to create mechanisms through which the poor could help themselves, mechanisms that are critical to long-term poverty reduction. This is the area in which short-term safety nets can make some of their most important permanent contributions and the one in which the most work remains to be done.

CHAPTER THREE

The Politics of Protecting the Poor during Adjustment:
Bolivia's Emergency Social Fund

IN BOLIVIA, as in Chile, institutional structure determined the kind of safety net implemented during adjustment.[1] In the case of Bolivia, as the public institutions delivering social services were notoriously inefficient, a demand-based safety net program was implemented outside the public sector. The Bolivian experience demonstrates the contributions that safety nets can make to the political sustainability of reform, and to poverty reduction, when they operate in a nonpartisan and transparent way and incorporate the demands and participation of the poor into their design and implementation.

Bolivia's safety net, the Emergency Social Fund (ESF), was the first multisectoral program of its kind. It was a compensatory scheme that was part of a dramatic structural reform plan, and it attracted a great deal of national as well as international attention because of its new demand-driven approach to allocating resources. Rather than designing and executing projects, the fund responded to proposals for projects from local and municipal governments, nongovernmental organizations (NGOs), and grass-roots groups. The idea of applying market-oriented principles to an assistance program was nothing short of revolutionary, and it turned out to be a remarkable success, both in its positive economic and social impact at the local level and in the attraction of international donor finances at the central administrative level. The main drawback of the scheme was that those in the poorest areas—those traditionally neglected by the Bolivian state and by NGOs—were the least capable of submitting viable project proposals. Although the ESF clearly employed poor people and the works executed indirectly benefited more poor, in general it did not reach the poorest decile.

Despite the fact that the program administered an enormous amount of money for a resource-poor country like Bolivia, in general it operated in a transparent and efficient manner. This is unusual for such programs in developing countries and was all the more impressive in Bolivia, where the management of the state tends to be dominated by the politics of "cargos y puestos" (positions and posts).[2] Control over scarce resources in countries where the demand for funds and services far outpaces availability often opens the door to political patronage. In such cases the state ceases to act as an impartial guarantor of the public interest.

The ESF was successful in part because it was outside the normal bureaucracy, and thus was able to avoid the "dirty" realm of politics. This does not mean that it was totally isolated from politics. The ESF was both affected by politics and had significant effects on politics at both national and local levels, a relationship that has not yet been fully evaluated but is key to understanding the program's effects on poverty alleviation. This chapter explores that relationship. It also examines the extent to which the ESF helped sustain the adjustment process. Not only did the agency project an image of efficiency and transparency, but it was able, at least temporarily, to reverse deep-seated mistrust in the government resulting from a record of unfulfilled promises. With the ESF many poor people in regions long neglected by the state saw the government come through for the first time, and saw it trying to make the adjustment process less painful and costly. This perception may not have created political support for the adjustment process per se, but it certainly created necessary support for the government at a critical political time.[3]

Since then the ESF approach has been tried elsewhere in Latin America and in Africa, but with mixed results. ESF supporters cite its demand-based approach, its efficiency and transparency, and its rapid results. Critics object to the program's temporary nature, its inability to target the poorest sectors, and its institutional position outside the public sector. The following analysis addresses the issues underlying that debate.

The Political Context

Until five years ago, Bolivia had one of the most unstable political systems in the world. Throughout its history, the nation led the South American continent in numbers of military coups. After several failed attempts at democratic transition in the late 1970s, democracy was achieved in 1982, when the military government was thoroughly discredited by the corrupt, drug-trafficking Garcia Meza regime of 1980–82.[4] Yet the succeeding regime, under President Siles Zuazo, had such a fragmented base of support that elections had to be called one year early, in 1985.

At present Bolivia has three major political parties: the centrist Nationalist Revolutionary Movement (MNR); the centrist Leftist Revolutionary Movement (MIR), led by current president Jaime Paz Zamora; and former dictator Hugo Banzer's Nationalist Democratic Action (ADN), which is slightly right of center. The left is splintered into a host of highly sectarian, overideologized, and personality-based parties. From 1958 to 1989, 418 new political parties were formed in Bolivia.[5] This fragmented system makes it extremely difficult to govern the country, particularly since some organized interest groups, such as the Bolivian Workers Confederation (COB) and the military, are still powerful enough to destabilize the political establishment.

Coexisting with the formal political system are a vast number of NGOs and grass-roots groups that have a strong ideological bent—usually to the left—and firm bases of popular support. Many of these groups grew out of opposition to the Banzer dictatorship in the 1970s but few have ties with political parties. Bolivia's traditional political parties are preoccupied with vying for control of state resources and for the most part are out of touch with the needs and concerns of poor urban or remote rural communities. Informal groups have become key actors in the local political arena. They were also tapped by the ESF, for in many remote communities they were more in touch with the local population than central or local government agencies.

In the 1985 elections, Hugo Banzer and the ADN won a plurality of 28 percent, but were closely followed by Victor Paz Estenssoro and the MNR with 26 percent, Jaime Paz and the MIR won 9 percent, and the United Left (IU) 2 percent. The constitution stipulates that in the absence of a clear majority the final results must be decided by the Congress, which has had to perform this task in all elections since 1979. In

1985 the MNR was able to unite a majority in opposition to Banzer, and Paz took the presidency. Ironically, because he needed a strong mandate for orthodox economic reform, he then turned to the ADN to form a pact for governing, the Pacto por la Democracia. One of the benefits of the pact was that it gave the MNR access to an economic plan the ADN had designed with Harvard professor Jeffrey Sachs. The Paz government implemented this plan as the New Economic Policy (NEP). In exchange for its support in Congress, the ADN was given control of several government agencies and access to certain municipal governments, as well as a tacit but ultimately unmet promise that power would be rotated from the MNR to the ADN in 1989. Through the Pacto, the ADN was also able to legislate a new electoral code that reduced the role of small parties, most of which were on the left.[6]

Although the NEP was a severe stabilization and adjustment program, several opportune factors made its implementation possible. Foremost was Paz's stature in national politics. As the father of the 1952 MNR revolution, he was able to carry out a dramatic reversal of his "own" revolution, something that few other politicians could have done. Second, he had a strong working majority in Congress in matters relating to the Pacto. This allowed the government to control labor and other opposition forces through congressionally sanctioned states of siege. Third, he recognized the need to compensate the country's large population of poor, who were not only hard hit by the adjustment program but had already suffered almost a decade of economic decline. Paz was determined above and beyond any short-term political goals to end the nation's crisis.

Although the NEP stabilized hyperinflation, economic reactivation was much slower to follow. Increasingly, displaced workers had to rely on the informal sector for employment; many former miners, for example, turned to coca growing in the absence of other alternatives. These trends contributed to the general disaffection with established parties that only grew worse in the electoral campaign of 1989, which brought mud-slinging between the major candidates to record levels. Economic issues were supposed to be their central concern, as indicated by their common theme of "stability with social justice," but in one way or another those became secondary to personal attacks.[7] The left offered little more than a return to pre-NEP economics.

The growing importance of politics *outside* the formal system was demonstrated by a surge in support for populists such as "Compadre" Palenque and his National Conscience (Condepa) party, and for beer

Table 3-1. *Municipal Election Winners in Bolivia, by Department Capital, 1987, 1989, 1991*

Department capitals	Party[a]		
	1987	1989	1991
Sucre	MBL	IU-MBL	UCS
C. de La Paz	MIR	Condepa	Condepa
El Alto	MIR	Condepa	Condepa
C. de Cochabamba	ADN	UCS	AP
C. de Oruro	MIR	AP	UCS
C. de Potosi	MIR	AP	AP
C. de Tarija	FRI	AP	MNR
C. de Santa Cruz	ADN	AP	MNR
C. de Trinidad	ADN	AP	MNR
C. de Cobija	ADN	AP	AP

Source: Communication from officer in Bolivian embassy, referring to an article in *Hoy*, December 2, 1991.

a. MBL: Bolivia Liberation Movement; IU: United Left; UCS: Civic Solidarity Union; MIR: Leftist Revolutionary Movement; Condepa: National Conscience; ADN: Nationalist Democratic Action; AP: Patriotic Accord (alliance between MIR and ADN); FRI: Revolutionary Leftist Front.

king Max Fernandez and his Civic Solidarity Union (UCS). Both men were critical of the system, but neither had a specific program. Antisystem messages were particularly effective in poor urban areas, which had been devastated by hyperinflation as well as the costs of adjustment. Whereas in 1985 hyperinflation bought support for stability at all costs, by 1989 stagnant growth was less attractive.

This rejection of the traditional political parties was evident in electoral results. In 1989 Condepa became the fourth largest political force in the nation and the first in the capital, La Paz, after only four months in existence. In the 1989 municipal elections, the UCS took Cochabamba, and by 1991 it came in second place nationwide, with 26.9 percent of town council seats (see table 3-1).[8] Voter absenteeism and abstention was also telling: only 66 percent of eligible voters registered, and of those, 27 percent abstained from voting in the 1989 national elections.[9]

Although the MNR won a plurality of 23 percent in 1989, an unlikely alliance between Banzer's ADN (which garnered 22 percent) and Paz Zamora's MIR (which garnered 19 percent) colluded, along with Condepa, to elect Jaime Paz to power in the Congress. Although this unholy alliance arose primarily out of opposition to MNR candidate Gonzalo Sanchez de Lozada, Banzer presented it as an effort to let the younger generation take power.[10] The end result was a power-sharing agreement between the MIR and the ADN, known as the Acuerdo Patriótico (AP, patriotic accord), in which the two parties agreed to divvy up ministerial and cabinet posts.

Ministries were divided by levels, rather than turned over in entirety to particular parties. Thus if the minister of health was of the MIR, then the vice-minister would be ADN.[11] Although this may have been an equitable solution where power sharing was concerned, it hardly made for an efficient system. If anything, it promoted patronage more than ever. In addition, since there were two parties vying for the control of public posts, both of whom had little experience in power but were eager for opportunity, the system left little room for non-Acuerdo actors and opened the door to a great deal of sectarianism.

Although the Paz Estenssoro government had a power-sharing agreement with the ADN in the Pacto of the preceding regime, the dynamic was different then. First of all, ministries were not divided. Since the ADN did not want to be a formal part of the MNR government, the "price" for its support was control of several state enterprises rather than ministries. More important, Paz Zamora owed his victory to the ADN's support in Congress. A left-wing weekly correctly described the arrangement as "Jaime in the government, Banzer to power."[12] The Paz Estenssoro government, however, had been elected in Congress by a coalition of groups in opposition to Banzer, and only turned to the ADN after the election to build a support coalition for the NEP.

That is to say, whereas the dynamic in 1985 stemmed from a need for unity in the face of an economic crisis that was threatening Bolivian society and its polity, 1989 signified a return to traditional patronage-style Bolivian politics. This return was facilitated by the electoral system, which does not call for a second round of popular elections between first- and second-place winners to obtain a clear popular mandate but allows personal rivalries and ambitions to dictate the electoral outcomes in Congress. Alliances such as that between the MIR and ADN suggest that co-governing parties need not share agendas or ideologies because their main objective is to seek control of the public administration. The ESF was not completely isolated from this political context.

Origins and Structure of the ESF

The ESF was established in late 1985 as part of the Paz Estenssoro government's New Economic Policy (NEP), a stabilization and adjustment plan designed to end hyperinflation and more than five years of negative growth rates. The ESF was not intended to be a comprehensive solution to social problems, but rather a temporary measure for protecting the needy until economic growth could begin and a more permanent solution to the problems could be found.[13] Under the direction of Fernando Romero, a highly successful entrepreneur, the ESF was set up as a three-year emergency program (it was later extended to four) to provide, first, short-term employment for those most affected by the adjustment plan and, second, basic social services that the government did not have the full capacity to deliver for the time being. The program covered four broad areas: economic infrastructure, social infrastructure, social assistance (such as school food programs), and productive support (such as group credit schemes).[14] During its entire operation the ESF attracted US$239.5 million in foreign resources, mainly in the form of grants, channeled largely through the World Bank.[15]

One of the keys to the fund's success was its timing. Bolivia was experiencing a severe economic crisis that threatened the viability of its recently reconstituted democratic system. In addition, President Paz, being in his fourth term in office, had the national status to implement sweeping economic reforms. He was also personally committed to restoring to health the nation's long-crippled economy. More important, he saw the ESF as a vital part of the NEP, and he and Romero both agreed that it should be totally independent from politics.

The administrative unit of the ESF consisted of a small group of well-paid and highly qualified personnel, who have often been credited with the program's success.[16] Not only did the fund manage to issue an enormous amount of support extremely quickly, but the results of its efforts were unprecedented by Bolivian standards. At full capacity the program generated 20,000 man-months of employment per month. The infrastructure that was created—the sewerage, low-income housing, schools, and health posts, among other improvements—benefited 1.2 million people in low-income rural and urban areas, and came after almost a decade of economic decline.[17] In a total population of just under 7 million, this is a significant figure.[18] These results drew political support for the adjustment program and made the fund a potential instrument for patronage.

The function of the ESF was to respond to proposals submitted by local governments or NGOs and to enlist subcontractors from the private sector to implement them. Because the ESF team had a great deal of freedom to administer its funds, it was particularly concerned with avoid-

Table 3-2. *Emergency Social Fund (ESF) Beneficiaries, by Poverty Area and Income Level*

Poverty area	1985 population (millions)	ESF commitment		Approval rate (percent)
		Total (millions of U.S. dollars)	Per capita (U.S. dollars)	
1 (least poor)	2.3	56.1	23.97	24
2	0.7	20.3	27.77	23
3	1.3	17.3	13.51	25
4	1.4	16.3	11.67	33
5 (poorest)	0.6	6.2	9.45	28
National	6.4	116.1	18.20	26

Source: Julie Van Domelen, "Working with Non-governmental Organizations," in Steen Jorgensen, Margaret Grosh, and Mark Schacter, eds., *Bolivia's Answer to Poverty, Economic Crisis, and Adjustment: The Emergency Social Fund* (Washington, D.C.: The World Bank, 1992; and the Emergency Social Fund offices, La Paz).

Table 3-3. *Family Income of ESF Workers in Relation to the General Population*

Decile of total family earnings	Percent in EPH sample[a]	Decile of total family earnings	Percent in EPH sample[a]
First	6.25	Sixth	14.25
Second	7.75	Seventh	8.00
Third	13.25	Eighth	7.25
Fourth	21.50	Ninth	3.75
Fifth	15.50	Tenth	2.50

Source: John Newman, Steen Jorgensen, and Menno Pradhan, "Worker's Benefits from Bolivia's Emergency Social Fund," Living Standards Measurement Study, Working Paper 77 (Washington, D.C.: The World Bank, 1991), p. 14.
a. EPH: Encuesta Permanente de Hogares (Permanent Household Survey).

ing corruption and inefficiency, particularly in its initial years, when there was pressure to disburse large sums and to reach as many people as quickly as possible.[19] At times, the projects that emerged in the push to act rapidly and keep administrative costs low were of variable quality.

One problem was that beneficiaries were difficult to target. The founders of the ESF had intended the program to assist those directly affected by the adjustment program—the former tin miners—rather than to be a buffer for the poor in general, which is what the program evolved into.[20] Even after the Department of Promotion was set up in 1988 to reach out to the poorest and most remote regions, per capita ESF expenditures remained lowest in the poorest regions, and there was a disproportionately low representation of ESF workers in the poorest two income deciles (see tables 3-2 and 3-3). The fund did not altogether reach those most affected by the adjustment program, either. Former tin miners, for example, accounted for only 10 percent of those employed by the ESF.

After enjoying a privileged position in relation to other workers in the days before reform, many of them felt the ESF wage was too low. Many also preferred higher-paying alternative employment available in the informal coca-growing industry. However, 44 percent of the program's beneficiaries were construction workers, whose industry had been very hard hit by the economic reforms. The extent to which a demand-driven program can target the poorest is not clear and may well be a trade-off for not imposing what is "best" from outside.

Because of its decentralized, demand-based administrative structure, the ESF offered little opportunity to manipulate beneficiaries politically. Workers were hired by subcontractors and many did not know they were working for a government program. Only 29 percent even knew what the ESF was. By contrast, the bureaucracy of centrally administered programs not only administers resources but also designs and implements projects and hires the necessary labor. Program officials often use their control over resources and employment for political patronage purposes.[21]

Although the ESF did not employ the poorest of the poor, it clearly employed persons in need of both income and employment. Ninety-nine percent of ESF workers were male and were on average poorer and less educated than the urban population. The majority were heads of the household and the sole income earners for the family. ESF wages varied but in general were on the low side of the spectrum for similar work. Eighteen percent of those working would have been unemployed if they had not been working for the ESF, and, had they been working in the informal sector, their wages would have been 45 percent lower. Whereas many of the poorest households were headed by women, only 1 percent of ESF workers were women.[22]

More than half of the beneficiaries expressed satisfaction with ESF work. They complained mainly about the low pay and temporary nature of the work. For the most part, ESF workers were not organized, which is not so surprising given that the work was temporary and that many workers were relocated from other communities or occupations owing to recessionary conditions.[23]

Beneficiary communities were more aware of the origins of ESF projects and more positive about their impact than were the individual workers. More than 70 percent of the indirect beneficiaries of community projects knew that the projects were from the ESF. Communities usually organized themselves to bid for projects for their neighborhoods, whereas workers were often from outside the community or had not been involved in bidding for the projects. Of the communities interviewed for a 1988 study, 80 percent said that the community had benefited from ESF projects, 33 percent said that the projects strengthened community organization, and only 9.8 percent said that they had created problems for the community.[24] The ESF also provided opportunities for small businesses in state projects that would normally have been precluded by their informal status. The subcontractors hired by ESF solicitors were primarily from the informal construction sector. Only 2 percent of them were registered in the Chamber of Commerce. More than 50 percent cited experience and professional prestige as a positive aspect of working with the ESF.[25]

Although the ESF was a temporary program, it strengthened the ability of many communities to administer projects over the long term and to organize a movement to solicit essential services from the state. This was a positive political development in a nation where community organization and autonomy from the central government have traditionally been weak. Enhancing the effectiveness of the political voice of the poor was a means to break the traditional dependence on patronage politics.

The ESF and Politics

The political effects of the ESF are difficult to define in precise terms. For one thing, the political context in 1990 was very different from that in 1985, when the ESF was set up. Although politicians did not necessarily change, the dynamics of the AP power-sharing agreement intensified intraparty competition within the public sector in general. And although the ESF had a special status, it was still part of that sector, and it controlled large resources. Second, the role that politics played changed from one period to another. The 1989 election was a critical time, and the MNR clearly used ESF works, and even its beneficiaries, to bolster the campaign of its candidate, Gonzalo Sanchez de Lozada. Because of the way the ESF was structured, however, the government was not the only actor that could make such use of the ESF. Indeed, the soliciting agencies—municipalities, state development corporations, NGOs—could often claim as much if not more credit for projects than could the ESF. Thus the ESF was also a factor in municipal elections in 1987 and 1989. Nevertheless, the results showed that there was no direct correlation between a high number of ESF projects and victory at the polls. Some mayors with ample ESF funds were reelected; others were not.

National Politics

The ESF originated at an exceptional time in Bolivian politics, which was reflected in both its mandate and its leadership. The success of Fernando Romero in keeping the ESF out of politics has been noted by his employees, by a variety of soliciting agencies, and even by observers of the political opposition.[26] Romero was clearly under political pressure: needs were infinite, resources were not. Every congressman, city mayor, and local official wanted to get involved in the ESF. Romero, who had respected status as a businessman, had no qualms about refusing to meet with politicians—or even ministers—if he felt that the intent was political rather than technical. He also had no interest in advertising, stating, "We will publicize with our results."[27]

Subsequent directors took a different approach. In general, they attached more importance to public relations, both with politicians and the press. There was a belief that people *should* know that the works executed by the fund pertained to the fund. This change also reflected a different political context from the early years of the Paz government, when severe economic and political crisis seemed to dictate exceptional leadership. Indeed, during the ESF's early days there was a certain mystique among its staff, created by the sense of crisis, by the leadership of Fernando Romero, and by the dedicated cohesive nature of the original team. As the agency grew and became more organized and bureaucratized, this aura faded. Nonetheless, after Romero left in September 1988 and was succeeded by Adolfo Navarro, the team at the ESF continued to function with more efficiency and dedication than most public officials in any country. This was due in part to the high payment scale and skill of the team, but also to the ESF's image of a public agency putting forth an exceptional performance.[28]

Although politics was not a force within the fund, it was always being subjected to some level of political pressure. Before 1989 there were cases in which MNR municipalities expected to receive ESF funds automatically, without putting in projects, as if it was their right.[29] After 1989 pressure came from the MIR-ADN ranks. As one former director stated: "The irony is that before if you were correct, a technocrat, and

didn't respond to party pressure, you were accused of being MIR. . . .
Now you are accused of being MNR!"[30] This pressure increased sharply
at the time of the 1989 elections, as pointed out by program officials and
beneficiaries alike.

The 1989 Electoral Campaign

Views about how the fund was used by the Sanchez de Lozada campaign vary. Campaign advertising consultants and a few ESF officials
thought that the program was not used enough. Yet several ESF staff
members resigned during or just after election time because they felt that
political pressure had increased too much. That pressure came not only
from the MNR in general but also from different wings of the MNR, all
of whom wanted particular favors.[31] One official was reprimanded by the
vice-presidential candidate of the MNR because she visited an MIR
municipality in Oruro just when he was campaigning there. The purpose
of her visit was to clarify some problems with a project; when this was
done, she approved the project. She was then called by the MNR candidate and reprimanded for "saving face for the MIR municipality!"[32]

According to another official, the way that ESF projects were put to
political use was demoralizing to much of the staff. The then executive
director, Adolfo Navarro, began to personally inaugurate ESF projects
in order to increase publicity. Until then it had been the privilege of the
regional zone chief, who was the actual director of the project from start
to finish. If the zone chief belonged to the opposition and a project was
inaugurated as part of the MNR campaign, it was difficult for him to
participate. The same sorts of tension were created when opposition
municipalities inaugurated projects during their campaigns. In addition,
a small number of people within the fund wanted to use fund equipment—such as jeeps—for the campaigns. This created enormous tension
within the fund, which until then had been free of internal political
debates. There was also a great deal of pressure on the fund to finalize
works prior to the electoral campaign.[33] In another case, a new US$1
million ESF fund providing rotating credits to campesinos was instituted
in late 1988 and increased during the campaign. Yet the works of the
fund—particularly school breakfast programs and the building of
schools—were not used exclusively by the MNR, but by a host of regional
politicians.[34] There was no consistent correlation between ESF works
and electoral success (see table 3-4). In El Alto, for example, which was

Table 3-4. *Bolivian National Elections, 1985, 1989, and Correlation of ESF Funds and Results, by Department*

Department	Winner[a] 1985	1989	ESF funds per capita (before 8/6/89; U.S. dollars)[a]
Chuquisaca	MNR	MIR	54.96
La Paz	ADN	Condepa	1.77
Cochabamba	ADN	MNR	22.94
Oruro	MNR	ADN	34.19
Potosí	MNR	MIR	22.71
Tarija	MNR	MNR	48.55
Santa Cruz	MNR	MNR	12.66
Beni	MNR	MNR	53.06
Pando	MNR	ADN	123.65

Results	ESF funds per capita Low (<$20)	Medium ($20–$40)	High ($40–$60)	Very high (>$60)
Party stays in power	1	0	1	0
Opposition party wins	1	3	2	1

Sources: Nation Electoral Court data, La Paz, August 1990; and Emergency Social Fund Office, La Paz, August 1990.

a. Per capita figures are taken from number of votes. Because the absenteeism rate is extremely high—approximately 33 percent in 1987—the total population is larger than indicated. The funds were solicited by the regional development corporations of each department.

the focus of a large part of the MNR's campaign, ESF spending was greater than that for most departments as a whole; Condepa won the elections by a large margin.

The fund was also drawn into television campaigns in the 1985 and 1989 elections, which were the first in Bolivia to become mass media competitions. In 1985 television was used to support the democratic system and denounce possible military coups, but in 1989 it carried the candidates' personal campaigns. Regardless of the expenditure on TV, it did not guarantee victory. The MNR spent the most on TV spots, followed by ADN, MIR, the IU, Socialist Party One (PS-1), Condepa, and the Bolivian Socialist Falange (FSB), in that order. Yet Condepa, which concentrated its forces on radio campaigning, became the fourth political force in the nation and the first in La Paz.[35]

On the advice of the Sawyer Miller advertising firm, the MNR followed the style of U.S. political campaigns. Sanchez de Lozada was presented as a new kind of leader, imaginative and innovative, in comparison with the "corrupt" Banzer or the "dreamer" Paz. Continuity in the economic program and stability were key issues, as was the promise of 250,000 new jobs. Several TV advertising slots featured Sanchez de Lozada as the architect of the recuperation, and three of those used the ESF.[36] They juxtaposed scenes of political violence with images of people working under ESF signs and images of Sanchez de Lozada; or they showed Sanchez de Lozada distributing milk and bread at ESF school breakfast projects. This use of the ESF was in keeping with Bolivian political tradition in that the state apparatus was expected to be at the service of the official candidate.[37] At the same time, other forces were also free to use the ESF for their own ends, as was evident in many opposition municipalities and departments.[38]

As for the effects of the fund on politics, this was more striking in smaller communities. Beni, for example, is a long-neglected region that received a substantial amount of ESF funds in relation to its size. After the Department of Promotion launched efforts in March 1988, US$3 million was approved for projects in Beni up to August 1989. People from the department even contributed to the Sanchez de Lozada campaign![39] The MNR won in the provinces of Beni, even though the ADN took the capital, Trinidad.

These attempts at politicization began to tarnish the image of the ESF. The MIR mayor of El Alto, for example, complained that despite an extremely good relationship with the fund, after December 1988 disbursement for several projects stopped. He blamed the electoral climate, and interpreted this as an MNR attempt to discredit his MIR municipality.[40] Although the delay in projects coincided with a cash-flow shortage that the fund experienced in late 1988 and early 1989 and thus may have been the explanation, the fact that the MNR had begun using the ESF so publicly at this point led the opposition to suppose that the ESF was being run differently because of the upcoming elections. With the change of government, the attempts by the MIR and ADN to politicize the ESF increased substantially, as was reflected in the changes in ESF directorship.

The Change in Government

As already discussed, the MNR won a plurality in the elections but failed to swing a victory in the congressional runoff, and the ADN-MIR took power on August 6, 1989. Mario Mercado, a former ADN senator for La Paz, replaced Navarro as director. Under the new government the

ESF director was given the rank of minister without portfolio. From this point on there were new political pressures on the fund. Mercado took a much more public approach than had past directors Romero and Navarro. He apparently once said that he would not work with the municipality in Sucre because it was aligned with the Bolivia Liberation Movement (MBL).[41] Yet Mercado was known for protecting the staff, and there was no large staff turnover with the change of government. It is not clear what approach the new director appointed in July 1990, Luis Alberto Valle, will take. It is significant that Jorge Patiño, the second in command, resigned in September 1993. In addition, whereas earlier directors were allowed to approve their own contracts, Valle has insisted that all contracts must receive his prior approval before they are accepted.[42]

After August 1989 the government's attitude toward the fund clearly changed. When one director received a call saying that General Banzer wanted a particular project, she responded, "He doesn't work here, I understand." However, political pressure was apparently strong enough to prompt her to resign shortly thereafter. Although directors are free to turn projects down independently, there is no longer the sort of protection from the leadership that Fernando Romero provided. This support made it possible for the staff to resist political pressure from higher levels. For example, when a La Paz zone director was approached with a proposal from the health minister requesting US$70,000 to remodel the health ministry, the zone chief told the minister that the project was hardly one that falls within the ESF's mission. However, US$16,000 was later approved by the directorate.[43]

In the allocation of funds to municipalities, political affiliation seems to have become a new consideration, although not a determining factor. Even an MIR representative in Congress noted that after 1989 there were a lot of complaints about the fund within his party in parliament: that the fund was not assisting municipalities aligned with the government but rather those supporting the opposition.[44] This was probably due in part to the fact that the MIR at first perceived the ESF as an MNR program and tool, which aroused a certain amount of suspicion. It was also due to the general political climate after 1989, which was marked by intense intraparty competition for the spoils of the state.

The fund was indeed the focus of rivalries between the ADN and the MIR. In June 1990, in the midst of a debate over restructuring the cabinet, MIR party official Gaston Encinas launched a publicity campaign against Mario Mercado's running of the ESF, after Mercado refused to receive him. Encinas criticized Mercado's management as feudal and inefficient and repeated Senate President Gonzalo Valda's complaint that the ESF was being run in an indiscriminate manner.[45] Although it is not clear that Mercado refused to receive Encinas for partisan reasons, the issue demonstrates how in many instances the ESF became a political football.

The MIR or ADN were probably no more political than the MNR, but partisan competition *within* the government sparked a change in the political context. In addition, the executive branch was no longer determined to insulate the ESF from political pressure, as is demonstrated by its using the directorship as a political appointee position. Inasmuch as the ESF was a creation of the previous government, there was little incentive to maintain it as an "exceptional" institution.

The Municipalities

An unanticipated side effect of the ESF was that it strengthened local institutional capacity, as it provided NGOs and local governments with experience in project design and implementation. Municipal government is still evolving in Bolivia. The first nationwide municipal elections were held in 1987, and even now mayors are not directly elected.[46] The ESF played a large role in revitalizing municipal governments, which rarely had access to resources not directly controlled by the central government. Municipalities gained experience in administering projects in a wide variety of sectors, such as health, education, and sanitation, whereas before their experience had been limited to urban infrastructure. The ESF had the most impact on small, less developed municipalities that had a high level of demand for services in comparison with their capacity to provide them. Municipalities in Latin America in general tend to act more as political power brokers distributing scarce central government resources than as independent governments with development agendas.[47] The opportunity to move beyond a patron-client relationship was extremely valuable for municipal governments. What is less clear is whether such lessons can be lasting if resources remain concentrated in the center.

Because the ESF's primary criteria for allocating funds were technical and project oriented, it was usually able to work with municipalities of all political persuasions, although political issues were more prevalent in

Table 3-5. *Correlation of ESF Funds and Bolivian Municipal Election Outcomes, 1989*

1980 results	ESF Funds per capita[a]			
	Low (<$25)	Medium ($25–$40)	High (>$100)	Very high (>$500)
Party in power wins	1	1	2	0
Opposition party or coalition wins[b]	5	11	2	2
Governing party wins in coalition	4	5	1	1

Sources: See table 3-4.

a. Funds per capita are in U.S. dollars and represent ESF funds solicited by municiplities before August 6, 1989. The municipalities used are *only* those that solicited ESF funds. Per capita figures were taken from total number of votes. Because absenteeism in Bolivia is high—approximately 33 percent in 1989—the actual population is larger. Figures may be skewed by higher relative rates of absenteeism.

b. MIR and ADN contested the 1989 municipal elections as a coalition.

some cases, and there was no correlation between ESF fund allocation and political affiliation of particular municipalities. Regardless of their political affiliation, municipalities, as the solicitors and supervisors of ESF projects in their localities, were in a far better position to claim "credit" for the works than were ESF personnel or the central government. Indeed, as noted earlier, beneficiaries often failed to understand the ESF's role in the provision of projects and benefits. The fact that municipalities were best positioned to claim political credit by no means indicates that they were able to translate those claims into electoral victory. In some municipalities with a high level of ESF funds per capita, such as San Ignacio de Moxos and Palmar, the party in power was re-elected. In others with a high level of ESF funds, such as El Alto–La Paz, Quillacollo, and Frias, the party in power was not reelected (table 3-5). In El Alto, which was an MIR municipality, both the MIR and the MNR tried to use the ESF to their credit and, ironically, neither party won.[48]

There seems to be no direct correlation between ESF works and votes. This correctly indicates that people vote for many different reasons. What may be most beneficial at the community level, such as sewage systems or roads, may actually be less popular at the individual level, where football fields and school desks may be in demand. A case in point is the popularity of beer king Max Fernandez and his UCS in Trinidad, who made a great deal of impact by building football fields. Meanwhile, after the 1987 Department of Promotion was set up, Trinidad became a beneficiary of a relatively high quantity of ESF funds. In some cases the use of the ESF became an effective campaign strategy. In one Oruro city, where the candidate was losing by a large margin one month before the election, he caught up and won the election after changing his campaign strategy and focusing on the ESF.[49] If one considers that ESF funds often increased the independence of local groups in relation to local or central governments by providing resources that they would normally have had to solicit through traditional mechanisms, it is not surprising that those resources did not translate into votes for established political parties.

The ESF and ESF works had more impact—which often did translate into electoral results—in smaller cities than in larger ones. Small, remote communities were accustomed to receiving barely any government attention and projects at all. Political concerns tended to be more prevalent in larger, more urban and more politically conscious towns. In larger towns, with a large cast of different actors competing for funds and projects, it was much harder for the population to have a positive general feeling about the ESF and even harder to translate that into votes for any one particular candidate.

This dynamic can be seen in the contrasting cases of the San Ignacio de Moxos and El Alto municipalities. The mayor of San Ignaicio de Moxos, Ana Maria Ruiz Antelo of the MNR, who was elected in 1987, was one of the first provincial mayors to present projects to the ESF and became very effective at doing so. Subsequently, San Ignacio became the city with the most ESF funds per capita, receiving 20 percent of all ESF funds for its department, Beni, which amounted to US$169,206.54. San Ignacio was small enough that ESF projects and funds had a sizable impact on the town's infrastructure and economy. Although Banzer took San Ignacio in the national elections (August 1989), Ruiz Antelo and the MNR took the municipal elections in December 1989 with a large margin: 196 votes in a total of 1,410 valid votes. Even though there is no direct correlation between the ESF and elections at a general level, it seems quite obvious that Ruiz Antelo was associated with the arrival and promulgation of ESF projects in San Ignacio. In a town where people were unaccustomed to government attention, the introduction of ESF projects and funds clearly had a political impact.[50]

A contrasting case is that of El Alto, a larger town that has received quite a bit of government attention in recent years. Until recently El Alto was a poor suburb of La Paz, with a dire need for basic services of all kinds, but it is now Bolivia's fastest-growing city (since October 1988 its population has jumped from 100,000 to 350,000 people). El Alto received US$12 million in ESF funds—which was more than some entire departments were given. It also figured prominently in the MNR's 1989 campaign. Even so, the race was won by Condepa. Thus ESF funds do not necessarily determine elections.

Many projects were channeled to El Alto through a variety of soliciting agencies, including both MIR and Condepa municipalities. In 1987–89 the ESF enabled the MIR municipality to play a new role in the provision of social welfare infrastructure. Yet with the election campaign, "the war began between municipal and MNR projects."[51] The MIR's successor, Condepa, seemed to have no problems with the ESF, although it did complain of some politicization among ESF staff at lower levels. On several occasions the Condepa mayor clashed with the ADN-run municipality of La Paz and the central government as well.[52] Because of the diversity of the soliciting agencies (NGOs as well as municipalities played an active role) and the many projects implemented in El Alto, all sides complained about the lack of coordination of ESF activities. At the same time, the Condepa mayor did see the ESF as playing a positive and facilitating role in relations between the government and NGOs. Beneficiaries had mixed opinions: some felt the ESF served as a "political act," but to others it had no clear relationship to the projects that they were working on.[53]

Despite all of the bickering and accusations at the central level, it seems that, with the exception of a few instances at election time, the political use of the fund did not really affect the way it operated at the municipal level, nor did these uses prevent local-level officials, including those from the opposition, from using the fund to their own advantage. Furthermore, the use of ESF projects or subcontracts for political or personal clientelistic goals did not have the same impact on the fund as its use at the national level. In some instances, politics or cronyism determined the allocation of subcontracts, largely because of the freedom in the allocation process, which did not require public bidding.[54] Yet such instances seldom affected ESF efficiency because many local actors were competing for ESF resources; moreover, the fund carefully supervised project execution. These practices by local leaders also had little impact on the fund as an institution. In contrast, party leaders viewed the fund as part of the intraparty struggle for the control of state spoils. While such attempts had limited impact on the fund's operations, they clearly put a great deal of pressure on fund personnel. In the longer term, this eroded the fund's institutional vision of itself as having an exceptional mission above and beyond partisan concerns. Thus although politics at the national level did affect the fund as an institution, at the municipal level the fund was more likely to have impact on politics than the other way around.

Relations with NGOs

The role of nongovernmental organizations has expanded markedly in Latin America in the past decade. In the same way that the inadequacy of formal state and legal institutions has led to a surge of informal economic activity, so the limitations of fragile young democratic institutions have given rise to a great deal of "informal" political activity at the grass-roots level. In many countries NGOs encourage democratic practices at the local level that form a fundamental basis for consolidating democracy at the central level. One of the most widely cited achievements of the ESF is that it improved relations between NGOs and the state, relations that had traditionally been hostile. Yet this accomplishment is seldom mentioned in the context of the development of democratic institutions in Bolivia. The fostering of cooperation between the state and local organizations was a positive step and in the short term may have contributed to the sustainability of adjustment. In some cases, however, problems in administration alienated or angered particular groups. In such cases, politics often was—or at least was *perceived* to be—a factor.

There are four kinds of NGOs in Bolivia: religious or church-affiliated NGOs, national NGOs, international private voluntary organizations (PVOs), and grass-roots organizations. Religious organizations have a long tradition of working in Bolivia and tend to be apolitical. International PVOs tend to be technocratic and focus on the provision of basic services. The 600 or so national NGOs, most of which are small, are far more political, although few have partisan ties.[55] They are more *ideological* than they are partisan.

National NGOs have a deep-seated mistrust of government institutions—whether democratic or not. This mistrust stems from a tradition of corrupt and incompetent governments that continuously neglected pressing social needs.[56] NGO opposition to the Paz Estenssoro regime also has an ideological basis. Most NGOs are ideologically if not politically affiliated with the left. The NEP was seen as a reversal of the MNR revolution and as a distinctly "antipopular" policy. Yet it was clear from the start that the ESF was going to have to rely on NGOs, because of the inefficiency of the line ministries. The need for cooperation with

NGOs was particularly acute in the poorest and most remote regions, where state institutions were the least developed. Only with a great deal of effort on the part of the ESF staff and the positive example that they set by working successfully with some of the better-known NGOs was the NGOs' initial mistrust gradually eroded.[57]

The results were striking. After three years in operation, out of 551 entities working with the fund, 81 percent were NGOs and 19 percent were state institutions. While 68 percent of the resources invested by the fund were channeled through state institutions, 32 percent were channeled through NGOs.[58] The role of NGOs was particularly prominent in the areas of social and productive assistance, while the municipalities and regional development corporations implemented the bulk of economic infrastructure projects. NGOs were responsible for more than 50 percent of social assistance projects and 99 percent of productive schemes.[59] Religious organizations received the largest share of financing, as they were most adept at presenting projects, and in the poorest and most isolated communities they were typically the only organized institutional presence.[60]

Working with the ESF clearly had an impact on the NGOs. Experience was gained in presenting proposals and in administering projects and budgets. In many cases a new trust in working with the state was created, whether it was the line ministries or municipalities and prefectures. The ESF represented only a small portion of total NGO budgets.[61] In general, the smaller the NGO and the more it depended on ESF financing, the greater the impact.[62] Cooperation was greatest in the health and education sectors, where NGOs are fairly strong. While NGOs were able to administer programs and provide key investments, line ministries could provide equipment and staff.[63] The role that the ESF played in creating a rapprochement among state institutions, NGOs, and local actors had a positive and revitalizing effect on local democratic government, although it is one that was not foreseen by the original architects of the ESF. Yet this process was not without problems, nor is it irreversible.[64]

For one thing, most NGOs differed from the ESF in their view of the role of aid. Whereas NGOs saw their role as a long-term developmental one that was part of the process of structural change, the ESF's vision was that of short-term relief during an adjustment process. This difference was just as much politically based, however, and was especially prevalent among the more ideological NGOs. It was much less common in the religious organizations, whose operations leaned toward short-term assistance, which in part explains their predominance in ESF projects. NGOs also had to adapt their speed of operations to that of the ESF. Because the institutional and executing capacity of NGOs often varied, many tensions arose.[65] Yet the ESF's ability to work with all kinds of NGOs and its innovative style of responding to local demands may well have modified the visions of both parties. In the context of mutual suspicion, the intermediary role of international organizations was a critical one.

The relationship between the ESF and the NGOs was by no means free of politics, particularly since many NGOs were ideologically motivated. In addition, even when politics was not a factor in ESF decisions— for example, when projects turned down for the lack of technical capacity—the NGOs often felt that politics had played a role. This was particularly true when the ESF's evaluation had been poor or hasty, or the results had been poorly explained and communicated.[66] Because ESF supervisors and evaluators were not always familiar with local conditions, misunderstandings often occurred when projects received negative evaluations. One reason was that the ESF did not take into account the longer-term effect that its funding—or a reduction in funding—could have on NGOs. At the same time, when the ESF ran short of funds in late 1988, owing to a government cash-flow shortage, ESF staff may have unwittingly tightened up technical criteria without realizing the impact that this could have on NGOs.[67] Few beneficiaries understood the NGO-ESF financial relationship, with the result that when there were financial or disbursement problems, the NGOs received most of the blame.[68]

The *perception* that politics was playing a role was often more important than the actual politics. The IPTK, for example, is an NGO affiliated with the Marxist left and has a basis in Sucre, a city controlled by the MBL. Yet the IPTK was one of the first NGOs that the ESF worked with, because of its high technical qualifications and its timely presentation of projects. On the one hand, NGOs criticized the ESF for letting the IPTK use the ESF for its political advantage; on the other hand, Congress criticized the ESF for having political designs on opposition-run Sucre.[69] In a few cases, ESF inefficiency was perceived to be a result of political favoritism.[70]

At the same time, NGOs did recognize that the ESF was under pressure at particular times of the *political* agenda, such as election time.[71] NGOs were well aware of how the ESF was used by the MNR in its 1989 campaign, and also of the partisan competition generated by the MIR-

ADN Acuerdo Patriotico. Some NGOs saw the ESF as part of the "so-called distribution of power quotas".[72] The instances in which the ESF was blatantly used for political purposes, for example, during the election campaign, undermined the trust and relationship that the ESF had built with the NGOs, and thus their longer-term trust in the state.

Despite some failures, the ESF contributed to the democratic process at the local level by actively incorporating municipal organizations in its operations rather than imposing initiatives from the center. This approach enhanced the ESF's ability to respond to local needs and allowed the fund to avoid the mistakes of many centrally implemented aid efforts, which often undermined or duplicated the work of local groups, usually arousing their hostility in the process. This also made it much easier to elicit their support—through their involvement—for ongoing economic reform. From the standpoint of NGOs and other local groups, the opportunity to establish a cooperative relationship with the state had political as well as economic ramifications. It tangibly demonstrated the benefits of independent local participation in state activities, narrowing an age-old division between society and state in Bolivia. The ESF created the potential for increased independence among local groups, in contrast to the traditional and generally ineffective mechanisms for soliciting services from the state, because they could avoid partisan intermediaries and go directly to the ESF. This newly gained independence may go a long way toward explaining why ESF funds did not necessarily translate into votes for established political parties.

From the ESF to the SIF

Before any conclusions can be drawn about the politics of the ESF, it is also necessary to consider the successor to the ESF, the Social Investment Fund (SIF). The SIF was intended to provide a sense of permanence to the ESF experience, but with a viable long-term administrative framework. Thus its objective is to adopt the most positive aspects of the ESF—its demand-driven approach and its goals of efficiency and transparency—but to work with the line ministries, specifically in the health and education sectors. The SIF has continued to depend on the presidency and has retained the highly qualified ESF staff. The coordination with the geographic and sectoral priorities of the ministries was intended to solve the targeting deficiencies of the ESF and supplement the works of the two weakest ministries at the same time. The SIF was to receive US$99 million in funding from the World Bank and other international agencies for its first three years, as well as substantial counterpart funds from the Bolivian government. In addition, the SIF has more built-in bureaucratic mechanisms to protect it from corruption and political manipulation than did the ESF. Public bidding is required for all subcontracting, for example, and sectoral criteria have been established to impose qualitative norms. Yet, to prevent delays, ministries are given only one week to intervene before a project is approved.[73]

What allowed the ESF to avoid politics to the extent that it did was clearly not regulations, since there were very few. Rather, it was the sense of mission of the ESF staff, the commitment of the president to a nonpolitical institution, and the sense of crisis that united much of the nation. With less sense of urgency and two parties in government competing for spoils-sharing power, it was going to be far more difficult for the SIF to achieve the same unique status and relative freedom from politics that the ESF had.

Conclusion

It is difficult to draw simple or straightforward conclusions about the effects of the ESF on politics or the effects of politics on the ESF. It is even more difficult to establish any direct causal relationship between the ESF and the political sustainability of the adjustment program. However, given the amount of resources administered by the ESF, the numbers of people that it reached, and the prevalent position that it had in national and local politics, it is plausible to assume that it played a role in strengthening support for the Paz Estenssoro government, if not directly for economic adjustment.

The ESF and Political Sustainability

The *perception* that the government is doing something to make the adjustment process less painful or costly is important to the political process of sustaining adjustment. The important distinction is not necessarily whether this support is for the adjustment process per se or for the government implementing it. The ESF reached unprecedented numbers of the poor, and local organizations and public offices established a cooperative working relationship with the central government for the first time. Groups that traditionally had been in the opposition discovered that they could benefit from working with the government. If this did not create direct support, it at least reduced potential opposition to the government and its program. And concentrating on the previously marginalized was more cost-effective from the perspectives of both political sustainability and poverty reduction. If the government had instead focused all its compensation efforts on the less poor and more vocal and organized groups such as the tin miners, it would likely have had difficulty persuading them to support its policies, regardless of the level of compensation, because their relatively privileged positions were being permanently undermined by the adjustment program. The unwillingness of these groups to work for ESF wages because they were deemed to be too low demonstrates that they were clearly better off than those who did work in the ESF.

The significance of the support generated by the ESF varied, depending on the beneficiaries. The low level of organization of ESF workers coupled with their lack of knowledge about the ESF meant that as a group they could hardly be counted on to form an organized base of support for any political party, the government, or the adjustment program. Yet the employment of substantial numbers of people who would otherwise have been out of work helped sustain the adjustment process. The experience of several countries suggests that the isolation and frustration that accompany unemployment contribute to political discontent and social unrest.[74] In addition, it is likely that support for, or at least a more positive view of, the government was generated among those workers who did understand their relation to the ESF.

Beneficiary communities had a better grasp of what the ESF was all about than the workers did, for communities often participated in the solicitation of particular projects. The awareness and general positive opinion of the ESF at the community level provided a significant base of potential support for the government during the adjustment process, although this support did not necessarily translate into votes at election time. And in general the ESF enhanced NGO-government relations, even though it aroused political hostility or opposition among some NGOs. This also translated into indirect support for the government, or at least it led groups that would otherwise have been hostile to the government's "orthodox" economic policies to take a more neutral view of them.

Again, this was a form of indirect support for—or at least less opposition to—the adjustment process.

As for the general political impact of the ESF, it was strongest in small remote communities or municipalities that had traditionally been neglected by the state; and it was less significant in larger, more politicized communities with highly organized bases of opposition, such as those made up of former miners, or those in major cities where a large number of political forces were competing for political support, such as El Alto. In such communities, it was much more likely for hostility toward the ESF to be generated by politics.[75]

What the outcome would have been without an ESF can only be guessed. Although it might have been possible to implement economic reform, Bolivia's fragile democratic institutions would probably have been substantially weakened. Instead the ESF not only contributed to popular support for the national government but also promoted participation in the democratic process at the local level.

Some caution must be exercised when using the ESF experience as an example for other countries, however. The ESF did not build support for the government among those most directly affected by the adjustment program—the miners in particular. Rather, it gave a political voice to large numbers of the nation's poor, who had been previously neglected by the state. This strategy was successful because the miners were a minority, and the ESF had sufficient financial resources to reach a significant number of poor in relation to Bolivia's total population. If the organized base of opposition had been somewhat larger, or resources more limited, the political dynamic might not have been the same. In that case, very different criteria would have been used to determine whom to target so as to ensure the political sustainability of adjustment.

Politics, Poverty, and the ESF

Although it is as difficult to evaluate the effects of the ESF on politics as on poverty, a few clear conclusions emerge from Bolivia's experience. The Emergency Social Fund was unique in several respects: its demand-based approach, its effectiveness in attracting and channeling resources, its ability to isolate the project selection process from politics, and its success in achieving a cooperative relationship with the state. These achievements were particularly notable in a country where most poor areas had rarely, if ever, received government attention; where state institutions were known for their inefficiency, lack of responsiveness, and pervasive patronage; and where relationships between the government and NGOs had traditionally been hostile. It is not surprising, therefore, that the fund had a strong political as well as economic and social impact. The fund affected politics and politics affected the fund. Not all politics is bad, and not all of the political effects of the fund were bad. As mentioned earlier, the fund helped make the adjustment process more sustainable. It also contributed to the development of Bolivia's local institutions, which are key to poverty reduction.

The fund had diverse effects on state institutions. Because it operated outside public sector institutions, its effects at the central government level were minimal. Indeed, its highly visible presence may have provided the government with an excuse to avoid politically difficult social reforms. In contrast, at the local level, the ESF's effects on the capacity of both the state and NGOs to organize and administer its programs were substantial and enhanced the ability of these institutions to alleviate poverty. In many cases ESF funds allowed municipal governments to broaden their activities and pursue independent development agendas. This was a positive achievement in terms of both poverty reduction and political development. Although the exception rather than the rule, there were also cases in which conflicts of a political or personal nature obstructed working relations between local groups and the fund.

Meanwhile, politics had both positive and negative effects on the ESF. For the most part, fund personnel and projects were selected for technical rather than political reasons. Political pressures on the fund increased slightly after the departure of Fernando Romero, and markedly after the 1989 change of government. Yet there were limits to the extent to which the fund could be "used" by politicians, because of its demand-based design. And although the "results" of the fund were used by politicians at election time, the fund as an institution was not. This by no means guaranteed success. The effect of the ESF on elections depended in part on the nature of the municipality. In small, remote communities unaccustomed to government attention, ESF funds had more impact in general, and therefore were more likely to influence electoral outcomes than in larger, more politicized communities. Even then, because the ESF provided such communities with the opportunity to increase their independence through autonomous initiative, ESF funds did not necessarily translate into votes for established parties.

The ESF as an institution was also affected by politics to a certain degree. On the negative side, political pressure from the central government in some cases led fund staff to resign or to approve inappropriate projects. On the positive side, local politics were an important and positive aspect of the fund's operations. Reacting and adapting to local needs and demands were critical to the fund's operations, to its success as an institution, and to its effects on poverty alleviation.

By encouraging independent interaction with the state, the fund may have made local organizations and groups more willing to go beyond traditional party politics and exercise autonomous political choice. This may explain the lack of correlation between ESF funds and votes for established parties and the surge in electoral support for regionally based independents such as Max Fernandez and Compadre Palenque. The rise of "populists" such as Palenque and Fernandez was not necessarily a positive outcome, but it may have alerted centralized institutions such as political parties to the fact that they must be more responsive to local needs and concerns. To the extent that these are long-term effects, they constitute a positive trend in Bolivia's political development. And by enhancing the political voice of the poor, they increase the capacity of the poor to help themselves and therefore to reduce poverty.

In a nation where the practice of political patronage is the norm and where political economy is perceived as a zero-sum game, the ESF managed to remain remarkably free of political constraints and influence. Moreover, it conducted most of its operations in an efficient and transparent manner. The ESF experience does have relevance for implementers of similar programs in other countries: it demonstrates that a decentralized program based on local demand and administration increases the political voice of the poor and limits the extent to which the program can be used for political patronage by the central government or by any one political force. Such a program encourages the kind of independent local initiatives that are critical to reducing poverty. By taking such initiative and prompting an effective response from the state, the poor increase their stake in the "system," if not in economic reform per se. The ESF reached more than 1 million poor in a nation of just under 7 million people, either directly through hiring or indirectly through the works that it generated, which suggests that it had some direct impact on poverty in addition to enhancing the capacity of the institutions involved in reaching out to the poor. Although the demand-based nature of the program made it more difficult to target the poorest groups, on balance this may be a trade-off worth making, especially in view of other experiences with programs for the poor.

CHAPTER FOUR

The Politics of Reform without a Safety Net:
The Case of Peru

FEW countries in the world have suffered economic deterioration as extreme as that suffered by Peru in the late 1980s; fewer still have implemented as dramatic a stabilization policy to correct their macroeconomic distortions. Coming to power after the economic debacle and the hyperinflation of the 1985–90 government of Alan Garcia, Alberto Fujimori, a political unknown who had run on an antishock platform, had little choice but to implement an exceptionally harsh orthodox stabilization and adjustment program. The process of reform is far from complete, and the nation's democratic institutions have been in a state of flux ever since President Fujimori closed down the courts and the legislature in April 1992. Although elections for a constituent assembly were held in November 1992, the legal and legislative systems are not yet fully democratic.

As in many of the other cases discussed in this volume, the reform effort in Peru was largely shaped by the political context. Because of the extreme nature of the political and institutional crises, there was a limit to what any government could do from within the public sector. This suggests that a Bolivia-style program—independent of the public sector and insulated from political pressures—would have been the most appropriate approach to implementing a safety net. Yet for a variety of reasons detailed in the following pages, the government was very reluctant to act on the safety net front. The result, not surprising in the Peruvian context, was that most action on the compensatory front was by and large a private endeavor. In part because the poor had low expectations of the traditionally inefficient and unresponsive Peruvian state, a widespread grass-roots effort was independently launched to implement emergency feeding programs and other schemes to protect vulnerable groups.

Another unusual aspect of the Peruvian case is the congruence of circumstances that produced a political dynamic that fostered public tolerance of the costs of adjustment over the short term. Ironically, that tolerance gave the government even less incentive to implement a safety net, resulting in even greater hardship for Peru's most vulnerable groups and permitting the further erosion of democratic institutions. The case of Peru vividly demonstrates the costs of failing to address the social dimensions of adjustment—a strategy that makes it all the more difficult to sustain economic reform in the long run.

The chapter opens with a discussion of the political context and then moves on to the social costs of the pre-reform economic policies and of the adjustment measures that were subsequently necessary. These measures were implemented under two regimes: the 1985–90 Garcia government and the Fujimori government of 1990 onward. The Garcia regime attempted a "heterodox" stabilization experiment, but with dismal results. That may explain in part the Fujimori government's skepticism about the usefulness of safety net programs. The experiment also demonstrates how clientelism and partisan management can undermine the effectiveness of safety net programs, in sharp contrast to the Bolivian example. The discussion of the Fujimori approach explores the dynamics of dramatic economic reform with high social costs but without a viable safety net program.

The Political Context

As mentioned at the outset, economic reform in Peru failed to include any significant compensatory measures. In most successful cases of economic adjustment under democratic auspices—notably, Bolivia, Costa Rica, Spain, Thailand, and Turkey—governments made such programs an integral part of their adjustment effort, negotiated social pacts establishing the terms of compensation, provision of basic services, and increased spending on the social sectors.[1] Even many authoritarian regimes, such as those in Chile, Ghana, and the Philippines, introduced safety net programs to complement adjustment efforts.[2]

In Peru the absence of popular protest against the economic measures is as notable as the absence of a safety net. Indeed, Fujimori retained approval ratings as high as 64 percent in 1992 and 69 percent in mid-1993.[3] This is particularly striking in view of the extensive protests the Peruvians mounted against far less severe austerity measures in the late 1970s. Their subsequent behavior had a great deal to do with the extreme economic shock that preceded adjustment and with the violence perpetrated in the continuing war with Sendero Luminoso, or Shining Path, a group of fanatical Maoist insurgents. In this atmosphere of pervasive Sendero-linked violence, strikes and street protests became associated with terrorism rather than with economic policy and destroyed the incentive for social protest. The issue on which the population was evaluating the government was of higher priority than the economy.[4] Yet their reluctance to protest against stabilization policies did not necessarily translate into sustained public support for longer-term structural reforms.

Although populations often remain neutral or give the government tacit consent after extreme crises, once the move is made from stabilization to adjustment, this support tends to erode in the face of pressure from various interest groups that are negatively affected. As the "honeymoon" following stabilization comes to an end and structural reforms require continued sacrifices, it becomes increasingly difficult to maintain that support. A government's ability to deliver immediate results *and* to convey a sense of equity is often the critical factor in generating popular support at this point.[5] Compensation can help gain that support: safety nets are ideal tools for delivering immediate results on the social welfare front, as well as for addressing equity concerns.

The Peruvian government's awareness of the transient nature of its support—it had no institutional base in any party or front—explains in part its temporary closing of democratic institutions in April 1992, known as the *auto-golpe*, or self-coup.[6] Just before the closings, the opposition in Congress had organized as a coherent force for the first time since Fujimori came to power to protest the "antipopular" nature of the government's economic program. Ironically, the leaders of the opposition were none other than those who had been largely responsible for the economic debacle of the late 1980s: Garcia and the American Popular Revolutionary Alliance (APRA) party. Recognizing how vulnerable he was to an organized opposition, the president condoned the systematic persecution of APRA party leaders after the coup.[7]

One reason for the strong support for Fujimori, as mentioned earlier, was the extent of the crisis that made adjustment necessary. The social costs of Garcia's mismanaged heterodox economic policies, after almost a decade of steady decline in the standard of living, resulted in an unprecedented deterioration of the economy, marked by hyperinflation, and of the state's capacity to deliver essential services at a time of rapidly increasing demand. As living conditions grew even worse, there was a *desborde popular*, or popular overflow, on the social front.[8] By the time Garcia left office in 1990, the provision of basic services had virtually ground to a halt. Exacerbating the situation, political violence on top of economic chaos generated a general sense of turmoil and instability. The stabilization efforts of August 1990 rapidly stemmed hyperinflation, which fell from an annual rate of 8,000 percent that year to 556.6 percent in 1992, the lowest level in fifteen years.[9] Although the price stability that ensued did not bring political stability, its swift halt of inflation at least provided some semblance of economic stability, which had important effects on all societal sectors, in both economic and public confidence terms.

By the end of the APRA regime people had such low expectations of the state and had suffered such severe economic decline that it made little sense to oppose the government's adjustment policies. As a result, measures such as the early retirement of public sector workers drew surprisingly little protest. In addition, salaries in the state sector were so low that most public sector workers were forced to supplement their income in the informal sector.

Indeed, when the August shocks were administered the general feeling was that there was no real alternative. While Mario Vargas Llosa campaigned on a pro-shock platform and lost, his loss was due as much to his association with Peru's traditional elite and the parties of the right as to his explicit economic platform. In contrast, Fujimori's campaign slogan of "Work, Honesty, and Technology" was a deliberately vague "alternative" to Vargas Llosa's promises of a shock. Fujimori also profited from the split of the United Left coalition into moderate and radical camps in 1989, which meant there was no viable alternative from the left. Two weeks after coming to power, Fujimori, who of the two candidates was considered to be the man of the "pueblo," implemented precisely the shock that he had campaigned against.[10] By that point, almost everyone felt that a shock was inevitable. Politically, the shock was more acceptable coming from the candidate supported by the majority of the poor than from Vargas Llosa, who had links not only to the aristocracy but also to the severely discredited traditional party system.

Another important factor that led people to accept the shock program was the charisma of the first economics minister, Juan Carlos Hurtado Miller, who had a rare ability to communicate with the public. In a two-hour address on national television in which he presented the shock measures, Hurtado Miller stressed the unprecedented nature of Peru's crisis and made it clear that there were simply no alternatives to the stabilization policies. From that point until his resignation in early 1991, he remained more popular than most politicians in the country—including President Fujimori.[11] In his presentation of the measures, Hurtado Miller also called for a social emergency program to complement the shocks. His highly visible and charismatic presence—which contrasted sharply with the withdrawn and serious persona of the president—sold the stabilization policies to the public and ensured the success of the early stages of the reform program.

Ironically, however, because there was no organized popular protest against the economic program, the government saw no threat of social unrest and no longer felt compelled to act on the safety net front. Its decision seemed justified, at least in political terms, as community organizations and NGOs demonstrated an enormous organizational capacity for self-help, distributing quantities of food aid and other services to millions of poor in shantytowns in Lima and other cities. The need for social safety nets seemed greatly reduced, and the government took no serious action to increase its hopelessly inadequate levels of social expenditure until late 1992.

At that time the Fujimori government decided to more than double expenditure on food aid and on the newly revamped social fund, Foncodes, thereby giving it a much more prominent position. The total social expenditure was raised to 10 percent of the government budget for 1993.[12] Perhaps by then the government had become aware of the need for a more institutionalized base of support.

The Peruvian government also had an enormous amount of freedom to make policy by decree, some of which was provided to the executive in the 1979 constitution. In addition, from the initiation of the Fujimori government until November 1991, the president had "emergency powers" that allowed him to make virtually any kind of policy by decree. Congress only had after-the-fact review privileges. In the month before the emergency powers were to expire, Fujimori issued 126 decrees—which was more than Alan Garcia had issued in his first three years in office. In a special session two months later, the legislature modified or repealed only 28 of these, most of which dealt with counterinsurgency rather than with economic policy. And although the legislature had censured more than fifty ministers during Fernando Belaúnde Terry's first term in the 1960s, under Fujimori it censured only one minister in twenty months.[13] Despite Fujimori's claims to the contrary at the time of the *golpe*, Congress did not pose a serious obstacle to the implementation of the reform program. Indeed, in comparison with other countries, Fujimori was able to push through a large number of significant reforms, including a reform of the labor code, a substantial increase in tax collection, and the privatization of some state-owned enterprises. Moreover, he did it in a very short time and with little organized opposition. Yet the freedom accorded to Fujimori early on served as a disincentive to any effort to build a coalition in favor of reform in Congress. Ultimately this made him more vulnerable to opposition once it began to organize in early 1992, and in part explains his closing down of Congress in April of that year.

By mid-1992 the public's tolerance of the effects of prolonged recession and unemployment was eroding, and a number of strikes were held in the public sector. At the height of the cholera epidemic in 1991, public sector health workers were on strike for more than two months. That same year, school children lost almost an entire academic year because of strikes in the public education sector.[14] And some of the most difficult structural reforms—such as privatization of the major state enterprises and reform of the sectoral ministries—had yet to be implemented. Opposition was even on the rise in the business community, where many industries were becoming insolvent because of the increased foreign competition sparked by trade liberalization, on the one hand, and the overvalued currency, on the other. The steady inflow of coca dollars that had opened up with a more aggressive monetary policy led to a sustained overvaluation of the new currency, the *nuevo sol*. There was much debate over whether the Central Bank could counter this trend with a more aggressive monetary policy. There was clearly also concern about the lack of progress on the safety net front within the international financial institutions (IFIs). In a rather interesting reversal of traditional roles, the

IFIs were more concerned about the social issues than was the government implementing reform.[15]

In this context Fujimori implemented the surprise April 1992 *auto-golpe*. Although this move brought him significant support immediately afterward, that support gradually faded as people began to recognize that the *golpe* was not a miracle cure. Whereas approval ratings for Fujimori were approximately 75 percent after the coup, in May the approval rating fell to 56 percent, and by June it was 41 percent.[16]

The erosion of political democracy—the closing of Congress and the continued harassment of the press and of opposition leaders, for example—was one rather negative result of the government's approach both to economic reform and to antiterrorism, which was to rely on secretive tactics and unilateral actions rather than consensus building, tactics that may be suited to short-term shock policies but not to a program for sustaining structural reform. A more open government concerned about generating consensus would most likely have addressed the social costs of reform much sooner. Only in late 1992 did the Peruvian government begin to pay attention to the social issue. Yet by then it lacked credibility on the social front; its effort may well have been too little, too late.

Of course, the public psyche at this time was also consumed with the threat from Sendero Luminoso. As a result, people placed a much higher value on strong leadership and decisive action than on forming a political consensus. The population's desire for a strong force against Sendero, as demonstrated in the widespread support for the president's *auto-golpe* in April 1992, diverted attention from their economic woes. In opinion polls taken from 1991 through early 1993, terrorism was seen as by far the nation's number-one problem, followed by unemployment and poverty. Human rights violations ranked tenth, and the interruption of constitutional regime ranked last.[17]

Timing was also critical in the political dynamic of this period. The capture of Abimael Guzman and several other members of Sendero's top leadership in September 1992 sent Fujimori's approval ratings skyward. This occurred at a time that there were almost daily car-bombings or other explosions in busy commercial sections of Lima and it looked as though the government was losing the war against Sendero. Much of the population was beginning to realize that the *auto-golpe* would not provide any kind of miracle solution. That may explain in part why Fujimori's approval ratings had fallen markedly by June of that year. People were also growing more frustrated with the prolonged poststabilization recession, as demonstrated by the prolonged public sector strikes.[18] Then the sudden capture of Guzman provided Fujimori with a second "honeymoon," something that most governments implementing reform are unlikely to have.

For several months after Guzman's capture, there seemed to be a widespread perception that even if the recession was bad, the government was doing well in the fight against Sendero Luminoso.[19] Having thus restored some of its popularity, the government gained the political momentum to continue with its potentially controversial economic reforms, such as its plan for reducing the size of the public sector. As late as March 1993, Fujimori's approval ratings in opinion polls were well over 60 percent.[20] In addition, in the elections for a Constituent Assembly in November 1992, Fujimori supporters garnered 48.5 percent of the popular vote and forty-three of eighty seats.[21] Although the electoral process apparently gave the government some unfair advantages and several opposition leaders and members of the press were harassed, most observers doubt that the results would have been noticeably different with cleaner elections.[22] The opposition, meanwhile, had no credible alternative economic plans to offer.

Following the second honeymoon, there were still no clear signs that the economy was emerging from its poststabilization recession. By March 1993 recession and unemployment had replaced terrorism as the nation's number-one problem in national polls. Forty percent of the population polled said they approved of the economic program, and 40 percent did not, with positive opinions directly correlated to higher income levels.[23] It seemed a matter of time before people would lose tolerance for the high social costs of reform, particularly in the lower-income groups, and would begin pressing the government for some form of compensation.

While in the early 1980s it was typical of most economic reform programs to neglect the social dimensions of adjustment, a consensus on the need to address social issues concurrent to implementing reforms has since developed in the international financial community. "This neglect of poverty alleviation may have stemmed from a failure to recognize that adjustment is a longterm process that benefits the poor only after several periods and that, furthermore, may be jeopardized if its interim social costs are considered too high."[24] Yet President Fujimori, who adopted orthodox economics with the fervor of a convert to a new religion, hardly approached social issues, which he considered marginal to his reform program.

Despite the severity of the adjustment measures in Peru and the Fujimori government's evident lack of concern for their social costs, there was virtually no popular protest against the government's economic policies, as explained earlier in this section. The absence of social protest and the high levels of support for the government in Peru seem to challenge an implicit assumption of this book: that there is some relationship between the political sustainability of adjustment and measures implemented to alleviate its social costs. At closer look, that challenge is less straightforward.

Although the autocratic Fujimori was quite adept at the tactics and strategies required to implement rapid stabilization, these are not the same strategies that generate support for sustained structural reforms, which usually depend on an organized base of political support. The lack of protest against stabilization measures is not the same as an institutionalized core of support for a prolonged period of economic social change. President Fujimori lacked a party or an organized political base of support, and his primary supporters in the campaign remained critical of orthodox shock therapy. A prolongation of the highly centralized and secretive decisionmaking that is often necessary to implement shock stabilization at a time of extreme crisis is likely to undermine policy effectiveness and create destabilizing expectations.[25] Such expectations—and the popular desire for immediate "miracle" solutions—were evident in the high levels of popular support for Fujimori's April 1992 *auto-golpe*. Yet it soon became clear that this was *not* a miracle solution. Even after the surprise capture of Sendero leader Guzman, it was difficult to imagine how Fujimori's resurgent approval ratings would translate into a broadly based and lasting core of support for reform. The sustainability issue, however, is not the only one of great concern in this case. Peru faces high human *and* economic costs arising out of the drastic increases in poverty, which will affect the quality and competitiveness of Peru's labor force in the future.[26]

The Social Costs of Adjustment—and of Avoiding Adjustment

Essential to the explanation of the rather singular political dynamics of adjustment in Peru is the extremity of the crisis that predated reform, as well as the social costs of the corrective policies that were implemented to stabilize hyperinflation and to eliminate extensive macroeconomic dis-

Table 4-1. *Basic Economic Indicators in Peru, 1981–90*

Year	GDP (1988 dollars) per capita	Average annual percent growth in consumer prices	Annual percent change in real wages[a]
1981	1,846	75.4	1.7
1982	1,804	64.4	7.9
1983	1,515	111.2	−14.3
1984	1,549	110.2	−8.0
1985	1,540	163.4	−8.4
1986	1,681	78.0	22.0
1987	1,814	86.0	3.8
1988	1,629	666.2	−22.1
1989	1,383	3,398.9	−48.3
1990	1,312	7,481.7	−19.4

Source: Inter-American Development Bank, 1991, pp. 150, 273.
a. These numbers apply only to the small percentage of workers who are in the formal sector. The vast majority who are in the informal sector may earn much less, or more, than this amount.

tortions. Owing to a combination of poor macroeconomic management and external shocks, the Peruvian population has been undergoing a steady erosion of its already poor standard of living since the late 1970s.

From 1977 to 1985, gross domestic product fell by 20 percent; in 1985 GDP per capita stood at the same level it was at in the late 1960s, when Peru was already one of the region's poorest countries. By 1985 inflation, which was at 30 percent in 1977, reached 160 percent; formal sector wages were at 64 percent of their 1979 level, and unemployment and underemployment had increased, respectively, from 5 to 10 percent and from 48 to 54 percent of the population. The share of social expenditure in the budget, meanwhile, dropped from 26 percent of the total in 1968–76 to 18 percent in 1977–85.[27] By the time Alan Garcia and his APRA government came to power in 1985, Peru was already experiencing a grave economic crisis, and political violence and social discontent were on the rise, as was most vividly demonstrated by the increasing number of insurgent groups and activities.[28]

After a two-year growth boom, which was the result of expenditure of the reserve stock and utilization of excess capacity, Garcia's poorly managed attempts to implement a heterodox reactivation resulted in an economic collapse of unprecedented proportions. From 1987 to 1990 per capita output fell by 25 percent (see table 4-1) and government expenditures fell by 43 percent, with a disproportionate decrease in social expenditures of 50 percent. By 1990 social expenditure in per capita terms was at 21 percent of its 1980 real value, at US$12 per person per year.[29]

Table 4-2. *The Extent of Poverty in Lima, 1985–86, 1990*

Poverty line[a]	Value of poverty line, June 1, 1990 (intis)	Percent of population below poverty line 1985–86	1990
Poverty line 1	1,447,650	0.5	17.3
Poverty line 2	1,447,650	12.7	54.7

Source: Paul Glewwe and Gillette Hall, "Poverty and Inequality During Unorthodox Adjustment: The Case of Peru, 1985–90," Living Standards Measurement Study, Working Paper 86 (Washington, D.C.: The World Bank, 1992).

a. Based on monthly real adjusted food and total expenditures per adult "equivalent." Poverty line 1 defines as poor any household for whom per capita income is less than the value of the minimum food basket. Poverty line 2 defines as poor all households where per capita food expenditures are below this amount.

Table 4-3. *Percent Change in Per Capita Monthly Consumption in Lima between 1985–86 and 1990*

Characteristic	Percent change	Characteristic	Percent change
Sex		Occupation of head	
Male	− 54.5	Agriculture	− 50.4
Female	− 54.9	Sales and services	− 56.7
Education level		Industry and crafts	− 52.3
None	− 58.7	White collar	− 54.1
Primary	− 59.1		
Secondary general	− 55.1	Unemployed	− 65.9
Secondary technical	− 46.4	Retired	− 50.2
University	− 54.0		
Other postsecondary	− 38.9	All Lima	− 54.6

Source: Ibid.

Indeed, one of the most crucial and devastating effects of the APRA government was that although in theory it was expanding the role of the state, in practice it was destroying the state's capacity to function. Between 1985 and 1990 the tax burden, for example, fell from 15 to 3 percent of GDP.[30] From 1985 to 1990 all social groups experienced declines of approximately 50 percent in their real values of food and total consumption; the decline was regressive, with the poorest deciles experiencing decreases of 58 percent and 62 percent in food and total consumption, respectively.[31] Using a minimum basket of goods or a minimum wage definition of poverty, 12.7 percent of the population of Lima was below the poverty line in 1985. This figure increased to 54.7 percent by 1990 (see tables 4-2, 4-3 and 4-4); real wage and minimum wage figures are somewhat limited in their representation of actual living standards owing to the high percentage of workers in the informal sector, some earning more and others less than the minimum wage. And whereas 53 percent

Table 4-4. *Change in Average Annual Consumption in Lima between 1985–86 and 1990, by Decile*
Thousands of constant June 1, 1990, intis

Decile	1985–86	1990	Percent change
1	2,258.6	848.9	−62.4
2	3,181.1	1,345.2	−57.7
3	3,808.0	1,731.9	−54.5
4	4,386.9	2,015.2	−54.1
5	5,164.7	2,349.7	−54.5
6	6,098.9	2,739.6	−55.1
7	7,128.5	3,218.5	−54.9
8	8,669.9	3,970.8	−54.2
9	11,451.5	5,311.0	−53.6
10	25,657.8	11,796.0	−54.0
All Lima	7,774.4	3,531.7	−54.6

Source: Glewwe and Hall, 1992.

of the capital city's population was fully or "adequately" employed in 1985, in 1990 the figure was only 5 percent.[32] Nationwide, it was estimated that more than 50 percent of the Peruvian population were below the poverty line, and that one-third of the national population—or 7 million people—were in conditions of extreme poverty.[33]

The corrective shocks that were necessary to stabilize hyperinflation of 8,000 percent—which was driven largely by increases in the public sector deficit—also had enormous costs for popular consumption levels. In August 1990 the price of gasoline rose by 3,000 percent and that of most basic foods by 500 percent overnight. Consumption levels dropped another 24 percent across the board, placing large numbers at the margin of the poverty line below it, and with marked health and nutritional consequences for the poorest groups (discussed below). The crisis was further exacerbated by a cholera epidemic in 1991 that claimed hundreds of thousands of victims and caused a US$1 billion loss in potential export revenues and other related costs.

The impact of economic deterioration across households was directly related to education levels and access to foreign transfers, both of which resulted in smaller declines of per capita consumption. There was no apparent benefit in being linked to a domestic transfer network, and employment type was only moderately significant in mitigating the impact. Unemployment, meanwhile, rose most significantly in the bottom two income quintiles.[34] There has been a gradual impoverishment of the middle class and an erosion of differences between it and the upper-income quintiles of the poor. Whereas income per capita in the middle sectors in 1993 was twice that of the poor, the average percentage of income spent on food was about the same for the middle sectors and the higher poverty quintiles—on the order of 45 percent.[35]

Despite the crisis and the shocks of the 1985–92 period, there was no general deterioration in anthropometric measurements or increased incidence of acute malnutrition (defined by a deviation from standard weight for height, a measure that reflects sudden or abrupt reductions in food consumption, as in the case of famine). The infant mortality rate actually dropped eighteen points during those years, from 73 deaths per 1,000 live births in 1986 to 55 per 1,000 in 1991, and the child mortality rate also fell significantly.[36] However, studies done between January and March 1991 in the poor, peri-urban areas of Cajamarca, Lima, Cusco, and Piura did find moderate changes in the nutritional status of the very poor. In comparison with 1984, chronic malnutrition or "stunting" (defined as deviations from standard height for age) increased 27 percent in Lima and 11 percent in Cajamarca, whereas chronic malnutrition in Piura and Cusco declined. The percentage of children *at risk* of chronic malnutrition (that is, with a deficit of height between 1 and 2 standard deviations from the norm) increased between 7 percent and 39 percent in all four cities.

The increase in chronic malnutrition in urban areas, which tends to be linked to prolonged conditions of poverty and poor nutritional and health standards, can in part be explained by increased migration from the impoverished sierra regions, where nutritional conditions are worse in general and average heights are lower. It also may reflect a general deterioration in the quality of diets of the poor during the crisis years. In the face of escalating inflation in the late 1970s, the urban poor were able to adapt their expenditure patterns and continued to consume a nutritionally adequate diet, but budgets may have been stretched to the breaking point by the late 1980s.[37] This is reflected in the higher incidence of chronic malnutrition among the lowest socioeconomic quintiles in the sample, the same households that were less likely to meet total nutrient requirements. The sharpest deteriorations and incidences in acute malnutrition seem to have been among the poor rural population, whose standards were already worse than those of urban areas.[38] Mean calorie consumption in the urban areas remained between 92 percent and 119 percent of recommended levels, with expenditure on food accounting for

47 percent of expenditure among the wealthier quintiles and 60 percent in the lowest quintile.[39]

The greater vulnerability of the poorest socioeconomic quintiles in urban areas, as well as the poor in remote rural regions, is not surprising. Yet it is worrisome in view of the fact that information is limited to the four regions in the study, and conditions in other rural or peri-urban parts of the country might be worse. The role of food aid in providing some sort of safety net has been concentrated in the capital. The proportion of families that used food programs, of either donated or bought food, was high only in Lima, where 47 percent of families of the lowest income strata participated. In the highest strata of Lima families in the sample (the sample excluded the wealthiest 20 percent in Lima), almost 9 percent used a food program, a percentage that exceeded that of even the *lowest* socioeconomic levels in the other cities.[40] In Lima programs such as the Vaso de Leche and millions of dollars in donated food from abroad have been critical to maintaining the consumption levels of the urban poor.[41]

The lack of a *generalized* decrease in nutritional status and the continued improvements in infant and child mortality trends can be explained by several factors. The first is that while social expenditure decreased sharply, ongoing vaccination campaigns, which are funded primarily by external agencies and are key to reducing infant mortality, did not. Related to this, and slightly ironic, the public awareness campaign in the aftermath of the cholera outbreak was quite effective in training the majority of the population in oral rehydration techniques. Second, the poor of Peru have consistently demonstrated a remarkable ability to adapt purchasing practices and diet to changing economic conditions and to seek out the most nutritious buy at the best price. Only when budgets are stretched to a breaking point is a decrease in nutritional value of the diet noted.[42] Third, the poor of Peru have also demonstrated a remarkable organizational and self-help capacity, with a large number of communal kitchens and other community groups playing an important role throughout the 1970s and 1980s. After the August 1990 shock, the number of communal kitchens in Lima at least doubled, and, coupled with millions of dollars in food donated from abroad, played a key role in maintaining the general nutritional, if not the economic, status of the poor.

It is also important to note, however, that the poorest of the urban poor, as well as the remote rural poor, are far less likely to participate in these self-help schemes or to have access to food distribution networks, as the concentration of food aid in Lima demonstrates. Reliable or timely information on socioeconomic status is also much scarcer for these groups. As a result, the most vulnerable of the poor have suffered declines in nutritional as well as economic status, declines that could have been avoided if adequate safety net mechanisms had been established.

Peru's poor have demonstrated a remarkable capacity to adapt and to survive amid dramatic deteriorations of income. Yet indicators also point to a marked deterioration among the poorest sectors, which have the least margin to absorb economic shocks. In addition, there are longer-term effects, which include neglect of expenditures on health and education and basic social services such as water and electricity. The deterioration of nutritional standards among the poorest socioeconomic quintile was one notable effect, as was the outbreak of cholera in February 1991. And the lack of access to government-provided services acts as a regressive tax on the poor, who end up paying much more for informally provided services, which are of lower quality and less quantity, such as obtaining water from trucks and "electricity" from kerosene and candles.[43]

A key question for Peru is how the general deterioration of living standards and the erosion of economic opportunities will affect political stability in the long term. The pragmatic voting behavior and general social stability of the increasingly large numbers of urban poor (more than two thirds of Lima's population of 7 million lives in shantytowns, for example) has long been explained by migrants' increased access to education and opportunities for advancement for their children.[44] Some frustration with the erosion of opportunities for advancement was evident in the dramatic increase in terrorist violence and support for insurgent movements in poor urban areas since the late 1980s, particularly among youth. At the same time, there were no street protests after the dramatic August 1990 shocks, even in poor urban areas, and the government managed to maintain approval ratings of 60 percent or more over two years. Tolerance for stabilization policies was due in part to the immediate benefits that they bring, particularly for the poor, who are taxed regressively by hyperinflation.[45] But how long popular tolerance can last in the face of marked deterioration in economic and health standards is unclear. This is the arena in which the politics of adjustment in Peru may grow far more complex and in which the government's lack of attention to the social costs of its policies may jeopardize the viability of the longer-term process of reform.

The politics of adjustment in the Peruvian case cannot be fully understood without examining the dubious record of the country's past social programs. The Fujimori government's half-hearted approach to the safety net issue may in part be explained by the social policies under its predecessor, the APRA government. The following review of the APRA government's policies focuses on the urban poor for two reasons: first, because of the obstacle that political violence poses to conducting field research in rural areas of Peru; second, because the urban poor are more directly affected by adjustment policies than are the rural poor, as is generally accepted.

Safety Net Policies under the APRA Government

The steadily increasing numbers of urban poor in Peru have long attracted the interest of political leaders and parties—beginning with the APRA party in the 1940s and continuing through the 1990 electoral campaign of Alberto Fujimori—in their efforts to build a support base in that group.[46] The methods used to address urban poverty in the past were by and large vertical and clientelistic. They ranged from the dictator General Manuel A. Odria's use of charity and gifts for the poor to the 1968–80 military government's highly publicized National System of Social Organization (SINAMOS). The APRA government of 1985–90 began with a policy that, in theory, differed from the programs of past governments. It proposed to incorporate the marginalized urban population into the formal economy through the extension of credit and employment by the state. In practice, however, the government's policies were characterized by an unprecedented degree of sectarianism and were implemented in a centralized, authoritarian manner.

Because of the lack of attention to detail and to local needs, the work of most local organizations was soon disrupted and the groups eventually alienated. The way in which the APRA implemented its policies for the poor, in conjunction with its disastrous performance in government, was largely responsible for a general discrediting of established parties among low-income groups. As a result, they shifted their support to the virtually unknown Fujimori and his Cambio 90 front in the 1990 elections: support for Fujimori was much higher in poor urban areas than in wealthier ones.[47] A brief description of the organization of the urban poor and of how they were affected by the APRA government's policies will help explain this phenomenon and may also serve as partial explanation for the attitude of the Fujimori government toward safety net or pro-poor programs.

There are several forms of local organization in the *pueblos jovenes* or shantytowns of Peru, some autonomous and some related to municipal governments or political parties. There are more than 1,300 communal kitchens and more than 7,500 committees of the Vaso de Leche, or Glass of Milk, program, which was established by the 1983–86 United Left (IU) municipal government.[48] Mothers' clubs in a variety of *pueblos* are involved in sponsoring communal kitchens. The kitchens not only are an effective survival strategy for their communities but also promote the independence of women as organizers and leaders. Different political organizations have often tried to promote these kitchens for partisan benefit. During the 1985 presidential campaign, the APRA and Accion Popular (AP) competed with each other in sponsoring the kitchens. The wizened response of the poor is summed up by the slogan "Comedores APRA-AP: facil aparecen, facil desaparecen." IU seems to have focused more on promoting autonomous kitchens, perhaps because of the experiences of many of its leaders with grass-roots organizational activities. Although these organizations are heterogeneous, most observers agree that they play a critical role not only in the day-to-day survival strategy of Peru's poor but in democracy at the local level. Their importance increased enormously as the economic crisis deepened in the late 1980s, as well as in the aftermath of the 1990 shock.[49]

The APRA government implemented two major programs for the urban poor: the Program of Direct Assistance (PAD) and the Program of Temporary Income Support (PAIT).[50] The government set up the PAD to deal with community concerns in the *pueblos jovenes*. The program was designed to help equip communal kitchens; provide primary health care, supplementary education, and community infrastructure; and organize local craft industries. The program created fifty-three centers in Lima's shantytowns, but was run from the government palace, as it was a pet program of the president's wife.[51] The program often failed to coordinate with the municipalities and existing neighborhood organizations and was largely out of touch with their needs, as even officials of APRA-run municipalities privately admitted. A prime example was the government's decision, under the auspices of the PAD, to spend 350 million intis (more than US$3 million) on building two Olympic-sized pools in two *pueblos jovenes*.[52] Although there is clearly a need for recreation facilities in low-income areas, swimming pools that require expensive imported equipment and can only be used for half the year seem a poor and ad hoc use of funds in districts that lack water and sewage facilities.

The PAD claimed to be supervising the normal, institutional development of the mothers' clubs.[53] This attitude, coupled with certain new restrictions imposed to make clubs eligible for its support, made the PAD an affront to the autonomy of existing kitchens and mothers' clubs. Comments from various mothers' clubs about the PAD ranged from "The PAD is marginalizing some communal kitchens and mothers' clubs because they are sometimes mistakenly identified with the United Left" to "They insist that the three directors be Apristas [middle-level functionaries involved in local program administration] and hold party cards."[54] The party's attempts to impose external control on autonomous community organizations so as to channel popular demands were clearly resented by local organizations as a direct threat to their autonomy and created substantial ill will toward the APRA party. This dynamic is precisely the opposite of the bottom-up manner in which demand-driven social funds, if properly managed, contribute to institutional development and result in sustainable projects. Not only did control imposed from above give rise to poorly designed projects in the case of the PAD, but it served to keep the urban poor on the margins of society and alienate them from the established political system and the state.

The PAIT employment program was a central part of the government's strategy of raising the domestic capacity for consumption. The program was initiated with a great deal of propaganda and fanfare and was allocated a large budget.[55] The program was modeled on Chile's employment programs and consisted primarily of public works within the *pueblos jovenes* themselves. Unlike workers in Chile, whose wages were set well below the minimum, PAIT workers were paid the equivalent of the minimum wage for forty-eight hours of work. This tactic temporarily drove wages upward in the urban informal sector and eliminated self-selection as a targeting mechanism. Approximately 500,000 workers were employed by the program. They were selected through a lottery system and were primarily female (76 percent), young (33 percent were between sixteen and twenty-five), and poor (living standards among workers, in

Table 4-5. *Characteristics of Workers in Program of Temporary Income Support (PAIT)*

Characteristic	Percent of total	Characteristic	Percent of total
Sex		*Civil status*	
Male	24	Single	21
Female	76[a]	Married	64
		Widowed/divorced	14
Age			
16–25	33	*Household status*	
26–35	34	Head	33
>35	30.5	Spouse	47
		Son or daughter	13

Source: J. Billone: EL PAIT: Funcionalidad y Metodologias (Lima: INP 1986), p. 75.
a. Estimates of female participation vary, with others as high as 80 percent.

terms of access to basic services, were below the average for inhabitants of *pueblos jovenes* (see table 4-5).[56]

The PAIT came in with a bang and went out with a whimper. In January 1988 President Garcia announced that Cooperacion Popular—the agency that administered the PAIT—would be turned over to the municipalities. The 147 Cooperacion Popular offices nationwide were to be dissolved, but the PAIT was to continue, run by the municipalities: "Who could be better than a mayor to run the PAIT, choosing the truly most poor and needy to give them a job . . . without political criteria?"[57] Garcia's assurances were hardly credible, for in many regions municipalities were very weak and controlled by local party bosses or power brokers. Often local PAIT office directors had more power than the mayors themselves. Meanwhile, the PAIT had no official budget, but was merely an allocation in the central budget, which had to be renewed annually.[58] In view of the ensuing economic crisis and deficit of funds, it was highly unlikely that a large budget would be approved for a project that corresponded to municipalities, which in poor areas were already short of funds for most basic services, and that would allow the municipalities rather than the central government to reap political benefit.

In the end the program was never transferred to the municipalities, and it remained under the auspices of Cooperacion Popular, which was not dismantled. The PAIT continued to function on a much smaller scale, using primarily the labor of existing program staff. Officials assured people in the shantytowns that the program would continue, but none could specify how or with what funds. Those who had participated in the program and hoped to continue were thus left in a state of flux, and the promised work acted as a disincentive for seeking alternative employment. There were two explanations for the proposal to transfer—and in reality dissolve—the program. One was that Garcia wanted to curb the power of PAIT functionaries, many of whom supported Luis Alva Castro, Garcia's main rival in the APRA party. More important, though, the proposal was an indication that in the face of an impending budgetary crisis, the government was no longer willing to invest the funds necessary to keep the PAIT running on a full scale, particularly as the program had no political usefulness in the short term: the next elections were not until November 1989.

Despite this fading out, the PAIT had lasting implications. In many cases it gave desperately poor workers—primarily women—the chance to earn a stable if temporary salary. Unlike other employment opportunities, the program did not discriminate between men and women and gave women the opportunity of working near home; the reported shortages of domestic servants in wealthy Lima neighborhoods at the height of the PAIT reflect this.[59] The program provided necessary although temporary income relief for its workers, who were the poorest among the poor.[60]

Yet there were a variety of negative effects as well. First, the program acted as a disruptive force in many communities. Workers were selected by lottery, since there were usually more applicants than posts. The uncertainty proved disruptive both to families hoping to join the PAIT and to those hoping to continue working there; a dependence on PAIT income emerged in many cases, as some workers had given up previous employment to work in the PAIT.[61] The PAIT also disrupted many existing community organizations, such as mothers' clubs and communal kitchens, because responsibilities in these organizations were often dropped—which is not surprising—when the opportunity to earn PAIT income arose, even though it was only temporary. Indicative of the lack of concern for existing organizations was the PAIT's decision to create its own kitchen facilities rather than have its workers use the existing local ones at lunchtime. (Details on a typical PAIT community and the workers' opinions of the program appear in tables 4A-1 and 4A-2.)

The program had many additional effects: male-female relations were affected by women having a salary for the first time; because the work was designed for men, women often suffered health problems; because of the low productivity of the work, skills training was rarely provided. In addition, the often negative attitude of PAIT functionaries toward local organizations was criticized by many women in mothers' clubs. Others pointed out that young people refused to return to school when given the opportunity to earn PAIT income.[62] Despite its drawbacks, temporary nature, and the disruptive long-term effects that it might have had at the community level, the desperate nature of the population targeted made the program a highly popular one.

The willingness of Garcia and the APRA to use the program for political ends was demonstrated by the increase in enrollments before the November 1986 elections and by his announcement, in September 1988 while his cabinet was implementing a harsh austerity plan, that 200,000 PAIT posts would be created in the near future, positions that never materialized.[63] The fact that workers were desperate made it easier to use the PAIT as a political tool, as was done by many Apristas. Furthermore, program funds were widely misused.[64]

In keeping with the hierarchical nature of the APRA party, programs were highly centralized. There was little coordination with local government, particularly in municipalities run by Izquierda Unida. Instead the posts of PAIT zone directors were used as vehicles for young Apristas. The first director of the program had a reputation for using the program to build up his own—and the APRA's—political base.[65] There was a substantial bureaucracy in the directorate, which lent itself to politicization. For every thirty workers, or *cuadrilla* (squadron), there was a chief, and another chief for every four of those. In total there were 4,000 functionaries; most of them were either Apristas or APRA sympathizers.[66] These bureaucrats wielded a great deal of power in remote and poor regions and became cards in the intraparty power struggle between Alan Garcia and Luis Alva Castro. The growth of a parallel bureaucracy, which duplicated and undermined the activities of local governments and organizations, was precisely the opposite of the institutional development that successful poverty alleviation programs should have.

Not only was the PAIT bureaucracy politicized, but its workers were put to various political uses. At times they were used to disrupt strikes; for example, they broke picket lines when public sector doctors and teachers went on strike in 1986. Such acts made organized labor hostile toward the PAIT. In Villa El Salvador, PAIT officials persuaded workers to march against the IU mayor, Miguel Azcueta, claiming that he was opposed to the program.[67] Aprista functionaries paid by the PAIT were

Table 4-6. *Enrollments in PAIT Programs, Nationwide and in San Juan de Lurigancho and Huascar*

	Number of workers	Investment (intis)
Nationwide[a]		
October–December, 1985	35,114	99,400,000
January–March, 1986	33,931	53,976,156
April–July, 1986	41,949	107,925,806
September–December, 1986	150,824	630,444,000
January–March, 1987	12,273	66,219,932
April–June, 1987	100,000	584,000,000
Total	374,091	1,541,965,894[b]
San Juan de Lurigancho		
September–December, 1986	4,526	17,706
April–June 1987	2,450	11,588
November–December, 1987	584	5,350
Huascar		
September–December, 1986	423	2,068
April–June, 1987	554	2,638
November–December, 1987	122	1,090

Sources: Nicholas Houghton, *Empleos de Emergencia* (Santiago: PREALC, 1988, p. 209); and PAIT District Office, San Juan de Lurigancho.

a. The proportion of posts in Lima ranged from 20 to 30 percent of the total.

b. Equivalent to about 100 million U.S. dollars.

used in the November 1986 election campaign, and PAIT workers were often transported to APRA political rallies. The number of workers hired just before the November 1986 elections rose sharply, then fell equally as abruptly after the elections (see table 4-6).[68] At the time, there were allegations of a link between the allocation of PAIT posts and the areas where IU was strong, although the data do not demonstrate a significant correlation (see table 4-7). Also, it was rumored that in many cases an APRA *carnet* (party card) was required to register for the PAIT lottery. More believable were the rumors that *cuadrilla* chiefs had to be APRA members.[69]

The way in which the PAIT and PAD were administered exposed the sectarian and top-down manner that the APRA, a supposedly pro-poor party, operated and clearly undermined their ability to contribute to poverty alleviation. The blatant political manipulation of the programs also limited their ability to generate popular support for any economic policy. The penchant for expensive and grandiose gestures that had little to do with the realities or needs of the poor demonstrated the risks of a centralized approach to poverty alleviation, lending credence to a

Table 4-7. *Enrollments in PAIT Programs and Support for Opposition Parties in Low-Income Lima Districts*

District	Party with most votes[a] 1983	Party with most votes[a] 1986	Number of PAIT posts	Number per inhabitant[b]
Carabayllo	IU	APRA	4,080	0.085
Ate	IU	IU	4,600	0.043
San Juan de Lurigancho	IU	APRA	4,910	0.031
Comas	IU	IU	7,795	0.025
Independencia	IU	IU	4,400	0.022
Chorrillos	IU	APRA	3,100	0.019
El Augustino	IU	IU	3,930	0.018
San Juan de Miraflores	IU	IU	3,100	0.016
San Martin de Porres	IU	IU	2,830	0.007
Villa Maria del Triunfo	IU	APRA	1,800	0.005
Lurigancho	IU	APRA	1,800	n.a.
Villa El Salvador	IU	IU	5,570	n.a.

Sources: Carol Graham, "The APRA Government and the Urban Poor: The PAIT Programme in Lima's Pueblos Jovenes," *Journal of Latin American Studies*, vol. 23 (February 1991), pp. 91–130; and PAIT program offices, Lima.
n.a. Not available.
a. IU: United Left; APRA: American Popular Revolutionary Alliance.
b. Number of PAIT posts per inhabitant, October 1985–June 1987, from highest to lowest; based on a total population of 6 million. These figures are not entirely accurate, because the population expanded in the 1980s.

demand-based approach. The system of inscription by lottery made the acquisition of a job a function of luck and of government patronage, and promotion within the program was possible only for party members, a practice that was pervasive throughout the state bureaucracy during the APRA regime. The PAIT program raised expectations and caused disruption within communities and then was ended without warning. People were kept in a state of uncertainty with false promises that the program would continue, and thus were discouraged from seeking alternative employment. This manipulative approach to management served to undermine the poor's already weak faith in the state and in the established system, which is precisely the opposite effect of demand-based safety net programs like Bolivia's. There the poor saw the state follow through quickly and in a nonpartisan manner for the first time and felt they had a stake in "the system." It is little wonder that in the Peruvian context Fujimori's vague but telling campaign slogan, "Work, Honesty, and Technology," had a great deal of popular appeal in poor urban areas.

Ironically, the general discrediting of state institutions made it easier to initiate substantial reform of the system and in part explains the public's tolerance of the shock therapy. Sustaining such reforms—or any other coherent set of policies—however, was made far more difficult by the APRA's record: the discrediting of relevant institutions, such as political parties, and the poor performance of government efforts to protect the poor in the face of a dramatic impoverishment of the majority of the population. When Fujimori came to power, his greatest weakness, despite his popularity, was that he lacked any organized base of support to sustain his policies and his program, and consequently he relied increasingly on the military to govern, both indirectly and directly, as he did on April 5.

Safety Net Programs under the Fujimori Government?

Because of the APRA government's economic mismanagement, the Fujimori government had little choice but to implement a shock stabilization program. It did, however, clearly have a choice in its approach to the social safety net issue. That it did not try to protect the poor can be blamed in part on the weak record of such programs under the APRA regime and their reputation for partisan manipulation. Yet it also stemmed from the political beliefs and leadership traits of Fujimori himself. First, the promised social emergency program was victim to the rivalry between Fujimori and the highly popular Hurtado Miller. Second, the lack of popular protest and the remarkable autonomous efforts on the part of the urban poor and the NGO community to organize into communal kitchens and other self-help organizations on a wide scale eliminated the government's primary incentive—fear of popular unrest— for organizing a program. Third, the program was victim to Fujimori's desire to maintain authoritarian control over it. Thus, despite the availability of foreign resources, no viable safety net program got off the ground for more than two years.

The social emergency program, or Programa Social de Emergencia, was originally set up under the auspices of the prime minister, and a former colleague of Hurtado's, Percy Vargas, was appointed director.[70] Yet the budget for the program, which was minimal at best, remained under the president's direct control.[71] It was evident from the beginning that Fujimori wanted to control the program, no doubt because of the potential political benefits attached to the distribution of desperately needed social services. Although in theory the program was to concentrate on the provision of emergency employment, in practice few, if any, projects were implemented. Only 14 percent of what was originally programmed was actually spent in the first year, a total of approximately US$89 million for a target population of at least 7 million—slightly more than the government was spending *per month* (US$60 million) on repaying Peru's external debt arrears. Eighty percent of that expenditure, meanwhile, was in the form of externally donated food aid, and only 15 percent was spent on employment generation.[72]

In conjunction with the so-called social emergency program, a Transitory Coordinating Commission, organized to address the social costs of hyperinflation and deep recession in 1989 by the Catholic church, the NGO community, and the private sector, continued to function actively. At first the commission sought to cooperate with the social emergency program, but by the end of 1990 most of the main actors in the commission concluded that the social emergency program was little more than an increase in bureaucracy. The director of the program, meanwhile, was ousted by Fujimori in September 1991 and replaced two months later by an academic with little practical or management experience. Management of the program's budget remained separate, in the hands of a Fujimori loyalist with no experience in the social sectors.[73] Despite the constant reshuffling of management posts, or perhaps because of it, the program never materialized beyond the rundown Lima offices from which it was administered. In March 1991, after it was publicly clear that the social emergency program was a failure, the government announced a national system for social development and compensation to incorporate all ongoing efforts and activities of government ministries in the social realm. The national system had no more success than its predecessors.

A final effort was made to get the social emergency program off the ground in mid-1991, pushed largely by external donors, in particular the Inter-American Development Bank (IDB). In conjunction with a US$425 million dollar trade sector loan, the first new loan from an international agency to Peru since the Garcia government limited external debt payments, the IDB sent an advisory team to set up a new social program structure, obtained a US$4 million dollar grant for a pilot period for the program, and allocated US$25 million of the trade sector loan for the program, on the condition that the pilot phase was completed. On August 15, 1991, the National Fund for Development and Social Compensation (Foncodes) was announced.

The IDB team was clearly influenced by the success of Bolivia's Emergency Social Fund and the number of social funds that had since then been set up throughout the region. Peru's fund, Foncodes, was to be, like Bolivia's fund, an autonomous institution outside the public sector that reported directly to the president. The fund was to respond to proposals from community organizations, NGOs, and local governments for the construction of socially useful infrastructure, such as schools and health posts, using labor-intensive techniques that would maximize employment generation. It was also envisioned that, as in Bolivia, the director would be someone from the private sector with the capacity to run the fund according to efficiency rather than political patronage criteria.

President Fujimori, however, insisted on appointing the former secretary general of his Cambio 90 party, Luz Salgado, as head of Foncodes. While Salgado was a good political organizer, she clearly lacked experience in the social sectors or international finance.[74] Again this underscored the president's vision of the social emergency program as a potential political tool rather than as a serious social program. The IDB team then suggested—and made release of the additional US$25 million conditional on—the appointment of a general manager with private sector experience to manage the program.

Foncodes was officially launched in mid-1991, but a private sector manager was not hired until June 1992. In the meantime, Foncodes disbursed only a few projects with pilot funds, rarely according to the original demand-based design of the program, and often alienating local NGOs.[75] A credible agency could not develop because the government did not have a firm commitment to fund it and to keep it out of politics. The program received no external support, for not only the IDB but the World Bank and other donors were hesitant to channel money to an organization that seemed to have explicitly political objectives. The program was in theory allocated US$120 million in the government's 1992 budget, 80 percent for employment creation and 20 percent for social support, but the full amount was never disbursed.[76]

In June 1992, in part as a response to international financial community pressure, President Fujimori replaced Luz Salgado with a director from the private sector, Arturo Woodman. From that point on, Foncodes took on a more active role. For the first few months Woodman aimed to raise the program's reach and visibility. In 1992 Foncodes funded slightly more than 3,000 projects at a cost of US$75 million, with projects in all regions of the country. It has targeted its projects in three ways: investing US$29 million in the fifty poorest provinces in the country; investing US$55 million in the fifty most violence-ridden provinces; and financing 315 projects worth a total of US$7 million for non-Spanish-speaking groups.[77] The program's budget was expected to double in 1993, and program management planned to revamp its targeting and evaluation procedures. Foncodes was planning to receive more than US$200 million from government funds in 1993. The change in the program's visibility and efficiency was quite evident six months after the change of management, as was the government's increase in resources and focus on the program. Including the increase for Foncodes, the government planned to spend 1–1.5 percent of GDP, or US$43 million (equivalent to 10 percent of the government's budget and a 92 percent increase over 1992) on social programs for 1993.[78] If it actually did so, then it would be an effort on par with Mexico's widely noted solidarity program, which spent 1 percent of GDP (6 percent of the government budget) on social programs in 1992.[79] The government's commitment to the expenditure increases, as well as to keeping the program out of politics, however, remained to be seen, and was called into question by continuous rumors about Fujimori's attempts to continue to manipulate the program.

The delays in the implementation of Foncodes cannot be attributed to foreign resource constraints.[80] IDB funds available for Foncodes were not disbursed for more than a year in objection to the president's blatant attempts to manipulate the program for partisan purposes through the appointment of Luz Salgado. The experience of other countries has shown that donors are usually very willing to support safety nets during a time of extreme crisis if the government's overall macroeconomic strategy is on track *and* if a credible agency is set up to channel the funds. Bolivia's Emergency Social Fund is a case in point. The Fujimori government either was not aware of this—which would be surprising given the strong message from external agencies—or, more likely, just did not have a commitment to the program. In the short term, this may have been due to the government's initial opposition to a shock program; therefore little research had been done within its ranks on how to address the social costs of such a shock. In the longer term, though, a wealth of information was available both within and outside Peru about appropriate programs.

In sharp contrast to the government's half-hearted attempts to address the safety net issue, popular, NGO, and church activity at the time of the shock was remarkable. In the late 1980s there were approximately 1,700 communal kitchens—with 70,000 beneficiaries—and 3,500 neighborhood Vasa de Leche program committees—delivering approximately 1 million glasses of milk per day in Lima. It is estimated that the number of communal kitchens at least doubled after the August shock, and that Caritas (Catholic relief services) alone was channeling food shipments (largely from U.S. AID) to 1.2 million people (before the shock it had been delivering approximately 700,000 rations).[81] U.S. AID officials estimated that approximately US$41 million a year in its food aid was channeled through Caritas, the NGO Prisma, and the Seventh Day Adventist church philanthropic branch, OFASA, with US$71 million programmed for 1992. After the shock, the agency estimated it was feeding one in three Peruvians.[82] Although there was some competition within certain shantytowns between Catholic and evangelical groups involved in food distribution, or sometimes between autonomous kitchens and outside sponsors, in general the extent of cooperation and national solidarity was remarkable. The extensive nature of grass-roots and community-based organizations in Peru has often been noted by outside observers; their ability to expand markedly and efficiently at a time of extreme crisis lent strong credence to these observations. Yet, as mentioned earlier, the poorest of the poor and those in remote rural regions were far less likely to benefit from such efforts.

Paradoxically, the poor's remarkable ability to organize led to two unfortunate results. The first and most critical was that, in the absence of the fear of popular unrest and given the extent of autonomous activity, the government completely devolved itself from responsibility for implementing a program to address the social costs of its policies. Clearly, it was in a resource bind, as the proportionate amount of money going to pay debt arrears indicates. Yet the manner in which the program was managed and the government's lack of support for it precluded the cooperation of various willing external donors, who had resources earmarked to help Peru but could find no credible government agency to which they could channel those resources. Thus some money went to the church and other NGO groups; some resources were just not spent.

The second result—which was a confluence of disasters of sorts—was that autonomous social organization was so successful that Sendero perceived it to be a threat to its strategy of establishing a base in Lima. In late 1991 Sendero began an all-out assault on the heads of communal kitchens and shantytowns, threatening to sabotage all efforts that made the government's policies more viable. Dozens of communal leaders and organizers were assassinated: one of the most effective leaders of Villa El Salvador, Maria Elena Moyano, was shot and then blown up with dynamite in front of her children.[83] Although attacks on communal leaders subsided somewhat by mid-1992, they continued to pose a substantial threat to popular organizations, particularly because most such organizations were rarely, if ever, able to obtain security or judicial services from the state.[84]

At the time of this writing, the popular perception remained, not surprisingly, that the social emergency program was just another empty promise by the Peruvian state. The poor of Peru have long since ceased expecting that the state will provide them with any kind of services and rely largely on informal systems of service delivery for virtually everything from transportation to criminal justice. And, as already mentioned, the need to rely on informal services acts as a regressive tax. Given the extremity of the economic shocks as well as Sendero's assault on popular organizations, the absence of any state support became all the more critical and created a vacuum that was increasingly filled by the radical group. Although many urban poor did not necessarily support Sendero, they also had no means of protection from the group and increasingly defaulted to Sendero presence and control of popular organizations in the shantytowns. The fate of those who attempted to resist, like Maria Elena Moyano, was a stark reminder of the poor's lack of alternatives when challenged by the group.[85] And in the context of a deep, post-stabilization recession, employment opportunities could not serve as an alternative for most of the poor: less than 10 percent of the economically active population of Lima were adequately employed in 1992.[86] In few contexts was the need for a safety net more evident, which makes the lack of government attention to the issue all the more striking.

The government's failure to follow up on its promises of a social program also made it vulnerable to the opposition's focus on the anti-popular nature of its policies. Most paradoxical was that the opposition was led by none other than former president Alan Garcia, whose macroeconomic mismanagement had necessitated the shocks, but whose criticisms of government policies seemed to pose a threat to Fujimori. Indeed, as stated earlier, Garcia was a primary target of government repression in the aftermath of the coup.

The mid-1992 changes in the social fund made it more likely to obtain substantive international support and therefore to provide some sort of safety net during the future course of economic reform in Peru. And, as the process of reforming the sectoral ministries was just beginning and would take several years to complete, there was a critical role for an extraministerial effort to deliver on the social welfare front in the short term. The newly implemented Ministry of the Presidency, for example, was just beginning to reorganize and to establish its role as coordinator of social and development policy. The emergency fund had a clear role until social sector reforms could be completed and the economy recovered enough to generate substantial growth and employment. What remained in question was the sincerity of the government's commitment to a safety net, as well as its ability to establish a credible image for the revamped social fund.

Conclusion

The data that are available on the social costs of economic mismanagement in Peru—and on the corrective shocks it necessitated—are alone sufficient justification for a safety net. An additional justification is the challenge that Sendero Luminoso poses to the credibility of the Peruvian state, particularly among the poor, who rarely see the state follow through on its promises. In the face of such formidable obstacles, anything short of a full-fledged government commitment to launching a viable safety net program is likely to fail. After two years of neglecting the safety net issue, the Fujimori government changed its approach and increased its emphasis on the social fund, Foncodes. Unfortunately, the government's largely political rationale for revamping the program, coupled with the program's tainted image from earlier years, made it less likely to have the kinds of effects that some other social funds, like those in Bolivia and El Salvador (see chapter 8), have had on poverty reduction and on political sustainability. Successful funds have been far less politicized and were integral parts of reform efforts much earlier in the process in those countries than in Peru.

When Foncodes was revamped, it remained possible for a significant safety net effort to contribute to the sustainability of structural economic reform in Peru, because political challenges were likely to increase with further reforms and the slow pace of economic recovery. After several years of low inflation, the memory of the preinflation crisis was likely to fade, making the political debate more susceptible to "populist" promises and the government more vulnerable to criticisms of the social costs of its policies. This had already begun to occur before the close of Congress in 1992, with the reemergence of Alan Garcia as the leader of the opposition. And it is more difficult to implement structural reforms that permanently displace large numbers of workers, particularly from the public sector, than to implement stabilization policies, which usually yield immediate benefits by ending hyperinflation. Fujimori first met this political challenge by closing down Congress in April 1992, and later in the year by increasing social expenditure, not coincidentally in the months before the November Constituent Assembly elections.[87] International pressure for attention to the social dimensions of reform may have also played a role. The sincerity of the government's commitment to the social safety net, however, remained unclear at best.

The final course that democracy, economic reform, and poverty trends will take in Peru remains uncertain. Political democracy exists only in a limited way, yet in the current international political context some maintenance of democratic institutions will remain a prerequisite to IFI and international donor support. And although the absence of a social safety net did not significantly affect the launching of economic reforms, the recent revamping of the social fund may play a role in sustaining reform in the future.

All the same, Fujimori's new commitment to the social aspects of economic reform seems to stem from concerns for his political position rather than from any sense of their inherent importance to the sustainability of the economic program. Thus it is particularly critical—but also difficult—for the social fund to establish and maintain an autonomous and nonpartisan image if it is to contribute to poverty alleviation and to the sustainability of economic reform. As the first few years of reform demonstrated, major noneconomic factors, primarily the presence of Sendero Luminoso, will continue to alter the usual dynamics of the politics of adjustment, and thereby distinguish the Peruvian case. Thus reform in Peru may be sustainable without a safety net, but the costs in terms of poverty and the further erosion of state credibility—both fundamental causes of support for Sendero and other insurgent groups— would be extremely high. And if, in the face of an erosion of popular tolerance, reform is not sustainable, the resulting policy reversals and economic uncertainty may have devastating effects on the nation's already fragile democratic institutions and political balance and may erode even further the living standards of the nation's severely impoverished majority. Although it is impossible to predict which scenario will result, the implementation of a viable safety net program would be an obvious way to avert a dangerous gamble.

Table 4A-1. *Socioeconomic Characteristics of Huascar and Bayovar*[a]

Characteristic	Number	Percent	Characteristic	Number	Percent
Owns home	300	92.0	Number of floors		
Does not own home	26	8.0	One	312	95.7
			Two or more	14	4.3
Wall construction			Roof construction		
Cement or brick	155	47.5	Cement or brick	35	10.7
Straw matting	152	46.6	Straw matting	228	69.9
Cardboard or tin	4	1.2	Cardboard or tin	57	17.5
Other	15	4.6	Other	6	1.8
Where buys water			Kind of light		
From truck	322	99.1	Electric	312	95.7
Other	3	0.9	Candle or kerosene	14	4.3
Belongs to a			Participates in		
mothers' club			communal kitchen		
No	231	70.9	No	290	89.0
Yes	94	28.8	Yes	35	10.7
Doesn't know	1	0.3	Doesn't know	1	0.3
Belongs to Vaso			On communal		
de Leche			directorate		
No	101	31.1	No	229	70.2
Yes	224	68.7	Yes	81	24.8
Doesn't know	1	0.3	Doesn't know	16	4.9
Does communal work					
No	100	30.7			
Yes	224	68.7			
Doesn't know	2	0.6			

Source: Interview with Dr. Francisco Lazo, Instituto de Investigacion Nutricional, March 1988.
a. Total cases, 326: Huascar, 195 (59.8 percent); Bayovar, 131 (40.2 percent).

Table 4A-2. *Characteristics of PAIT Workers in Huascar*[a]

Characteristic	Number	Percent	Characteristic	Number	Percent
Number of times in PAIT			How entered the program		
None, but tried	1	4.3	By lottery	12	52.5
One	2	8.7	Signed up	3	13.0
Two or more	7	30.4	Both	7	30.4
Why entered the program			Invalid	1	4.3
Need for income	20	86.9	Mother abandoned by spouse		
Other	1	4.3	Yes	3	13.0
Invalid	2	8.7	No	20	86.9
Was in PAD or mothers' club			Member of community kitchen/ Vaso de Leche		
No	10	43.4	No	10	43.4
Yes, still	4	17.4	Yes, still	0	0.0
Yes, dropped	7	30.4	Yes, dropped	3	30.4
Invalid	2	8.7	Invalid	10	43.4
First work with income			Quality of PAIT work		
Yes	10	43.3	Easy	4	17.4
No	11	47.8	Hard	7	30.4
Invalid	2	8.7	Too hard	7	30.4
Previous work (of the 11 above)			Invalid	5	21.7
Selling food	1	9.1	Went to political rallies		
Washing	2	18.2	Yes, obligated	11	47.8
Street sales	4	36.4	Yes, voluntary	2	8.7
Lima job	1	9.1	No	2	8.7
Domestic servant	1	9.1	Invalid	8	34.8
Invalid	3	27.3	Went to rally and did not mind		
Wants to work again			Yes	8	61.5
Yes	17	73.9	No	5	38.5
No	3	13.0	Disadvantages		
Invalid	2	18.2	Work too hard	2	8.7
Advantages			Instability or lottery		
Near home	10	43.4	system	5	21.7
Income	3	13.0	Only party people		
Gives woman work	1	4.3	in	1	4.3
Fixed salary	1	4.3	Rich get work	2	8.7
Improves			Invalid	13	56.5
community	1	4.3	Was sole salary		
Illiterate or no job	1	4.3	Yes	7	30.4
Invalid	5	21.7	Had other	9	39.1
Felt party favoritism			Invalid	7	30.4
Yes	12	52.2			
No	1	4.3			
Invalid	10	43.5			

Source: Author's, Huascar, January–March 1992.
a. Total cases (valid observations): 23

CHAPTER FIVE

The Vocal Versus the Needy:
The Politics of Poverty Alleviation during Adjustment in Senegal

AFRICA is one region of the world where, on the whole, adjustment has moved slowly and without much success, resulting in many countries caught between "state and market."[1] The reasons are both political and economic. Political leaders lack the will or the institutional capacity to implement structural reforms in addition to stabilization measures, and the economic problems that necessitated adjustment remain unaddressed. As a result, adjustment has had little effect on poverty, which in many countries has simply grown worse. There are many other problems as well: patronage politics plays an extensive role in policymaking, managerial capacity is poor, and few countries have the institutions they need to operate a market economy. Furthermore, many politicians and civil servants have a greater stake in preventing or postponing adjustment than they do in implementing it. The poor, who in theory should benefit from structural changes—such as improved rural terms of trade and a reorientation of social welfare spending to primary education and preventive health care—usually do not, because the reforms are stalled or are being poorly implemented. If anything, the programs designed to protect "poor" groups during adjustment tend to evolve into opportunities for rent-seeking within the public sector. This is particularly true when programs have focused on compensating those hard hit by adjustment rather than on protecting the poor.

Of the countries on the continent, Senegal is one of the few with a long-established multiparty democracy. It is also among the nations with the most pressing poverty problems. Its experience with prolonged and postponed adjustment in the 1980s illustrates the difficulties of sustaining economic reform and of protecting vulnerable groups—much less the poorest—in the process. The slow pace of reform in Senegal—and thus the lack of positive results—has made political sustainability far more difficult. A central problem here is that the political context has played a large role in determining who benefits from safety net efforts. Groups strongly opposed to adjustment retain privileged positions within the public sector and governing party and as a result have been able to monopolize the benefits of most compensatory efforts. Yet the concentration of all safety net efforts on the vocal opponents of reform rather than on the poor in Senegal has not proved to be an effective strategy for sustaining adjustment, an outcome that confirms a basic proposition of this study. And despite the resources spent on compensation, there has been little reduction of poverty.

Violent protests and the arrest of several opposition leaders in the aftermath of national elections in February 1988 shook Senegal's democratic image and brought the issues of the social costs of adjustment and its political sustainability to the forefront of the political debate. Since that time the government has made substantial concessions to the opposition. Most notably, it has reversed several key reforms, some having to do with the prices of urban consumer goods, and has introduced two programs that address the grievances of the "victims" of adjustment.

One of those programs is the Délégation à l'Insertion, à la Réinsertion et à l'Emploi (DIRE). Although it was established in 1987, the DIRE received increased public attention after the political unrest of 1988. It was aimed at parastatal workers who were laid off (*deflates*); civil servants who voluntarily retired; and university graduates (*maitrisards*), who, before adjustment, would have found jobs in the civil service. The other program is the Agence d'Exécution des Travaux d'Intérêt Publique contre le Sous-Emploi (Agetip), a semiautonomous government agency analogous to Bolivia's Emergency Social Fund. It was designed to fund labor-intensive public works executed by private sector companies that hired unemployed and primarily unskilled youth. Those without skills were considered to be a frustrated and potentially explosive element of society, largely because of their role in the February 1988 protests. It is widely accepted that the DIRE, for a variety of reasons detailed later in this chapter, was on the whole a failure. In contrast, Agetip, through rapid, transparent, and efficient management, has created a revolution of sorts and has even been cited as a model for the reform of Senegal's notoriously inefficient public administration. A primary reason for its success is that it has been insulated from politics and from Senegal's highly partisan and clientelistic public sector. Furthermore, its designers recognized that the employment issue had to be addressed if reform was to be sustained, because the opposition was extremely effective at tapping the frustration of unemployed urban youth. It is important to note, however, that although a great deal of the infrastructure built by Agetip has benefited poor areas and has created temporary jobs for poor and unskilled youth, the program is not specifically targeted at the poorest groups.

Indeed, the growing numbers of poor living on the perimeter of urban areas, in *bidonvilles* (shantytowns), have been almost ignored in the public policy debate. Yet they are the ones least able to absorb the rising prices of consumer goods and least likely to find steady, long-term employment. They have experienced greater declines in income during the adjustment period than have rural groups.[2] Like the rural poor, their political voice is much weaker than that of most other groups. Although it is not clear that public resources can reach the poorest of the poor effectively, little if any attempt has even been made to distinguish between poor and nonpoor groups in the allocation of compensatory benefits.[3] The purpose of this chapter is to examine the politics of adjustment in Senegal and the two main programs designed to address its social costs, with a view to determining whether such programs can help sustain the adjustment process and alleviate poverty over the long term. Another central question to be considered is to what degree political and institutional context determines the weight placed on each of these objectives.

The Political Context

Senegal's long-lasting political pluralism and stability may be described as an imperfect democracy that has nonetheless "served Senegal well in terms of social peace."[4] Although political freedom has been revoked at times, as it was during the 1968–74 period of one-party rule, Senegal has made impressive strides in the liberalization of the one-party state, and has managed to avoid the civil strife common in many of its neighboring countries.[5]

Senegal's political system, like its culture, is a complex mix of traditional and modern practices, religious fervor coupled with a high degree of tolerance, and internationally based ideologies infused with nationalism and pragmatism. Unlike most other colonies, Senegal did not have to endure a violent struggle for independence, and the members of its elite held office in the French National Assembly. Thus the roots of a democratic system were already in place. In addition, ethnic divisions are mitigated by the unity that the Islamic religion provides. The predominant tribe is that of the Wolof, whose empire fell to the French. During the colonial period, Wolof religious leaders—marabouts—replaced tribal chiefs in village hierarchies. They still play a large role today, issuing *ngidal*, or orders, before elections to indicate how the rural population and even some in urban areas should vote. The influence of the marabouts is more limited in urban areas, where the politically active urban youth seem to accept the religious function of the marabouts but disapprove of their involvement with the governing party.[6]

No politician, even the most extreme Marxist, seems willing to challenge the marabouts, however, and many even credit them with preserving Senegal's stability and providing an alternative to civil strife and dictatorship. Although the marabouts may not be democratic, they do support the existing system of government. Because of that support and their control over the rural population, no such challenge—even a military one—could hope to succeed. For the largely illiterate rural population, the marabouts also serve as an alternative to the seemingly oppressive and unintelligible state bureaucracy. Yet religion can also be a destabilizing force, and Islamic fundamentalism is apparently on the increase, particularly among frustrated groups such as the urban poor and unemployed youth.[7]

Islamic fundamentalist tendencies in Senegal seem to be tempered with a high degree of tolerance. Although only 15 percent of Senegalese are Catholics, the first president and leader of the independence movement, Leopold Senghor, was a Catholic, and the current president, Abdou Diouf, a Muslim, is married to a Catholic. These are but two examples of the interaction and mutual tolerance between the country's religious groups.

Another prominent characteristic affecting Senegal's political structure is a high degree of clientelism and clanism. Personal and family ties are so strong that Senegal is said to have an economy of affection: noneconomic factors that affect economic decisions and "impose social obligations on individuals that limit their interest and capacity to support public concerns outside the community."[8] Although such ties exist in many African countries, in Senegal they cut across religious, class, and ethnic lines. Clientelism and clanism are at the base of the political-administrative system. The Parti Socialiste (PS), for example, which has been the predominant political party for decades, is in theory anchored in socialist ideology. In practice, however, it acts as a clientelist political machine. Its main rival, the Parti Démocratique Sénégalaise (PDS), also depends on clientelist ties for its political base. Even unions, traditionally quite strong in Senegal, are part of the clientelist system.[9]

Although Senegal's religious leaders and clientelistic politics provide stability for the regime, they are not necessarily supportive of democratic principles or of economic and administrative reform. Many members of the political elite remain uncommitted to a reform process that threatens their base of privilege. The clientelistic system benefits three groups in particular: trade unions, civil servants, and students. Civil servants have been a strong political force ever since the French granted them political rights before independence. Their ties to the PS made them an important base of support for the government after independence. University students, meanwhile, have traditionally been granted free tuition, subsidized meals, and a guaranteed job in the civil service. This is a regressive distribution of resources in a country where many are without access to basic health, education, and services such as running water. The students have become an organized and vocal group that can mount a formidable political opposition. Trade unions have also held a privileged position in relation to the average worker and have contributed to the inefficiency that pervades both the public and the private sectors. Few people trust or support private enterprise, which they associate with the French or with other foreign interests.[10]

To some extent, even the poorest groups accept clientelistic politics. Competing factions of the PS, for example, have traditionally tried to control urban shantytowns by offering them services, the most prized being the acquisition of *bornes-fontaines*, or common water spigots. With the prolonged economic decline since the early 1980s and the state's decreasing capacity to deliver services, clientelism has begun to lose some of its force as a source of political stability, at least at the level of the urban poor.[11]

The prevalence of clientelism does not augur well for efficient public administration and economic management. Through their effective political opposition, civil servants who have lost status and income because of adjustment have been able to slow the pace of reform. Indeed, the number of civil servants has continued to increase throughout the adjustment period, although real wages have fallen steadily.[12] In the economy, the clientelist-based influence of the marabouts has been cited as one of the main reasons for the precarious condition of the banking system.[13] The economy of affection has also had negative effects on wage earners' ability to save and has thus created a major obstacle to economic growth. Workers in any case have an extremely difficult time saving much of their earnings, because many of them support several extended family members, either in the city or in their rural hometowns.[14]

The links between society in general and the formal political-administrative system and the elite who benefit from it are limited at best. Most people live on the margins of the system, frustrated by a stagnating economy and shrinking economic opportunities. It is little wonder that violence erupted during the elections of 1988 or that the campaign slogan of the opposition was *Sopi*, the Wolof word for change.[15] When the Diouf regime in 1991 invited six parties to join the government, it received a positive reply from the main opposition party, the PDS, and one Marxist party, the Parti de l'Indépendence et du Travail (PIT). To the majority of the splinter parties, as well as to those disaffected from the political system in general, however, the PS and the PDS are not that different, and the new governing alliance is merely "old wine in a new bottle."[16] Even the poor have felt that bringing the opposition into the government has not signaled much of a change in the system or its policies.[17]

At the same time, another kind of change has taken place: "As 'social forces, expectations, and grievances have been unable to find a means of expression in the structures and organizations that Senegalese democracy has made available to them,' the gap between civil and political society has widened, and the people have begun to channel their demands through other institutions and processes."[18] These are nongovernmental institutions and autonomous grass-roots organizations that are democratic in character. The phenomenon is analogous to the informal economy: unable to meet their demands within the system, people are resorting to similar activities in a parallel or informal arena. Yet, as in the informal economy, there are legal and institutional limits to vertical links. These limits, particularly in the political arena, can lead people to become frustrated, as they did during the February 1988 violence, or can lead them to look for alternative systems, such as those founded in religious extremism.

The Adjustment Process

From the time it gained independence in 1960, Senegal has had the slowest growth rate of any African country not prone to extreme civil unrest. At the same time, it has received the largest amount of foreign aid per capita.[19] This, coupled with reasonably good economic conditions and deficit spending in the 1960s and 1970s, allowed the "system" to remain stable. Indeed, high levels of donor aid permitted Senegal to postpone necessary economic adjustments. Since the onset of the economic crisis of the early 1980s, however, President Diouf has been trying to implement reform from within the system, although there has been some criticism of these efforts: "Judging from trade and industrial policy in the 1980s, the leaders of the Diouf administration perceive their best defense in the face of economic crisis to be one that accommodates the powerful but does not focus on the frustrations of the poor (who are strong in numbers if nothing else) with the regime itself."[20]

The prolonged economic crisis and the adjustment efforts have both entailed social costs, such as rising prices for consumer goods and fewer employment opportunities. The government's initial response to these costs of adjustment was to "take care of its own." As mentioned, its first adjustment program, the DIRE, was clearly aimed at groups within the system: civil servants and *maitrisards*. Aided by donor funds, the DIRE was an expensive "sweetener" designed to buy off these groups.

At least in the short term, this may not have been a bad political strategy, since the groups who stood to lose the most from adjustment were those that had a stake in an increasingly unsustainable system. Yet no effort was made to explain or "sell" the concept of reform to these groups or to the party rank and file. The problem was that the government's technical team was poorly organized and insulated from the rest of the government, with the result that even the cabinet had a poor understanding of reform.[21] Thus most groups within the public sector remained opposed to reform, despite the attempts to buy them off. A 1986 survey of Dakar residents singled out civil servants and salaried workers as the most dissatisfied groups.[22]

Less privileged groups had also felt the negative impact of the economic crisis and of adjustment and were gradually becoming more vocal about their problems. In the February 1988 elections and their aftermath, the opposition, united behind the Alliance Sopi, was able to tap into the frustration of the urban poor. Unemployed youth, in particular, mobilized against the government following a sharp increase in unemployment in the 1980s. By 1991 open unemployment in Dakar stood at 24 percent.[23] Underemployment was higher but is more difficult to measure. The unemployment was due to a gradual reduction in new civil service jobs and to a general economic downturn. It was exacerbated by migration from drought-ridden zones in the late 1980s, which increased the number of workers relying on Senegal's saturated informal economy.[24] This also placed an increased burden on an already inadequate urban infrastructure, which had deteriorated visibly in the 1980s.

The opposition was led by Abdoulaye Wade of the PDS, which in theory is a neoliberal party but in practice is center-left. Wade complained that the adjustment process was being imposed from outside and countered the government's proposed changes with a series of unrealistic promises, one of which was to cut the price of rice in half if he was elected.[25] His message found a great deal of sympathy among the urban population. In fact, the Alliance Sopi itself had emerged from the 1988 election campaign in an attempt by the PDS, the Ligue Démocratique-Mouvement pour le Parti du Travail (LD-MPT), and the PIT to capture the popular mood in favor of change. Wade and the PDS, in particular, made inroads into urban areas, capturing 24.74 percent of the national vote, almost 40 percent of the vote in Dakar, and more than 45 percent of the vote in the region of Zinguinchor (see table 5-1).[26]

Violence broke out when the government refused to allow PDS supporters to hold demonstrations before the February elections, and the protests spread to several cities. After the election, the opposition disputed the results. Wade accused Diouf of massive fraud and claimed that he had won the election. In response, the government declared a state of emergency and imprisoned Wade for "inciting insurrection." Although Wade was released in April, civil unrest and the stalemate in government continued for twenty months.[27] At this time, the Alliance Sopi was expanded into a larger and more organized movement, CONACPO, that included most of the sixteen parties other than the governing PS.

The events surrounding the February elections had significant political impact, both at home and abroad. During the next few months the gov-

Table 5-1. *National and Municipal Election Results, Senegal, 1988, 1990*[a]

Percent of total

	1988				1990[b]
Region	PS	PDS	LD-MPT	PIT	PS
Dakar	54.20	38.40	2.97	2.22	69.8
Ziguinchor	49.82	45.85	2.90	0.56	65.4
Diourbel	86.26	12.39	0.52	0.39	73.7
St. Louis	84.45	12.71	0.60	1.06	82.7
Tambacounda	71.12	24.99	2.26	1.11	70.1
Kaolack	72.85	24.62	0.43	0.30	77.7
Thies	73.76	22.85	1.27	0.66	70.2
Louga	88.68	9.34	1.15	0.11	77.1
Fatick	69.85	25.71	1.74	1.23	69.1
Kolda	59.24	34.11	1.07	0.62	69.7
Total	71.54	24.74	1.41	0.84	72.6

Sources: *Le Soleil*, March 4, 1988 (Dakar, Senegal); and *Le Soleil*, November 27, 1990.
a. Figures for abstention were not available. PS: Parti Socialiste; PDS: Parti Democratique Senegalaise; LD-MPT: Ligue Démocratique–Mouvement pour le Parti du Travail; PIT: Parti de l'Indépendence et du Travail.
b. The PDS and other opposition parties boycotted the 1990 municipal elections.

ernment endeavored to conduct a "dialogue" with the opposition and by January 1991 had given in to virtually all its demands. The government even agreed to change the electoral code, allowed the opposition to have more access to the media, and invited several parties to join the government.[28] The accord seemed—at least temporarily—to buy peace with most of the opposition and helped the government resolve the insurrection in the Casamance, where the PDS had strong support.

Those who remained outside the government accused the PDS and the PIT of being co-opted. In any case, the CONACPO alliance seemed to have lost the primary reason for its existence. Wade, meanwhile, who was given the third most powerful position in the government, took on the role of the preeminent statesman and received far more media attention than he had as the leader of the opposition. Nevertheless, he remained critical of the International Monetary Fund and what he called IMF-imposed policies, and of privatization in particular, no doubt, in an attempt to retain a political niche for himself.[29] However, the political liberalization actually increased the strength of Diouf in comparison with that of the party old guard opposed to adjustment. In parliamentary elections held in May 1993, the PS was able to retain the national majority that it had in 1988. Of 130 parliamentary seats, the PS obtained 84 seats and the PDS only 27 seats.[30]

In the aftermath of the February 1988 violence, the government made the social costs of adjustment its first public and political priority, and the donor community seemed more sympathetic to these concerns.[31] The government decided to focus its attention on a group that had played a critical role in the postelection unrest, the urban unemployed youth. Together with the World Bank, the government laid plans for the Agetip program, which it presented to a May 1989 donors' conference in Paris. The program was to provide rapid, visible, short-term employment to a frustrated and potentially destabilizing group and was to demonstrate the government's concerns with the social costs of adjustment at the same time. Before discussing Agetip in detail, however, it is necessary to examine the extent of poverty in Senegal and the record of the previous program designed to address the social costs of adjustment, the DIRE.

Adjustment and the Poor

Despite significant rural-urban migration in recent years and the well-known negative effects of adjustment on the urban poor, there is no comprehensive measure of the extent of poverty in Senegal or of its rural-urban breakdown. And the effects of adjustment per se were probably far less damaging to the poor than was the prolonged period of economic decline that necessitated the adjustment, as well as the long-term neglect of basic social welfare services.

By most socioeconomic indicators, Senegal ranks quite low among developing countries. Its infant mortality rate, at 82 deaths per 1,000 live births, is on the high end of the scale, and its adult illiteracy rate is 72 percent (81 percent for women), which is extremely high even by regional standards.[32] Despite a notable increase in enrollment in the 1980s, only half of Senegal's school-aged children attend school.[33] Health is also a low priority, traditionally receiving 6 percent or less of the government budget. In the 1980s conditions deteriorated from 7.7 to 6.1 hospital beds per 10,000 people, and 4.9 to 3.5 doctors for the same number.[34] While the worst poverty is in rural areas, the usual migratory trends have been exacerbated by the drought in the Sahel, and Dakar is now home to approximately 2 million people, or one third of Senegal's population. There is still a gap in living standards between urban and rural regions, but it narrowed in the 1980s, as the price of groundnuts increased more than urban wages did. Income is also more evenly distributed in rural areas than in urban ones.[35]

Although there is as yet little comprehensive information on the extent or severity of urban poverty, a recent study of living standards and income levels in six communities on the outskirts of Dakar—*bidonvilles*—provides some anecdotal evidence of its extent. These areas have a growing population of squatters displaced from rural zones. Most of them live in *baraques*, houses made of straw, and the poorest or most recent arrivals live in the open air. The average number of inhabitants to a room measuring 1.5 by 2.0 square meters is seven to eight adults, and the adult women are accompanied by small children. Households live from hand to mouth, with intermittent periods of fasting. Inhabitants find employment mainly in informal services, such as laundry and domestic work, watch repairs, part-time chauffeuring, and in some cases prostitution and drug trafficking. None can afford any form of health care, and most spend between 25 and 80 percent of their income on food. Their earnings are extremely irregular, ranging from 2,500 to 5,000 CFA (300 CFA = US$1) a month for launderers, 6,000 to 15,000 for domestic servants, and 40,000 to 50,000 CFA per transaction for drug traffickers. Sewage and water services are virtually nonexistent.[36]

Of an economically active population of 585,522 in the Dakar region, approximately 143,090 were estimated to be *chomeurs*, unemployed, in 1991.[37] The number who either voluntarily resigned from the civil service or lost their jobs in parastatal industries in the 1980s, the *deflate* population, is somewhere between 5,000 and 15,000.[38] A surprisingly large percentage of the urban population appears to be without access to a steady income, and thus many in a family may have to depend on the one member with a full-time job. It is estimated that there are ten to fifteen dependents for each such person.[39] This phenomenon probably helps to mitigate the political effects of increasing urban poverty and unemployment. Under the circumstances, many people are resigned to economic decline and foresee no reversal. Usually the only way this "culture of poverty" can be reversed is by severe economic shock or by some kind of external influence.[40] The Sopi movement, which broke with years of uninterrupted political stability, may have temporarily provided such an influence.

As mentioned earlier in this book, the poor tend to be among the least politically vocal groups in society, with the rural poor being even less vocal than the urban poor. Although the urban poor tend to be disorganized politically, they can be mobilized at times, but they rarely provide a permanent base of support for political parties.[41] In general, the urban poor are concerned with day-to-day survival and will support whatever political force can deliver essential services in the short term. The poor of Dakar are no different. Interviews with forty-five women from three neighborhoods in and around Dakar revealed that the central-level political changes of the past few years had made no difference to their lives. What mattered were day-to-day material concerns: the price of rice, the need for a health post in a peri-urban village (that is to say, a *bidonville* on the outskirts of the city), and the need for education and basic training.[42] One woman said that political changes would be significant only when their "dossiers"—rather than those of people with connections—actually moved within the state.[43]

The poor who were interviewed had low expectations of the state, and most did not know of the government's DIRE and Agetip programs. Those who did know either had no idea of how to obtain benefits or assumed that they were for people with government connections. Many felt that autonomous local groups were doing something to help themselves. One such group is the Set Setal (meaning "be clean and make clean"), which is composed of urban youth who have organized voluntarily in cities around Senegal to clean up their neighborhoods.[44]

Although these interviews can provide no more than anecdotal evidence, the trends they suggest are neither surprising nor inconsistent with the results of similar research in other countries.[45] The poorest groups rarely have a coherent political organization to represent them and are seldom given any consideration in government policy. Most government programs for low-income groups do not even reach the poorest. Senegal's first public housing project, implemented in 1964, is a case in point: it was designed for the military and civil service *fonctionnaires*. Most of the Marxist parties, which in theory should represent the interests of the poor, are heavily influenced by external trends and are not particularly attuned to needs of the poor, whom they consider the lumpenproletariat.[46] Credit programs have either targeted the skilled and educated, as the DIRE did, or require guarantees that the poor cannot provide. According to the director of the Office of National Professional Training, it is more difficult for a person with a university education or a former civil servant to be poor, because they have expectations, than for the poorest, who do not.[47] Even most donor-sponsored programs do not target the poorest. U.S. AID's Agence de Crédit pour l'Entreprise Privée (ACEP), for example, has achieved a 98 percent repayment ratio, but only on loans to individuals who can provide guarantees. Clearly, these are not the poor.[48] Agetip and the Caisse Central, for example, have taken steps to sponsor microenterprises, but, again, these efforts are on a relatively small scale and have had little effect on the poor, who in Senegal are clearly the majority of the population.

Yet the poor are quite well organized at the community level, and minimal support for local efforts can have significant long-term results. The benefits of a small-scale project of this kind can be seen in Senegal's ABACED (Association des Bacheliers Chomeurs pour l'Emploi et le Développement), an NGO that helps the illiterate learn how to save. Bolivia's ESF is a good example of nongovernmental and community self-help efforts on a much larger scale. The Microprojects Unit in Zambia, which is funded by the European Community (EC) and the World Bank, and the Community Initiatives project in Ghana (a component of the Program of Action to Mitigate the Social Costs of Adjustment, PAMSCAD) are two further examples of the effectiveness of providing minimal support for NGO and community organizations.[49]

Unless government safety net programs are specifically targeted at the poorest groups, their members are not likely to even be aware that they exist. This lack of information is one of the many barriers to their participation. The information that is available to them is often manipulated—by marabouts, by local politicians, and by other third parties—and thus many of the poor are extremely distrustful of any intermediary institutions. The most effective way to reach the poor is to use their networks. That is why NGOs, despite their limitations, play an important role in this arena.[50]

The Agetip program, which to some extent relies on community initiatives, is an important first step in addressing the social dimensions of adjustment in Senegal. However, the issue of poverty has not yet received the attention it requires from either the government or donors. Perhaps quite justifiably, the government has been preoccupied with political sustainability rather than poverty alleviation because it is still in the early stages of adjustment. Public debate has focused mainly on employment and has ignored broader poverty issues, such as the state of public education and health services.[51] Even the DIRE and Agetip programs are primarily concerned with employment in urban areas. Employment clearly is a critical issue, and the pace and scale of urbanization in the

1980s suggest that many of Senegal's poorest inhabitants now live in urban areas and are likely to be negatively affected by adjustment in the short term. Although the circumstances justify an urban bent to policies designed to address the social costs of adjustment, these efforts should not substitute for a comprehensive poverty alleviation strategy. And although some progress has been made in redirecting health and education expenditures to the poor, the nation's weak social welfare indicators, even in relation to those of other African nations, are sufficient evidence that a great deal more needs to be done. As the case of Senegal amply demonstrates, protecting the poor during adjustment is an absolute necessity. It is difficult to imagine a country becoming competitive in the world economy when a large proportion of its population is uneducated and in poor health.[52]

In view of the slow pace of reform in Senegal, the benefits of adjustment are not likely to reach the poor in the near future.[53] A change of focus is clearly in order. A systematic evaluation of where the poorest are, such as was done in Ghana before the implementation of PAM-SCAD, would be a good starting point. It is paradoxical that, in a country that has received as much outside aid as Senegal, so little is known about the poor: who and where they are, and how many there are. Although Senegal's political concerns are legitimate, the country has spent an inordinately large amount of money and effort on short-term strategies to placate politically vocal and relatively privileged groups while ignoring its vast poor population.

Délégation à l'Insertion, à la Réinsertion et à l'Emploi

The government created the DIRE in November 1987 in response to the negative effects of adjustment policies on civil service and formal sector employment. As mentioned earlier, the DIRE was supposed to ease the transition to other employment for public sector workers (the *deflates*) and civil servants who had been laid off and was to help university graduates (*maitrisards*), who before adjustment would have been virtually guaranteed jobs in the civil service, find alternative employment.[54]

From the outset, the DIRE had a serious institutional problem. Although at least four ministries were in charge of employment policy, the DIRE was created as a separate agency, but with no clear mechanism for coordinating policy and thus no clear sense of direction.[55] From 1987 to 1989 the DIRE disbursed approximately 3 billion CFA, about half of which came from abroad (U.S. AID, the World Bank, and the African Development Bank) and the rest from the government. The money was channeled from the Public Treasury to the BCEAO, a state bank, and then to the DIRE, but no mechanism was in place by which to account for expenditures or follow up on the results of the aid. Since the DIRE's financial flows were never clear or guaranteed, about US$3.5 million was lost or had "filtered" through the bureaucracy. Furthermore, there is no existing account of the exact number of loans made or any list of beneficiaries.

Of the 11,000 to 16,000 people who were eligible for DIRE loans, approximately 5 percent received loans from 1988 to 1990. The enterprises set up under the program had a mortality rate of 32 percent. Information on the failed enterprises is not available, because only the dossiers of the 496 projects that were financed and recovered were retained at the DIRE offices. These projects created approximately 1,500 jobs, at a cost of US$11,000 per job, which is expensive for public employment program standards. Loans were made in amounts of US$10,000 and US$50,000.[56] While the eligible groups were clear enough and only 18 percent of borrowers did not fall within the eligible group, the number of eligible borrowers far exceeded the available loans, and there was no systematic selection process.[57] Thus lending was based largely on personal or clientelistic criteria, as most observers agree.[58]

It was therefore extremely difficult for the average person without connections to get a loan. Eighty percent of the loans were made to Dakar residents, and less than 19 percent of the borrowers were women. Less than 10 percent of the beneficiaries were required to give a personal contribution in order to get a loan. Also there was little control over the projects chosen or attention to their economic viability over the long run. Because no training was provided, the probability that inexperienced college graduates or civil servants could run successful private enterprises was low. Of the eight projects visited by the author, only one offered training and follow-up (from the International Labor Organization). This was a sewing firm in a low-income zone that had begun as a one-woman shop and grown to employ ten others and to produce for export. It was the most viable of the projects and the only one that was expanding.[59]

Although precise figures are unavailable, the amounts squandered under the program must have been enormous when one considers that the smaller loans were worth the equivalent of twenty months of minimum wage salary and that the larger ones were worth eight years of minimum wage salary.[60] Indeed, it is difficult to imagine a recent college graduate with no job, training, or guarantees being eligible for the full disbursement of a US$50,000 loan in a wealthy industrialized country, much less in one of the poorest countries in the world. Of the businesses that were set up, the most profitable were pharmacies, bureaux d'études (law offices), and farming ventures. Small businesses were the least profitable. The larger US$50,000 loans seemed to generate more stable and profitable enterprises and in general created more jobs.

The program's designers apparently ignored the lessons from the loan or credit schemes of other countries, such as the importance of group guarantees and of disbursing funds in small tranches that are only increased upon successful repayment. In addition, they paid no attention to the financial, macroeconomic, and cultural conditions in Senegal. The financial sector was mired in a deep crisis, in large part because loans were granted on the basis of personal friendships and guarantees rather than economic viability.[61] A loan program that used similar criteria in this context was destined to fail. The DIRE also neglected to consider whether the firms it sponsored were appropriate to the economic context. That is to say, little attempt was made to introduce industries other than those already predominant in Senegal's small formal sector: furniture, textiles, and commercial services such as pharmacies. In addition, family and friendship ties placed a severe strain on incomes, since loans or parts of loans were soon filtered to brothers, uncles, or friends rather than put toward productive activities. Such abuses were difficult to prevent because there were no provisions for accountability or follow-up in the program. Also, it was a serious mistake to place the DIRE's funds in the public treasury rather than in a viable financial institution. The state is not necessarily well suited to serve as a bank, because there will always be pressure to allocate program funds to other public or private uses.[62]

Since the DIRE produced only a small improvement in permanent employment, its political impact is probably of greater interest. It was, above all else, a "sweet deal" to vocal groups who were opposed to adjustment, particularly those within the system: its civil servants. Considering the size of Senegal's public sector in comparison with that of the private sector ("almost everyone in Senegal has at least a relative in the civil service"), it is not difficult to see that the DIRE had a strong political impact.[63] At its inception, the DIRE was a highly public and visible agency, which gave the impression that the government was doing something to make the adjustment process less costly.

The government targeted politically vocal groups, but they were certainly not the poor. (Actually, these groups had already cost the state a great deal of money in terms of defrayed university costs.) Most DIRE projects, such as the travel agencies supported in central Dakar or the high-technology chalk factory in the industrial zone of Dakar, had no connection with the poor and should have been supported by credits from the banking sector rather than with government and donor funds.[64] Also, many projects were in wealthy urban or industrial areas, where the program neither produced small viable enterprises nor redistributed income to low-income groups. It was clearly an expensive "buy-off" scheme for the politically vocal. Furthermore, little was accomplished in the way of sustaining political adjustment. Rather than stimulate autonomous microenterprises, the DIRE perpetuated a tradition of government handouts for a privileged sector of society. Nor did the program staff make any kind of effort to generate support for economic reform among beneficiary groups.

It was bad enough that most people did not even know about the program, but when those who did applied for group credits for microenterprises, their dossiers were often "lost," or they were told that the agency could lend only to individuals.[65] Although the DIRE was not designed to reach the poorest groups, it can be criticized for acting as a regressive tax. It channeled state money to privileged groups that had already benefited from the state and allocated these funds largely for patronage purposes. There were undoubtedly countless other ways in which the money could have been better spent.[66] Even a condition as simple as requiring beneficiaries to make counterpart contributions in order to qualify for loans would have given rise to more sustainable projects. Instead, the DIRE merely served to appease those who had the most to lose from adjustment in the short term. And in the final analysis its effectiveness can be judged by its lack of sustained political impact.[67]

Agence d'Exécution des Travaux d'Intérêt Publique contre le Sous-Emploi (Agetip)

In contrast, the Agetip program had more positive results—in part because it grew out of the mistakes made by the DIRE. The Agetip designers also drew on the experiences of Bolivia with the ESF and of

Ghana with the PAMSCAD. After receiving donor pledges at the May 1989 Paris conference (the World Bank pledged US$20 million), Agetip was set up as a semiautonomous agency responsible to Senegal's president. This arrangement was similar to Bolivia's ESF. Furthermore, in both cases the director was appointed from the private rather than the public sector. The director of Agetip, Magatte Wade, had previously been the head of IBM's West Africa office and had a mandate to run the agency using private sector criteria and methods. Remembering that Ghana's PAMSCAD program had lost a great deal of momentum because it was overambitious and lacked focus, Agetip designers opted for simple and visible activities, largely in urban areas. Unlike the ESF, which was involved in activities ranging from infrastructure to health and education to small credit schemes, Agetip and its advisers began with a small range of activities—labor-intensive public works.[68] In view of Senegal's lack of experience with such an agency, this was a prudent decision.

Agetip's objectives were fourfold: to generate a substantial number of temporary jobs for a critical group, unemployed youth; to improve the skills of the workers hired and the competitiveness of the firms; to demonstrate the feasibility of labor-intensive public works; and to generate economically and socially useful projects. The last objective, which focused on Senegal's deteriorating urban infrastructure, had a political dimension as well: to restore civic pride, particularly in poor areas where there was a great deal of need. To meet those objectives, Agetip was to maintain a small but skilled and well-paid staff (a maximum of twenty), keep costs low and visibility high (administrative costs are less than 5 percent of total costs), lend support to but not replace other development programs, and demonstrate flexible procedures. It was designed to function *outside* the government so that it could avoid bureaucratic delays and political pressure. In all these respects, it resembled Bolivia's ESF. Donors emphasized that Agetip was to stay out of politics, and the president made this clear in presenting Agetip to the public, the parliament, and the ministries: Agetip would rely strictly on its manual of procedures and nothing else in selecting projects.[69]

In the first year or so of operation, from June 1990 to September 1991, Agetip demonstrated remarkable efficiency and tangible results. It generated approximately 11,103 jobs lasting an average of thirty days each, or 332,438 worker-days of labor. This was equal to an average monthly minimum wage of 54,390 CFA per worker, which represents a significant distribution of income. Agetip channeled funds to and supervised the implementation of 119 projects, which were implemented by seventy-eight enterprises. Ninety-nine of the projects were completed in full, and twenty are continuing. The projects have an estimated value of 2.3 billion CFA, and the labor ratio per project is 33 percent. The projects have been in health, education, sanitation, waste collection, and transport infrastructure. Fourteen of forty enterprises surveyed in a World Bank evaluation had created thirty-one permanent jobs as a result of Agetip support. Several of these enterprises were newly formed Groupements d'Intérêt Economiques (GIEs), which would probably not have got off the ground had it not been for Agetip, given the weak state of Senegal's financial and construction sectors.[70] The projects range from socially beneficial canal drainage, septic tanks, and other sanitation facilities in poor neighborhoods to the renovation of income-generating projects for municipalities, such as markets and stadiums. Agetip has also supported food-for-work programs and voluntary clean-up programs (Set Setal) in poor low-income neighborhoods around the country. Agetip has implemented projects in each of Senegal's forty-eight municipalities.

Like the ESF, Agetip does not implement its own projects. It receives project proposals from mayors and municipal governments and subcontracts them out to architects and engineers for supervision, and then to private sector firms for execution. The relatively low profit margin allowed has favored small and medium-size firms over larger firms with higher operating costs. Although firms have complained about the profit constraints of labor-intensive production, to date all but 17 percent have met the required labor ratio (30 percent of the total costs must go to labor), and 65 percent actually exceeded the ratio![71]

One of the more problematic aspects of Agetip has been labor recruitment. This is not so surprising because there are only a limited number of jobs to go around. Agetip hired a small NGO, Junior Enterprise, to compile lists of unemployed workers by age and location, and to make the relevant lists available to entrepreneurs implementing Agetip projects in particular locales. There is a three-month waiting period for placement on Junior Enterprise's lists. The final decision of who to hire is left up to the firm, however, which usually also has its own list of recruits. The municipalities that solicited the projects may also have their own lists of people. The Agetip team has attempted to reduce the "traffiques d'influence" in the process by putting nonelected district governors rather than the elected mayors in charge of the recruitment lists. All enterprises that participate must undergo a qualification process but can obtain help from Agetip in doing so. During this process, Agetip hopes to improve the methods of labor recruitment.[72] Personalism and clientelism are so prevalent in Senegalese business and politics, however, that some of this behavior is bound to enter into the allocation of Agetip jobs. Thus at times firms have hired their own "trainees" rather than unskilled youth. Yet if this results in permanent employment, it may not be a negative result. Because targeting the poorest is not in Agetip's mandate and would create substantial delays in implementation, the existing recruitment process may be an unavoidable cost.

The Agetip team is well aware that temporary employment is not a wholly satisfactory solution in the face of unlimited demand. The only long-term solution is economic growth. Nevertheless, Agetip is able to serve two important functions: it provides training, and it redistributes income through the rotation of jobs. Some rural communities have proposed this rotation themselves, so that all community youths can have an opportunity to earn income.[73]

Agetip was designed to have visible political impact, which it has achieved both through its projects and through its sophisticated public relations system. It displays Agetip placards on all project locations, for example, and is in constant touch with the mass media.[74] This contributes to a popular perception that the government is doing something to make the adjustment process less costly. At the same time, Agetip has managed to avoid becoming a tool of the governing party, in contrast to many employment and public works programs, largely because of the approach and stature of its director, Magatte Wade. Also, as mentioned, Agetip's functions and objectives were clearly defined by the president from the outset and its manual of procedures was circulated publicly before the agency went into operation. Nevertheless, it was still subjected to some political pressure, particularly at the beginning, as ministers attempted to get "pet" projects through.

Agetip continues to battle political pressure. At the time of the November 1990 municipal elections, for example, the demand for Agetip projects increased markedly, but the agency pointed out that it had to abide by the manual of procedures in selecting projects.[75] This pressure continued even after the election, and in many instances came from municipalities that had previously worked with Agetip and were familiar with its operating procedures. At the time the author interviewed Agetip staff, the mayor of the second largest city in Senegal, Thies, paid a visit to the president to ask for an Agetip project, but the request was turned down.[76] Agetip's conscientious staff and the rigid project approval procedures, together with the president's apparent willingness to protect the agency from political pressure, helped keep the agency out of politics to the extent possible.

A commitment from the highest level of government, coupled with a nonpolitical, private-oriented directorate, seems critical to the effective nonpolitical management of social welfare programs outside the government, such as Agetip and Bolivia's ESF. In the case of the ESF, President Paz Estenssoro and Director Fernando Romero were clearly committed to keeping the ESF out of politics. In contrast, Zambia's President Kenneth Kaunda was determined to use the Social Action Programme (SAP) in an electoral campaign, with the result that the program was eventually discredited and donor support withdrawn. In Peru, the lack of presidential commitment to the Fund for Development and Social Compensation (Foncodes), coupled with the appointment of the former head of the president's party as the fund's director, led to long delays in program implementation and upset relations with the donor community.[77]

Not surprisingly, by operating outside the government, Agetip has aroused some suspicion and even animosity within the government bureaucracy, for although it benefits the government, it also reduces the traditional patronage and clientelistic means of building political support.[78] Members of the Agetip management team have said that this new method of operating has presented a difficult challenge. Others say the program has created a minirevolution and suggest that Agetip's method of operating be used as a guide in reforming the Senegalese state.[79] One member of the Agetip management team, who had worked for the government for twenty years, noted, "If we had had more Agetips and less state for twenty years, we would be a much wealthier country today."[80]

Agetip is, of course, not without flaws. Although targeting is not in its mandate and would be quite difficult to do in any case because of the nature of existing data, Agetip does not even have a system for identifying the neediest areas. Thus its contact with the poorest urban sectors, which are most vulnerable to adjustment-induced price increases, for example, has been very limited. Of the forty-five poor women interviewed in three neighborhoods (two urban, one rural), only a few of the urban women in one neighborhood had even heard of Agetip; none of the rural women had. The general perception among those who were aware of it was that "you had to know someone to get into Agetip."[81] There is no contact between Agetip and the Ministère de l'Aménagement du Territoire, which has a substantial amount of up-to-date data on regional disparities in the basic social welfare infrastructure.[82] Agetip could easily use some of this information to identify regions with a particularly poor basic infrastructure. In the absence of such information, Agetip does not necessarily concentrate its efforts on the most infrastructure-poor areas but looks primarily at those with a high level of unemployment (see tables 5-2 and 5-3).

Agetip has successfully targeted the poorest groups in its food-for-work program, which is run in several cities in conjunction with the World Food Program. This is a pilot program that has been implemented in Kaolack–St. Louis, Durvel, and Thies, all cities with a high level of unemployment. The food-for-work program pays workers in food, plus a monthly stipend of 10,000 CFA (a not insignificant sum in view of what some of the poor earn, as noted earlier) for labor-intensive public work to upgrade basic sanitation facilities in poor neighborhoods. The program has thus far been successful and has also managed to eliminate cholera from the St. Louis–Kaolack area.[83] Providing food for work is one of the most effective ways to target beneficiaries through self-selection, because only the poorest people will work for food rather than cash. Food provides an important income supplement for needy families, and concurrently neighborhoods benefit from improvements in basic sanitation facilities.[84] If this program were expanded, Agetip would be able to reach more vulnerable groups.

A labor profile of Agetip beneficiaries could be generated through Junior Enterprise, and a more scientific procedure involving collaboration with the relevant sectoral ministries could be used to allocate benefits between regions.[85] The problem with trying to reach the poorest and most remote communities, however, is that it entails high administrative costs and considerable staff time. An EC project directed at the poorest communities in the Fleuve spends 70 percent of its total outlay on technical assistance.[86] Although the costs of reaching the poorest groups are a concern for all demand-based programs, Agetip's operations could easily pay more attention to those groups without sacrificing efficiency.

Agetip and Local Governments

Agetip is designed to work through municipalities but has run into problems with this arrangement owing to the nature of municipal government in Senegal. Ever since the opposition boycotted the November 1990

Table 5-2. Schools and Agetip Projects, by Region[a]

| Region | Enrollment (percent) | Teachers per school | Schools per 1,000 square kilometers | | | Agetip projects | Estimated cost (thousands of U.S. dollars) |
			Elementary	Middle	Secondary		
Dakar	87.6	11	581.8	190.9	47.27	51	34,216.67
Ziguinchor	102.2	4	42.3	2.3	0.40	14	6,010.00
Diourbel	29.9	4	25.2	2.2	0.22	2	123.33
St. Louis	46.5	4	6.3	0.4	0.13	9	836.67
Tambacounda	30.8	3	3.0	0.1	0.01	2	120.00
Kaolack	39.3	4	13.9	0.9	0.18	7	620.00
Thies	55.8	6	43.3	4.3	1.00	22	980.00
Louga	30.1	4	4.3	0.3	0.03	2	103.33
Fatick	41.4	3	26.5	1.3	0.12	7	280.00
Kolda	44.8	3	15.4	0.3	0.04	2	166.67

Sources: République du Sénegal, Ministre de l'Interieur, *Esquisse du Plan d'Aménagement du Territoire* (New York: United Nations, 1989); and République du Sénegal, Agetip. *Rapport d'Evaluation Provisoire* (Washington: World Bank, September 1991).
a. Agetip: Agence d'Exécution des Travaux d'Intérêt contre le Sous-Emploi.

Table 5-3. *Health Posts and Agetip Projects, by Region*

Region	Hospitals	Health centers	Health posts	Total	Agetip project	Estimated amount (thousands of U.S. dollars)
Dakar	6	7	73	86	51	34,216.67
Ziguinchor	1	3	66	70	14	6,010.00
Diourbel	1	4	41	46	2	123.33
St. Louis	3	4	91	98	9	836.67
Tambacounda	1	4	66	71	2	120.00
Kaolack	1	4	61	66	7	620.00
Thies	2	9	66	77	22	980.00
Louga	1	4	42	47	2	103.33
Fatick	0	5	60	65	7	280.00
Kolda	0	3	43	46	2	166.67

Sources: See table 5-2.

Table 5-4. *Results of the 1990 Municipal Elections and Number and Cost of Agetip Projects, by Region*

Region	PS votes (percent)	Number of Agetip projects	Estimated cost (thousands of U.S. dollars)
Dakar	69.8	51	34,216.67
Ziguinchor	65.4	14	6,010.00
Diourbel	73.7	2	123.33
St. Louis	82.7	9	838.67
Tambacounda	70.1	2	120.00
Kaolack	77.7	7	620.00
Thies	70.2	22	980.00
Louga	77.1	2	103.33
Fatick	69.1	7	280.00
Kolda	69.7	2	166.67

Sources: Agetip, *Rapport d'Evaluation Provisoire*; and *Le Soleil*, November 27, 1990.

municipal elections, because of the purported fraud in February 1988, all mayors have been from the PS (see table 5-4). Thus Agetip deals exclusively with PS mayors and is perceived as a PS and government tool by the opposition. Since there was no competition in the 1990 elections, and accountability to the electorate was thereby reduced, the quality of municipal government varies from place to place. Much depends on the personality of the mayor, as is typical of local government in any authoritarian system.[87] Local government is modeled on the French top-down system, which makes municipalities extremely dependent on the center, also similar to many authoritarian regimes.[88] Another feature of Senegal's local governments is that they have little contact with NGOs, which usually provide the state's closest link to the poor but often sympathize with the opposition rather than the PS.[89] Even so, party competition at the local level is virtually nil and Agetip has to deal mainly with competition within the PS.

Voting behavior at the municipal level, particularly in rural areas, is dictated by the marabouts, who to date have supported the PS. Thus when Agetip receives proposals from municipal governments, they are not necessarily the result of community participation, as they would be in a genuinely demand-driven program. At the same time, independent local organizations like the Set Setal movement are on the rise and are gaining local government support, despite some initial concerns about the potentially volatile youth who might join them.[90] Such groups can play an important role in reaching out to the poor, since the mayors appear to be out of touch with their problems. As one rural woman commented during an interview, "There are local elected officials, but these people don't do anything for us."[91]

Agetip has given impetus to local development by providing municipalities with access to funds other than erratic resources from the Fonds Concours (the central municipal fund). In addition, by sponsoring economically sustainable projects, such as renovating town markets or stadiums or providing cold storage facilities for markets, Agetip is helping municipalities expand their long-term resource base.[92] Its contribution to autonomous local development efforts is expected to increase following municipal elections in 1994, coupled with the reform of the municipal electoral code and decentralization legislation that is currently being drafted by a national commission. These changes should yield a much more dynamic local political framework. But further political and institutional benefits could be gained from having multiparty actors involved in the project proposal process, as in Bolivia, where municipalities of diverse political bent participate in the ESF. Their input has helped sustain the adjustment process and has limited the government's ability to use the ESF for patronage purposes.[93]

Agetip and Nongovernmental Organizations

One way to work around Senegal's entrenched political elites, as well as to reach its poorest population, would be to improve Agetip's links to

NGOs. These organizations may not be homogeneous or without flaw, but they are quite good at some of the things that Agetip needs, such as outreach and training. NGOs in general provide the most extensive—and often the only—links available to the poorest groups. Also, NGOs tend to have longer-term objectives that allow them to incorporate local participation in a manner that most government programs cannot adopt.[94] Other programs such as the ESF in Bolivia and the EC's Micro-projects Unit in Zambia have benefited greatly from NGO participation. If anything, that participation has enhanced relations between NGOs and the state. This is the kind of lasting contribution to institutional development that demand-based programs like the ESF and Agetip can make.

Community participation can also improve a project's chances of remaining viable over the long term, as is amply demonstrated by the experience of countries such as Bolivia, Zambia, and Ghana.[95] Agetip would do well to follow their example in dealing with its maintenance problems. To stop people from throwing garbage into newly built canals, for example, it could have encouraged beneficiary communities to participate in the implementation of the projects through some kind of cash or labor contribution, something the Agetip has done in some rural projects and in the food-for-work program.[96] NGOs are extremely well positioned to play an intermediary role in this arena.

NGO activity has increased in the past ten years in Senegal, and today there are approximately 129 registered NGOs, 45 of which are national in scope.[97] The Conseil des ONG d'Appui au Développement (CON-GAD), the national umbrella organization of NGOs, is dedicated to the professional development of NGOs and seems extremely wary of admitting purely partisan or party-linked NGOs. Although the quality of NGOs varies, there are many highly motivated and well-trained Senegalese in the national NGO community, and they are a source that Agetip should tap.[98]

The problem for Agetip, however, is that NGOs tend to be suspicious of government attempts to control them. For its part, the government tends to view NGOs as being aligned with the opposition. As an extension of the government, Agetip has been caught between the two.[99] Furthermore, Agetip's rigid procedures, which are designed for private enterprises, are difficult for NGOs to comply with because their operating budgets are limited and their strength lies in the variety of activities they undertake. Relations between Agetip and NGOs were soured early on when a World Bank consultant doing preparatory work for Agetip indicated that it would be operating much along the lines of Bolivia's ESF; that is, with NGO participation in a wide range of activities. NGOs were asked to present proposals, which they put time and resources into preparing and which became a major part of the document sent to the donor's conference to evaluate the Agetip program. It was then decided that, at least as a starting point, Agetip's activities would be limited to labor-intensive public works and that NGOs would be excluded from participation. Although this move was probably made in the interest of efficiency, it permanently tainted Agetip's relations with Senegal's NGOs.

The NGOs felt they had put their credibility on the line by agreeing to work with the state, with no tangible results. While the World Bank wrote a letter to CONGAD explaining the change in approach, a more tactful public relations strategy might have avoided the resentment and bitterness that the incident caused. Despite the letter, most of the NGO leaders interviewed for this study did not fully understand what had actually happened and felt they had been "used" by Agetip to secure donor support.[100] Many NGOs, including those that had implemented projects with Agetip, complained that Agetip staff—exclusive of the director—tended to have an arrogant approach: "We have the money, we have the authority."[101] Given the NGOs' history of working with the poor and their expertise in that arena, their complaints may be warranted.

Agetip clearly benefited from the relations that it did have with NGOs. Without the NGO links to the community, it would not have been able to implement certain projects, such as the National Council of Negro Women (NCNW) project in the Casamance. Agetip's links and outreach to the poorest groups would be enhanced, however, if these relations could be expanded. It would also benefit from NGO training activities and, more important, would improve its image by association with these organizations.[102]

Some NGOs actually believe that the World Bank created Agetip to finance the government's reelection campaign, and there were rumors of Agetip funds being diverted to fund electoral campaigns.[103] This is clearly *not* the case, as is demonstrated by the lack of correlation between Agetip projects and electoral support for the PS (table 5-4), as well as by Agetip's accountability for all its funds. Yet the perception exists, and any effort to improve relations with NGOs would visibly demonstrate Agetip's nonpartisan and transparent nature, which would enhance its long-term potential to contribute to the political sustainability of the adjustment process. At present it seems that opinions about Agetip vary depending on one's position toward the government. There is no reason why Agetip could not bring groups of all political bents into its fold, as the ESF did in Bolivia. This, too would contribute to the political sustainability of adjustment.[104]

The Agetip directorate is aware of the benefits that could come from working with NGOs and is about to launch some new collaborative activities such as a small artisans and handicraft project in conjunction with UNICEF. NGOs could try to "make peace" as well by accepting Agetip as a different kind of state operation. Better working relations would certainly help Agetip escape some of the risks associated with expanding its operations.

Although mistakes will undoubtedly be made along the way, such collaborative efforts would have a beneficial effect on politics, institutional development, and poverty alleviation that would far outweigh the risks. Agetip has already had institutional impact. Even critics of the program note that despite the weakness of both central and municipal institutions, "Agetip is the only means for people to get things done."[105] This reflects the extent to which Agetip has demonstrated efficiency and visible results, although it also places a great deal of pressure on the agency. Because its strength lies precisely in its small staff and narrowly defined objectives, the agency could overextend itself if it branches out into too many other activities. Yet the need for institutional development in Senegal is unlimited, and Agetip has the potential—even via demonstration—to make an important contribution. One way to develop this potential without overextending the agency would be to expand its links with NGOs.

Perhaps a more difficult challenge would be to increase Agetip's collaboration with relevant ministries, along the lines that have evolved in Bolivia. Yet this would be a risky undertaking, as Agetip threatens to undermine entrenched interests by introducing a completely new method of operating into public institutions, one based on efficiency criteria. Even Agetip beneficiaries are already complaining about having to adapt to Agetip criteria and losing their discretionary privileges.[106] Although Agetip should clearly not link its fate to that of the state sector, it could cooperate with appropriate ministries or departments, such as the Aménagement du Territoire or the health and education ministries, so as to take their priorities into account in its operations. Agetip's method of operations could have demonstrable effects on state institutions.[107]

Conclusion

Until now, Senegal's experience with both adjustment and poverty alleviation has been frustrating, largely for political reasons. Not unlike many other African countries, Senegal has a political and administrative system dominated by entrenched interests that are more concerned with maintaining their privileged positions than with reforming the system. Nowhere is this more evident than in the experience of the DIRE.

The DIRE was set up as yet another government agency with responsibility for employment, but it had no links with existing government and nongovernment efforts. At the same time, the program's resources were channeled through the public treasury. This arrangement plus the fact that no criteria had been established to govern its operations opened the door to clientelistism in the granting of loans. In the absence of training and follow-up, there was no incentive to repay loans or to create viable enterprises. Thus an enormous amount of money was used unproductively to "buy off" relatively privileged groups. Such a strategy can only have short-term effects and will do little to ensure the political sustainability of reform.

As the ACEP's 98 percent repayment ratio demonstrates, however, successful credit programs can be run in Senegal. Although at present credit programs rarely reach the poorest, they can do so if they are based on group guarantees, as the Grameen Bank experience in Bangladesh demonstrates. They would have to meet several other conditions as well: stay outside the established bureaucracy; establish and stick to clear and detailed eligibility criteria; provide training and follow-up; and lend small amounts in tranches rather than large lump sums, which become victims of the "economy of affection." Schemes such as the DIRE, if brought up to these standards, have the potential to get viable microenterprises off the ground. They in turn could provide the employment and income that are sorely needed during a prolonged economic crisis and during adjustment.

Agetip has had better success—in fact, it has created a small-scale institutional revolution, which has given rise to autonomous initiatives for local development and has helped build vital infrastructure for many middle- and low-income communities. The agency has temporarily employed a large number of unskilled and unemployed youth and distributed a substantial amount of income. Whether rightly or wrongly, increased unemployment is associated with the adjustment program in the mind of the public, and this has had some impact on political sustainability. Agetip has also had some impact on the state by demonstrating a completely different method of operating. Its designers seem to have learned from the mistakes of the DIRE as well as from those of agencies in other countries. That is why they placed Agetip outside the established bureaucracy and gave it a mandate to run the agency like a private sector firm. Thus, in contrast to the DIRE, it was able to operate efficiently and to remain clear of the influence of entrenched political interests.

Like most other government programs in Senegal, however, Agetip has not yet been able to reach the poorest groups to any great extent. The reasons for this failing are also political. Because project proposals come primarily from municipalities, which are not competitively elected and depend on the central government for both resources and authority, genuine community participation does not take place, as it should in a demand-driven program.

Unlike other government programs, however, Agetip is extremely well positioned to reach the poorest. Being outside the government and having a demand-based design, it has the flexibility needed to include community organizations and NGOs in its operations. Since communities in Senegal are not highly organized, the best strategy for reaching the poorest in the short term would be to expand Agetip's links with NGOs. This would not mean changing its efficient operating methods, but rather incorporating new elements of activity, such as outreach and training, where NGOs could play a major role. NGOs are not particularly good administrators; Agetip is. NGOs' links with the poorest are the most extensive in Senegal; Agetip's are very limited. Both stand to benefit from collaborative activities.

By building institutional development goals into its operations, Agetip would also be better equipped to provide temporary employment and income in the face of unlimited demand. By strengthening its links to the poorest, stimulating autonomous community initiatives, and working with municipal governments, Agetip can help alleviate poverty over the long term while also providing desperately needed employment and income in the short term. In view of its strong record and unique position,

Agetip has an opportunity to lead others into new ways of alleviating poverty.

Perhaps the most important contribution such programs can make is an institutional one: they can help improve the state's (as opposed to the government's) method of operating in a more permanent sense, and give previously marginalized groups a stake in the ongoing process of reform—and thus make reform more sustainable in the long term. This was one of the primary contributions of Bolivia's ESF. Not only did it demonstrate that the state could operate transparently and efficiently, but it also showed that a program of this kind could collaborate with municipal governments and NGOs of all political bents, to the benefit of all groups. On this front, the DIRE failed, for it weakened the credibility of public agencies and reached only a small and relatively privileged group of beneficiaries. By contrast, Agetip has clearly demonstrated that the state can operate in an efficient and transparent manner. It has also shown that interaction with nongovernmental organizations is vital.

These are valuable lessons for countries throughout the world. The story of Senegal also points to the difficulty of reaching the poorest groups, particularly when most of the politically vocal are also those with entrenched interests in the existing public administration. At times these interests have been challenged by sporadic outbursts of the public, as occurred after the February 1988 elections in Senegal. Even then, however, the government tended to direct its attention to the vocal rather than the needy groups. In Ghana, for example, the PAMSCAD was seen as a political sweetener for vocal groups; it was an afterthought tacked on to an adjustment program that the government was committed to. Dramatic political or economic change, such as the landslide election of the pro-market Chiluba government in Zambia, may be the only way to undermine groups with entrenched interests in the public administration. In Zambia a public consensus has since developed on the need to identify and target the poorest and most vulnerable groups during adjustment, as people increasingly recognize that resources are limited and that poverty is widespread. Yet such a consensus seems the exception rather than the rule in Africa.

In Senegal economic deterioration has been far less dramatic than in Zambia, adjustment has been more gradual, and political changes have occurred within the established, semidemocratic system. Yet there is no coherent political voice speaking on behalf of the poor. Agetip is a first step, but it does not offer a coherent strategy for alleviating poverty. In the absence of dramatic domestic political change, it may be that, at least in the short term, external support is a necessary impetus to developing such a strategy. Yet if such resources are channeled to politically vocal nonpoor groups, that clearly gives the wrong message about the political economy of adjustment.

It should also be remembered that political and institutional constraints impede poverty reduction in Senegal as much as does the lack of necessary resources. Being outside the government bureaucracy, Agetip is able to overcome some of these constraints, but much more must be done to reach the poor. The need for a broad poverty strategy has already been mentioned. The critical point to mention about such a strategy is that it not only focuses directly on the poor but can serve to build support for reform among previously marginalized groups, as similar programs have done in Bolivia. Yet without progress on the reform front and sustained economic growth, it is unlikely that any safety net program in Senegal can have a lasting impact.

CHAPTER SIX

The Politics of Adjustment and Poverty in Zambia: "The Hour Has Come"

THE CASE of Zambia demonstrates how dramatic political change can facilitate adjustment and provide unique opportunities for redirecting resources to the poor. It also sheds light on the formidable obstacles to reform in countries bearing the legacy of the one-party state. The relationship between safety nets and political context is not the only theme of this case study, however. Another lesson that emerges is that effective communication about the social costs of reform can increase the public's willingness to accept adjustment measures and thus help sustain the process. Safety nets, too, are shown to contribute to sustainability: like Bolivia, Zambia directed compensatory benefits to previously marginalized groups and at the same time relied on their participation in safety net projects; such an approach helped create new coalitions of support for economic reform. And as in Bolivia, such a strategy succeeded, in part because the program was insulated from partisan politics. In Zambia the importance of insulation is made clear by the contrasting approaches of the Kaunda and Chiluba regimes. Yet another lesson is that the political and poverty-related effects of safety net policies can be as important to local institutions and initiatives as they are at the central level. While this also resembles the Bolivian case, in Zambia these effects form part of a difficult rebuilding of local structures after the demise of the one-party state.

This chapter examines the politics of adjustment in Zambia and the extent to which the political "revolution" of October 1991 resulted in sustainable economic reform efforts in conjunction with adequate safety net programs to protect the poor. Zambia implemented several programs to address the social costs of adjustment. The programs were initially part of the Kaunda regime's half-hearted attempts to adjust and often fell victim to the ruling party's partisan approach to government. With the subsequent election of the Chiluba government, a new approach to the implementation of safety nets was taken, and early indications are that the government is genuinely committed to assisting the poor rather than the vocal groups of the country. However, the Chiluba government is still relatively new, and any conclusions drawn from its present efforts are tentative ones.

The Political Context

From the time of its 1964 independence until the elections of October 1991, power in Zambia was controlled by Kenneth Kaunda and his United National Independence Party (UNIP), which imposed a one-party state in 1973. Both the party apparatus and government bureaucracy had entrenched interests in managing the economy and polity according to patronage principles. The system of market distortions and inflated civil service payrolls was easy enough to support when copper export revenues flowed in during the boom years of the 1960s, but became unsustainable once the terms of trade began to deteriorate in the 1970s. Thus in the late 1970s, Zambia launched a prolonged process of adjustment. The first agreements (see table 6-1) were quickly rescinded, however, because of strong public opposition.[1] In the latter part of the 1980s, the government introduced several programs to address the social costs of adjustment, one being the food coupon system for maize meal of January 1989 and another the social action program of early 1990. Like many other government programs in Zambia, these two were inextricably linked to the party and were used more for political patronage purposes than for alleviating poverty.[2]

The political context for both adjustment and poverty alleviation changed dramatically when Kaunda and the UNIP party were voted out of power by a margin of more than two to one in the national elections held on October 31, 1991. The electoral margin by which Frederick Chi-

Table 6-1. *Chronology of Adjustment Programs of Zambia, 1973–91*

Year	Program
1973	One-year stand-by agreement with the IMF for SDR 19 million.
1976	One-year stand-by agreement with the IMF for SDR 19 million.
1978	Two-year stand-by agreement with the IMF for SDR 250 million.
1981	The IMF offers help without preconditions: three-year Extended Fund Facility for SDR 800 million.
1982	IMF plan canceled because objectives are not met.
1983	Return to the IMF after failure to find alternative sources of funds; one-year stand-by agreement with the IMF for SDR 211 million.
1984	Twenty-one-month stand-by agreement for SDR 225 million.
April 1985	IMF agreement suspended for noncompliance.
February 1986	"Shadow program" transformed into twenty-four-month stand-by agreement with the IMF for SDR 229 million.
January 1987	Kenneth Kaunda backs away from reform measures; the IMF and World Bank programs are suspended.
March–May 1987	Discussions with the IMF to get program back on track.
May 1987	Kaunda announces suspension of IMF reform effort.
1988	Informal talks with the IMF and World Bank.
February 1990	Zambia reaches preliminary agreement with the IMF and World Bank.
September 1991	The IMF and World Bank suspend agreement in response to Zambia's failure to make payments in July.

Sources: Joan M. Nelson, ed., "Economic Crisis and Policy Choice"; and Cherry Gertzel, ed., "The Dynamics of One-Party State in Zambia."

luba and the eclectic Movement for Multiparty Democracy (MMD) defeated Kaunda, as well as the peaceful manner in which Kaunda turned over power, signified a revolution for Zambia and was a surprise to virtually all observers. It was the first peaceful and complete democratic transition in English-speaking Africa.[3] Chiluba took 76 percent of the votes, as well as 125 of 150 parliamentary seats. Nineteen of UNIP's 25 seats, meanwhile, were concentrated in Eastern Province, where Kaunda had a strong base of support. In the aftermath of the election, the UNIP party virtually collapsed, with thousands of party members resigning or defecting to join the MMD—even in Eastern Province.[4] Chiluba and the MMD had run on a pro-adjustment platform and made the elimination of inefficiency and corruption in government a major issue of the campaign and of the new government's early policies.

To date, the government seems committed to bold economic reform and has initiated debate on how to protect the poorest and most vulnerable groups in the process.[5] Yet, because the UNIP party held such a monopoly on all matters of government and was deeply involved in the implementation of programs at the local level, Zambia is now suspended in an institutional vacuum and is thus finding it difficult to move ahead with its policies. As one observer noted, "Party and government structures that had emerged during the 1976–83 period of the 'command economy' could hardly be expected to support a sharp change in policy orientation aimed at dismantling government controls."[6]

The Politics of Adjustment

Pervasive patronage at all levels of government and policymaking is at the root of these institutional problems. The phenomenon is certainly not uncommon in Africa. At independence, most nations on the continent lacked fully developed markets and bureaucracies through which to implement policies, and found patronage an easy means to build bases of political support. Moreover, African culture places more value on friendship and family ties than on public service. Since neither participation nor accountability to local structures had been a concern of the colonial administrations, it should not be surprising that little importance was attached to them after independence.[7] Thus, from the beginning, many African nations were caught in an institutional quagmire that led them to subordinate social and economic policy objectives to those of patronage politics.[8]

Zambia was no exception. Indeed this pattern may even have been more extreme there than in other African countries, since its indigenous political and institutional structures were very underdeveloped at the time of independence: only 4 percent of Zambia's top civil service posts were filled by Zambians, in sharp contrast to the 60 percent filled by the indigenous population in Ghana.[9] Kaunda and his UNIP party had a great deal of support because they were nationalists, not because they were well equipped to govern. Kaunda's philosophy of "humanism" took little interest in the role that the market or an entrepreneurial class could play in economic development. The party built and relied increasingly on an extensive network of patron-client ties, financed by copper revenues, and more than US$2 billion left in reserves by the colonial administration. Access to the party system and the state resources that it controlled became the primary route to social advancement in postindependence Zambia.[10]

Kaunda's postindependence popularity and the UNIP's access to a lucrative pot of state funds guaranteed widespread political support for years. By the early 1970s, however, the economic tide had turned, and the UNIP began to face more credible challenges, in particular from the United Progressive Party (UPP), which had splintered from the UNIP in 1971. The UPP was a populist movement representing the disadvantaged groups that were discontented with the control exercised by the politicians and the bureaucracy.[11]

In response, Kaunda outlawed all opposition parties and dissolved Parliament in 1972, and in 1973 he declared the Second Republic a one-party state. At that point, several of the original UNIP government members left office and entered the private sector.[12] Meanwhile, the international financial agencies and some domestic critics began voicing the concern that government policy and spending practices were far out of line with changing economic realities. Ignoring the warnings, the UNIP government instead imposed a command economy and increased party control over all aspects of society. Government structures were matched by party structures at all levels: provincial planning units, district councils, ward development committees, and village productivity committees. Many of Zambia's local institutions grew out of this process, which Kaunda called "decentralization in centralism"—although it was essentially a means of extending party control from the center to the local level and it neither decentralized power nor supported local initiatives.[13]

Virtually all party structures were designed to facilitate political patronage rather than achieve development objectives. The rural cooperatives that were sponsored by the government in the late 1960s and early 1970s are a case in point. Not only did production loans tend to favor the peasants and cooperatives that were better off, but the cooperative mortality rate was highest in areas where party organization and influence was strongest.[14]

After the one-party state was established, the UNIP's influence became pervasive. The patron-client system crept into most transactions, from getting permission for a stall in the local market to conducting

Table 6-2. *Income Distribution in Urban Areas, 1975, 1985*
Percent

Households	1975	1985
Poorest 25%	7.1	3.5
Second poorest 25%	12.8	18.1
Second richest 25%	19.1	18.5
Richest 25%	61.0	60.0

Source: Venkatesh Seshamani, "Toward Structural Transformation with a Human Focus: The Economic Programmes and Policies of Zambia in the 1980's," UNICEF, Innocenti Occasional Papers 7 (October 1990), p. 11.

business at the highest level. Although a few businessmen joined the UPP or were active in the opposition in the mid-1970s, most remained in the UNIP because it was the only way to get things done. It was easier to use party ties to circumvent the rules than to attempt to change them.[15]

Less privileged groups without the resources to buy their way into the patronage system did not fare as well. Their access to markets was highly regulated, and they were forced to turn to illegal trade and informal markets.[16] Another telling statistic is that Zambia's income distribution was among the worst in the world. That also signified that the poorest 25 percent lost the most during the economic downturn of the late 1970s (see table 6-2).[17]

In the political realm, the UNIP's monopoly on power reinforced clientelism in local politics, particularly in poor municipalities that lack basic services.[18] Most developing countries are familiar with clientelism. In Zambia, because there was no genuine competition and thus no way of challenging overall policy, clientelism dominated national politics as well: "In the absence of a competitive party system, voters, behaving rationally, [would] therefore pay more attention to the ability of candidates to do things of an immediate local value rather than to their stands on national issues."[19] Debate on issues of national concern—such as how to reverse Zambia's precipitous economic decline—was postponed for almost two decades, that is, until the October 1991 elections.

The UNIP's monopoly of power was not tolerated by everyone, however. Some opposition was voiced at the polls in the 1970s.[20] It then gathered strength in the 1980s, as the economic crisis deepened, and culminated in the formation of the MMD. A key player in the opposition movement—and an important interest group that the UNIP was never able to fully control—was the union movement, which had been in existence for some time before the UNIP. The Mineworkers of Zambia (MUZ) are the best organized of the unions, and their strikes along the rail line in the 1930s and 1940s began a tradition of union protest that had a lasting effect on urban politics. Although the UNIP received union support in the struggle for independence, it was not able to control the unions for its political objectives.[21] The UNIP attempted—and failed— to create a rival mineworkers union in 1963 and met with the same rebuff in 1966 when it tried to take control of the unions through the union elections. The unions had their own traditions and organization and the criteria they used in selecting their leaders were different from those of the patronage-based party. Union members followed company rather than party rules, in general distrusted political leaders, and believed that the union defended them better than the party.[22] In 1978 the chairman of the Zambian Congress of Trade Unions (ZCTU)—none other than Zambia's current president Chiluba—stated: "Politicians are all the same. They promise to build a bridge where there is no river. In fact, politics is the conduct of public affairs for private advantage."[23] Unions were at times able to influence important policy changes by the government. In November 1974, for example, they successfully pressured the government into reversing measures introduced to hold down urban wages and cut subsidies for urban areas.[24]

The UNIP's inability to control the unions reflects its general lack of support among the more educated and organized sections of the population. This failing ultimately proved to be its downfall, because these were the groups that formed the MMD.[25] By the time of the 1991 elections, the MMD, strongly supported by the unions and headed by a former union leader, recognized the dire need for reform and campaigned on a pro-adjustment platform.

The UNIP and Adjustment

The decision to adjust is often reluctantly made by governments at their weakest moment. Thus it is not surprising that the same institutional structure that was unable to implement a coherent economic strategy finds it difficult to sustain politically painful adjustment measures. In addition, the slower the pace of adjustment, the greater the opportunities for entrenched interest groups that oppose reform to become "institutionalized".[26] In the early 1980s the Zambian government lacked the political base and even more the will to sustain an adjustment program. By the time it finally recognized that adjustment was imperative, the economic decline had eroded its support among all the key groups of society, including the business community that it had been able to co-opt before. And the UNIP party had little to gain from a process that would ultimately undermine its position.

The UNIP government also had a history of troubled relations with the donor community going back to 1973 (table 6-1).[27] The most marked break with donors occurred in December 1986, after a poorly designed attempt to raise the price of maize meal caused widespread riots in which fifteen people were killed. Zambia broke off relations with the International Monetary Fund and the World Bank in May 1987, reimposed a regime of price controls and import restrictions, and followed Peru's example of limiting debt payments to 10 percent of export earnings. By late 1988 most donors were reluctant to deal with Zambia while it was out of accord with the international financial institutions, and relations were only reestablished through long and arduous negotiations.[28] In June 1990 a doubling of the price of meal was met with more riots, twenty-three deaths, and an attempted military coup, although Kaunda still resisted a policy reversal.[29] In the 1991 preelection atmosphere, however, the president abandoned the spending limits of the adjustment program by raising salaries for civil servants and increasing subsidies on maize meal and on housing. In July Zambia failed to make a US$20 million payment to the World Bank—after several exceptions had been made for Zambia—and the Bank and the Fund suspended scheduled disbursements of US$75 million in September 1991. At this point, even Zambia's most generous donors, the Scandinavians, were extremely reluctant to finance further operations.[30]

The Kaunda government was unable to stick to an adjustment program for a number of reasons. To begin with, the UNIP's political base was eroding because opposition to the reforms was now building within the UNIP party and the government itself. Most UNIP members had little to gain from a program designed to eliminate a host of opportunities for rent-seeking. The privileges granted to nonpoor urban groups through generalized maize meal subsidies, housing subsidies, high civil service wages, and special prices on items such as maize and beer for the military and certain unions gave several key interest groups a stake in the "system." The system also guaranteed universal free health care and education.[31] The perception that the program was being imposed from abroad and a lack of understanding of the measures within UNIP certainly helped to undermine the reform effort. The December 1986 riots, for example, strengthened the hand of the anti-IMF people in UNIP. This lack of understanding may explain why measures were often implemented at inopportune times, with little research into their short-term effects. To add to the problem, the government simply announced measures in the press as decrees, rather than explaining them to the public. The government's consistent failure to seek public consent for its policies also led to considerable uncertainty within the private sector.[32]

This was the approach taken in the December 1986 maize price increases. The subsidy was removed from breakfast meal, the more expensive of the two meals, and retained on roller meal, the meal that the poorest buy. Yet the subsidies were still channeled through the millers after they had ground the maize. Since the millers had no confidence that they would be promptly reimbursed for the subsidized meal, they stopped the production of roller meal and increased that of the more profitable breakfast meal. So almost overnight, no roller meal was available, and breakfast meal cost twice as much as before, a situation that was complicated by panic buying and shortages.[33]

Also contributing to the erosion of political and popular will, often called "adjustment fatigue," was the government's lack of attention to poverty issues or to the equitable distribution of the burden of adjustment.[34] The perception that the government is doing something to make the adjustment process less painful can generate important public support at a critical time, even if the public disapproves of the adjustment process per se. This was not the case in Zambia.[35] By the end of its tenure, the UNIP regime was in such poor standing that no economic policy it implemented could inspire public confidence. "A key ingredient in the sustainability of reform is the government's credibility and the confidence that 'the economic policymakers know what they are doing.'"[36] Nothing demonstrates the extent to which the UNIP had lost the public confidence as much as the 1991 elections.

The 1991 Elections and the Challenges Ahead

The extent of the opposition's victory, the peaceful manner in which Kaunda transferred power, and the strongly anticorruption and pro-free market bent of the Chiluba government surprised most observers. The opposition began as an eclectic movement of professionals led by a group of economists from the University of Zambia Research Foundation, the private sector, unions, and even disaffected former UNIP leaders. The MMD was formed in the aftermath of a 1990 forum on multiparty democracy organized by several members of this movement. It was the only significant opposition to challenge the government, despite the existence of twelve other minor parties. The MMD's factions were held together primarily by their opposition to the UNIP and their belief in the need for dramatic reform. By this time the UNIP had lost the support of the private sector, the unions, and the general population; the only supporters left were political appointees in the civil service.[37] The MMD's call for change through its slogan, "the hour has come," captured the popular mood. Zambians were given a political voice for the first time in decades, while all around them the standard of living was deteriorating in the face of widespread UNIP corruption. It is not surprising that the vote was staunchly anti-UNIP.

The extent of the victory is still remarkable, however, because the opposition began mustering its forces only in December 1989, when it called for multiparty politics. Moreover, Kaunda took control of the new process, and did not announce the October 31 election date until early September. The increases in freedom of the press and in independence on the part of the judiciary in the two years before the election played a major role.[38] In the words of one observer, "Just three years ago, one would never even dream of talking about politics in the office, and now we have had a revolution."[39]

The results apparently took Kaunda by complete surprise, which demonstrates how out of touch both he and the UNIP were with the mood of the people. His visits around the country were always preceded by his organizers, who bused people in or gave away free T-shirts in order to draw crowds. Although it was common to see children wearing UNIP T-shirts, many of them were holding their hands in the MMD victory sign. The fragile nature of UNIP's support became clear when thousands of UNIP members deserted the party immediately after the elections. No doubt it never occurred to Kaunda, as it had not to Pinochet in Chile, that he could lose. He might not have put himself up for election had he thought events would turn against him. Yet once the process was launched, it was impossible to stop without resorting to force and widespread bloodshed.[40]

In its campaign, the MMD warned, albeit in vague terms, that the proposed reforms would require the public to make substantial sacrifices.[41] The MMD also called for an investigation of the allegations of massive fraud in the state copper parastatal, Zambia Consolidated Copper Mines (ZCCM), and raised the possibility of privatizing the major parastatals.[42] The UNIP, meanwhile, warned of fragmentation, disorder, and chaos if the MMD won. It manipulated the social action program for political purposes and even wrote into its party manifesto that the price of maize meal had fallen by 20 percent in its last year in office.[43]

Chiluba's statements upon taking power indicated a new approach: his cabinet members were going to work, not reap benefits from their office, and, unlike Kuanda, Chiluba would be called Mr. President rather than His Excellency. Although he was harsh on the topic of UNIP's corruption, he also strongly condemned the attacks of MMD zealots on UNIP party members. He ordered a new currency to be issued without Kaunda's portrait or his own, in order to play down the personality cult, and he stressed MMD's accountability to the electorate.[44] Chiluba also sought an immediate rapprochement with the international financial community, although he stressed that initiatives and reforms must be internally generated above all else.[45]

Yet some of the former UNIP leaders in the MMD and the cabinet sought to operate the way they had previously. Michael Sata, minister of local government and a former UNIP leader, made public statements about the MMD's ability to act like a one-party state.[46] At the same time, overzealous MMD members attacked UNIP members' property and even urged the government to abandon Eastern Province because it had voted for the UNIP![47] Given the MMD's electoral margin and Zambia's lack of experience with democratic government, it is little wonder that the MMD showed some signs of operating like its predecessor.[48] When the UNIP attempted to stir up anti-MMD activity among the military in March 1993, Chiluba imposed a ninety-day state of emergency.

Also a challenge for the MMD government were the various unrealistic measures passed in the last months of the UNIP government.[49] The UNIP gave the 150,000-strong civil service a 100 percent pay raise just before the elections, which the workers accepted only on the condition that they would receive another one in June 1992.[50] The Chiluba government did not have the resources to meet these promises, nor did it have room for them in its economic strategy, which proposed to downsize the civil service. The UNIP also spent billions of kwacha during the election campaign, much of which cannot be accounted for because the UNIP shredded vital documents in the days before surrendering power. Finally, the most recent report of accounts available from the Central Bank in 1991 dated back to December 1987, which meant that it would be some time before the government knew how bad Zambia's financial situation actually was![51]

Yet there was room for cautious optimism about the MMD's capacity to implement a viable adjustment program. First, the government had a strong political mandate: it had more than 76 percent of the vote and 125 out of 150 seats in Parliament. The experience of several countries indicates that political change of a relatively dramatic nature may facilitate the implementation of far-reaching economic reform; in this case the newly elected government enjoys a much longer "honeymoon" period than is normal. Second, people were aware of the extreme nature of the economic crisis, and the government made no false promises in its electoral campaign. As a result, unpopular measures met with less resistance.[52] Third, Chiluba's labor background guaranteed him a certain amount of union support.[53] Fourth, with the UNIP in disfavor, there was no credible alternative. Fifth, the new government received support from the international financial community early on.[54] Also, after the UNIP's experience with food riots, donors were willing to support safety net policies. And at least in the arena of economic reforms, Chiluba realized that it was essential to move quickly while the government had political momentum.

There were also some obstacles to adjustment. First of all, despite his promises to reduce the size of the government, Chiluba found that he had to appoint at least twenty-one ministers because he needed the support of a variety of provincial and sectoral factions.[55] The MMD was a movement more than a party and thus consisted of several factions, including the radical free marketeers known as the Group of Seven, which had quite a bit of influence on Chiluba; former UNIP party elites with sufficient influence to get government posts; and the Caucus for National Unity (CNU), a pressure group that sought political support among influential MMD members who did not receive posts in the government. By its second year in office, the government felt that these factionalist tendencies were threatening its cohesion, and in early 1993 decided to remove Finance Minister Emmanuel Kasonde, even though he was one of the strongest proponents of adjustment in the government, as well as an advocate of safety net policies, and was respected in international financial circles. His removal, the result of political infighting, was a blow to the adjustment program and to donor relations.[56]

Nevertheless, the government made remarkable progress in its first year. Structural reforms, trade liberalization, and privatization all moved ahead far more quickly than most observers would ever have predicted. In addition, in its first few months in office the government proved that it could administer relief aid on a massive scale when the country was struck by a severe drought.[57] It also freed the exchange market, removed price controls and subsidies on most commodities, and balanced the budget for 1992. Difficult measures remained to be implemented, however. It still had to fire as many as 50,000 civil servants, who accounted for about half of the public sector's wage bill.[58] And perhaps most worrisome, despite its early rhetoric, the government was not fully addressing the social costs of its policies. By the end of 1992 it had still not appointed anyone to run the social action program. Indeed, at December 1992 consultative meetings with external donors, the pressure to address social issues came primarily from the donors rather than from the government, as had occurred in Peru. It may be that many MMD members, because of their old aversion to the UNIP, were so opposed to state planning that they made it difficult for agencies and ministries to formulate a coherent strategy for addressing the social costs of adjustment.

As the government's honeymoon period drew to a close, these social costs were becoming something of an obstacle to adjustment. Because Zambia is more urban than most African countries, its political and poverty considerations are more typical of those in the adjusting countries of Latin America. Unpopular measures are likely to elicit a much more explosive reaction in urbanized societies than in more rural societies, as past experience in Venezuela and Zambia itself has shown.[59] A larger percentage of the urban population relies on the market for food and other goods and is thus much more vulnerable to price rises than are the rural poor. Like most other African countries, however, Zambia is one in which the poor constitute a high percentage of the population (70 percent). When "everybody is vulnerable" but little information is available about this segment of society, it is extremely difficult to target the most vulnerable groups or to design strategies to protect them.[60]

Donors clearly seemed willing to lend support. Yet any strategy to address the social costs of adjustment entails domestic political economy trade-offs. Under the UNIP, while donors financed social expenditures, the government squandered an enormous amount of public funds elsewhere.[61] A sustainable strategy for protecting the poor must entail Zambians themselves exercising political choice and setting priorities for public expenditure.

While adjustment may be more politically volatile in an urban society like Zambia's, it is often the *manner* in which measures are implemented or presented that makes the difference, as demonstrated by the willingness of Peruvians to accept great price shocks. That is why the first finance minister under the MMD insisted that the difficult measures required in Zambia needed to be clearly explained and presented as a package that provided a sweetener to make them more palatable to the public.[62] As a result, the Chiluba government did not merely unleash unpopular measures overnight, as the Kaunda government had done. Instead, it made a concerted effort to inform the public about its reforms. In the case of privatization, it "mount[ed] a massive publicity campaign, like they did for the privatization of British Telecom or British Gas, to tell the public the merits and demerits of buying shares."[63]

This new approach explains the lack of protest when the government doubled the price of maize in December 1991. Since then, the price of breakfast meal has been liberalized and has risen almost fourfold. The subsidy on less refined roller meal remained in place temporarily, but eventually subsidies were removed from all grinds except donated yellow maize. This enhanced popular acceptance of the measures, as did the government's playing up to the people's historic willingness to pay high prices for meal on the black market whenever official pricing policy caused a shortage. Before the price rises, the government also gave millers more incentive to produce the less expensive meal in order to ensure an adequate supply.[64]

The maize meal issue had been the political bête noir of the Kaunda government, which spent almost 17 percent of its total budget (see table 6-3) on maize subsidies.[65] Eliminating that burden had to be a central objective of any adjustment program, from both an economic and a political point of view. Since much of the urban population spends up to 70 percent of its income on food, however, it cannot afford the increase in the price of meal.[66] Identifying a viable strategy for protecting the truly vulnerable in the face of continued price rises was one of the most immediate—and difficult—challenges facing the Chiluba government. The discussion now turns to the economic legacy of the UNIP that the new administration had to contend with in its search for such a strategy, the potential effect of price increases on the poor, and some possible strategies for identifying and reaching the vulnerable.

Table 6-3. *Maize Subsidies in Relation to the Total Government Budget and Budget Deficit, 1986–90*
Millions of kwacha

Year	Government budget	Budget deficit	Maize subsidies	Maize subsidies as percent of government budget
1986	5,383.6	1,025.7	565.0	10.5
1987	5,837.5	2,146.8	638.4	10.9
1988	8,359.3	1,531.2	1,413.0	16.9
1989	9,838.0	3,699.0	1,585.6	16.1
1990	24,503.3	2,801.4	3,363.9	13.7

Source: Ministry of Agriculture, "Evaluation of the Performance of the Maize Sector, June 1990."

The Economic Legacy of the UNIP State

Zambians were considerably worse off at the end of UNIP's term than they were at independence in 1964. The per capita annual income at that time was US$540, which was among the highest in the countries of Africa. Today it is US$390, which is among the lowest in the world. In the 1980s GNP per capita declined by 50 percent and inflation was expected to top 150 percent by 1991.[67] Although countrywide data are in short supply, credible estimates place up to 42 percent of the urban population and anywhere from 20 to 80 percent of rural households below the poverty line (52 percent of the country's population is urban).[68] Basic social welfare services barely function; hospitals are without drugs, beds, and personnel; most schools are without books and desks. Real per capita health care expenditure in 1989 was one-third of its 1982 level; education expenditure was one-quarter of its 1982 level. Expenditure in health care remains skewed toward curative care, and in education it goes toward tertiary education, despite the fact that this costs the government 130 times as much per pupil as does primary education.[69] Of the mothers attending antenatal clinics in urban areas, 25–30 percent are HIV positive. There are yearly epidemics of cholera and dysentery. Yet in 1991 hospitals in one of the nation's major cities, Livingstone, closed down because water shortages made it impossible to conduct diagnostic blood tests![70] The mortality rate from cholera in the 1990–91 rainy season ranged from 5.6 percent in Eastern Province to 11.2 percent in Northern Province.[71] In contrast, the mortality rate in a 1991 cholera epidemic in Peru was kept to less than 1 percent.[72]

Table 6-4. *Government Employment as a Share of Total Employment, Selected Years, 1975–90*[a]

	Employment			
Year	Government	Parastatal[b]	Total	Government share of total (percent)
1975	124,760	116,150	361,230	34.54
1977	126,260	128,350	353,340	35.73
1980	106,100	n.a.	379,300	27.97
1981	106,040	n.a.	373,720	28.37
1982	106,510	n.a.	366,480	29.06
1983	106,930	n.a.	364,160	29.36
1984	105,000	n.a.	365,190	28.75
1985	108,030	n.a.	361,520	29.88
1986[c]	104,870	n.a.	360,540	29.09
1987[c]	108,680	n.a.	361,830	30.04
1988[c]	108,570	n.a.	369,390	29.39
1989[c]	109,440	n.a.	371,800	29.44
1990[c]	111,630	n.a.	376,950	29.61

Sources: Prices and Incomes Commission, Lusaka, Zambia, 1991; and for 1975 and 1977, Morris Szeftel, "Political Graft and the Spoils System in Zambia," *Review of African Political Economy*, no. 24 (December 1982), p. 6.
n.a. Not available.
a. The table only includes data on formal employment, which represents 20 percent of the labor force in 1984 and 10 percent in 1990.
b. 1980–90 data do not provide a breakdown of the parastatal component of employment. It is estimated that parastatals make up 80 percent of Zambia's economy.
c. Estimated value.

The precipitous decline in the state of Zambia's infrastructure and welfare can be attributed in large part to misallocated spending, to cuts in recurrent expenditure rather than consumption in the face of decreasing government revenues, and to pervasive corruption.[73] It was also due to a 50 percent decline in the terms of trade for copper just when oil prices rose. From 1975 to 1986 copper generated 85 to 90 percent of Zambia's foreign exchange, which the government continued to spend lavishly despite the decline in the terms of trade. This behavior, coupled with rapid population growth (3.7 percent a year), proved disastrous.[74] Formal sector employment peaked in 1975, with 120,320 positions, and fell to 98,730 in 1979. During this same period, government employment grew from 124,760 to 126,260, and parastatal positions from 116,150 to 128,350. Parastatal salaries were 60 percent higher than those in the private sector in 1977. Even with the economic decline and attempts at adjustment of the 1980s, government employment continued to grow (see table 6-4).[75]

Although the UNIP regime mismanaged the economy, it did promote a certain level of institutional development, which distinguishes Zambia from many of its neighbors. First of all, the UNIP expanded the basic infrastructure, such as health facilities and schools, to even the most remote parts of the country, although it failed to maintain them. In many other parts of Africa, such infrastructure just does not exist.[76] In addition, urban settlement policy in Zambia in the mid-1970s was concerned with organizing squatter residents into community-based, self-help groups that could provide voluntary construction labor and with developing primary sanitation, health, and education infrastructure. By matching its settlement policy with the available space, Zambia has had a less haphazard, crowded, and precarious peri-urban situation than have many other developing nations.[77]

Kenneth Kaunda's rather vague philosophy of "humanism" dictated that the state would take care of every Zambian. At the time of independence, when funds were readily available, this precept did indeed lead to better living conditions and access to services for a large majority, but when economic trends turned downward and the effects of misguided government policy were finally felt, these improvements all but evaporated. In addition, the politics of the one-party state, which made party membership a prerequisite for virtually all basic services, at times isolated the poorest and most vulnerable from the very programs that were designed to benefit them.[78] At the same time, the belief that the state should dictate and provide all services free of charge made people less willing to help themselves or to maintain their infrastructure. Donors, meanwhile, sanctioned such policies for decades with large flows of assistance.[79] Indeed, decades of party and government handouts have all but destroyed Zambia's tradition of self-help, with the result that indigenous organizations such as NGOs remain weak. One of the primary challenges in implementing programs for the poor will therefore be to revive community initiative.[80] Although the extended family plays a major role in providing a social safety net in many African nations, Zambia is much more urban than most, and thus the links to families in rural areas may be less important here.

No episode in Zambia's experience demonstrates these various problems as well as the politically explosive maize crisis. Zambians, even the very poor, are so accustomed to subsidized maize that they are unwilling, in the short term, to adapt their consumption habits to any other product. Rice, for example, which is the main staple for much of the world's population, is considered an inadequate food by the majority of Zambians. As the price of higher-quality foods increased in the 1980s, most Zambians began substituting maize for other foods.[81] Only the poorest people buy the less processed roller meal; most opt for the more expensive (but less nutritious) breakfast meal.[82] In many other countries the poor usually look for the most nutritious buy at the best price.[83]

All these factors have made it doubly difficult to protect the poor in Zambia. To make matters worse, there are few reliable data on the actual extent of poverty, although three recent studies have provided enough data for a rough estimation of who the vulnerable are. This provides at least a good starting point for devising a policy that would protect the poorest groups as an accompaniment to adjustment policies.[84]

Poverty in Zambia

Health and nutrition data indicate that over the past few decades poverty in Zambia has increased both in extent and severity.[85] Per capita income is at one third the level it was in 1964, and, to judge by various social indicators, Zambia is now no better off than most low-income countries, despite having been considered a middle-income country in 1981. Estimates of the number of households under the poverty line range from 35–40 percent to as high as 70 percent.[86] The price of a food basket for a family of six increased in cost forty-six times from 1975 to 1989, owing to various bouts of inflation, and there is good reason to believe that today many low-income households spend up to 70 percent of their income on food. Thirty percent of the deaths of children aged one to fourteen are nutrition related, and infant mortality is still high (82 per 1,000).[87] In addition, adult literacy is about 25 percent, and income distribution is poor: the top 20 percent of the households hold 63 percent of national income, whereas the bottom 20 percent hold 4 percent.[88]

In 1991 an estimated 67 percent of Zambians were below the poverty line, as opposed to 60 percent in 1974–75.[89] If one uses the Price and Incomes Commission's rather controversial poverty line of 1,556 kwachas per month and abject poverty line of 778 kwachas per month, then 42 percent of urban households are below the poverty line (of these, 68 percent earn their living in the informal sector); and 24 percent are below the abject poverty line (6 percent of these households are in the formal sector and 31 percent in the informal sector).[90] While only 24 percent of the economically active population was in the formal sector in 1980, this figure dropped to about 10 percent in 1990. The greatest increases in poverty have been in traditionally better-off urban areas, and inequality between rural and urban sectors has actually narrowed in recent years.[91]

Seventy-five percent of female-headed households are poor.[92] Because of gender discrimination in the labor market, most working women in Zambia are in the informal sector. Seventy-two percent of those in low-paid occupations such as food sales are female, and workers in low-paid occupations make up one third of all female-headed households. Thus it is likely that a significant percentage of those in abject poverty are female-headed households. The 1990 income figures may be too low if the current prices of basic goods are taken into account.[93] Incomes adjusted for inflation or poverty levels are probably higher. In the formal sector, approximately 110,000 workers are below the poverty line, and 11,000 are in extreme poverty; in the informal sector, 161,000 are below the poverty line, while at least 98,000—many of whom are female—are in extreme poverty.[94]

The percentage of rural households below the poverty line is probably much higher—estimates vary from one-fifth of all households (1989) to 80 percent of the population (1980)—but even less information is available on the situation in rural areas. These households appear to have been less affected by price trends, with the important exception of some of the poorest rural households, which buy a large proportion of their food. Household surveys taken in 1975 and 1985 found that per capita income fell by only 4 percent in rural areas, whereas in towns it fell by 30 percent, and in former squatter areas it fell by 22 percent.[95] The greatest numbers of rural households living in abject poverty are in the four provinces least served by physical infrastructure: Luapula, Northern, North-Western, and Western.[96]

Despite the lack of precise numbers, the trends are straightforward enough: the largest numbers of urban poor are in the informal sector, particularly among female-headed households. It also seems that the effects of economic decline have been worse for the urban poor, particularly women.[97] In addition, any household with only one adult working or with one adult who is ill (such as AIDs households) is likely to be vulnerable.[98] These households would also be the ones most negatively affected by adjustment—or at least they would be the least equipped to absorb price increases and other negative shocks.

Income distribution is also more skewed in the informal sector than in the formal sector. The incomes of the self-employed in the informal sector are comparable to or higher than those of low-income workers in the formal sector. Those who are employed by others in the informal sector, however, earn less than those at the lowest level of the formal sector. These trends are particularly significant because the percentage of the population that is employed in the formal sector has decreased dramatically, from approximately 20 percent in the early 1980s to approximately 9 percent in 1992.[99] With a high percentage of the population already in the informal sector, there may be a limit to how many workers it can absorb at a time of increased unemployment. Given the relatively small size of the market in Zambia, the informal sector is likely to expand in a lateral direction; that is to say, when more low-skilled workers enter the sector, wage levels will fall.[100]

Another important aspect of poverty in Zambia is that basic services such as health and education have also deteriorated. Interviews with a small number of randomly selected urban and rural poor groups in Lusaka indicate that the lack of health services is a primary concern of the poor, followed in order of importance by the state of schools.[101] Especially since the introduction of user fees in some cases, many people simply do not go to the doctor or send their children to school because the quality of the service is so low.[102]

On a more positive note, the living conditions of the urban poor in Zambia, though hardly adequate, are somewhat better than those of the poor in other cities in developing countries because of both the available space and land and the government's settlement policies in the mid-1970s. In addition, although the level of organization varies among shantytowns—or compounds, as they are called in Zambia—all of them have parent-teacher associations (PTAs), cooperatives, and some kind of church-related organization.[103] Such groups can play an important role in helping the poor devise survival strategies and in helping the state protect the most vulnerable groups.

The Poor and Adjustment

It may not be possible to predict who will suffer most during adjustment in Zambia, but it is possible to determine who can least afford to suffer. The most vocal opponents of adjustment measures are often not the most vulnerable. Traditionally, these vocal groups are university students and laid-off civil servants. Yet given the extent of deterioration of living standards before the implementation of major structural reforms, the "vocal" may also be vulnerable in Zambia.[104] There is no doubt that there will be losers in the adjustment process: as many as 30,000 civil servants need to be laid off, and the price of maize has already quadrupled with liberalization.[105] Whatever side is taken in "the vigorous debate over the impact of adjustment," it is clear that the trend is toward "a more explicit policy emphasis on reaching the poorest."[106]

For almost a decade, reform in Zambia moved at an extremely slow pace, however, which means that it will take longer for the positive impact to be felt by the poor. Moreover, as mentioned, wages tend to decrease in the informal sector during the crisis that necessitates adjustment.[107] Stop-and-go efforts at reform have merely sped up the deterioration of the living standards of the poor, at least of those in urban areas. And the impact is probably being felt the most by workers in the nontraded informal sector, precisely those who have been identified as most vulnerable in Zambia.[108] At the same time, genuine attempts at adjustment may actually bring the needs of the poor and vulnerable to the political forefront.

To date, few countries have made social welfare policy an integral component of their adjustment packages. What has been done is often too small to have a significant effect on poverty.[109] This was the case in Zambia under Kaunda, whose Social Action Programme (SAP) failed to get off the ground. The SAP had a poor record because the government tried to politicize the program and failed to stick to it, so the donors withdrew their support.

For the Chiluba government, the challenge is to identify and protect the poorest and most vulnerable from the negative impact of the adjustment measures. To achieve this goal, it must address three key issues. First, it must buffer the poorest from the effects of rising maize prices. People at the margin, who spend up to 70 percent of their income on food, cannot afford to see that figure go any higher. If it did rise, they would probably reduce consumption instead and thereby risk an even greater incidence of malnutrition and related diseases. Zambia's health infrastructure is not equipped to cope with such an increase, as the high mortality rates in the cholera epidemic demonstrated. Without some protection, people forced to withstand continued price increases might eventually succumb to the kind of rioting that took place in 1986 and

1990. Second, the bulk of the government's social welfare expenditure was spent on subsidizing maize, and a large amount of that subsidy went to nonpoor groups. If that expenditure could be released for other purposes, some progress could be made toward achieving a social welfare policy that is focused on the needs of the poor. Third, precisely because it is so important to get beyond the maize issue, protection should concentrate less on coupons or subsidy schemes, and more on income-generating activities or food-for-work schemes.[110]

Some steps have already been taken in this direction. Currently, the World Food Programme in conjunction with a nongovernmental organization, Human Settlements of Zambia (HUZA), is implementing extensive food-for-work programs in low-income peri-urban settlements, employing primarily women, and paying them in kind, to build pit latrines and other essential basic infrastructure.[111] This, coupled with the World Bank's Social Recovery Fund and the Economic Community's Microprojects Unit (MPU), which provide income-generating activities and renovate infrastructure, is a starting point for protecting the poor and vulnerable. In addition, a host of church organizations and NGOs play a vital role in providing services for the poorest sectors. Their links to grass-roots groups must be incorporated into any strategy to reach the poor. Perhaps the most vital next step was to find a viable long-term solution to the maize meal issue, thereby allowing the government to focus on more important social welfare issues.

The Politics and Poverty of Maize

Because services have deteriorated to a virtual standstill, the only thing the poor have been able to count on in recent years is the low price and ready availability of maize. Indeed, by 1985 the maize subsidy "was the only welfare measure the government was providing."[112] Yet the nation has enough land to produce, "a maize surplus anytime it wants."[113] The bulk supply and distribution problems it has are due to policy distortions.[114] These distortions have had a number of important effects. They were all linked to the UNIP's political objective, which was to provide cheap maize to urban areas. In the 1970s low producer prices discouraged production, necessitating imports. In the 1980s producer prices were raised, but most of the profit went to inefficient marketing parastatals. The net result of the maize policy was an enormous amount of leakage to nonpoor groups and lasting disincentives to production and distribution.

The heavily subsidized price of maize in Zambia was one-third what it was abroad; thus an enormous amount was smuggled.[115] Maize was so cheap and plentiful that a great deal of it was wasted: in 1988 an entire ton rotted in storage. Most farmers and distributors preferred to sell maize abroad illegally than to store it. The result was a continual need for imports, and the Chiluba government had to import large quantities from South Africa upon taking office in order to avoid famine.[116] Also, under the UNIP's panseasonal, panterritorial uniform producer price, free transport to the line of rail was provided. In remote rural provinces this move eliminated the incentive for farmers to produce the grain more cheaply for sale in the region or to store it for sale later in the year. The maize marketing board, meanwhile, had a statutory obligation to buy all the maize offered to it.[117] Subsidies on fertilizer created similar distortions.[118] Approximately 25 million kwacha were lost daily between producer prices and processed meal.[119] Without these distortions, production and distribution would be more efficient, and Zambia could diversify from maize production and consumption.

The maize issue has been so important to both the politics of adjustment and the welfare of the poorest that it has been the cause of bloody food riots—in December 1986 and June 1990. While most people assume that an increase in the price of maize automatically hurts the poor, the issue is not that straightforward. Initially, when Zambia tried a general subsidy scheme in the early 1980s, it was expensive but had progressive effects. High-income groups spent 2.2 percent of their incomes on maize whereas low-income groups spent 7.5 percent, and the percentage has risen quite sharply since then.[120] In January 1989 price controls were removed on most other basic commodities and a coupon system introduced to replace the general subsidy on maize, which by then had become unsustainable. Food coupons could be exchanged for set quantities of either breakfast meal or the less refined and less expensive roller meal at state retail outlets and some private shops. There was no targeting between urban households, although the wealthiest ones were less likely to participate in the system because of the time it took to obtain and trade in coupons. When targeting was not used, it became a rationing system, with long queues for both coupons and maize. In addition, registration closed after two months, with the result that many needy families—also the most likely to be poorly informed—were left out. In addition, under this arrangement no provision was made for new family members.

Rural areas, which were presumed to be self-sufficient, were not included in the coupon system. This discounted the importance of food purchases for the poorest of the rural poor, who either do not produce enough for their own consumption, or cannot afford to store their production, and thus need to purchase food after the harvest period.[121] In general, though, price increases improved the situation for many rural farmers. In addition, by making village grinding financially viable, it encouraged farmers to keep food for their own consumption and for local sales. Before the 1990 price increase, a bag of milled meal cost the same as a bag of unmilled meal, so farmers were quick to sell their harvests for cash.[122]

In July 1989 the government made an attempt to redesign the coupon system, setting a limit of 20,500 kwacha in annual income for eligibility, but this target income level was rapidly made obsolete by inflation. Formal sector workers received the coupons at their places of work, and all others at the local civic center, where they were distributed by UNIP party officials. The revamping of the coupon scheme coincided with the June 1990 rise in the price of maize meal and riots in several cities.[123] Because it was difficult to determine the income levels of formal sector workers, the coupon system eventually became yet another tool for party patronage. It seemed that "the Party vigilantes . . . coopted in the system to ensure law and order . . . favoured some households."[124] Since the poor were rarely party members, they were unlikely to be those favored.[125] Many of the poorest households, meanwhile, found the transport costs to the civic centers too high, or they had no means of carrying the heavy bags of maize back to their compounds. And the opportunity costs of the poor's time, especially in single-parent households, is often underestimated. Many poor were forced to buy maize from black marketeers who sold it in the compounds at two and three times the price. Finally, because the poor can usually afford only small quantities, middlemen were subsidized far more often.[126]

The coupon system did not do much for the very poor. The expenses of households receiving the maximum of six coupons went up 477 percent after the introduction of the coupon system. The expenses of the poorest families, who consumed much more of their total food intake as maize and who were often bypassed by the system, went up even more. And in the last few months of the UNIP government the coupon distribution system broke down. Its one positive benefit was that it reduced the costs of maize subsidies by one-third.[127]

Since the December price liberalization, the system has been in transition. (In addition, in 1992 drought reduced the availability of maize.) The system could be reformed in several ways: a monitoring system could be introduced; private traders could be allowed to trade in coupons, and the number of available retail stores could be increased; some provision could be made for registering new entrants; and the value of coupons could be linked to an overall consumption basket reflecting the needs of the poor. Targeting could be improved by choosing specific locations and by subsidizing only roller meal, as the government has already done. Yellow maize, donated from abroad and seen as an inferior commodity by Zambians, is also subsidized.[128]

To a certain extent, the price liberalization appeared to hurt middlemen more than the poor, who were already paying more than the official price. The public seemed to show no reaction when the price was raised in December. Yet the poor no doubt felt the increase: the official price, when the new government took office, was 215 kwacha per 25 kilogram bag, while the poor paid approximately 500 kwacha per bag. Without the subsidy, the price would go to 2,000 kwacha per bag.[129] A longer-term solution may be to promote the consumption of other products. Rice, for example, grows well in some of the remote parts of Zambia. From 1980 to 1990, meanwhile, the production of maize increased by only 3 percent, and the production of soya increased by 21 percent.[130] Because of the time lag involved, however, this is not an option that can serve to protect vulnerable groups in the short term. In any case, maize price liberalization was certainly a necessary and timely first step toward addressing social welfare issues.

Programs for the Poor: The SAP, SRF, and MPU

In view of the urgency of the poverty problem and the need for adjustment, action on the social front must be both rapid and visible. To a large extent, it will be necessary to rely on continuing efforts and programs. Among these are the Social Action Programme, the Social Recovery Fund (SRF), and the Microprojects Unit.

The SAP was unveiled at the April 1990 donors' meeting in Paris. It was to provide protection for the poorest and most vulnerable groups through temporary and targeted measures consisting of social sector and income-generating activities designed to mitigate the effects of adjustment.[131] In 1991 the SAP set up six sectoral working groups, in health, education, water and sanitation, food security and nutrition, income generation and employment, and women in development. Each group comprised representatives from the government, relevant ministries, donors, and NGOs. The Steering Committee for the SAP was chaired by the Division for Economic Cooperation in the Ministry of Finance. In addition, provincial SAP working groups were set up to establish priorities for the program within the context of provincial development plans. In contrast to Bolivia's highly successful Emergency Social Fund, the SAP did not have an autonomous secretariat, a unitary source of funds, or a mechanism for ensuring financial accountability for those funds.[132] It was primarily an institutional structure at the national level designed to act as a liaison among the government, the line ministries, and the donors.

Donor commitments to the SAP were disappointing, which severely limited its scope. Most donors instead decided to continue with their country projects.[133] One reason for their action was that the UNIP government had failed to abide by the conditions of the structural adjustment program after April 1991. Another was that donors and the government had fundamentally different conceptions of the SAP. Whereas donors were seeking a program that targeted the poorest and most vulnerable groups of Zambia, the government apparently saw the SAP as a sort of "wish list" for spending in the social sector. Donors also complained that the SAP ignored the glaring problems of administration in Zambia. One water project, for example, was supposedly being managed by five different ministries. Seeing that the Zambian government was not complying with the adjustment program, donors were reluctant to put money into a vaguely defined "slush fund." The only donor money approved for the SAP was US$14 million provided by the Dutch, the Swedes, and the European Community for targeted support for the health sector. The third and perhaps primary reason that the program did not get off the ground was that the UNIP used it as a political tool before the election.[134]

The government of Zambia was thus forced to fund the SAP on its own. It disbursed 465 million kwacha of a total of 550 million committed for 1991; 44 percent of the amount went directly to the provinces. In the

absence of viable, functioning ministries, provincial planning units were
the only agencies that could actually get things done.[135] The first 165
million was released in February, 200 more in August, and a final 100 in
October. The government initiated more than 200 SAP provincial projects and set up at least three in each district in the country. Most were
in primary education, rural health care, and water and sanitation, and
their priorities were set by the provinces. The remaining projects were
implemented through the working groups. Lusaka Urban District Council, for example, received 45 million kwacha, and Lusaka's main hospital,
the University Teaching Hospital, received 138 million kwacha. The largest percentage of funds went to emergency water and sanitation projects,
women and household security, NGO projects, and Urban Self-Help Push
(discussed below).[136]

Although the government endeavored to draw ample attention to these
projects in the hope of strengthening its political support, the public was
soon aware of the lack of substance behind the publicity. At the time of
the program's inception, party politicians were sent out to the provinces
to publicize it and instead made a series of promises that had nothing to
do with the SAP's priorities. Access to the SAP was politically valuable
because it was one of the only sources of government funds available for
delivering services at the local level. However, it appeared that the funds
were being allocated at the discretion of the UNIP rather than the SAP.
Of the 100 million kwacha disbursed by the government in October, for
example, 40 million was committed directly by the UNIP at the district
level. Although this does not necessarily imply that all the funds were
wasted, the bypassing of normal procedures meant that provincial priorities were ignored and there was no mechanism for preventing the money
from being used for political purposes, particularly since the UNIP controlled all levels of government.[137]

Because of the great lack of social services in the country, the SAP
became a useful tool in the election campaign. The UNIP devoted an
entire section of its political manifesto to the SAP, and the politicization
of the program was one of the MMD's major criticisms in its campaign.
The UNIP even tried to impose party cards on SAP women's groups at
the district level. One UNIP chairperson for women's issues in Northern
Province stated that she should get the SAP funds for the district because
she knew best how to help people, and she needed five new vehicles in
order to do so![138] Large sums of government money that had nothing to
do with the SAP were also channeled directly to district councils for

political purposes. In one case, the UNIP wrote checks for 10 million kwacha for district governors.[139]

Because the government had discretionary use of whatever funds were available, working groups had little, if any, money to work with. After responding to government requests for proposals, NGOs and other groups would be told that there was no money for projects, but that they had the SAP's approval to petition donors. Most felt that it would have been far more efficient to do so directly. Some NGOs complained that the top-down approach even extended to working committees. Moreover, the government took no interest in research or targeting. Its main concern was, "How can we spend money to get out of this problem?" NGOs also noted that the bulk of the money was spent on large and visible projects that would have maximum political impact. They also criticized the bureaucratic approach and excessive requirements of the SAP.[140]

Most NGOs also recognized, however, that the working groups brought government, nongovernment, and donor actors together to discuss sectoral priorities and the effects of adjustment, and in this sense they were an unprecedented and positive step. Before the SAP the government had little contact with the NGOs. The NGOs credited the expatriate SAP coordinator with persisting in getting the process launched. Partly as a result of the discussions held by the SAP, the message that something had to be done to identify and protect the poorest and most vulnerable groups began to find an audience.[141]

The one SAP-funded program that many observers considered an exception in terms of having a positive impact on social welfare, reaching the poorest, and avoiding political pressure was Urban Self-Help Push.[142] The program, which began before the SAP, was administered jointly by the World Food Programme and the local NGO HUZA. The UNIP government gave Push 27 million kwacha. The program provides food for work and technical assistance for labor-intensive projects designed to improve sanitation in poor urban areas. Under the Kaunda government, Push funded 150,000 workdays to build 800 pit latrines, 70 kilometers of drainage, and provide 1,500 people with food rations for two years. Under the Chiluba government, the World Food Programme gave Push US$1.6 million in food in 1992–93 to counter the effects of a severe drought, and the government contributed 60 million kwacha (US$300,000) in counterpart funds. In 1992 the program employed 3,800 people in Lusaka and Ndola, 95 percent of them women; it was expected to expand to 10,000 the next year, and to receive US$13 million in food aid over a period of five years.[143] The communities that benefit also provide support in the form of voluntary labor on weekends. Technical assistance is provided by NGOs, the International Labour Organization, and the United Nations Development Programme. The main factors keeping Push from expanding to an even larger scale are its shortage of engineers and the quality of its infrastructure.

HUZA, though an independent NGO, works out of the Lusaka Urban District Council. This provides it with necessary infrastructure, but also leaves it open to political pressure from the government, which the regional director of the World Food Programme has complained about as well.[144] The fact that the program has been kept out of politics at all is due mainly to its expatriate and nongovernment management. The expatriate representative of the World Food Programme can afford to resist political pressure from the Zambian government, and the local implementing agency is an NGO that is removed from the reach of politicians, at least in a formal institutional sense. This enables the program to draw on specific expertise and grass-roots links, on the one hand, and distances it from the political patronage network, on the other.

Push has been successful on two fronts: it has reached a group that is clearly both poor and vulnerable—urban women, and indirectly, their children; and it has built a sense of self-help and community spirit among the poorest groups. It is providing sorely needed community infrastructure and income support through food for groups that are usually overlooked by the government. Yet, because Zambia has a tradition of government handouts, there has been substantial debate about the appropriateness of payment in kind rather than in cash. Nevertheless, the program continues to give impetus to self-help efforts.[145] The Push program is one that should be a part of the new government's efforts to protect the poor and vulnerable.

A large problem for the SAP was that it was not part of the adjustment program from the beginning. Thus many members of government and critics alike saw it as "the sugar coating to make adjustment palatable" or as a "shopping list" used to get money from donors.[146] Once it became politicized, no one considered it a serious effort. Despite its flaws, the SAP yields some important lessons. The first is that dialogue is vital in placing the issues of poverty alleviation and protection of the poorest at the forefront of public debate. The working groups set up for the SAP also provided a good mechanism for designing long-term sectoral strategies. Another lesson is that it is essential to strengthen local implementing capacity, particularly when mid-level ministries are weak. The SAP worked with the provinces precisely because they were more effective at implementing projects than Zambia's mid-level institutions. The SAP's implementation problems were greatest in areas that cut across ministerial or sectoral responsibilities, such as women in development, direct income support, food security, and monitoring and targeting. In addition, because it concentrated strictly on projects, it tended to ignore broader policy issues such as food security.[147]

Donors, meanwhile, saw the SAP as a good way to rationalize and target the social sector budget.[148] Although the UNIP government did not share this vision and the SAP did not serve this purpose, this does not preclude it filling such a role in the future. The new government stated that the SAP would be given priority and gave it 1 billion kwacha in its initial budget, yet it has ceased to exist as a coherent program because a new director has not been appointed to date. The SAP experience under the UNIP should not discredit social action programs in general. Yet it does identify the risks of overambitious and poorly targeted programs, as the experience of the PAMSCAD in Ghana also demonstrates (see the appendix). Another important lesson to draw from this experience is that placing such programs under the state bureaucracy exposes them to enormous political pressure. For this very reason, the semiautonomous Push program has fared much better.

The SRF and the MPU have managed to avoid most of the problems encountered by the SAP but have had to define their objectives quite narrowly in order to do so. The question being debated in Zambia is whether such a narrow approach is the most effective way to address the social costs of adjustment. Some would still argue that the program should be one component of a broader strategy that employs at least some of the mechanisms established by the SAP—even though it ceased to exist as a coherent program under the Chiluba government after supposedly being given high priority.[149]

Demand-Based Programs: The MPU and the SRF

The MPU was set up in 1986, and until 1989 it operated with a staff of three to manage 100 small projects. Since then its activities have expanded, owing to the World Bank's decision to implement its Social Recovery Fund from within the same government agency—the National Committee for Development Policy, under the Office of the President.

The program was to be managed with the same approach and core staff, however. In February 1992 the operation was formally divided into two demand-based programs, to respond to demands from local community organizations and NGOs for the construction of basic social infrastructure, such as primary schools and rural health posts. The two programs have a budget of US$40 million, most of which comes from the World Bank and the European Community, and counterpart funds from the Zambian government. Under the two programs, 250 projects have been implemented across the country.[150] World Bank funding also provided for the introduction of monitoring services, including a household priorities survey and a beneficiary assessment.[151] Because Zambia has an extensive but poorly maintained infrastructure, the programs focus more on renovating existing infrastructure than on launching new projects. Being a small operation trying to cope with the virtually unlimited need in Zambia, each program has had to establish clearly defined objectives. The primary purpose in both cases is to generate sustainable projects that will encourage communities to help themselves. This contrasts with other similar programs in Africa and Latin America, which have at the same time tried to reach the poorest groups or to create temporary jobs or employment. Because resources are limited and autonomous community initiative is sorely lacking in Zambia, the objectives of the MPU are to use the resources that it has to generate a small number of sustainable initiatives that will have demonstrable effects. While operating in the same vein, the SRF also seeks to counter the negative effects of adjustment and drought, through labor-intensive public works in drought-stricken areas. All labor receives payment under the SRF, in contrast to the MPU's requirement of a 25 percent community contribution, which is usually in the form of voluntary labor. (The SRF still requires community contribution in some form, but it is not a strict 25 percent requirement.) The MPU has had 1,000 requests for projects since its inception and has approved 300 of them. The average project size is US$30,000. More than 100 community groups and 21 NGOs are currently involved in the program. Approximately 30 percent of the projects are being implemented by NGOs, most of which are church related.[152] Most of the local groups involved are parent-teacher associations and church mission groups. Since February 1992 the SRF has implemented 131 projects with 400,000 beneficiaries, 47 percent of them women.[153]

The programs are equipped with mechanisms that promote local government and community participation. The procedure for submitting a project proposal, for example, begins with local groups, which must organize themselves into project committees (PCs) and then seek the approval of the district councils and provincial planning units, whose task is to ensure that the projects fit in with local government priorities (NGO projects go directly to program headquarters).[154] Although this system can create delays, the MPU and SRF may question local governments about why a project is delayed or not approved, since a copy of every project proposal goes directly to the program headquarters. Of course, this puts programs at the mercy of the local governments, which in many cases do not have the skills required to aid in the presentation of viable proposals. In one case, an MPU project in Western Province failed when the mayor misled the population about what the project entailed and what kind of contribution was necessary.[155]

Another problem is that approval has to be obtained from institutions that are not necessarily known for their efficiency or dedication to service. Furthermore, the programs have only a small staff to process a large number of proposals. Thus the rigors of the procedure may have inhibited many poor groups and less experienced community organizations from participating in the programs, especially if approval depended on political patronage. Even professionals have complained about the time it takes to obtain approval. In general, though, most communities in Zambia are fairly well organized, while many of the less developed community organizations rely on some sort of outside aid (from parish priests, for example) to find out what the programs entail and how to put together a proposal.[156]

Community contribution is required to ensure that projects are sustainable and infrastructure maintained. MPU projects in rural areas usually require voluntary labor, which is quite plentiful, especially during the dry season when farmers are not busy tending their fields. In contrast, the SRF pays wages for all labor for the duration of the drought period. In urban areas, where the opportunity costs of the poor's time may be higher because they rely more on the market, contributions are usually in cash. When skilled labor is necessary, workers from outside the community are paid market rates; if the necessary bricklayer or other technician is available locally, then compensation is provided at less than the market rate. Community contributions are designed to avoid practices of the past, when the state—aided by donors—provided everything free of charge, and communities had little stake in maintaining or improving infrastructure. Teachers, for example, usually came from other regions for a short time and had no interest in maintaining schools. Because the average person was alienated from the governing party, there was little respect for public property. The resulting deterioration of infrastructure invited vandalism. Now PTAs are allowed to collect contributions, which are often used to continue with community improvements even after a project has been completed.[157] Indeed, because the PTAs are so well organized, education projects have been posting a better record than health projects. Education projects have accounted for 72 percent of projects, health 12.6 percent, water 8.6 percent, infrastructure 3.4 percent, credit 2.2 percent, and food security 0.57 percent. With community contributions, procurement practices become more cost-effective, since communities are unlikely to pay for overpriced services with their own funds.[158]

In general the community contribution approach seems to work best in tighter, better-organized communities: "Whenever the Project Committee is a genuine representative of a rather close-knit community who has been working together on the micro-project, a potential has been opened for future community development."[159] Although at times local jealousies jeopardized the functioning of programs, this was the exception rather than the rule.[160]

Community participation is usually led by one or two prominent persons in the community, and, as mentioned, cash and labor are the most common form of contribution. In general, the contribution of rural areas is higher than that of urban areas. Strong outside presence in the management of projects, by line ministries or churches, for example, tended to reduce the community ownership of the projects. Where projects were difficult to complete, it was usually because building materials were not available, there were delays in receiving documents from the district or provincial units, funds were misused, or the community contribution was poorly organized. The quality of workmanship was apparently another problem, which was due to the shortage of qualified personnel.[161]

The main drawback of a demand-based approach is that it is biased toward the most organized and vocal communities. Because resources and administrative time are limited, the programs cannot help communities prepare proposals or fund extremely small projects. It also takes a great deal of administrative time and staff to reach the smallest and most remote communities.

One criticism that has been leveled at the MPU is that its outreach activities are too haphazard. The government made an attempt to address this problem when in October 1990 it introduced more refined evaluation criteria, a computer-based accounting system, and more efficient procurement procedures and assigned more staff to follow-up activities. The World Bank assisted with this effort by adding the SRF and hiring a few additional staff members.

The programs have had a noticeable impact on communities. For years, local governments had no money, and now they are enjoying the largest programs of government assistance in existence. In addition, most observers—both in and outside the government—commend the programs for their efficiency and the works created. Because the programs remain quite small, however, their most lasting impact will be of a long-term institutional nature. To reach more people, the programs would have to expand the scale of program activities, and therefore staff. But that might pose a threat to their operations because their success is in part due to the very fact that they are small and have limited objectives. This dilemma has been resolved in part by the division of the two programs and by concentrating on expanding the SRF.

Although the programs have relied on NGOs to implement projects, it may be difficult to expand their responsibilities because indigenous NGOs tend to be weak when it comes to administrative capacity. Local governments, although they are likely to become more efficient in the long term now that accountability has been introduced by the electoral process, will be in a state of flux in the short term and can hardly be counted on to take on more administrative responsibility.[162] Yet the extent of need in Zambia and the successful record thus far of the programs' staff suggest that continued expansion is both feasible and desirable, and may even be worth some trade-offs in efficiency.

To date, the programs have managed to avoid political pressure quite successfully. In theory, there should have been less pressure on the program in the one-party state because it would be expected to have fewer factions. Quite the opposite was true, however, because Zambian politics had a long tradition of patronage, while the program was one of the few providers of basic infrastructure. From the start, the MPU tried to disassociate itself from the political process by emphasizing the technical nature of projects, but this proved difficult. In the early stages of the program, political pressure was particularly strong. One reason was that the technical criteria for project selection were not fully spelled out, and therefore projects were selected on a "first-come, first-served" basis. In addition, many layers of political pressure were brought to bear on the program. If a member of Parliament was not successful in getting a project, he would get a minister to come to the MPU, and so on.

Adjustments were subsequently made in the project's administration to address these issues. To begin with, clear and strict mechanisms were applied to project selection. Perhaps even more important, this information was made public, especially to MPs and other politicians. Also, more power was given to local administrations by involving district councils and provincial planning units in project approval. Although this did not eliminate political in-fighting and competition, it at least channeled it to the local level and freed the MPU of involvement in political decisions. This process not only helped depoliticize the program but also contributed to project sustainability. An MP who requested a project for political purposes was unlikely to follow up on it at the local level; nor was a local government that had not been involved in submitting a project proposal. Under the current system, even if an MP requests a project, he must go through the appropriate local channels, to give the local government a say in the matter. The MP's support may then give the project a positive boost.[163] Political pressure by no means ended with these reforms, for there were many more cases of ward chairmen or MPs trying to interfere in project selection. At least the process now had technical criteria and a transparent system of selection to limit some excesses.

One of the most difficult tasks was to establish performance and merit criteria in a system in which the party had always dictated that need alone qualified everyone for state resources. These criteria were somewhat easier to introduce at the local level, but at the party and ministerial levels the message of equal distribution continued to dominate. Although communities were not accustomed to competition, they soon adapted and moreover began to realize that they could get things done without the party. Of course, their efforts were often sabotaged at the district and province levels when the party wanted to maintain control. The two clear lessons from this experience are that the more straightforward the rules, the freer the program is from political pressure; and the greater the community participation, the better the record in terms of maintenance, responsibility, and program viability.[164]

Needless to say, the changing political context has had an impact on the programs. Since planning has fallen out of favor with the new government, poverty programs have not been given sufficient attention or publicity. In addition, multiparty competition initially created some conflict over program projects. If the ward committee was pro-UNIP, for example, there was a tendency to say the project came from the party. Since the committee was usually chaired by a member of the UNIP, in many cases people refused to work on the projects. This divided communities and slowed project implementation.[165] Still, the programs seemed to avoid political pressure from the center at election time, and there is no correlation between number of program projects allocated to provinces and electoral margin (see table 6-5). Although this is also due to the MMD's overwhelming electoral margin, it stands in sharp contrast to the performance of the SAP.

The postelectoral context is different, however, and introducing political competition into the process may encourage people to try to "outdo each other in implementing projects."[166] If such competition remains within limits, it could be positive. But excessive local political competition might divide communities and run counter to the kind of initiative the programs are trying to promote. This is something that program staff should keep an eye on, particularly in view of the aggressive nature of the MMD's anti-UNIP campaign immediately following the election.

To conclude, the relative success of the programs, both in avoiding political pressure and in stimulating autonomous community development, provides important lessons for those attempting to reach the poor in Zambia. If the SRF expands further, it will have to increase the staff that it has available for monitoring. Equally important, it will have to develop an outreach system for the poorest communities. It may also need to develop a different line of activities that require less complex procedures for presenting and implementing projects and are designed specifically for poorer groups. Public works programs are a good first step, and the experience of Self-Help Push with food for work is also relevant. In the Push program, 1.7 million people who would have been receiving government handouts after the drought worked instead. The program has relied on community participation as well: the villagers decide what works should be given priority. This approach has garnered support for the MMD in rural areas: "Our community will have something lasting to show for our effort as well as us all receiving food equally. Under Kaunda, you only got food if the village headman liked you."[167] Since the drought, self-formed community groups have also come to the SRF requesting food for work. Perhaps the greatest challenge for the programs at present lies in adapting to the changing local political context.

Table 6-5. *Allocation of Microprojects and Election Results, by Province*
Amounts in millions of kwacha

Project	Central	Copperbelt	Eastern	Luapula	Lusaka	Northern	Northwest	Southern	Western	Total Zambia
Election results[a]										
UNIP votes	0	0	19	0	2	1	3	0	0	25
MMD votes	14	22	0	14	10	20	9	19	17	125
Total votes	14	22	19	14	12	21	12	19	17	150
Education projects										
Number	15	10	9	11	9	16	1	24	10	105
Amount advanced	13.8	18.6	7.2	7.4	18.5	25.9	4.4	17.1	3.2	115.8
Amount justified	10.5	18.0	5.7	5.5	13.5	17.4	2.8	9.4	2.3	85.0
Health projects										
Number	7	3	5	7	5	7	3	8	1	46
Amount advanced	9.2	5.9	5.8	10.0	6.7	18.6	7.3	12.0	0.8	76.2
Amount justified	9.0	3.2	4.0	7.2	4.5	14.0	5.7	9.9	0.8	58.3
Infrastructure projects										
Number	0	2	7	0	0	4	0	2	0	15
Amount advanced	0	3.0	9.0	0	0	1.7	0	0.8	0	11.8
Amount justified	0	0	5.3	0	0	0.9	0	0.6	0	6.8
Water supply projects										
Number	0	2	2	0	0	1	0	5	0	10
Amount advanced	0	3.9	1.5	0	0	0.1	0	1.2	0	6.7
Amount justified	0	2.8	2.1	0	0	0.1	0	0.6	0	5.6
Other projects										
Number	0	0	0	0	4	0	0	2	1	7
Amount advanced	0	0	0	0	11.5	0	0	4.5	0.1	16.1
Amount justified	0	0	0	0	9.1	0	0	0.8	0.1	9.9
Total projects										
Number	22	17	23	18	18	28	4	41	12	183
Amount advanced	23.1	28.7	23.5	17.4	36.6	46.3	11.7	35.5	4.0	226.7
Amount justified	19.6	24.0	17.1	12.7	27.0	92.4	8.6	21.2	3.2	165.7

Source: Data were compiled during an interview with Robin Hinson Jones, political officer at the U.S. embassy in Lusaka, Zambia; November 14, 1991.
a. Congressional seats. UNIP: United Progressive Party; MMD: Movement for Multiparty Democracy.

Figure 6-1. *Party and Local Government Structures under the United National Independence Party*

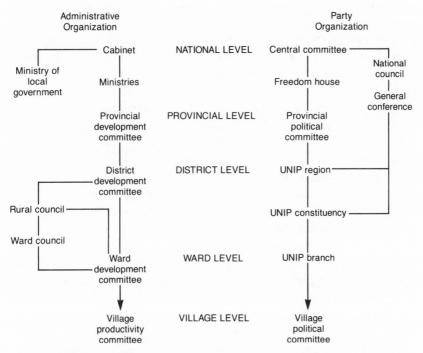

Source: Michael Bratton, *The Local Politics of Rural Development: Peasant and One-Party State in Zambia* (Hanover: University Press of New England, 1980).

The Changing Local Government Context

It has been said that "a feature of African politics is that political stability at the center is compatible with the deepening of social stratification and the persistent unfolding of rural under-development in the locality."[168] The UNIP party's policy of "decentralization in centralism," which was an attempt to consolidate central government control by extending party structures to the local level, created precisely such a system. That is to say, the institutional framework consisted of complementary party and municipal structures down to the province, district, ward, and village level (see figure 6-1). The top-down manner in which these organizations were set up and controlled put them completely out of touch with the communities. Thus the party was a party "with more leaders than followers at the local and rural levels," and therefore was poorly equipped to implement effective poverty reduction programs.[169] In

Ghana, for example, the Provisional National Defense Council's lack of grass-roots ties proved to be a major obstacle to the implementation of the PAMSCAD program, particularly in rural areas (see the appendix).

The party monopolized the channel by which central resources flowed to the locality. Material resources from the center were used to purchase political control in the locality, with rewards concentrated in the hands of selected local leaders who, in turn, ensured that the participation of peasants in local political organizations was held to manageable levels. The result was that much of the population remained under the same control it was subject to during colonial times. Particularly in remote villages where the party was weak, the traditional powerholders—the tribal chiefs—were able to dominate new structures created by the party and maintain their previous systems.[170]

Although a system of elected local authorities (rural councils) was established just before independence, it was revamped in the late 1960s with the consolidation of UNIP control. In 1969 a civil service reform was implemented that was designed to decentralize and depoliticize local politics. A cabinet minister was appointed for each province and a district governor for each district. In 1971 ward development and village productivity committees were set up, and in 1975 a complementary party structure was introduced to match state structures at the provincial, district, ward, and village levels. A few changes were made in 1980: political power was concentrated in the district governor, and the district executive secretary was to be in charge of administration. The district council was elected indirectly—it was composed of ward chairmen—and this arrangement limited its accountability. The idea was that the party would mobilize and the state would implement, while the UNIP would have control over both the central government and local participation. The result was a great many mismatched organizations, with no consistent chain of command or representation. The potential for conflict between local party and state representatives was high, and consequently local authorities were easily co-opted by local power brokers.[171] The confusion and conflict that the system caused can be seen in the dispute over the control of markets that broke out in 1970 between the Lusaka urban district council and the party. Out of this conflict came a series of inconsistent regulations that increasingly forced marketeers to abandon legal markets and establish informal ones.[172]

Of the local structures set up by the UNIP, the ward development committees seem to have been the most active and viable. Yet even they were dominated by prominent party men or ambitious farmers who were grafted onto the UNIP party machine; a relatively small, closed leadership tended to dominate in other organizations such as cooperatives and PTAs. Thus the UNIP lacked a base among the rural poor below the leadership level. "The commitment of peasants to the UNIP political machine was instrumental rather than moral or ideological, as illustrated by [one farmer] who referred to his party card as his 'passport for fertilizer'."[173] The UNIP tended to be authoritarian in its relations with the poor, particularly in rural areas, where political awareness is generally much lower and where the UNIP seemed less concerned with building a base of political support than with maintaining control.[174]

Despite the limitations of the ward and village committees, they were much closer to the rural poor than the often distant district councils, and they provided unprecedented opportunities for access to the state, which is unusual in Africa. The desperate need for basic services, meanwhile, made access to the resources that these organizations could broker from the center extremely important: "The low level of living conditions that afflicts most of Africa makes provision of basic amenities one of the central themes of life. Consequently, demands for roads, housing, water, electricity, schools, and medical dispensaries create vast new opportunities for accrual of power to those who dispense these blessings."[175]

Although clientelist politics and dependence on the center for resources are typical of municipalities in most developing countries, the situation was more complex in Zambia because of the dual party-state structure and the economic breakdown of the late 1970s. Like municipal governments throughout much of Sub-Saharan Africa, Zambian municipalities had virtually collapsed by the 1980s owing to excessive population growth, the lack of expertise, weak management, and constant political interference from the center.[176]

Since the 1991 elections and change of government, the local institutional context has changed significantly. In the campaign both parties called for direct mayoral elections, to replace the system of appointed district governors.[177] The MMD government held local government elections in 1992. District councils were directly elected; they then elected mayors to replace the currently appointed district governors. The electoral results mirrored those at the national level: the MMD swept most council seats in a landslide, with the exception of Eastern Province, the

UNIP's traditional stronghold.[178] The district councils have the authority to levy taxes to generate their own resources. Attitudes toward this system may change because Zambians are used neither to paying taxes at the local level nor to demanding accountability from the government.[179]

Although direct local elections are a positive first step, they will not in and of themselves generate autonomous local development. Particularly in rural areas, people do not fully understand what their rights are and what they can—and cannot—expect from the government. Program financing is the second step, since people are much more likely to be exigent about the performance of a service if they are actually paying for it. Taxation at the local level is analogous to community contributions to projects at the MPU level. Another positive step is the dismantling of the party-state structure. Whereas before NGO representatives had to go to the party to get things done at the local level, now they can go directly to the district council. In addition, all the district money channeled to the party for political purposes in the old days should now be freed for local use.[180]

Above all, the recent election did a great deal to promote political awareness and force people to take their fate into their own hands. The mandate for the MMD was as strong in remote rural areas as it was in urban areas. The very process of voting for change and then seeing it come about dramatically and rapidly has had an effect on all of society, bringing political awareness even to remote rural regions, which is rare in Africa. The UNIP can at least be credited with creating the atmosphere that drove local people to organize themselves. Self-governance still has a long way to go, however, especially in remote regions where the tribal chiefs or local power brokers still hold enough sway to distort democracy.[181] To the extent that the chiefs supported the UNIP, the electoral process weakened their political influence.

Perhaps a more serious obstacle to effective local government is the institutional vacuum that has developed since the crumbling of the UNIP. Rapid decentralization may be difficult to achieve precisely because the UNIP party structure was thoroughly integrated into the government, right down to the local level. Although communities know how to organize, they have no policymaking experience, NGOs and local governments seldom interact, and personnel and institutional problems are grave. Even the electoral rolls have been in total disarray, which is why local elections had to be delayed. Finally, there is the danger that the MMD will attempt to fill the institutional vacuum at the local level with its own party people, which could easily happen because political experience at the local level is so poor.[182]

Yet there are some things to be optimistic about. The opportunity to develop viable and independent local institutions has at last presented itself and could have an important impact on poverty alleviation in general. By giving beneficiaries a stake in the continuing process of change, demand-based programs could contribute to the political sustainability of reform. At the same time, by introducing independent choice, taxation, and accountability into local politics, Zambia may find demand-based social programs such as the MPU and the SRF more feasible. On the one hand, the programs will have to be extremely flexible with regard to approval norms and institutional requirements until the local structure is consolidated. On the other hand, previous programs did not have to worry about partisan competition. Although competition may generate better project proposals, it may also create tension among local government structures, because in the short term they will be the only institutions still linked to the UNIP party structure. It will be very important for the programs to accept proposals from all political actors, to prevent prolonged UNIP control at the local level or its being replaced by an MMD monopoly. The requirement that program proposals obtain local government approval should be reevaluated after local elections are held and the nature of political competition at that level becomes more evident. Indigenous as well as international NGOs are sure to play an important role in filling the institutional vacuum.

The Nongovernmental Organizations

As in much of Africa, the number of NGOs has grown considerably in Zambia in recent years. There are now 130 indigenous and international NGOs, 1,093 registered cooperatives, and an unknown number of PTAs and community organizations. Although in many other countries the government and NGOs have troubled relations, since independence the Zambian government has sought pragmatic collaboration with the country's NGOs. Collaboration is most widespread at the provincial and district levels and is related to concrete projects, but NGOs seem to want to avoid the bureaucracy at the middle level. Zambian NGOs and the government seem to be on good terms largely because these organizations are apolitical and tend to be implementing agencies rather than advocacy groups. Although the government has done little to sponsor NGOs, it seldom, if ever, tries to impede their activities.[183]

It is also important not to overestimate the capacity of NGOs, particularly the local ones. The most prevalent NGOs, such as UNICEF, which supports the implementation of 80 percent of public health projects in Zambia, are international organizations.[184] Local NGOs, meanwhile, depend almost entirely on foreign funds. Their strength lies in their emphasis on self-help initiatives at the community level, their links to the poorest groups, their dedication, and their ability to operate with low budgets.[185] Yet most of them also suffer from funding constraints and limited administrative capacity.[186]

These qualities put the NGOs in an ideal position to help programs like the MPU and SRF reach the poorest groups, through services, training, and assistance with the presentation of viable proposals. By and large, NGOs have been favorably impressed by the way in which the programs operate. In particular, they note that the World Bank sought to establish a dialogue with them before expanding its activities through the MPU, and that the dialogue improved their relations with the government and led to the formation of the NGO-Zambia forum. They also saw the SAP discussions as an important means to link the local work of the NGOs to national policies, but then soon became frustrated with the SAP's reluctance to follow through. Some also criticized the MPU for what they saw as excessive concern with projects and inadequate attention to sectoral policies, as well as an unwillingness to invest in NGOs as institutions.[187]

Until now, the SRF and MPU took an approach that above all supported local capacity, while recognizing that NGOs were most efficient at delivering services to the poor.[188] Nevertheless, it may be necessary to rely on NGOs in the short term if the program is to be expanded at a time of weak institutional capacity and dire need. In the current atmosphere of institutional flux, they will be critical actors for reaching vulnerable groups and the poor. Because there is no coherent national strategy at present for reaching these groups, NGOs are a good starting point. To the extent that investment in NGOs as institutions fosters capacity-building activities, their activities will complement, rather than duplicate, the development of local institutions. Finally, the new government's openness and willing recognition of its own limitations provides an excellent opportunity for developing government-NGO relations.

Conclusion

The dramatic political changes in Zambia and the growing awareness of the importance of adjustment and poverty alleviation suggest that this is an opportune time to implement extensive structural reform. However, the economic crisis poses formidable challenges. Innovative efforts will be required to identify and reach the poorest and most vulnerable groups, both to protect their welfare and to ensure that the adjustment process is sustained. The MPU, the SRF, and some elements of the Social Action Programme, will be critical to the success of such efforts. At the same time, the antistatist philosophy that pervades the government and discredits state planning—a phenomenon similar to that of many former socialist countries in eastern Europe—seems to have limited the government's efforts to take a more pro-active approach to formulating safety net and poverty reduction strategies.

The government should continue to take advantage of its political strength and the popular sentiment in favor of change and should move quickly to implement difficult adjustment measures. The foremost among these, for both budgetary and political reasons, was the maize meal issue, which the government already tackled by liberalizing the price. To a certain extent, this move may not have hurt the poor, who were already paying two and three times the official price and are equally as concerned about availability of maize as about its price. Thus in the long term they stand to benefit from a liberalization of the pricing, marketing, and distribution systems, and in the short term could probably absorb a twofold increase in the official price. But since the price will continue to increase, some sort of protective mechanisms need to be adopted. The government's decision to maintain the subsidy on roller meal and on donated maize, both of which are consumed primarily by the poorest, was a good first step. The distribution of coupons also needs to be improved, both to allow private traders to accept coupons and to establish a monitoring system that will ensure that the coupons are accepted by outlets and traders in peri-urban areas, since the transport costs to civic centers will keep many of the poorest groups from participating in the coupon system, as they have in the past.

The reform of the maize pricing system was explained to the public in a way that did not incite unrest. And the public needs to be continually reminded that the revenue previously used to subsidize maize will now flow into health and education services, both paramount concerns of the poor. Also, some kind of "sweetener" should be presented when other difficult policy measures are implemented; for example, eliminating school uniforms, which place a financial strain on poor households.

Protecting the poor also means focusing on income generation rather than compensation. Other countries have had ample experience with labor-intensive public works schemes to draw on. In Zambia the Urban Self-Help Push program seems a viable means of targeting the poorest households in urban communities, as does the SRF's public works program, which operates in both urban and rural areas. The experiences of the MPU provide a good basis on which to build a community organization and self-help program, as well as local institutions. The widespread increase in political awareness and independence gained through the electoral process should act as a stimulus to such efforts. In view of the institutional vacuum created at the local level by the dismantling of the old system of local governments, NGOs will be of vital assistance to demand-based programs like the SRF and MPU. In the longer term, as accountability among elected local authorities increases, the institutions needed to fill the gap should evolve more rapidly. Although the SAP was by and large a failure, the dialogue that it initiated among the government, donors, and NGOs was extremely valuable. The working groups set up by the SAP should be maintained, because they provide a sound basis for policy reform in the social sectors.

Perhaps most important, the scope and rapid pace of political change in Zambia should make it easier not only to move ahead with economic reform but also to redirect more resources to the poor than is the case in contexts of stalled economic change and semidemocratic systems, such as in Senegal. Sustaining such changes, however, will also require strengthening the political voice of the poor. This can be done—at least in the short term—through the participatory, demand-based approach of safety net programs such as the SRF and the MPU. The electoral process and the extensive dialogue concerning economic reform that it stimulated have made much of the public aware of the need to protect the poorest and most vulnerable groups of Zambian society. Although actually doing so is no easy task, this awareness, coupled with the new data on poverty available in the Central Statistics Office and the Prices and Incomes Commission, should provide a sound basis on which to take decisive action. From a political perspective, the moment is opportune. From a poverty perspective, the need is imperative. The hour, indeed, has come.

CHAPTER SEVEN

The Political Economy of Safety Nets in Post-Socialist Economies:
The Case of Poland

THE POLITICAL sustainability of any transition from a state-run to a market-based economy is linked to the population's ability to tolerate the social costs of adjustment. The degree of tolerance depends on how the population—and its political representatives—view those costs. As in many other countries, distributive issues and social policy remained at the margin of the political debate in Poland during the first two years of its market transition.[1] By mid-1992, however, the social costs of economic reform had moved to the center of that debate: the public's growing frustration had become *the* issue from which various opposition groups sought to reap short-term political gains. This forced the government to rethink its strategy in an important area of public policy that had obviously been receiving too little attention. Until then public discourse had focused on wage grievances, rather than on concrete proposals for implementing safety nets or social reform. The lack of progress on this front caused a political backlash—most evident in the electoral victory of the former communists in the September 1993 parliamentary elections—which now threatens to jeopardize the entire reform process.[2]

The case of Poland reinforces the three themes that run through this volume. First, once again, political context seems to be the factor determining the kinds of safety nets that are implemented. Second, safety nets—and a better public understanding of adjustment policies—could contribute to the political sustainability of reform, especially in light of recent political trends. And third, from a poverty standpoint, a targeted system is needed to protect the increasing numbers of poor and unemployed.

Most post-socialist countries have a well-developed institutional network for the delivery of social welfare services, although in many cases it is too extensive to sustain financially under present economic conditions. The obstacles to changing the focus of these institutions from the provision of universal service to targeted safety nets for the growing numbers of poor and unemployed are primarily political. For one thing, the public is understandably unwilling to give up a system of free access to all social services—despite its obvious and growing flaws—at a time of extreme economic uncertainty. For another, the administration has had no experience with democratic government, particularly with communicating with the public. It has made little attempt to inform the public of the financial nonviability of the current system, or the potential benefits of reforming it. Lack of public understanding has resulted in widespread anxiety about the social costs of reform, and as a result the political opposition to it is rising.

Together with other countries in the region, Poland is facing serious economic, poverty, and employment problems. However, its political system is more coherent than many, its economic transition has been far more rapid, and there seem to be fewer noneconomic obstacles to success, such as cultural and ethnic divisions. Poland neglected to give the social safety net issue serious attention at first because of timing: the government was preoccupied with managing an economic crisis and implementing a stabilization program whose effects were unclear. The high social costs of the January 1990 stabilization and the prolonged recession since then, however, have surprised even the strongest supporters of the economic program. The public's willingness to tolerate almost any cost in exchange for a transition from the communist system gradually disappeared.[3] The governing Solidarity coalition became fragmented in 1990 owing to disagreement about the pace of reform, as well as its social costs. This was coupled with "intense political competition to articulate new social grievances" among former communists and other opposition groups.[4] Although the country had made impressive progress in stabilizing inflation and implementing macroeconomic reforms after 1989, considerably less has been done in the way of structural change, such as privatizing state enterprises. As in many other countries, slow or stalled reform efforts gave groups with a stake in preventing them more opportunities to build an effective opposition.[5]

In Poland the very *threat* of impending change caused increasing anxiety among organized labor. A series of costly industrial strikes in mid-1992 revealed that the reform program was vulnerable to popular discontent. Not surprisingly, the strikes were strongly supported by the opposition, which, together with the unions, made the Solidarity movement's position on market reforms all the more difficult to hold. These developments brought the safety net issue to the forefront of the political debate and culminated in the September 1993 backlash against reform.

The safety net issue is particularly complex in Poland because of the conception of social welfare under communism. Before the transition, social security rights were not based on any scale of needs but rather on one's position in the occupational or social structure.[6] Benefits had no relation to individual work efforts or contributions. Because they were perceived as "rights" granted by the state, there was—and still is—no connection between political demands for benefits and the obligation to pay for them. Under this system, significant sectors of society had "privileged" access. And, although the system was known to be inequitable and its services to be of poor quality, free universal access to those services provided an important guarantee of social security for the entire population. This was especially important in a context where standards of living were in general low, and where financial rewards were neither abundant nor particularly useful. This guarantee became even more important in the atmosphere of uncertainty generated by the transition. Labor Minister Jacek Kuron once stated: "I realized that people think it depends on me where they work, how much they will earn, and how much their company will sell. . . . They used to live wretchedly, poorly, but safely. And all of the sudden that order has fallen down."[7]

By failing to educate the public about the reform process, the government made this uncertainty all the worse. One reason for the neglect was that the government had no experience of democratic practices; another was that it had received such a wide electoral mandate that there seemed to be no need to generate popular support for the measures. As a result, the general public knows surprisingly little about the economic reform program. When the reforms were announced, public expectations of immediate prosperity rapidly gave way to disillusionment as it became clear that the transition would be long and costly.[8] To make matters worse, the government unrealistically promised that there would be a marked improvement after only six months of belt-tightening.[9] These trends, coupled with widespread skepticism born of decades of unrepresentative government and a fragmenting Solidarity coalition, opened the door for opportunistic politicians.

Social welfare reform in the Polish context requires establishing market and efficiency criteria as the basis for determining wages and employment. A cash benefit system, not wages, should be the main tool for alleviating poverty.[10] At present, almost all social security benefits are linked to occupational status. Most information on individual benefits and earnings remains based in individual firms rather than in the central social insurance agency, ZUS. In addition, minimum insurance schemes in the social security and health sectors would have to be supplemented by private schemes giving individuals the incentive to save and invest.[11] Such changes—the January 1992 implementation of an income tax was a first step—would not only introduce efficiency criteria but also allow the government to divert the resources gained in this way to protecting the poor and unemployed. By contrast, the existing system has no adequate safety net, a principal reason why the managers of state-owned enterprises (SOEs) often retain redundant workers.

Such reforms cannot be implemented without the necessary resources and administrative capacity—or political support. This chapter examines the social safety net issue in the context of the politics of adjustment in Poland, with special attention to administrative capacity at the local level. Virtually all proposed social sector reforms, as well as the social assistance act passed in November 1990, envision a pivotal role for local institutions. They will indeed play a vital role in rebuilding a political coalition in favor of reform in Poland and thereby in resolving the social safety net issue. Without them, the transition could be undermined by political uncertainty.

The Political Context

The political context in postcommunist societies is one marked by rapid and dramatic change. Where redistribution and correction of market rules used to be the central goals of the government, the emphasis now is on market-oriented reform. This tremendous shift has wreaked havoc all along the political spectrum, making the politics of adjustment and of social welfare policy particularly complex.[12] The traditional position of the left, favoring increased state involvement in the economy and society, is now shared by the postcommunists and the far right, which blends that position with extreme nationalism. At the political center itself is a mixture of voices ranging from social democrat to Hayek-style liberal. The situation is even more complicated in Poland, where the government attempting to implement economic reforms originated in the Solidarity union movement, which developed into a broad social movement of approximately 10 million members from the intelligentsia, unions, and a variety of other groups. The cohesion of the movement was soon tested, however, as it quickly became clear that Solidarity's unity was based on opposition to communism rather than on support for market-oriented reforms.

To add to the problem, Solidarity leaders were inexperienced both in running a government and in promulgating market-oriented reforms, yet they were under pressure to make speedy changes that would simultaneously create democratic government and a market economy. There were five governments in three years (see table 7-1), and the most recent government, of Hanna Suchocka, was a seven-party coalition. In large part because of the fragmented party system, parliamentary debate was unable to move beyond particularistic issues and short-term political objectives, and most proposals for concurrent reform of the social welfare system fell victim to highly partisan wrangling. Economic reform, it seemed, was implemented almost in spite of Parliament. At the same time, the successive governments failed to communicate or "sell" economic reforms to the public. Consequently, only a small elite understood the political debate and the economic reform program being introduced, with the result that the changes heightened public anxiety. [13] It is precisely this anxiety that opponents of the reform program seek to tap. "This is a potential social foundation of 'escape from freedom' syndrome, which may result in some kind of a populist movement under authoritarian leadership."[14]

The Transition

The February–April 1989 round table talks between the last communist government in Poland and the Solidarity-led opposition focused primarily on the terms of the political transition rather than on economic issues. In the elections that followed in June 1989, the communists re-

Table 7-1. *Main Political Events in Poland since 1980*

Date	Event
August 1980	Following strikes, self-governing unions formed under the guidance of Solidarnosc.
December 1981	Martial law imposed and the Military Council of National Salvation, led by Gen. Wojech Jaruzelski, is set up. Trade union activity is suspended; Lech Walesa and other Solidarity leaders are detained.
June 1986	Poland joins the International Bank of Reconstruction and Development (the World Bank).
February–April 1989	"Round table talks" on the future of Poland. Solidarity regains legal status, and free elections are announced.
June 1989	Elections to new bicameral National Assembly are held.
August 89	President Jaruzelski accepts the proposal for a Solidarity-ZSL-SD coalition and nominates Tadeusz Mazowiecki of Solidarity as chairman of the Council of Ministers. Appointment approved by Sejm; ends almost forty-five years of communist rule.
September 1990	President Jaruzelski agrees to step down as head of state before his six-year term expires.
November 1990	First round of presidential elections.
December 1990	Walesa wins the second round of presidential elections. Jan Krzysztof Bielecki, a radical economist, becomes chairman of the Council of Ministers after the president's first nominee, Jan Olszewski, fails to form a government.
October 1991	Voters elect a fragmented Parliament. Former communists have substantial leverage, but no single political party has a dominant role.
December 1991	The Bielecki government resigns. Walesa nominates Jan Olszewski (as prime minister), candidate of center-right coalition opposed to free-market reforms.
May 1992	Prime Minister Olszewski resigns after Parliament ignores his pleas for fiscal prudence and approves $2.2 billion in salary and pension increases.
July 1992	Waldemar Pawlak resigns after being unable to form a coalition. New government formed, headed by Ms. Hanna Suchocka.

Source: Compiled from Simon Johnson and Marzena Kowalska, "The Transformation of Poland, 1989–91," paper presented to World Bank Project on the Political Economy of Structural Adjustment in New Democracies, edited by Steven Webb and Stephan Haggard, May 1992, abstact; *Europa World Year Book, 1991*; and *Washington Post Index*.

tained majority (65 percent) control over the lower house of Parliament, the Sejm, but allowed free elections for the newly constituted upper house, the Senate. Solidarity won all but one of the seats that it contested in those elections.[15] After this electoral victory, Solidarity graduated from a social movement representative of Polish workers into a broader political force that was held together by Lech Walesa's charisma, the church, and the democratic ideals of the opposition. Ultimately it was unable to maintain that unity.

In an unopposed vote, General Wojiech Jaruzelski was elected president. After an ill-fated attempt by Lieutenant General Czeslaw Kiszczak to form a communist-led government, Jaruzelski accepted Walesa's proposal for a Solidarity-led coalition government. Tadeusz Mazowiecki, a respected newspaper editor and moderate member of Solidarity, was named prime minister. To a large extent because of its links to Solidarity, the first noncommunist government came to power with a great deal of public support—but without a program. Mazowiecki soon appointed Leszek Balcerowicz, a proponent of orthodox economics and the Jeffrey Sachs school "shock" therapy, as finance minister. In January 1990 Balcerowicz introduced a rapid and extensive stabilization and adjustment program. Measures included the immediate removal of price controls, a restrictive incomes policy, a 40 percent devaluation of the zloty and a move to full convertibility, the liberalization of trade, the setting of realistic interest rates, and the reduction of the government's budget deficit from 8 percent to 1 percent of gross domestic product, largely through the removal of subsidies on all goods except coal.[16] There was virtually no public debate about the perspectives, costs, or potential benefits of the Balcerowicz stabilization and adjustment program.[17] Indeed, the only other economic program that was considered was a more radical transition plan proposed by Janusz Beksiak.[18] The reality was that there were few realistic alternatives. Besides, the government felt little need to strengthen what seemed to be a remarkable base of public support.

The initial results of the plan were impressive. A host of international observers commented on the speed with which Poland was adopting a free market trade and price structure. The total national industrial product of the fledgling private sector grew from generating 5.5 percent in 1989 to 8 percent in 1990, and it then shot up to 27 percent in March 1992. By that point, the private sector was in control of 73 percent of building and 32 percent of transport.[19] This transition was not without its costs, however. Real wages in January 1990 were only 56.7 percent of

Table 7-2. *Basic Economic Indicators, Poland, 1989–92*

	Cumulative numbers			
Item	*1989*	*1990*	*1991*	*1992[a]*
Industrial production index				
(1985 = 100)	111.1	82.1	69.8	70.1
Unemployment rate				
(percent)	. . .	3.4	9.1	12.2
Consumer price index				
(1985 = 100)	828.9	5,684.3	9,680.2	12,336.4
Trade balance (millions of				
U.S. dollars)	47	3,589	−711	382

Item	*Results of 1990 stabilization (percent)*
Change in real wage in five main sectors	−32
Change in gross domestic product	−12
Inflation rate	250

	Trends in real wages[b]			Trends in real wages[b]	
Month	*1990*	*1991*	*Month*	*1990*	*1991*
January	56.7	88.6	July	106.9	104.5
February	92.9	105.4	August	103.1	99.0
March	131.1	99.2	September	102.8	98.7
April	87.6	96.2	October	107.5	105.4
May	92.7	95.3	November	106.7	101.7
June	98.9	97.4	December	97.3	105.4

Sources: International Monetary Fund, *International Financial Statistics* (Washington, October 1992), pp. 426–29; and Simon Johnson and Marzena Kowalska, "The Transformation of Poland, 1989–91," Duke University, Ficqua School of Business, June 28, 1992.

a. January–April.

b. Index, with previous month = 100.

the December 1989 level; although they recovered somewhat in subsequent months, they finished the year with a 28 percent overall decline. Open unemployment, which had previously not existed, was expected to reach 6 percent by the end of 1991. Instead it ended up at 11.5 percent (see table 7-2). In some industrial regions the rate reached 30 percent. Gross national product fell by 13.5 percent in 1990 and continued to fall, in part in response to the drop in demand caused by price rises, and in part to collapse of trade with the former Soviet Union, which had previously been a major consumer of Polish industrial products. The government's financial condition worsened as heavily indebted state industries posted record losses and failed to pay taxes. This forced the government to continuously cut back a series of recently granted increases in benefits, from pensions to unemployment insurance.

If these were the costs of economic transition, the public increasingly speculated about the effects of the proposed structural reforms, such as privatization of state enterprises. The consensus among the political elite began to deteriorate. "Without doubt, some deputies became more radical in their opposition to the government as the perceived social costs of the Balcerowicz Plan increased. From mid-1990 there was consistently bad economic news: rising unemployment, falling production, and persistent inflation."[20]

The first crack within the Solidarity coalition appeared just before the November 1990 presidential elections.[21] By the end of 1989, many Solidarity members wanted General Jaruzelski to be replaced by a president from their ranks. The seven existing parliamentary clubs splintered in a debate over who should be president. This was the so-called war on top. The Solidarity movement formally split. The core supporters of the market transition and of deeper and accelerated reform backed Mazowiecki. Those behind Lech Walesa wanted the government to play a larger role in shaping the course of market changes *and* in reducing their social costs, although they were by no means opposed to economic reform. The split in the Solidarity coalition and the weakened political leadership left an extremely negative impression on the public, particularly since the economic team was much more liberal than the mainstream of the coalition.[22]

The unknown populist Stanislaw Tyminski was able to capitalize on the general discontent with the Solidarity government's policies.[23] In the first round, Mazowiecki garnered 18 percent of the vote, Tyminski 23 percent, and Walesa 40 percent. At this point Mazowiecki resigned and formed the Democratic Union, the party that was to be the basis for the Suchocka government's coalition. Although Walesa won the elections in the second round (see table 7-3), the coherence of the Solidarity movement and of the government coalition supporting market reforms was severely shaken by the war on top and by the extremely negative tone of the electoral campaign between Walesa and Tyminski.[24]

The second government, that of Krystof Bialecki, retained Balcerowicz as finance minister and attempted to continue with his economic plan, but was faced with the first serious challenges related to popular unrest: whereas a total of 159,000 days were lost to strikes in 1990,

Table 7-3. *Results of Elections, 1989–91*

Party or candidate	Seats	Percent of votes
June 1989, Parliament		
Sejm		
Solidarity	161	35.0[a]
"Communist" coalition (6 parties)	299	65.0[a]
Senate		
Solidarity	99	. . .
Independent	1	. . .
November and December 1990, president		
First round[b]		
R. Bartoszcze	. . .	7.2
W. Cimoszewicz	. . .	9.2
T. Mazowiecki	. . .	18.1
L. Moczulski	. . .	2.5
S. Tyminski	. . .	23.1
L. Walesa	. . .	40.0
Second round[c]		
S. Tyminski	. . .	25.8
L. Walesa	. . .	73.4
October 1991, Parliament		
Sejm		
Solidarity coalition (8 parties)	270	51.83
"Communist" coalition (4 parties)	137	26.11
Other parties and coalitions	53	22.06
Senate[d]		
Solidarity coalition (6 parties)	60	. . .
"Communist" coalition	16	. . .
Other parties and coalitions (22 parties)	24	. . .
Strongest coalitions in Parliament		
(total seats in Sejm plus seats in Senate)		
Solidarity coalition (5 parties)	325	. . .
"Communist" coalition (3 parties)	152	. . .

Source: Johnson and Kowalska, "Transformation of Poland, 1989–91."
a. Percent of seats.
b. Abstention rate was 39.4 percent. Tyminski received most votes in relatively undeveloped agricultural regions. Walesa received most votes in large towns, and least in small agricultural voivodships (regional governments) in eastern Poland.
c. Abstention rate was 46.6 percent.
d. Abstention rate was 56.8 percent.

150,000 were lost in the first quarter of 1991 alone.[25] This, coupled with a series of corruption charges, sapped the momentum of the government. And with the upcoming parliamentary elections, the Bialecki government expected only a temporary stay in office from the beginning.[26] By the October 1991 parliamentary elections, political forces again began to differentiate themselves through criticism of the Balcerowicz economic program. Some of the complaints came from the postcommunists (under the new banner of Social Democracy), and others from parties with Solidarity roots. In the Solidarity group itself, criticism came from the Center Alliance and traditional Catholic nationalists on the right and Labor Solidarity on the left. The economic program also came under assault from a growing independent movement, led by the KPN (Confederation of Independent Poland), which stressed the state instead of religion and nationalism. Left and right wanted to bail out dying state enterprises, protect agricultural policy, change employment strategies, and extend rather than reduce the system of universal social benefits.[27]

Solidarity failed to obtain a clear electoral mandate for the economic program in either the 1990 presidential or the 1991 parliamentary elections. Yet, to the extent that voting hinged on economic issues, abstention rates of more than 40 percent suggest that while people had doubts about the economic reforms, they refrained from voting in favor of vague alternatives. After the elections and a great deal of delay, the government of Jan Olszewski was pulled together from fifteen parliamentary caucuses and twenty parties with little experience in government. In the still politicized postelectoral atmosphere, the Olszewski government focused more on persecuting former communists than on economic or welfare sector reforms.[28]

Finally, in May 1992, the ill-fated coalition collapsed, after Olszewski resigned in protest of a parliamentary approval of $2.2 billion in salary and pension increases. At that point, the alternatives were to let Walesa take direct control of the government or to hold new elections. Thus seven parties led by the Democratic Union swiftly came together in a coalition and formed a government under the leadership of Hanna Suchocka. The Suchocka government had several advantages over its predecessors. First, because there was a great deal of pressure to deliver, members of the coalition were forced to unite behind reform if they did not want to see it derailed. Second, the government had the benefit of hindsight and experience: several of its members, such as the ministers of labor and privatization, had served under previous governments, which—under the pressure of a great many competing demands, limited time, and some fear of the media—had neglected to communicate with the public to explain the reforms. Faced with debilitating strikes in the summer of 1992, the government recognized it needed to build popular support for reforms, as well as to implement desperately needed changes in the social welfare sector. Third, the government had the firm leadership

of Suchocka, a respected lawyer who had the support of the church and
the reform-minded liberals in Parliament.[29] The Suchocka government
was able to make more progress in the social welfare arena than its
predecessors, particularly in initiating a social pact among business, government, and labor.

By May 1993, however, after a vote of no confidence, the Suchocka
government suffered a major setback and became a caretaker government
until the elections called for five months later. The vote, in protest at the
government's refusal to grant pay raises to public servants and to increase
pensions, was supported by the former communists, the KPN, and much
of Solidarity.[30] In the September 1993 elections, pro-reform forces were
soundly defeated: Suchocka's Democratic Union received less than 12
percent of the vote, while the former Communist Democratic Alliance
and other antireform forces together garnered more than 40 percent of
the vote.[31] From that point on, the fate of the reform program was
uncertain, at best.

In the atmosphere of political fragmentation after the 1990 elections,
the opposition grew increasingly vocal and organized, and the reforms
stalled. "The only well-articulated interests in Poland . . . , ironically,
[were] the residua of the ancien regime: the interests of the workers
employed in the mammoth, uncompetitive state enterprises, and the
interests of 'socialist private farmers.' " Yet, also important and somewhat ironic, "the fragmentation of the parliament [was] a blessing rather
than a curse, for had one or two parties been able to collect the whole
worker-peasant vote, economic reform would have come grinding to a
halt."[32] When the political and social pressure reached such a pitch that
it threatened to reverse the entire process, the Suchocka coalition was
formed. Although inflation was the key issue facing the first postcommunist government, social policy was clearly the primary concern for the
Suchocka government throughout its tenure.

Summer Strikes and the Pact on Public Enterprises

As the success of the Solidarity movement had demonstrated in 1980,
organized labor had the capacity to precipitate political change in Poland.
Attempts at economic reform under the communist regime had failed
because they did not contain real wage increases.[33] The traditional conflict in strikes was over wage-related grievances, with workers and managers on one side and the government on the other. As the economic

reforms began to erode the position and salaries of workers in the state-owned enterprises (SOEs), strikes took on an increasingly defensive and political tone, and in the summer of 1992 they left key industries debilitated.[34] This style of government-labor relations had clearly become unsustainable. The insolvency of state enterprises was the primary cause of the 1992 budget crisis: there were no funds to meet new wage demands.

From the beginning the Suchocka government sought to send a clear message to striking workers about a new style of labor relations. To prevent sectoral strikes from consistently evolving into political crises, the government tried to distance itself from negotiations between workers and enterprises.[35] It took a harsh stance on all the major strikes up to September 1992, when the Pact on State Enterprises was announced. While refraining from using force, which would have been anathema to a government with origins in the labor movement, the administration refused to yield any concessions and instead focused on building support among the "silent majority." Indeed, this majority was bought out quite early, and 13,000 workers signed petitions against the strikes. The government made clear that it would not take "sides" in wage negotiations, that it would not alter its macroeconomic policies, and that it would not allow strikers to obtain better settlements than those legally negotiated. Yet the extensive nature of the 1992 strikes and opposition support for them forced the authorities to seek a new mechanism for dealing with social discontent and for incorporating participation in the design of future reforms. These efforts came to fruition in the pact. The pact had two aims: to improve the economic viability of state firms, and to shift workers' attention from making demands on the state to taking responsibility for their own firms.[36]

Although the strikes were clearly costly for the firms involved, the government's gamble to maintain a hard line may have paid off politically, since the incidents did not develop into a general strike or widespread social unrest, as some of their more radical proponents wished and many observers feared they would. This is particularly important because the strikes took place in strategic industries—automobile, copper, and aircraft—where organized labor traditionally had strong influence. State workers decided to strike in part because they had genuine grievances over the decline in their standard of living, but also because the slow pace of proposed reforms had fueled their fear of what was to come. They had been part of a privileged sector of Polish society and stood to lose not only access to material assets but also their social position and prestige. Many therefore tried to maximize short-term political and economic gains through the strikes.

The opposition's move to capitalize on these grievances was a key factor in the government's decision to create the Pact on State Enterprises.[37] This was the first public agreement in which social policy was given central importance.[38] A second pact, the Pact on Social Safety Nets, was also to be negotiated with the unions. It pertained to the reform of the social welfare system and was announced a month later. The Pact on State Enterprises was drafted in the office of Labor Minister Jacek Kuron, the most effective public communicator in the government and arguably the most popular politician in the country. Kuron was the only member of the government who emphasized public relations and communication. Among other things, Kuron was known for his weekly television addresses, in which he attempted to explain government policy to the general public.

The first draft of the Pact on State Enterprises was presented to working teams of representatives of government, trade unions, and employers' organizations. The government was then to negotiate the proposals with each of the trade unions, because of divisions among them. The initial pact proposed changes in the law on privatization of public enterprises to allow workers to get 10 percent of the shares; a law on the financial restructuring of state enterprises and banks; a law on securing employees' financial claims in case of financial insolvency; a new framework for negotiating incomes policy, which was designed to be more flexible and included tripartite negotiations; a new law on collective bargaining, which established employees' representation when there was more than one union; changes in the regulation on work safety to include private companies; and a new law on the compulsory social fund of enterprises, which cut the size of the fund in all cases but made the law applicable to private enterprises. By lowering requirements such as the enterprise social fund, yet making them applicable to the private sector, the government hoped to begin to incorporate the private sector into its statistical and regulatory systems, while at the same time reducing the existing disincentives to reporting income.[39]

The pact also included a strategy for mass privatization in which all adults would be given an option to buy a share in one of several national investment funds created to purchase 400 or so state enterprises. The shares would have a low price—less than one-third the average national monthly wage—and options could be sold on the open market. It was assumed that most people would sell their options, so there would be some concentration of ownership and attraction of foreign capital. At the same time, it was hoped that the scheme would create popular support for privatization—so-called popular capitalism.[40]

Notably absent from the pact was any mention of unemployment insurance or compensation in the face of privatization, although the pact did allude to the necessary liquidation of some firms. The government's strategy seemed to be to treat all issues of social welfare and compensation in the second pact, and thereby diffuse the politically controversial link between privatization and unemployment. Several of the privatization proposals had been debated in Parliament before the pact was introduced and thus were less controversial than they might have been the first time around.[41] Nevertheless, unions were quick to raise the employment issue in their response to the pact. The deputy chairman of the communist trade union OPZZ, Waclaw Martyniuk, stated that negotiations with the government lacked substance and that it would have been "much easier to negotiate the pact had the government simultaneously prepared [the] 'pact on social guarantees.' "[42] The pact was also criticized by some elements of the center-right who felt that the government's approach to the strikes was "sluggish" and that privatization should not have been an issue for negotiation in the pact.[43] Thus the Center Alliance (PC) announced it would oppose the pact in the Sejm. Regardless, the government had little choice but to offer unions some "carrots" as a basis for negotiation. Minister Kuron and Deputy Minister Michal Boni had each previously served as labor minister and had experience dealing with labor, as well as some vision of how the situation could be resolved. In September, on his "Seven Minutes with the Labor Minster" weekly television program, Kuron stated that the pact was intended to " 'wrest workers from their morass and their feelings of despair and hopelessness,' " and rested his authority on the passage of the pact.[44] By November 1992, representatives of the government, Solidarity, and employers' organizations agreed to most of the terms in the pact, leaving only collective contracts for further clarification.[45]

Beyond its content, the pact was an attempt to change the nature of government-labor relations and diffuse the strategy of the more radical unions, which was to expand labor conflict into social conflict and thereby repeat the August 1980 pattern of general strikes and political conflict.[46] A tripartite framework would provide a government representative to diffuse the deadlock that often occurs between unions because there is no closed shop in Poland, while at the same time keeping the conflict at the sectoral level. Yet as long as workers demand that state socialism be restored, the pact will signify endless negotiations without meaningful results. Even so, the pact is an open-ended invitation to unions to negotiate, which reduces the incentive to pursue further strike activity. And for every concession unions gain through the pact, the government gives them "a heavier burden of responsibility."[47]

The pact by no means resolved all the government's problems. In December 1992 strikes against government plans to halve the 300,000-plus work force in the coal mines of Silesia over a period of ten years signified the largest individual protest since the fall of communism and created further tension in government-labor relations.[48] And in March 1993 the Suchocka government suffered another setback when Parliament defeated its plan to privatize 600 state companies simultaneously. The vote of 203 to 181 caught the government by surprise and revealed splits in the coalition. The measure was finally passed in May with an extremely close vote.[49] Later that month the government was dealt a major blow by the no-confidence vote in protest of public sector wage and pension levels. Although the pact served as an impetus to solving the problems of state enterprises and provided a framework for government-labor relations, it did not actually provide a solution to the difficult issues involved.

The political urgency of the state enterprise problem pushed it ahead of social sector reforms on the government's agenda. State workers were traditionally one of the most powerful organized forces in the country and continued to control strategic sectors of the economy. In 1992 SOEs still employed 50 percent of the population.[50] Furthermore, most politicians in the government had Solidarity roots and therefore some allegiance to organized labor. The social reforms of the second pact were to revamp the health, housing, social security, and unemployment systems. The Suchocka government had been working on them since it came to office. Here, too, negotiations depended on a stable budget because, as one adviser put it, "it is difficult to discuss such proposals when all you can do is cut," again demonstrating the government's need to include some "carrots" in order to generate support for negotiations.[51] Although by the end of 1992 there was little public mention of the second pact, there were several concrete proposals for the reform of the social sectors and for targeting universal benefits in the Labor Ministry. Clearly, the government planned to proceed with reforms regardless of the status of the second pact and despite substantial political opposition.[52]

A Constituency for Reform?

Ultimately, the success of both pacts, and of the government's reform program in general, hinged on its ability to communicate and sell its reforms to the public. Rather paradoxically, it is likely that the Democratic Union (Mazowiecki's party) would have done better if it had been "a bit less pragmatic and a bit more populist."[53] One Finance Ministry official noted that the government needed to implement reform "with the people not against the people." Communication was even a problem *within* the government: it was not uncommon for high-level officials to find out about key decisions in the press the next day.[54] This is not surprising in view of Poland's lack of experience with democratic government. Yet the problem needed to be addressed if market reforms were to be sustained.

Under the previous two governments politicians tended to focus public attention on partisan political issues such as decommunization, trials of security agents, and abortion rather than on economic reforms. In contrast, the Suchocka government attempted to begin a dialogue about the proposed reforms. In neighboring Hungary, soon after the Polish pact was announced, the government launched similar negotiations with its unions and the private sector, in an attempt to generate support for reform among the middle class.[55]

In addition to the pact, the Suchocka government opened a new office for press relations and attempted to involve diverse sectors of society in the drafting and negotiation of reforms. For example, it established a permanent dialogue between the housing lobby and the ministry.[56] Despite the anonymity of the typical Polish politician, the public seemed to respond to communication efforts—Labor Minister Kuron and his weekly television slots had an 80 percent approval rating. And when the usually staid Prime Minister Bialecki appeared on television after a frustrating series of negotiations with organized labor and launched an emotional tirade accusing the unions of jeopardizing the reform program, his approval rating skyrocketed. Apparently people were relieved to see the prime minister vent some emotion.[57]

Building a constituency for reform in Poland is no easy task. In the short term, the losers far outweigh the winners. The pro-reform coalition is neither large nor well organized, but it is an active minority. The main proponents are a small group of intellectuals, most of them with Solidarity roots, whose material situation may have worsened but who strongly believe that the situation will improve, and that there are few available alternatives. In general this group tends to be younger, educated, middle class, and urban. The supporters of reform also include members of the small but growing private sector and *some* workers in private and state factories who tend to support the idea of reform but are far less likely to do so if directly affected by its costs.[58] Managers in state firms tend to be pro-reform, but because most of these state firms are run by worker councils, managers usually do not have the authority or the incentive to implement reforms in their factories.[59] Thus, recognizing that unemployment is bound to rise if their firms are privatized or are forced to operate on a profit, they continue to pursue strategies to protect redundant jobs. These include holding down wage increases rather than laying off workers, firing only temporary or undisciplined workers, and introducing labor-sharing schemes. As a result, employment reduction has remained far behind the decline in output. Paradoxically, former party members, or "the nomenklatura," also tend to be pro-reform. They seem to have found a profitable if not privileged niche under the new system.[60]

State workers continue to have a more clearly articulated set of interests than the eclectic pro-reform forces. A 1991 poll found that 71 percent of Poles felt that unemployment was the most pressing national problem, in comparison with 62 percent of Hungarians and 36 percent of Romanians.[61] In some rural or industrial areas that used to depend on a sole industry or factory, unemployment rates are as high as 20–30 percent, and there is a growing sense of hopelessness and fear. It seems that the lower the education level, the lower the support for reforms and the higher the expectations of the state.[62] In the absence of a defined or tangible future alternative, many people tend to become nostalgic about conditions of the past, sentiments that opposition groups are quick to capitalize on.

Polish farmers are also well organized and are voicing more and more opposition to the market transition, because it has meant a flood of foreign competition coupled with an increase in the price of inputs such as fertilizer. These trends have tended to erode whatever gains resulted from the liberalization of consumer food prices. Pensioners, meanwhile, did well when in 1990 the system was indexed to the average monthly wage, but have lost a great deal since then with the erosion of that wage and may provide the opposition with yet another base of support.

Polls taken in 1991 found that 80 percent of the population deemed their positions to be poor, 75 percent found their standard of living to be worsening, and 38 percent expected it to get even worse. The majority of those interviewed also felt that the distribution of the costs of reforms was unfair. Trust in political institutions was quite low: 18 percent had trust in local institutions, 40 percent in the central government, 26 percent in the Sejm, 44 percent in the police, 57 percent in the church, and 71 percent in the army. Polls also indicated that many respondents had little understanding of the basic principles underlying democracy or markets.[63] A better understanding of the reform process from the beginning might have prevented people from expecting so much and then becoming disillusioned and could have encouraged them to prepare for the future.

Because the party system is fragmented and particularistic and elections can be called at any time, politicians are motivated to capitalize on grievances for short-term gain. And because most parties lack any kind of ideological base, they are more likely to take a popular stance on an issue such as pension reform than they are to remain committed to the longer-term goals of the market transition.[64] Antireform forces such as the KPN or OPZZ might have gained a great deal if elections had been held in the climate of the 1992 strikes.[65] Although unable to garner a clear majority, these forces dealt the government a severe electoral defeat in September 1993 and thereby cast doubt on the future of the reform program. There is also the question of the intentions of the president himself, who in theory supports reform but in practice has demonstrated a tendency to take populist or nationalist stances, as he did when he blamed the lack of Western aid for the state of the Polish economy.[66] In the war on top, he distanced himself from the most committed reformers. He remains at the margin of most economic policymaking, however.

As for Solidarity, both the union and the movement are in a very difficult position. The union tends to support the government. Yet its main constituency consists of workers in state enterprises or in the public sector, all of whom have legitimate wage grievances and fear for their jobs. Solidarity supported a hard-line stance against most of the strikes of the summer of 1992, as well as the collective bargaining structure proposed in the pact.[67] Although this support was important for the reform program, it also increased the risk that Solidarity's position in the union movement would be undermined by opposition unions. Approximately one-quarter of the union movement is affiliated with Solidarity, one-eighth with OPZZ, and one-half is unaffiliated. For some workers, Solidarity is part of the government and therefore cannot represent their interests. Others support Solidarity but do not want to affiliate formally.[68] In other sectors the more militant Solidarity 80 has more appeal than does the original union.[69] Another problem for the Solidarity movement is that the most skilled and talented people in the movement either entered the government or are serving as advisers rather than devoting time and energy to the union. Still, Solidarity's position in government—as well as its legacy—does give it a certain mystique and political power, and therefore appeal, that other unions just do not have.[70]

Solidarity's position reflects the paradox of the Polish situation: how to legitimize a new political and economic strategy that came about because of worker protests, but that must undermine workers' organizational and occupational structure in order to succeed. To shift the balance, the government will have to encourage the uncommitted majority to participate in the reform efforts. Communication and negotiation are critical. The Suchocka government's changed approach is an important first step, as are the autonomous local initiatives discussed in the next section. The most critical issue that remains to be addressed in order to sustain reform, however, is how to implement an adequate social safety net.

The Politics of the Safety Net

No other subject has generated as much debate in Poland as the social costs of the market transition. Yet the issue has received little serious political attention, in part because the philosophy of the transition has discredited state intervention. Among pro-market forces there is reluctance to examine the need for the state to provide a safety net; to the extent that it is discussed, responsibility is delegated to local governments. On the other side, critics of market reforms have unrealistic expectations of what even the most socially conscious state could afford, given its economic capacity and budget constraints. No political party has taken on serious reform of the social welfare system as a platform issue. Most parties react to government proposals rather than suggest alternatives.[71] The issue is politically explosive because it entails curtailing universal benefits—even if they are of low quality—in exchange for an intangible promise of a better system in the future. In view of the speed and dramatic nature of economic and political change in Poland in the past three years, it is not surprising that the general public is reluctant to give up even the most minimum guarantee of social security.

There is a great deal of uncertainty about the average person's ability to cope with economic change. On the one hand, warnings are issued about the effect of years of reliance on the state, which has been described as "learned helplessness." On the other hand, "the pathologies of the planned economy forced people to become resourceful in finding ways and means to produce and exchange goods and services outside the official economy. This is the greatest safety net (or set of nets) in postcommunist societies today."[72] Indeed, a higher percentage of the population (72 percent) in Poland appears able to "cope"—defined as getting by without spending savings or borrowing—than that in any other eastern European country.[73] These contradictions are the result of major differences in political ideology, peoples' situations in diverse regions, and occupations. Whereas in Warsaw the unemployment rate is between 2 and 5 percent, and there is a shortage of blue-collar workers, in other regions of the country, particularly in the east, whole towns face a future of structural unemployment because their defense or textile factories no longer have a market since the economic collapse of the former USSR.[74] Unemployment is highest among those with only a primary education, followed by those with only vocational training. It is also higher among women than men, and highest in the eighteen-to-twenty-four age bracket.[75]

Before the safety net problem can be discussed, much less adequately addressed, it is essential to distinguish between the poor and those most affected by economic changes. There are marginalized or residual poor in almost all societies. They are less likely to be directly affected by structural economic changes, but they will be hurt by rising prices of food and health care and other public services. In Poland this group has traditionally consisted of the elderly on limited fixed incomes, families with more than three children, single mothers, or families with social problems like alcoholism. With the possible exception of pensioners, these groups do not form a particularly strong political constituency.

The most vulnerable, however, are not necessarily poor; indeed, they were often quite privileged before reform. They are the occupational groups that depended solely on the state for employment and whose social benefits were directly linked to their place of work. This category includes university professors, public sector workers, and workers in state-owned enterprises. Many of these are skilled workers who are organized, have certain resources, and can find new opportunities in a transformed economy. The exceptions are workers laid off from the mammoth unproductive SOE conglomerates, who will not be able to find work near home or housing anywhere else even if they are willing to move.[76] Some of the people in this traditionally privileged group are entering the ranks of the new poor.[77] Ironically, this group of vulnerable and new poor were the backers of the political changes that ushered in economic reform. Unlike the residual poor, they form a strong potential political constituency for opposition politicians.

Another group that is vulnerable and has a strong political constituency consists of farmers. Between one-quarter and one-third of the Polish population is still linked to agriculture. There are 3 million farms, few of which are capable of competing with European Community farmers, and no more than 10 percent of them use modern techniques. The modern farms are even worse off: under the communist system, the state was the monopoly buyer and inputs were heavily subsidized. Now they are faced with inflation, EC competition, and increasing debts. They want tariffs, guaranteed prices, and debt reduction, none of which are likely to be seen in the current economic context, especially since farmers have traditionally received far less attention from the state than industrial workers.[78] Although they are vulnerable to economic changes, they always have the option to return to subsistence farming, a safety net that most unemployed workers do not have.

In the early stages of the transition, targeting the poor or vulnerable was not an issue. The primary concern was to protect people from inflation and then from stabilization-induced price changes through indexation. Wage and pension indexation went through several revisions in 1989–91, and an unemployment law appeared for the first time in December 1989, but its provisions reflect the government's lack of concern for targeting benefits. Under the original law, all those who declared themselves unemployed—even first-time entrants to the labor force—were eligible for benefits (initially 70 percent of the average monthly wage) for an unlimited period of time. By mid-1990 it was clear that the system was financially unsustainable and a disincentive for seeking alternative employment. Thus the law was reformed to limit eligibility and reduce benefits over time.[79]

Following the economic crisis of the 1980s, and particularly stabilization, more people found themselves below the poverty line (see tables 7-4, 7-5), and poverty became a political issue. With the passage of the November 1990 Social Assistance Act, the government publicly acknowledged that there was poverty in Poland for the first time.[80] At this point, the approach to social policy began to change. The government realized

Table 7-4. *Estimated Poverty Line and Headcount Ratios*

Year	Poverty line (zlotys per month)	Headcount ratio	Year	Poverty line (zlotys per month)	Headcount ratio
1980	25,452	0.144	1987	152,460	0.237
1981	29,196	0.093	1988	237,120	0.153
1982	58,452	0.139	1989		
1983	n.a.	n.a.	1st quarter	83,664	0.196
1984	87,960	0.299	2d quarter	110,798	0.232
1985	97,320	0.195	3d quarter	176,771	0.108
1986	114,720	0.188	4th quarter	406,742	0.133

Source: Tomasz Panek and Adam Szulc, "Income Distribution and Poverty: Theory and a Case Study of Poland in the Eighties: 1980–89" (Warsaw: Research Centre for Statistical and Economic Analysis of the Central Statistical Office and Polish Academy of Sciences, 1991). The social minimum income level used by Panek and Szulc—the official poverty line in Poland—is high by OECD standards.
n.a. Not available.

Table 7-5. *Percent Share of Different Social Groups in Total Number of Poor*

Year	Workers	Workers and farmers	Farmers	Pensioners	Total
1978	6.4	9.5	14.9	20.8	9.2
1979	6.1	12.8	16.7	17.1	9.7
1980	7.8	10.6	17.2	23.7	11.1
1981	11.4	11.4	16.4	29.2	13.9
1982	17.3	15.8	20.9	35.7	19.8
1983	19.1	13.4	29.7	49.0	23.7
1984	19.0	12.9	25.1	39.3	21.9
1985	17.3	11.3	19.5	32.4	19.1
1986	17.0	9.4	19.2	25.4	17.3
1987	25.2	12.6	21.4	27.6	22.7
1988	14.8	8.0	14.4	25.9	15.2

Source: Branko Milanovic, "Poverty in Poland, 1978–88," WPS 637 (Washington: World Bank, March 1991), p. 4.

that it could not provide universal benefits and at the same time deal with the budget crisis, rising unemployment, and social demands.

One of the government's great problems in dealing with poverty, however, will be simply to measure it. Before the market reforms, the standard of living was in a sense theoretical: salaries were higher than they are now, but there was very little that people could purchase because consumer goods were always in short supply. They had access to universal services such as health care, but the quality was very poor and waiting times often preclusive, and the "universal" access had been substantially eroded by a system of under-the-table payments to overcome the long waiting periods.[81] Now virtually all consumer goods are available, but

they are usually beyond the reach of the salary of the average Pole. Poles
have in a way shifted from one kind of poverty to another: from "gradual
pauperization" to fears of "mass poverty."[82] However, unlike many developing countries or even Western nations, where poverty on some scale
has always existed, Poland is unaccustomed to poverty. Indeed, it is an
anathema in a system that guaranteed social safety for forty-five years.
Even if standards of living were mediocre, everyone was guaranteed
minimum security.

Targeting benefits also has its political problems, as demonstrated by
the government's inability to limit family allowance benefits to the neediest. The benefit is minimal for wealthier families with fewer children,
but it is extremely important to larger, poorer families.[83] Even so, the
government has not been able to get proposals for limiting benefits to
pass in Parliament. Similar proposals to target benefits within the Solidarity union have also been met with strong opposition.[84] Yet another
concern is that while the budget crisis and low quality of services call for
reform, the changes are leading society deeper into poverty, which means
that there are fewer wage earners with the capacity to fund nonstate
services.[85]

In mid-1991 the government proposed to reform the pension system,
since its insolvency had by then become a major financial burden (10
percent of government expenditure) (see table 7-6). The debate over
pensions coincided with the October 1991 elections and thus turned into
a partisan and emotional event. Pensioners had already benefited from
the indexation implemented in 1990 by then labor minister Kuron; in
equity terms there was little reason for so much debate over refining the
system. Opponents of a more redistributive system warned of a return
to communism, whereas proponents noted that pensions were the base
for social not private insurance.[86] There were public protests over the
issue, and ultimately the substantive proposals for reform were withdrawn. The general public's understanding of state insolvency or of a
pay-as-you-go pension system is limited to begin with; this was exacerbated by politicians' claims that the state was failing to pay back pensioners what they were "owed."[87] The pre-electoral context was hardly
conducive to reforms that entailed short-term losses for longer-term
gains. A similar debate over subsidized medicines lasted over a year and
ended with a substantial watering down of the proposed reforms. The
debate centered on "revoking the right of several vocational groups and
pensioners to free medicines," rather than on essential drugs.[88]

Table 7-6. *Distribution of State Budget Expenditure on Social Safety Net and Cash Benefit Expenditure, 1990, 1991, 1992*
Percent

Item	1990	1991[a]	1992[b]
		Budget expenditure[c]	
Social insurance funds	n.a.	14.4	19.8
For nonfarmers (SIF)	n.a.	8.9	13.2
For farmers (SIIF)	n.a.	5.5	6.6
Alimony fund	n.a.	0.2	0.3
Labor fund	n.a.	3.0	3.9
Veteran fund	n.a.	0.1	0.1
Social assistance	n.a.	2.2	2.3
Other	n.a.	0.8	0.2
Subtotal	n.a.	20.7	26.6
Consumer price subsidy	n.a.	8.5	8.5
Total social safety net	n.a.	29.2	35.1
		Cash benefit expenditure	
Unemployment compensation	4.0	8.1	7.7
Unemployment benefit	3.9	8.0	7.5
Training benefit	0.1	0.1	0.2
Pension	75.2	73.2	77.3
Nonfarmer	63.7	63.5	67.1
Farmer	11.5	9.7	10.2
Social insurance allowance and benefit	19.0	17.1	13.3
SIF (nonfarmer)	18.2	16.9	12.5
SIIF (farmer)	0.8	0.3	0.8
Social assistance allowance and benefit	1.8	1.5	1.7

Source: Irena Topinska: "Social Safety Net in Poland," University of Warsaw, Department of Economics, June 1992, tables 7, 8.
n.a. Not available.
a. Estimate.
b. As appears in budget.
c. Total budget expenditure on the social safety net was 248,850 billion zlotys (estimate) in 1991, and 403,635 billion zlotys in 1992.
d. Total cash benefit expenditure was 61,705 billion zlotys in 1990, 138,991 billion in 1991, and 245,763 billion in 1992 (1991 and 1992 are estimates).

By mid-1992, with the growing fiscal crisis and the intense social unrest of that summer, it was no longer possible to postpone serious treatment of the reform issue. The important safety net in the public mind—and of concern to the government—is employment, particularly since the big loss-making state enterprises have yet to be privatized or liquidated. Thus excess employment—which is approximately 20–30 percent in large enterprises and 5–15 percent in small ones—serves as a safety net for great numbers of workers.[89] In addition, most social benefits are linked to participation in the work force and are administered by the firms.

The government has attempted to deal with the employment issue in various ways—one being to postpone it (it was omitted from the September 1992 pact). This move has provided fuel for the opposition and heightened anxiety and unrest among organized labor. And as long as the government continues to foot the bill for huge loss-making enterprises, it will not have the resources to implement the reforms desperately needed in the social sectors. Another strategy has been to promote local enterprises, but this has its limits in severely depressed regions.

To complicate matters, whereas before there was a great deal of hidden unemployment, now there is a great deal of "hidden work."[90] People who work in the "gray market" are reluctant to pay taxes and are also afraid that they will lose social assistance benefits if they declare informal income. Statistics on the private sector are unreliable, and firms have every incentive to underreport income and employment, especially since the social insurance and other benefits they are required to pay per worker are daunting: employers are required to contribute 45 percent of their payroll to social insurance payments.

There are few, if any, concrete proposals for dealing with regionally concentrated structural unemployment in Poland. The most viable option for addressing the employment and safety net issue is to differentiate among the "losers." The employment issue is very different for a sixty-year-old laid-off state worker than it is for a twenty-five-year-old. A great deal also depends on what is possible in particular regions and local contexts. Approximately 70 percent of the unemployed are under thirty. Training for new and emerging vocations is obviously a key issue for this group.[91] For depressed regions where there is no hope of foreign investment or local business, some sort of public works program should be envisioned, for political as well as economic and social reasons.[92] Although there has been some talk of public works programs, to date the authorities have been reluctant to look at relevant examples outside Europe, such as Chile.[93]

Social discontent has often caused major policy reversals in Poland.[94] The strikes of the summer of 1992, as already discussed, seriously jeopardized the reform program and forced the government to begin publicly addressing the social safety net issue. When Solidarity found itself in an awkward political position, it stopped backing unpopular policies, but this made it difficult for any government to implement reform, as the May no-confidence vote demonstrated. The September elections then called into question the fate of the entire reform program. Poor public understanding of proposed social welfare sector reforms and the absence of existing safety nets rapidly eroded popular tolerance for the costs of reform.

Poverty in Poland

As the preceding discussion suggests, poverty in Poland is a complex problem. In eastern Europe in general, it is difficult to assess real income levels or purchasing power before the transition to market prices and convertible currencies. And in societies that have had little experience with inequality, it is difficult to distinguish relative or absolute poverty from trends in income differentiation.

Yet poverty has several distinct traits in Poland. To begin with, it has a changing profile. Before the 1980s the poverty that did exist was primarily rural, but in the 1980s it became an urban phenomenon. Approximately 70 percent of Poland's 7 million estimated poor are now in the cities. Poverty also increased more in Poland during the socialist recession of the 1980s than it did in either Hungary (where it remained at 15 percent) or Yugoslavia (where it increased from 17 to 25 percent). Although unemployment did not increase at this time in Poland, household incomes declined. The number of people below the poverty line increased from 9.2 percent of the population in 1978 to 22.7 percent in 1987. With the hyperinflation of 1988–89, all incomes fell substantially.[95]

Poverty has also changed in terms of its societal profile. Previously, the poor belonged to the same social groups that constitute the "residual" poor in many societies: the elderly on small fixed pensions, female-headed households with large numbers of children, and those at the social margin, such as families of alcoholics. Now this profile includes young skilled workers (between the ages of twenty-five and forty) with families. As mentioned earlier, members of groups that were once considered privileged, such as state enterprise and public sector workers, are entering the ranks of the poor. To be sure, they are not as poor as the former group, and they are politically powerful. Pensioners and those with only primary and vocational education are more likely to be poor than other groups. The link between poverty levels and education levels contradicts the conventional wisdom in Poland that economic status is *inversely* related to higher-level degrees.[96] The poor also include floating or migrant workers, who do not even appear in household surveys but are very

vulnerable to price changes.[97] Although income distribution worsened
slightly from 1987 to 1990, there was no increase during the transition
years 1990-91: sharp falls in real incomes usually produce lower differentiation in the short run.[98]

Another point to note about poverty in Poland is its relationship to
unemployment. Because most benefits such as pensions were linked to
and administered by employers, the loss of one's job usually meant the
loss or drastic curtailment of these benefits. Most benefits are indexed to
average wage levels, but wages have deteriorated to such an extent that
it now takes two wage earners to keep families out of poverty. Real wages
fell 25 percent in 1990 alone and unemployment rose noticeably, which
suggests that poverty had undoubtedly increased from its 1987 levels.
Poverty is also regional and occupational; while there is little inequality
within regions, there is a great deal between regions. Poverty levels are
far lower in Warsaw and other cities where a new private sector is rapidly
developing than they are in industrial regions or towns that were largely
dependent on a particular industry or public enterprise that is now
defunct.[99]

Whereas in developing countries unions tend to represent a relatively
privileged section of the working class, in Poland the concerns of organized labor tend to reflect those of the average citizen. The standard
occupational categories are workers, worker-farmers, farmers, and pensioners. Since 1990 pensioners have consistently been the worst off. The
other three groups ranked, from most to least privileged are workers,
farmers, and worker-farmers. From 1985 to 1987 the relative position of
workers declined below that of farmers for the first time. In the first two
quarters of 1989, farmers and worker-farmers lost the most, and workers
again became the most privileged group (in relative terms). Yet by this
point differences between groups were quite small, and fluctuated as
changing macroeconomic policies took effect.[100] All groups suffered
losses after the 1990 stabilization. In 1990 pensioners received a temporary boost with the indexation of pension adjustments, but it was a boost
that could not be financially sustained.[101]

Yet another characteristic of poverty in Poland is that an increasing
percentage of the average salary is now being spent on food. It reached
a high of 57 percent of average incomes in January 1990 but then fell to
about 45 percent thereafter.[102] Self-supply of food is also increasingly
important among almost all worker categories, with the exception of
pensioners (see table 7-7). Another trait of poverty that is difficult to

Table 7-7. *Percentage of Different Social Groups That Supply Their Own Food Products*

Group	Percent	Group	Percent
Workers	10.54	Workers and farmers	65.36
Pensioners	16.63	Farmers	71.81

Source: Data compiled during interview with S. Berger, of the Warsaw Agricultural University, September 1992.

measure is the widespread anxiety that has accompanied the rapid transition from a system with guaranteed benefits to one in which income levels, benefit schemes, and occupational categories are in a state of upheaval.[103] Poverty in Poland is clearly not as extreme as poverty in less developed countries or even in some advanced industrial countries. In Poland millions of people receive some sort of benefit from the state, whether in the form of housing subsidies, family allowance benefits, or subsidized medicines. Yet the fact that poverty even exists in a society where there was little income differentiation in the past and where the economic future is highly uncertain has caused a great deal of anxiety.

The government's social minimum—the equivalent of the poverty line—is determined by the Institute of Labor Statistics, which reports that the level is high compared with average salaries. Actually, the government would like to replace the social minimum with a different poverty criterion, since approximately half the population is currently at that level, but unions are strongly opposed to such a change. The minimum used to be a simple accounting measure, for until the 1990 Social Assistance Act no special benefits were even assigned to those below the social minimum. In 1989 the minimum was 70,000 zlotys a month, while a more conservative estimate of the poverty line was 60,000 zlotys a month. In addition, the goods reference is quite high, since it includes appliances such as television sets. The erosion of the real wage since then, however, has probably placed the social minimum at about 800,000 zlotys, or approximately US$60 in December 1991, which is much closer to, or even below what would constitute a realistic poverty line.[104]

Yet another complicating factor in estimating poverty in Poland is that only a third of those on unemployment benefits shift to welfare when their benefits run out, in part because private sector employment and earnings are underreported.[105] Social assistance centers also report that many unemployed people repeatedly refuse jobs below their skill level: approximately 30 percent of those registered as "unemployed" in 1990 were unwilling to take jobs that were offered.[106] This implies that a

Table 7-8. *Percentage of Income Spent on Food, by Decile and Worker Group, 1992*[a]

Decile	Workers	Pensioners	Workers and farmers	Farmers
1	55	58	63	56
2	54	54	58	56
3	52	55	57	55
4	48	54	52	53
5	45	52	48	52
6	43	48	46	50
7	41	46	44	48
8	39	44	42	45
9	38	42	46	48
10	33	36	38	43

Source: See table 7-7.

a. Between 1980 and 1988, daily average available calories per person ranged between 3,307 and 3,495. Note that these numbers represent *available* calories rather than those *consumed*. Average consumption for an adult male in industrial countries is 2,600 a day.

segment of the "unemployed" must have some form of income or social security. And although the percentage of income spent on food has increased, there is no real hunger or malnutrition in Poland, and consumption levels have remained relatively constant since the 1990 shocks (see table 7-8).

Food subsidies, before their removal in 1989, accounted for 17 percent of the government's total budget and nearly 30 percent of the total value of food consumption. Yet their removal had less effect on nutritional status than might be expected. Although the consumption of milk, which was the most subsidized food before 1989, has fallen since the removal of subsidies, the consumption of meat, which was rationed before, has increased to the highest levels in recent history, at 73.2 kilograms per person.[107] Indeed, the proportion of the average food budget spent on meat and meat products (40 percent) is surprisingly high and hardly meets the profile of a typical "poor" household. The total energy content of the average Polish diet fell by approximately 2.3 percent per year from 1989 to 1991, but total calories still remain well above industrial country averages (table 7-8).[108] Meanwhile, those at nutritional risk are limited to small children in socially marginalized families and the poorest pensioners. Nutritional standards are becoming increasingly differentiated, and the occupational groups with access to self-supply, such as worker-farmers, are developing a distinct advantage.[109]

The Existing Safety Net

In Poland, as in most eastern European countries, the safety net was formerly based on a combination of consumer subsidies, universal benefits transferred from the central budget, and state sector wages.[110] In the 1980s social income accounted for 45–48 zlotys for every 100 of labor income in Poland. This created a major labor supply disincentive.[111] In 1991 the Polish government spent 30 percent of its total expenditure on the safety net, and in 1992 that percentage was closer to 35 percent. The bulk of expenditure went to the social insurance system, followed by subsidies (table 7-6).[112] All sectors of society, including private farmers and the clergy, were covered by the pension system. ZUS also administered a series of other universal benefits, including family allowance and nursing and maternity benefits. The public health system provided universal coverage, although both quality and access deteriorated substantially by the 1980s because of substantial funding problems. With the initiation of market reforms, Poland began shifting to a new type of safety net, marked by the introduction of an unemployment insurance law in December 1989 and of a social assistance act in November 1990.

Social transfers—unemployment compensation, social insurance, and social assistance—amounted to 11 percent of GNP in 1990, and more than 90 percent of these expenditures went to social insurance.[113] In per capita terms, pensioners received two times the average transfer, workers 80 percent, and farmers 70 percent. Although allowances were given without any income criteria, transfers had a redistributive effect. However, they did not change the ranking among socioeconomic groups. The wealthiest households received only 80 percent of per capita transfers going to the poorest, while their original income was nine times greater. Child care and family allowances—benefits related to the number of children—reduced inequality in Poland, while pensions and universal benefits contributed to it.[114]

Even before the market transition, the government was aware of both the social costs of the economic crisis of the early 1980s and of the increasing financial insolvency of the public social welfare system. "Several factors . . . [reflected] the government's attempt to avoid a dramatic increase in poverty. First, the government encouraged early retirement in fear of a possible emergence of unemployment. Second, in 1982 all low-income families were granted a lump-sum benefit supplementing family allowance. Third, the government compensated substantial price increases in 1982 by introducing special flat rate benefits paid out together with pensions."[115]

Despite the drop in GDP, social welfare's share of the public budget grew from the late 1970s onward. In 1978 social expenditure accounted for 19.9 percent of the budget, in 1982, 26.2 percent, in 1989, 20.8 percent, and in 1991 almost 30 percent. Cash expenditures increased in relative importance to subsidies during this time.[116] Until their removal in 1989, subsidies on food, transport, housing, energy, coal, medicines, and kindergartens accounted for 20–30 percent of current government expenditure. Subsidies still remain on energy, public transport, cooperative housing, and medicines, and they accounted for 8.5 percent of the total budget in 1991 (table 7-6).[117]

Until 1989 universal family benefits played a major role in the safety net system, while direct social assistance was virtually nil—only 1.2 percent of government expenditure was on social insurance.[118] By that time, however, the financial burden of the universal system could no longer be sustained. The largest consumer of public funds is now the pension system.

The Pension System

The social security system in Poland provides 27 percent of the population's net disposable income, and its importance has increased in the public psyche with the "rising public anxiety over the social costs of the transition."[119] Although many now realize that the current system is unaffordable, most people do not blame the system, but rather the general state of the economy. The system, which is administered by the ZUS, is rife with inefficiency and skewed incentives. It is partly funded by "pay-as-you-go" employer contributions. In 1990 contributions funded only 88 percent of expenditures, since the 1982 pension law set pensions as high as average wages regardless of contributions. As mentioned earlier, employer contributions amount to 45 percent of most company payrolls, and there are no counterpart employee contributions. Because of changing demography, there are 12 million contributors for 5.5 million recipients of pensions. Two percent of total contributions are passed on to the Ministry of Labor to fund unemployment compensation; the rest goes to the social insurance fund. Early retirement is very easy; 25 percent of pensioners retire early, and the average retirement age in Poland is fifty-eight for men and fifty-seven for women. It is also possible to work almost full-time while receiving a pension. Finally, because pension levels are based on an individual's wages in the final year before retirement, most companies boost salaries by 30–40 percent in the last two years, with the result that pension levels are often as high as average salaries. In addition, a variety of occupational groups receive an additional 15 percent of the average monthly earning as a bonus. These groups are chosen on the basis of their hard working condition (miners), social prestige (teachers), or political influence (journalists).[120] "The fairness of the system seems to have nothing in common with the relation between individual contributions and individual benefits. It is rather a matter of the concession distribution between occupational groups. This gives rise to continuous pressure for equalizing concessions to the level of the most favourable groups."[121]

Private farmers have a separate system. There are 2.5 million farmers in private agriculture and 1.5 million pensions. While the system is in theory based on contributions, 90 percent of the funding comes from the government budget.[122] Because the farmers are well organized politically, they have been able to consistently resist efforts to increase their contributions.[123]

Before 1986 the pension system actually yielded some surpluses. This was largely because benefits were indexed ad hoc. While this created some inequality among pensioners, depending on the timing of retirement and of indexation, it prevented the system from becoming financially insolvent. These inequalities were the target of a great deal of criticism, however, and made the fate of pensioners a high priority for the first noncommunist government. In 1990 automatic indexation of the pension system was introduced. To forestall an increase in the average pension up to the level of average earnings, the Ministry of Labor also introduced a modified benefit formula to prevent increases in the highest pensions. The proposal was presented shortly before the 1990 presidential elections, but it triggered strong public opposition and was withdrawn.[124]

By mid-1991 the pension system was in deep financial trouble because of the indexation of benefits, the growing numbers seeking retirement in anticipation of unfavorable changes, and the decline in the number of contributors because of the decline in state sector employment and tax evasion by the new private sector. The government was forced to expand its subsidization of the system from 10 to 25 percent while reneging on its policy of full indexation. In August of that year the president of ZUS resigned in protest over the lack of progress in reforming the pension system. A reform proposal was again introduced in October 1991, which would have reduced benefits to pensioners with high pensions—approximately one-fourth of the total—and placed a ceiling on pensions amounting to 250 percent of the average wage. It also eliminated concessions to occupational groups and differentiated between contribution and non-contribution years. The debate in Parliament over this reform, as mentioned earlier, was highly partisan and emotional. Ultimately, part of the law was approved for a two-year period, but only after it was challenged in the Constitutional Court by the former communist trade union OPZZ. In addition, some of the more fundamental problems, such as employee contributions and the need for a funded system, were not addressed.[125]

In most Western countries the pension system aims to spread earnings evenly over the life cycle and, in part, to redistribute income. In Poland the pension system serves as a safeguard against poverty, which is why there is such an outcry when people talk about changing it.[126] Until November 1990 there was no formal social assistance system for poor and vulnerable groups. The nonsocial insurance benefits were related to the pension system and administered by ZUS.

Family allowance is a subsidy paid to families for each child under the age of sixteen and up to the age of twenty-six if attending school full-time. Dependent spouses with children under eight also receive allowances. The benefit is fixed at 8 percent of the average monthly wage in the previous quarter and is paid monthly. Thus a family with three children would receive 24 percent of the average monthly wage in family allowance. Since families with more than three children are more likely to be in poverty than smaller families, the benefit is important to some families, particularly those with single parents. The benefit for a wealthier family with one child is relatively minimal. Family allowance is the most important of these benefits and accounted for 13 percent of all social insurance expenditure in 1991, but there are also universal nursing allowances, caring benefits, maternity benefits, birth benefits, survivor pensions, and funeral benefits. All these benefits tend to be more generous than their counterparts—if they exist at all—in the West.[127]

The Health System

The public health system in Poland in theory guarantees universal access to all citizens. In practice, however, the system has suffered from underfunding. Also, its incentive system encourages specialized care and hospitalization at the expense of preventive care and outpatient treatment. Waiting periods are very long; drugs, equipment, and facilities are inadequate; there are not enough hospital beds and specialist services; and patient relations with physicians and other health care workers are poor. There are few general practitioners, whose prestige in the Polish medical profession has now fallen, and in the absence of a referral requirement, people go directly to specialists. Although the number of hospital beds per person in Poland compares favorably with those in other countries, waiting lists for admission are long. That is the result of underdeveloped outpatient services: 20 percent of hospital beds go to patients who should be in nursing homes, for example. There is also excessive use of emergency ambulance services; in some regions more than half the calls for this service are unwarranted.[128] Regional differences are quite substantial, since funds are allocated on the basis of regional bargaining, historical allocations, and political jockeying that has little to do with medical disparities among regions. Many complain that patients are often required to pay for certain services. Since waiting lists are not available to the public, informal payments may be made to gain timely access to services. Certain occupational groups also have privileged access.[129]

Ninety percent of the managerial positions in the national health system are held by physicians without any economic training. Budgets are still administered on a line-by-line basis with no computerization. There is some reluctance to apply economic standards to health care, which is considered a public good. For example, there are no medical audits or peer reviews in the medical profession after the medical school stage. Although the deterioration in the quality and availability of services has focused attention on costs, quality control, and patients' rights, there seems to be little political interest in reforming the health care system, and the issue was not on any political platform in the October 1991 elections.[130] Officials concerned with the financial crisis in the system are far more likely to drive the movement toward reform than are politicians concerned with the poor quality of public health.

The Unemployment and Social Assistance Laws

The transition brought two major changes to the social safety net in Poland: unemployment benefits were introduced, and targeted assistance was provided for the neediest groups. The Law of Employment and

Unemployment was passed in December 1989 and later was substantially revised to make unemployment rules more restrictive. The original law provided in-cash and in-kind benefits from a labor fund financed by employer contributions and central government transfers (approximately 75 percent). Since 1992 income taxes have also provided a source of funds for unemployment benefits.[131]

Under the original law, almost anyone without a job could register as unemployed and was eligible for benefits of an unlimited duration. Since then the law has been revised to exclude those under eighteen, over sixty-five, pensioners, students, and farmers. A maximum income test is now used. Applicants must have worked at least 180 days in the previous twelve months and not been offered a suitable job, inclusive of public works or retraining. Before the revisions, individuals were allowed to refuse two job offers. Benefits are now limited to one year, at which point the recipient has to rely on the benefits provided by the Social Assistance Act. At first benefits were set at 70 percent of the previous wage and declined over time. Since March 1992 benefits have been set at 36 percent of the average monthly wage, equivalent to 737,000 zlotys, or just over US$53 a month, which is below the social minimum line. More generous rules apply in massive layoffs or for persons who have worked for at least thirty years.[132]

The labor fund spent 82 percent of its total on unemployment benefits in 1991, with the rest going to public works and training programs, including subsidies for youth employment. In 1990, 236,000 unemployed found jobs, 10,300 received vocational training, 106,900 participated in some form of public works, 27,900 loans were made to generate additional jobs, and 32,000 startup loans went to new businesses.[133] In September 1992 the Labor Ministry announced plans for a program of action to create new jobs.[134] To limit the strain on the state budget, payroll contributions to the labor fund were raised from 2 to 3 percent in January 1993.[135] The government also proposed shifting the administration of employment benefits from employment offices in the forty-nine vovoidships (regional branches of the central government) to the gminas (local governments that became fully autonomous in 1990). Although decentralization is appealing in theory, gminas are unlikely to have the resources and administrative capacity necessary to manage the growing employment problem.

The Social Assistance Act of November 1990 replaced a system of state-sponsored charities that previously cared for the "margin" of society that was poor. Expenditure on social assistance in 1990 was only 2 percent of the total spent on social insurance; it rose to 9 percent in 1991. The new law assumes that reform will result in poverty and unemployment and that social assistance will become the nationwide benefit of last resort. All individuals whose income falls below a poverty line or social minimum of 100 percent of the minimum pension are eligible for social assistance. Benefits are either centrally commissioned cash payments, financed jointly by the central and local governments, or in-kind services provided at the local level. In 1991 the central government spent 2,100 billion zlotys on social assistance benefits, and local governments spent 900 billion.[136] There are eleven categories of eligibility, including homelessness, unemployment, disability, and alcoholism.[137] Benefits are limited to 28 percent of the average monthly wage. In-kind benefits include health or home assistance services, or goods such as food or fuel. Other programs include housing subsidies, credit for new small businesses, and means-tested cash grants for medicines.[138]

There are 2,400 social assistance centers based in gminas, staffed by approximately 15,000 social workers. The discretionary judgments of these workers are a primary basis for the allocation of benefits. This is an insufficient basis for the expanded new system. Social workers in general either are poorly educated or have degrees in sociology or psychology rather than in social work. As a corrective measure, the law stipulates that by 1995 social workers will have to have professional degrees in social work. Gminas also vary greatly in their quality and administrative capacity.[139] Since the financial constraints on the government are increasing, it has been trying to delegate more to the gminas, but the ability of the gminas to administer social assistance benefits is becoming an even more critical issue.

The social safety net system clearly needs to be developed further. Unemployment and social assistance systems are currently administered independently of each other, but they should be more closely linked. Family allowance should be targeted, financed by general taxes, and administered by social assistance offices rather than by the state insurance agency.[140] Social insurance contributions should be shared between employers and employees. Several substantive proposals for reform of the system are being considered within government circles and have been or will soon be the subject of parliamentary debate. Although most proposals are grounded in the serious research of a talented team of advisers, the government's *political* strategy for pushing the reforms through will be as important as their content. It is very difficult to persuade people to give up whatever security they have in exchange for a vague promise of future improvement, particularly when economic and political changes have occurred quickly. And because services are provided by the state, and the general public has little idea of how they are financed, few people recognize that they have a stake in curbing demands for increased state expenditure. The public will have to be educated about the problems in the current system and about proposed reforms before the government can expect political support for change.

Another obstacle to implementing reform is that the lower standards of living in recent years have led people to think more about existing benefits, even if they are inadequate or of poor quality. A related issue is that the potential of privatization is limited as long as the capital market remains underdeveloped and poor living standards restrict the available pool of potential participants in private schemes. In 1990, for example, a law was passed allowing insurance companies to work as nonprofit institutions providing pension, accident, and health insurance. Twenty-two private companies were created, but only one of them offers mutual funds. Thus most of them are just not realistic options for most Polish consumers. And although the Polish pension system's replacement rate is high by Western standards, the standard of living is so low that many retirees are living in or near poverty.[141]

Proposed Reforms

Despite the obstacles, the Suchocka government made several efforts to change the social welfare system, both to complete the Pact on Social Safety and to reform the health and pension systems.[142] There are also proposals to reform the family benefits system and to reduce consumer price subsidies, especially in the public transportation sector, through the reduction of groups eligible for subsidized fares. A government attempt to reform the family benefits system, introduced by Labor Minister Boni just before the 1991 elections, caused a major uproar and had to be withdrawn. Reform proposals aimed to remove the family allowance from the social insurance system, so that it would become universal rather than employment-linked, and to introduce an incomes test.[143] In 1992 the level of allowance was frozen at 167,000 zlotys per beneficiary per month and would remain so in 1993. Eligibility for family allowance would be limited and would not extend beyond the secondary education level. The targeting system would be refined to increase the allowance for large families. The total 1992 budget—21.5 trillion zlotys—would not be exceeded in 1993.[144]

In the pension and health arenas, the proposed reforms assumed that a fully privatized system is nonviable in the short term, and they are based on minimum systems of state insurance in the social security and health fields, coupled with different mechanisms for allowing private providers for those who can afford it. In both previous instances of proposed pension reform, elections were pending. This was not the case early in the Suchocka government. And if the popular labor minister Kuron, the sponsor of most reforms, had acted as their salesman, the chances of their obtaining parliamentary approval would have been enhanced. The Suchocka coalition demonstrated resolve and coherence in the face of the strikes. Yet it also used up a great deal of government energy and attention, at the expense of progress on reforms. Finally, if changing the subsidy system for medicines took more than one year in Parliament, it is unlikely that the political debate over the entire pension or health systems will be much easier, regardless of political timing.

The disincentives in the current pension system are high.[145] In the last quarter of 1989, a time of hyperinflation, people were able to retire and get pensions that were higher than average salaries. In 1990 benefits were harmonized and indexed but had to be lowered in 1991, when the government could no longer afford them. Even though the benefits scheme was simplified and special privileges reduced, the basic solvency problem, with no upper limit on benefits, was not addressed.

To reform the pension system, employee contributions will have to be introduced. The public needs to understand that pensions are not a gift from the state but a return on contributions made on a pay-as-you-go basis.[146] "This would have no short-run economic effects but would matter in the longer run if it affected the perception of workers and so the political pressures in the pension determination process . . . such a change would have a moderating effect."[147] Yet introducing such reforms is not easy. Few politicians can afford to alienate the powerful pensioners' lobby, which maintains that the pension system would be solvent if benefits like family allowance were removed.

The pension reform proposal under the Suchocka government recommended a partly private system based on the Chilean model,[148] where the system applies to those making 120 percent of the average monthly salary, or 25 percent of wage earners, and 10 percent of pensioners. This bracket would be exempt from eligibility for the basic state-provided insurance and would have to opt for a private provider. This arrangement would ease the financial burden on the state and ensure that private systems had sufficient capital to operate. There would be compensation for those who shifted to the private system. The existence of a private option would give at least some sectors of the population a perceived stake in the reforms, just as "popular capitalism" did in Chile.

The private funds would have to be regulated, however. In Poland's underdeveloped capital markets, too many small and financially nonviable funds could develop. There would also be an upper limit on earnings of 120–300 percent of the average salary on which pension contributions could be paid, in order to remove the incentive that now exists to underreport income. Another aspect of the reform would be to enhance the financial solvency of ZUS by removing noninsurance benefits such as family allowance from its jurisdiction. ZUS should also ride "piggy-back" on the new tax system's individual earnings records. It is critical for earnings records to be centralized in the ZUS rather than in individual firms, or the evasion problem, as well as other administrative problems, will not be resolved. Among the reforms planned for 1993, the government hoped to tighten the eligibility procedures for disability pensions, reduce eligibility for early retirement, and lower the ratio of average pensions to average wages to 60 percent by reducing the base on which pensions are evaluated.[149]

As for the health care system, the flaws in the structure of the care provision have received much less public attention than the insolvency of the system. Yet unless structural and financial issues are treated concurrently, budget concerns will lead to haphazard reform and "to an explosion of the uncontrolled, chaotic methods of generating additional income, with all the inherent negative social consequences, such as a sense of social insecurity, uncertainties as to required out-of-pocket costs and social inequalities in access to health services."[150]

A principal barrier to reform of the health system is that politicians are much more interested in "hotter" issues, such as wage grievances, abortion, and decommunization. Besides, health care reform is a costly and time-consuming process. One problem is that patients' rights are totally unrepresented, in contrast to the strong organizational representation of physicians. Another problem is that dissatisfaction does not translate into sufficient information, and the general public remains poorly informed about the system or proposed changes.

The proposals for reform within the Suchocka government assumed that the basic incentives are askew. The Ministry of Health is both the provider and purchaser of services. Since it both allocates funds and administers policy, there are no incentives for quality control and the system is vulnerable to political pressure from diverse occupational groups.[151] The proposed reforms would separate the function of payer from that of provider and manager, and would establish medical and financial rather than bureaucratic and political criteria for quality control. At the same time, for the same reasons that a fully privatized pension system is inappropriate for Poland, a market health system would not be viable because of the unstable regulatory framework and the limited financial means of most of the population. Thus the reforms propose a basic national insurance system with incentives that would encourage both consumers and producers to use primary and preventive care. Such a system would give private providers and patient a choice but would also provide a basic level of insurance. Some proposals in government and parliamentary circles are based on regional rather than national insurance schemes. The risk in regional schemes is that they may emphasize the regional disparities that already exist *and* focus solely on the financial aspect of reform, and thus fail to address systemic incentives.[152] The government proposed that hospitals begin cost accounting, and was identifying medical facilities to be restructured, and tightening procedures regarding the prescription and payment of medicines.[153]

Another sector that is in desperate need of reform and that would enhance labor mobility, and thereby reduce unemployment, is housing. Here, too, attention will have to focus both on finances and on changing basic incentives. There is a tremendous shortage of affordable housing, because of bottlenecks in production (slow construction) and consumption (no affordable credit or mortgages). Subsidies, which are currently given to cooperative housing construction, should be indirect and focused on the development of a market-based construction sector. This would reduce construction costs and thus stimulate effective demand. Affordable credit will be essential, as will support for local efforts to construct rental housing units for those who cannot afford to buy.[154]

In education, a major objective of reform is to shift from the narrow, enterprise-specific vocational education of the past to a stronger emphasis on secondary education, as well as to devolve primary schools to local governments and provide new performance incentives for teachers.[155]

Until now, the reform debate in all sectors has tended to emphasize decentralized solutions based on the newly elected gminas and has paid less attention to the need for new systemic incentives at the national level. While decentralization clearly has benefits, there are limits to how rapidly a hypercentralized authoritarian system can be transformed into a representative, decentralized one. Unfortunately, the fate of all proposed reforms was made uncertain by the September 1993 change of government. Whether faster progress on reforms might have prevented the political backlash that now threatens to derail the entire program remains uncertain.[156]

The Role of Local Governments

The introduction in March 1990 of genuinely representative and autonomous municipal governments—gminas—and the subsequent elections of municipal authorities in May of that year were greeted with enthusiasm and expectation. Decentralization was the logical extension of the political philosophy of reducing the role of the state and increasing reliance on the market. In addition, the increasingly evident failure of the central government's ability to maintain the social welfare system led to de facto expectations that the newly created local governments would take over. The Social Welfare Act, for example, envisions a major role for local governments in implementing social assistance policies, as well as in providing primary education and health services. Proposals for the reform of the health and housing systems and the employment fund also envision a greater role for municipal governments. To many it has become clear, however, that the "hopes that followed the introduction of the local self-governments were great and not proportional to their real functions under [Poland's] complicated conditions. The features of the self-governments were too strongly idealized. The complex economic situation, which had to influence the speed and range of the gaining independence process was not, consciously or unconsciously, taken into account."[157]

Another problem is that local governments in Poland vary tremendously in their administrative capacity, leadership experience, and financial resources. The general population has an ambivalent attitude toward local government; abstention in the 1990 municipal elections was 56.7 percent.[158] Much progress needs to be made in institutional development before local governments can adequately fulfill their new role.

Before the March 1990 law, the 2,404 local governments, or communes, were merely extensions of the 49 regional vovoidships. They were
not genuine governments, since their authorities were appointed by the
center, either directly, in the case of the vovoids, or indirectly through
the vovoids, in the case of the communes. They merely served as local
branches of the central government in a hypercentralized system with
substantial deconcentration, similar to the French prefecture system or
to the "decentralized" municipal system in Chile under Pinochet. They
depended on the center for resources, and expenditure was allocated by
a mix of norms, negotiations, and discretion. There was also no clear
division of labor between vovoids and communes; both were involved in
the administration of various services, including health and education.[159]

The 1990 law created full-fledged local governments that would have
resources and autonomy. The only central government control is ex post
facto legal regulation. Municipal councils are elected directly and they in
turn elect the mayors. Gminas are responsible for water provision, sewerage, sanitation, roads, power, primary education, sports and parks,
community housing, urban planning, *and* the implementation of the social assistance act. Health care and secondary education remain the responsibility of the vovoid and center. There are, as yet, no plans to turn
the vovoids into genuine regional governments.[160]

Gminas also became the full owners of community-subordinated enterprises, including all public services. In addition, some gminas inherited
ownership of the services previously administered by state-owned enterprises, such as employee housing and health centers. Their capacity remains limited, however, in that many do not actually take over these
services, because "municipal authorities do not have the means to maintain these even when the facilities are offered free."[161]

The resource base of gminas is not entirely clear. Besides enterprise
taxes, which are required by the central government, gminas have taxes
of their own on real estate, cars and roads, high incomes, inheritance
and gifts, business activity, and dog ownership. Their capacity to administer these taxes varies with the gmina and its resource bases. Gminas
also receive transfers from the central government. They receive 50 percent of income tax payments and 30 percent of wage and salary taxes.
These transfers serve several uses. On the one hand, they are an attempt
to redistribute resources between rich and poor gminas and correct any
vertical resource mismatches, and on the other hand, they give the central

government some influence in gmina affairs. In theory gminas have access to credit. In practice the mechanisms necessary do not yet exist.[162]

The differential capacity of gminas as well as their continued dependence on the central government for resources are the main constraints to their taking on more responsibility. In their first year of operation 60.7 percent of their revenues were shared with the central government and another 18.8 percent were from block grants.[163] While some of the benefits that gminas administer do originate at the local level, they spend a large part of their time trying to get resources from the central government.[164] But the central government, because it needs to maintain control over fiscal policy, may be reluctant to devolve more resources to the local level, as can be seen in the slow transfer of health care to local authorities. Here the government blames the "professional weakness of local communities causing a reluctance to take responsibility, and also a lack of a clear picture with respect to finances."[165] That weakness may account for the fact that local governments played no role in the major strikes of 1992.[166]

In the past, central government investment helped reduce regional disparities. With decentralization, these disparities are likely to increase substantially.[167] A related problem is that the most depressed regions, which also have the greatest need for a safety net, are usually the ones with the least developed capacity for self-government. Conversely, gminas near or in relatively resource-rich cities, such as Warsaw, have financial advantages as well as access to skilled personnel in the intelligentsia and the universities.[168] For example, the BISE, a government-related institution that extends credit for local entrepreneurial initiatives, was unable to elicit much gmina interest outside of Warsaw, because few people understood credit schemes or how to promote local businesses. New gminas are unlikely to promote businesses in depressed regions, however. Some sort of impetus will have to come either from the central government or from foreign investment to create markets, buying power, and skilled labor so as to spawn other initiatives.[169] Thus while the introduction of autonomous gminas has constituted a revolution of sorts for Poland, there has been a concurrent tendency to exaggerate the potential of decentralization.[170]

An even greater barrier is the unclear legal framework. There is no legal definition of the gmina's role in health and secondary and vocational education, for example. Thus some gminas are involved in these activities and others are not. In addition, the legal system is still skewed toward centralized decisionmaking. For instance, the Ministry of Education still decides what kind of equipment local schools will get. The financing system is also in flux. At present, gminas are allocated 2 percent of central government company taxes and 15 percent of income taxes, but these allocations can be changed by the central government. In theory many politicians support decentralization; in practice they are less likely to vote for the devolution of resources and control.[171]

The speed with which political and economic change has come to Poland has also translated into problems at the gmina level. Immediately after the municipal elections, for example, there were high expectations. Then there were widespread attempts to impeach mayors when these expectations were not fulfilled. Inexperience was clearly a factor. Only one-third of the counselors elected believed they were competent or prepared enough to represent the electorate! Internal conflicts existed between new authorities and the towns, and broader conflicts about the appropriate role for local governments. Furthermore, particularly in the smaller and more parochial gminas where the same people have tended to maintain some power throughout the transition, authorities from the former regime who were reappointed or reelected often came into conflict with new entrants to the system. Although these conflicts stabilized somewhat as expectations became more realistic, they remain an issue in the day-to-day functioning of local governments.[172]

Perhaps even more worrying is the lack of experience with local government in Poland. Poles are used to looking to the central government for solutions, rather than to grass-roots democracy. They are not accustomed to cooperating at the neighborhood level in any organized manner. Their reluctance even to trust neighbors is a legacy of authoritarian government, although this attitude seems more pervasive in the large cities than in small towns. The lack of experience with compromise and negotiation is reflected in the large number of political parties. And because change has been so rapid, the current legal order seems vague.[173]

Although many of these difficulties can be blamed on years of communist rule, there were no democratic local governments under the pre-communist system, either. Regions continue to reflect the distinctions that emerged from the tripartite partition of Poland between Germany, Russia, and Austria, as well as religious distinctions. These differences were clear in the abstention rates and electoral results in the 1990 presidential elections.[174]

The relations between central and local politics tend to be complex in all countries.[175] In Poland these relations are not yet well established. In

general, parties have a weak presence at the local level. Whereas 72.1
percent of respondents in a 1991 survey felt that the local town council
had an influence on decisionmaking at the local level, only 10.1 percent
thought that political parties had influence, a ranking that was behind
that of the local parish (21.3 percent), the mayor (70.8 percent), the
regional Solidarity board (22.1 percent), social organizations (10.3 percent), and enterprises (10.3 percent).[176] At certain times—for example,
during local elections—partisan politics can become more of an issue
and can create strong tensions.

At present, the new system appears to be amalgamating with the old
bureaucratic power structure,[177] a phenomenon that has occurred in other
municipal systems in transition from an authoritarian to a democratic
regime. In Chile, for example, municipal governments remained in the
control of former Pinochet appointees well after the transition to democracy at the central level. Because of this and the weak presence of parties
at the local level, there was a slow transition to democracy at the local
level. Consequently, municipal governments have not been able to do
much in the way of alleviating poverty.[178] This is not to say that local
government capacity cannot be developed in Poland, but rather that
expecting local governments to simultaneously increase their responsibilities and become effective administrators and democrats may be unrealistic.

Despite the limitations of local government capacity, local initiatives
will be key to sustaining the transition to a market economy as well as to
democracy because of the overextended and discredited nature of the
central government. And while there are differences in capacity, they are
not necessarily linked to any one kind of gmina or region. Although
gminas of 80,000 people attempt to take on increased local initiatives,
gminas of 3,000 also do so. It is more likely that gminas in depressed
regions will have less capacity, but that may not always be true. The fact
is that gminas have often proved themselves to be better financial administrators than the central government, and local provision of services
often proves to be cheaper.[179]

A host of autonomous and government-linked initiatives have been
designed to increase gmina capacity, which cover a range of services from
legal advice to credit for small enterprise promotion.[180] In addition, in
mid-1992 the government announced a plan for special aid to 182 gminas
suffering from structural unemployment.[181] The proposals were not complete at the time of this writing, but their primary purpose was to attract

investment and provide public works, to be financed from resources redistributed from other gminas. This seems a step in the right direction, and as policymakers in Poland continue to move forward, they could benefit from the experiences of several Latin American countries with funds for social investment and employment creation.[182]

Nongovernmental Organizations

As other chapters have shown, nongovernmental organizations can play a vital role in the delivery of social welfare services. Unfortunately, the combination of authoritarian rule, coupled with the philosophy that all needs would be cared for by the state, discouraged the development of autonomous grass-roots organizations in Poland, other than those that attempted to topple the regime from underground.[183] Yet this very tradition of protest and underground activity reflects an underlying organizational capacity in Poland. During the four decades of communism, Poles had more voluntary organizations per capita than any other eastern European country. "The beginnings of civic culture existed in Poland in the form of numerous small, politically non-threatening social circles and clubs that never surrendered their spirit of voluntarism."[184] Poland was the only one of those countries to resist collectivization, to retain its church, and to have an independent union movement as significant as Solidarity. Yet the refusal to compromise that is usually characteristic of such underground organization is quite different from the skills required to build democratic organizations.[185] Another constraint to organizational development caused by the transition is that ordinary families are now forced to concentrate on mere survival. "The basic problems and difficulties undertaken by Polish NGO's stem from the cultural and socioeconomic conditions. Life in Poland is currently very difficult; people spend most of their time and energy trying to satisfy basic human needs."[186]

Foundations were dissolved in 1954, and NGOs only obtained the right to exist in 1984. In 1989 they were given the right to function in all areas. The exponential growth of NGOs since the 1984 legalization—3,000 new NGOs and 3,000 new associations have been created since then, and approximately 500 in each category deal with social policy problems[187]— indicates that the societal impulse to organize is still strong. It may not be shared by the "average" individual, but it does indicate that an or-

ganizational leadership class could take shape and lead to the development of a strong NGO movement in Poland.

Until 1989 most organizational efforts took an underground or protest
form; since then organizations have had to adapt to a more professional
and legal way of operating, a transition that was made more difficult by
an uncertain regulatory structure. It is still not clear if gminas can legally
subcontract services to NGOs. For their part, many NGOs, because of
their underground origin, are reluctant to cooperate with the state. There
is a mutual suspicion between NGOs and the state-run service provision
networks, such as the social assistance offices. In addition, because most
services were provided by the ministries until recently, many NGOs seem
to focus their efforts on cooperation with ministries rather than with
gminas.[188]

Most of the 3,000 NGOs currently operating in Poland are extremely
small and have only limited resources.[189] Seventy percent of the NGOs
are based in major cities: Warsaw, Cracow, and Gdansk. The provision
of public services by NGOs until now has been controlled by two large
quasi NGOs (kwangos): the Polish Red Cross and the Polish Committee
for Social Assistance. The care that such services provide (such as home-
care nurses) tends to be far more expensive than that provided by smaller
NGOs.[190] Yet the uncertain legal structure of the gminas, coupled with
the mutual mistrust between NGOs and the state, tends to perpetuate
the monopoly of the kwangos.[191] Because NGOs have only a small rural
and regional presence and there is no clear-cut regulatory framework,
gminas outside the major cities are less likely to "risk" the uncertainty
of cooperating with NGOs, at least in the short term.[192]

For the most part, NGOs seem to have stayed out of the political
realm since the establishment of the electoral process.[193] Some still maintain party or political links, but the vast majority are not political and
are often linked to the church (see table 7-9). Also, NGOs do not seem
to have strong ties to unions, no doubt because unions usually focus on
unemployment and until recently were able to provide extensive self-
contained social service networks. In the case of Solidarity, the union
has its own direct links to the government. Those NGOs that are not
church-linked tend to be oriented around issues such as homelessness or
the disabled. The apolitical character of Polish NGOs should facilitate
future cooperation with gminas. In contrast, in many countries ideology
is a barrier to government-NGO cooperation.[194]

Table 7-9. *Affiliation of Nongovernmental Organizations*[a]

Affiliated association	Number
Church, parish, religious order	190
Political party	5
Citizens' committee	30
Trade union	15
Other political and professional group	20
Foundation	110
Registered association	380
Unregistered association	10
Part or branch of other organization	190
Other formal organization (federation)	55
Other	110

Source: Data compiled during interview with Jan Jakub Wyganski, Klon Foundation, Warsaw, September 14 and 17, 1992.

a. There were 733 NGOs in the sample.

As the state's ability to provide social welfare services continues to decline, and as responsibilities are passed on to local governments that have their own limitations, the role of NGOs will no doubt increase, and they will become a partner in the implementation of the Social Assistance Act. It appears that a program such as the Emergency Social Fund in Bolivia, which did a great deal to improve state-NGO collaboration, would be useful in Poland.

Local Governments and Social Assistance: Case Studies in Ochota and Karchew

The Social Assistance Act of November 1990 recognized the existence of poverty and the need for mechanisms other than the social security system to address the needs of the poor. Yet the extent to which newly formed local governments are equipped to carry out all the provisions of the act remains in doubt. The act delegates the authority for running social assistance centers to the gminas and allocates central government funds to supplement local government resources for the provision of cash assistance benefits worth approximately one-quarter of the average monthly wage to the needy.[195] However, the act does not distinguish between two very different groups: families that are eligible for benefits because they are unemployed and families that receive benefits on other grounds. There is no systematic coordination with the employment offices run by the Employment Fund of the Labor Ministry. Benefits are granted to all those who do not have their own sources of income *and/or* to those whose household income per person does not exceed the minimum pension.[196]

There are several obstacles to implementing the act. The first is the variability of resources and administrative skills among gminas. In resource-poor gminas in depressed areas, the capacity to deliver benefits is far more limited. At the same time, the need is much greater; as a result, the outcome will differ across gminas.[197] In some gminas in poor areas, there are not enough funds to cover eligible applicants. These limitations affect both financial and technical aspects of social assistance centers:[198] in some gminas there are just no personnel available who know how to design and operate a budget, for example.

There is wide latitude in the design of the welfare programs, with much depending on the director and his or her relations with the town councils. The high level of social worker discretion and the lack of professional training also present implementation problems. The act is also vague about the relationship between the social assistance center and the gmina council. Since the social assistance center receives funds independently from the central government, it has a certain amount of freedom. Some town councils argue that all those who work in social assistance should be volunteers rather than professionals. In others the social assistance offices are seen as a tool for patronage, and gmina councils or mayors may seek to control their funds.[199] Social assistance centers are often embroiled in disputes between mayors and their councils. Political competition, parochial rivalries, and inexperience on the part of council members all affect the functioning of the social assistance centers.[200]

It is instructive to look in detail at the experiences of two social assistance centers, one in Warsaw in the Ochota gmina, and the other in its rural environs in the gmina of Karchew.

Ochota

Ochota is a gmina of approximately 200,000 people, many of whom depended for employment on the Ursus tractor factory, a large state-owned factory that is in the process of being privatized and is therefore laying off workers. Ochota's unemployment rate of 5–6 percent is high for Warsaw, where the average rate is 2.2 percent. Even so, the Ochota office has had to seek out its clientele and advertise its services, since the majority of needy people are not accustomed to using social assistance services. Under socialism, only the "dregs" of society were presumed to use social assistance offices, for virtually all other services were provided by the state. Perhaps more important, the social assistance office had to make outreach a major objective, by educating people about the kind of counseling and other in-kind services that it could provide and establishing a broader concept of social assistance—beyond that of cash handouts—namely, that of helping people help themselves.[201]

It has been difficult to establish a broader concept of social assistance, however. One reason is that people are reluctant to ask for help and are even more reluctant to take jobs that are of a lower skill level, even when in need. A social stigma used to be attached to seeking social assistance, and people were far more likely to seek help from the church or other such organizations than the social assistance office. Thus people only resort to coming to the social assistance office when they are in dire straits. Rather ironically, the most common complaints of visitors to the office are, "Why doesn't the state do more and more quickly?" and over the low levels of benefits. As state services in general precluded the need to seek assistance, people merely waited for the state to provide them when in need.[202]

The Ochota office's clientele has been gradually changing, in keeping with the general countrywide changes. Whereas formerly pensioners, the disabled, and families of alcoholics were the main clients, now more and more younger people are coming who are unable to cope with the changing system. The typical visitor is a family that has one member out of work and two children, and is suffering from poverty as well as other problems, such as marital stress. The average age is now thirty to thirty-five.[203]

In general, Ochota's clientele have had a difficult time with the transition and have a feeling of being lost; they tend to be frightened about ongoing and future changes in the welfare system. People seem to sense that they have to look for a job or be unemployed, yet the looking may require skills that are different from those needed under the previous system, when "being successful meant pulling strings to get ahead." Adolescents, for example, have no idea of how to seek a part-time job or to prepare a résumé. People are also reluctant to ask their families for help; the elderly will fall below the poverty line or visit the social assistance office before they ask their children—who may be quite well off—for help. But others take advantage of the system, for example by underreporting income (most of the people on unemployment benefits that visit the Ochota center have to find "moonlight" activities to make ends meet). Implementing a safety net in such a context thus implies adjusting attitudes as well as providing resources.[204]

The director of the Ochota office mentioned how difficult it is to find trained staff. Seventy percent of her office's staff have college degrees, but none of them are in social work. Working in a social assistance office in the past was considered an "easy" job that did not require a technical education. It was suitable for women who had small children at home, for example, since it allowed them to visit the children during the working day.[205] While this situation is gradually changing, and change is also mandated in the law, in rural gminas more remote than Ochota, one can only imagine that the difficulties of finding skilled staff are even greater. Besides being located in Warsaw, Ochota is a relatively wealthy gmina, and thus has the resources to hire skilled staff and to implement the provisions of the act without difficulty.

On a few occasions the Ochota community has become involved in the social assistance center's activities through community labor. Some new businesses also support the center's work, because doing so creates good public relations.[206] Building such community and private sector involvement into the operations of social assistance offices, which may be easier in smaller towns, will be a primary means of overcoming capacity and resource limitations.

Karchew

Karchew, in the rural environs of Warsaw, is a very different community from Ochota. It is a town of approximately 16,000 people: 4,000 of them live in the Wogie housing complex and commute to jobs in Warsaw, 6,000 are in rural areas, and the rest live in the town proper. The clientele group that makes the most demands on the social assistance office and has the highest expectations is from the housing complex. Second in importance are the townspeople. In contrast, the office has to seek out rural people in order to learn of their problems. This is quite difficult logistically: they are far away and the office only has a car one day a week, as is typical of social assistance offices in rural areas.

The director of the office had worked in social assistance for fourteen years before the change of government and was appointed director by the previous municipal council. Although she cited good luck in finding a small but talented staff, she had trouble with the new gmina council, which sought to control the finances of the social assistance office. The social assistance office is financed in part by the municipal budget but primarily by the state; of its 1992 budget, 1 billion zlotys came from the central government and 350,000 came from the gmina. Many members of the council attribute only marginal importance to the social assistance offices and would much rather see its resources going to roads or parks, for example.[207] In part, this may be due to the education levels of the town council: some members have a higher education, but most do not.

Political allegiances may have been another problem, since the director was appointed by the previous council. All meetings pertaining to the social assistance office were held without the director present; the council also determined that the social assistance center should not have an office separate from the gmina, even though the Social Assistance Act requires one. The director protested the council's ruling, in part because it was illegal and in part because she was having great difficulty running the office out of the one room she was assigned in the gmina. The whole issue ended up in the Warsaw Supreme Administrative Court, which ruled in favor of the director.[208]

Not surprisingly, relations with the town council have been difficult since then. Yet the director has managed to keep the council out of the office's day-to-day management. The social assistance office also had some success generating resources from other sources, such as the Labor Ministry, and had plans to start a foundation to raise funds for the office's activities, although not surprisingly, the town council was reluctant to approve any innovations in center management.

Like the Ochota office, the Karchew office has a mixed clientele that has changed in composition in recent years. Increasingly there are families that have no record of financial difficulties but are now having trouble because of unemployment. Typically, such families take anywhere from six months to one and one-half years to change their employment and financial situations.[209] Temporary benefits are usually not enough to sustain a family, particularly if there is any kind of expense-inducing problem, like the breakdown of a necessary appliance. There is also an increase of people with different kinds of financial problems seeking advice. The center provides the relevant contacts with health, employment, or legal offices. The office also offers a variety of in-kind benefits, ranging from meals for poor families to entertainment for senior citizens.

Karchew is also similar to the Ochota office in that some people come to ask for benefits, but when they are offered a job refuse to take it.

Many people are reluctant to seek assistance, even when they are in fairly difficult circumstances. Fear and hopelessness in the face of the current situation seem to be on the rise among the visitors to the Karchew office, reflecting a trend among the Polish population in general.

Conclusion

The barriers to implementing an adequate safety net in Poland are as much political and cultural as they are financial. The partisan nature and short time reference of the political debate have made it difficult to discuss long-term sectoral reforms. Uncertainty and the fear of change have blocked progress, as "populist" politicians have tapped those fears with unrealistic promises. Now that the social costs of economic reform have become increasingly evident, however, safety nets are a growing concern of the public, and politicians are beginning to feel more pressure to act. The Suchocka government's efforts to address the issue, particularly after the strikes of the summer of 1992 and the initiation of the social pact, were an important first step. Much more needs to be done, however, as the May 1993 Solidarity rift with the government over wage and pension increases indicated. Unless the public is educated about the proposed reforms and builds a consensus behind them, they will fail to win political approval and will become unsustainable.

Policymakers in Poland have tended to limit their outlook to Europe when seeking lessons on how to implement safety nets. The experiences of many Latin American countries with employment programs and social investment funds could also provide them with useful lessons, which would apply in particular to depressed regions with concentrated structural unemployment. Extended unemployment benefits are difficult to sustain in such regions because of fiscal constraints, and concerns about political stability call their utility into question. The public works employment programs that were used in the United States during the New Deal, and more recently in Chile during its 1970s and 1980s adjustment program, are relevant examples of how to alleviate poverty and deal with the threat of political unrest posed by regional concentrations of large numbers of unemployed with no prospects for the foreseeable future.

Ultimately, as in all countries undergoing adjustment and facing budget constraints, Polish policymakers will have to seek creative solutions to the poverty problem. Poland can no longer afford to have a social welfare system based on a universal service provision and will have to make progress in identifying the poorest and most vulnerable groups, as well as in developing strategies for reaching them. Existing systems will have to be revamped and targeted at the neediest groups, while wealthier groups must be persuaded to give up benefits that have little relevance to their incomes. At the same time, viable systems of social insurance and public health and education that can serve the entire population *must* accompany the targeting of assistance benefits to the neediest, for both social security and political sustainability reasons. Finally, in many regions of Poland, public employment or training schemes will be political as well as economic necessities. Although such schemes may not be able to provide links to future employment in regions of highly concentrated employment, they could provide needed social infrastructure and, more important, could help prevent the social frustration that would result from having a large percentage of the regional population inactive as well as unemployed.[210]

Delegating the administration of social assistance to local governments is a good idea in theory. In practice the central government must also give attention to the divergences in local government capacity, the inexperience of new local authorities, and the debilitating resource constraints in depressed regions with high levels of structural employment. It will be important to encourage nongovernment actors to complement the efforts of municipalities. One way to deal with these disparities would be to establish a fund, modeled on Bolivia's Emergency Social Fund, that provides technical and financial assistance in response to local government's or NGO's requests. Such a fund would provide an impetus to capacity-building in the weaker gminas, as well as to government-NGO relations, without imposing a centralized solution. It would also solve the problem of disbursing foreign aid, which currently goes to various ministries and agencies with little coordination.[211] In other countries, funds have been able to attract donor resources and yet prevent the donors or competing recipient agencies from duplicating or fragmenting their efforts. In areas where structural unemployment is a major issue, public works programs could be administered by the social fund. The role of social funds is to make up for temporary gaps in ministerial or government capacity in order to address social needs at a time of economic transition—a time in which government institutions are also in transition and facing financial constraints. This is clearly the case in Poland. A fund might also help make the reform of the health and pension systems more politically palatable.

Regardless of which proposals or instruments are chosen, reform of the social safety net in Poland will require a new political debate. Communication will be a critical element to consider in this debate because the public must be educated about the viability of various options, about the potential benefits of reform, and about the long-term costs of attempting to maintain a virtually defunct system of universal benefits. Approaches like the Pact on State Enterprises will be necessary to ensure that the majority of the population will be willing to support a dramatic restructuring of the system of social security despite the costs of the market transition. Slow progress on the reform of the system and the provision of an adequate safety net has already substantially strengthened the hand of the political forces that seek to derail the transition.

In the current political situation, it is unclear what course reform will take. But because the electoral results reflected a clear public mandate for attention to the social costs of reform, and continued deficit spending on the broader universal systems is not financially viable, some sort of targeted safety net system will no doubt have to be put into place by the new government, despite its antireformist campaign rhetoric and its promises to increase universal expenditures. If such progress were to occur, it could help Poland regain political momentum in favor of reform. The alternative—which would be to maintain and try to expand the current insolvent social welfare system—would be a costly policy reversal, both in social and economic terms.

CHAPTER EIGHT

Comparing Experiences with Safety Nets during Market Transitions:
New Coalitions for Reform?

MOST countries that have implemented successful economic reform have introduced a safety net or compensatory program at some point during the process (see table 8-1 and the appendix to the table). As this volume has made clear, the success of safety nets strongly hinges on political factors. On the policy front, establishing a consistent macro-level framework in which poverty reduction can take place requires economic adjustments that are often politically difficult to sustain.[1] On the program front, the implementation of targeted interventions—the allocation of scarce public resources—entails political as well as efficiency choices. The conventional wisdom is that the poor have a weak political voice. In addition, while the poor may bear some of the social costs of adjustment and have the least margin for absorbing negative shocks, they are often not the most negatively affected. Governments usually have legitimate concerns about sustainability in the face of opposition from organized or powerful groups, ranging from organized labor and political parties to the private sector, and thus have few immediate political incentives for helping the poor. An additional dilemma is that the poorest and most needy groups are often the most difficult and costly to reach. Therefore, for political sustainability reasons, compensatory efforts during reform

Table 8-1. *Adjustment and Social Welfare Programs, Selected Countries*

Country	Regime type[a]	Status of adjustment program	Safety net[b]	Status of net	Target group[c]
Argentina	Democracy	Sustained	Yes	Terminated	New and old
Bolivia	Democracy	Sustained	Yes	Sustained	New[d]
Chile	Authoritarian[e]	Sustained	Yes	Sustained	Old
Costa Rica	Democracy	Sustained	Yes	Terminated	New
Ecuador	Democracy	Sustained	Yes	Sustained	New
El Salvador	Democracy	Sustained	Yes	Sustained	New and old
Guinea	Semidemocracy	Sustained	Yes	Sustained	New
Guinea-Bissau	Semidemocracy	Terminated	Yes	Sustained	New
Guyana	Authoritarian[f]	Sustained	Yes	Sustained	New
Jamaica	Democracy	Sustained	Yes	Sustained	New and old
Korea	Democracy	Sustained	Yes	Terminated	New
Mexico	Semidemocracy	Sustained	Yes	Sustained	New and old
Morocco	Modified constitutional monarchy	Sustained	Yes	Terminated	New and old
Poland	Democracy	Sustained	[g]	. . .	New
Philippines	Democracy	Sustained	Yes	Terminated	New and old
Senegal	Democracy	Sustained[h]	Yes	Sustained	New
Spain	Democracy	Sustained	Yes	Terminated	New
Thailand	Democracy[i]	Sustained	Yes	Terminated	New
Turkey	Democracy[j]	Sustained	[k]	. . .	New
Venezuela	Democracy	Sustained	Yes	Sustained	Old
Zambia	Democracy	Sustained	Yes	Sustained	Old

a. Regime type at time adjustment program was implemented.
b. See the appendix to the table (starting on p. 272) for futher information regarding types and components of national programs.
c. Target group refers to the group (either new poor or old poor, or both) intended to receive coverage under original design of safety net.
d. Program was intended to reach the new poor but reached the old poor instead.
e. While begun under the authoritarian regime of Augusto Pinochet, the adjustment program has been sustained under President Patricio Aylwin's administration.
f. While begun under the authoritarian regime of Desmond Hoyte, the adjustment program has been sustained under the administration of newly elected president, Cheddi B. Jagan.
g. System in transition.
h. The adjustment program is sustained but with continuous policy reversals.
i. The democratic government of Thailand was replaced by the National Peacekeeping Council following a military coup on February 23, 1991.
j. The death of President Turgut Ozal has left Turkey with an unstable governing coalition.
k. See the appendix to the table (p. 278) for a description of the type of government program implemented.

tend to focus on vocal, organized, and privileged groups, at the expense of poverty alleviation objectives.

Yet, as this study has also shown, there is no adequate reason to assume that safety nets implemented during economic reform must inevitably be directed at vocal and organized groups at the expense of poverty alleviation objectives. In some cases safety nets can be designed so that they will help reduce poverty over the long term, as well as sustain the reform program. Some of the cases in this study yield valuable lessons about how to attain these goals. Dramatic political change or extreme economic crisis, for example, by altering or undermining the relative weights of powerful interest groups, can open political opportunities for governments to redirect public resources to less privileged groups. At such times, reaching out to previously marginalized groups rather than focusing on the vocal opponents of reform may allow governments to circumvent the traditional new poor–old poor dilemma. This may also require the participation of the poor, both in the implementation of safety net programs and in the political dialogue, in order to make resource shifts in their direction sustainable in the future. Effective communication efforts on the part of governments can be determining factors in such a process. In other cases, it may be necessary to extend safety net efforts to nonpoor groups that lose in relative terms during reform, in order to make the allocation of some resources to the poor politically salable. Ultimately, if reform efforts are abandoned for a return to unsustainable fiscal distortions or "populist" economic policies, the poor will suffer the most.

International trends in recent years support an approach of directing safety net efforts to the poor rather than to the vocal. Resource constraints as well as changing political views have had a great impact on social policy worldwide. The focus of government spending has shifted from development efforts relying on large-scale infrastructure projects and universal subsidies to the universal provision of only basic health and education services, along with targeted interventions—so-called safety nets—to help the neediest groups. Largely influenced by the experience of the Emergency Social Fund in Bolivia, social funds have become a primary means for the delivery of such interventions. Introduced by the ESF, the concept of incorporating market principles—via the demands of beneficiaries—into program design has proved to be an effective tool for reaching the poor and for building local institutions.

The most evident drawback of the social fund approach is that the poorest groups, which tend to be weakly organized, are the least equipped to solicit benefits from demand-based programs. While non-poor and poor alike can benefit from a variety of productivity-enhancing measures related to safety nets, such as credit schemes or increased investment in education, the poorest of the poor often face other obstacles, such as malnutrition or chronic diseases, that prevent them from benefiting from such policies. Concentrating all benefits on the most vocal groups is not the most effective safety net strategy; but focusing on the very poorest may not be either, since reaching them requires additional administrative time, resources, and targeted policies distinct from broader safety net programs.

Several broad lessons emerge from the field research conducted in the six cases in this volume—Chile, Bolivia, Peru, Zambia, Senegal, and Poland—and provide a basis for the analysis of the political economy of safety nets. The first lesson is that open political environments are more likely to be places in which there is a broad base of support for economic reform and therefore a policy atmosphere in which effective poverty reduction can take place.[2] In an open environment, the government is more likely to communicate with the public and increase popular understanding of the reform process, an effective means to create a political base of support for change.[3] The second and related lesson is that open political systems are more likely to encourage the participation of diverse groups such as nongovernmental organizations (NGOs) and local institutions in their antipoverty strategies. This enhances their capacity to reach poor and marginalized groups, thereby giving those groups a stake in the ongoing process of economic reform. The most effective poverty reduction efforts invite the poor to participate instead of treating them as passive recipients of government subsidies. And enhancing the political influence of the poor is essential to the sustainability of shifts in resource allocation that benefit poorer groups.

A final lesson is that strategies that rely on the participation of beneficiaries and the organizations that represent them—as social funds do—have the effect of strengthening the capacity of these institutions, thereby giving previously marginalized groups a more effective political voice and making longer-term contributions to poverty reduction. Giving previously marginalized groups a new stake in the system and increased influence may result in new coalitions supporting economic reform among previously disorganized but numerically significant sectors of society.

Such a strategy may be more cost-effective than attempting to placate relatively privileged groups whose positions are eroded by reform, since they are likely to remain opposed to reform regardless of compensation. This does not imply that such groups do not merit some form of compensation but suggests that all government efforts should not be concentrated on them.

The focus on short-term safety net programs raises a host of questions about their long-term sustainability and their relation to public sector institutions. Safety nets are often used as catchall terms, but they *cannot* be expected to substitute for coherent macroeconomic policy or efficient basic social welfare services, such as public health and education. Indeed, at times the existence of safety nets serves as an excuse for governments to postpone or avoid the more politically difficult processes of social sector reform. Theoretically, optimal central and local-level policies eliminate the need for social safety nets altogether. Yet because the reforms that are necessary to correct macroeconomic distortions and to revamp inefficient sectoral ministries take time to implement, there is a clear need for short-term, targeted interventions to protect poor or vulnerable groups during the process.

Poverty Alleviation during Adjustment: Field Experiences

The following review of experiences with various kinds of programs will shed some light on the relationship among safety nets, the political sustainability of reform, and poverty alleviation. The final section highlights lessons for policymakers involved in the implementation of safety nets in the context of economic reform.

Chile

One of the first and most effective efforts to protect the poor during adjustment was implemented in Chile.[4] Yet the authoritarian nature of the regime implementing that effort made the experience less useful as a model in terms of the political dynamics determining the allocation of public resources. Chile had an extensive social welfare structure before adjustment; the system was revamped and targeted to the poorest groups during the Pinochet years. While social spending per capita declined during the adjustment, it actually increased for the poorest two deciles.

Yet many people at the margin lost access to what had been one of the most comprehensive social systems in Latin America. This was not necessarily a positive result, nor is it one that a government more responsive to electoral pressure would be able to implement. Nevertheless, it proved extremely effective in protecting the poorest sectors during a severe economic crisis. The infant mortality rate, for example, not only continued to decline but accelerated in its rate of decline and is one of the lowest on the continent, below that of Colombia, Argentina, and Mexico.

From 1975 to 1987, Chile implemented large-scale employment programs in conjunction with targeted social sector spending. At the height of the economic crisis in 1982, with unemployment at almost 30 percent, the programs employed up to 13 percent of the work force. The programs paid one-fourth to one-half the minimum wage, thereby providing a self-targeting mechanism, although many critics argue that the subsidy was far too low. Implementation at the beginning was a bit haphazard, and labor was often not used productively, tainting the image of the programs. With time, program design was improved and incorporated some private sector hiring and training. Workers in the programs linked to the private sector were often able to find permanent jobs with the same firms, a positive effect in terms of poverty alleviation. Although the programs had several flaws—particularly the authoritarian manner in which they were implemented—even their harshest critics agree that the existence of the programs, and their sheer scale and duration, reduced the potential for social explosion at a time of unprecedented unemployment rates. It is unlikely that a demand-based program could attain the systematic coverage, scale, and speedy implementation that the Chilean programs did, particularly with the resources available in relation to population size.[5]

The Pinochet regime's protection of the poorest—through a variety of programs—is an example worth noting. Chile's record in comparison with that of its neighbors in protecting basic health and welfare of the poor during a period of adjustment, and targeting and reaching the very poorest, is indeed remarkable. Yet according to other indicators, such as income distribution and per capita consumption, Chile fared less well.

It is no coincidence that the government of President Aylwin made poverty reduction a primary objective of its economic program. The new government also set up a demand-based social fund, the Fund for Solidarity and Social Investment. Because line ministries are quite efficient and have extensive coverage in Chile, FOSIS can work the way that social funds are in theory intended to: to complement the works of line ministries with outreach programs for the poorest communities and for specific groups, such as unskilled youth in the case of Chile. In countries such as Bolivia or Senegal, because the public sector is so weak, autonomous, and efficient social funds become catchall programs and often get involved in providing services that line ministries are responsible for.

FOSIS also seeks to correct a major flaw in the Pinochet government's approach, its failure to incorporate any kind of beneficiary participation. The authoritarian government's top-down manner precluded the kind of participation from below that often enhances the sustainability of programs, and limited their positive political effects. Jobs were withdrawn from shantytowns that were active in political protests, for example. Finally, because the targeting of social welfare spending entails political as well as economic choices and the Pinochet regime was free of the constraints faced by most democratic regimes, its lessons on the political sustainability front are far less clear-cut and its targeting of the poorest at the expense of middle sectors not necessarily a replicable experience.

Bolivia

Bolivia's Emergency Social Fund was the first social fund of its kind and attracted a great deal of international as well as national attention.[6] Enthusiasts of the ESF commend its demand-based approach, its efficiency and transparency, and its rapid results. Critics question the program's ability to provide permanent poverty alleviation or to target the poorest sectors, as well as its position outside the public sector. The program did not reach those most directly affected by adjustment, the tin miners, and it also had a disproportionately low effect on the poorest two poverty deciles. The poorest regions benefited least from the ESF in per capita expenditures: the wealthiest of five income areas received US$23.97 per capita while the poorest received US$9.45. ESF workers represented 6.25 percent and 7.75 percent of workers in income deciles 1 and 2, respectively, but 13.25 percent, 21.5 percent, and 15.3 percent, respectively, in deciles 3, 4, and 5. By regional standards, however, deciles 3, 4, and 5 in Bolivia are still considered quite poor. And because it was situated outside the permanent public sector, the program did little to further the process of institutional or social sector reform at the central level. Indeed, its existence on such a large and visible scale may have even provided the government with an excuse to postpone more difficult institutional reforms. Yet the program clearly did have positive effects by demonstrating that a very different means of operating was possible in the public sector.[7]

The ESF administered US$240 million in its four years of operation, and the projects that it created, ranging from infrastructure such as health posts, schools, and low-income homes to services such as job creation and school lunch programs, benefited more than 1 million poor, a substantial number in a population of just under 7 million. Despite relatively weak targeting, the program had a considerable impact on the political sustainability of economic reform and on poverty alleviation.

To begin with, the ESF had a positive political impact in that it demonstrated that it could work in a transparent and nonpartisan manner— with local governments and NGOs of all political bents—in a country where aid programs were usually influenced by patronage politics. The ESF resulted in an unprecedented collaboration of efforts between NGOs—the groups with the closest ties to the poor—and the state. This allowed the fund to reach the poor in remote communities that had rarely, if ever, seen the state follow through on its promises. The fund also enhanced local capacity to carry out projects by providing municipal governments with independent funds. And because of its demand-based structure, the fund could not be monopolized by any one political actor at election time: a diversity of actors, from the governing party to local governments and NGOs, could claim credit for ESF projects. As a result, there was no correlation between ESF funds and the outcomes of the 1989 presidential and 1987–89 municipal elections.[8]

The fund provided the poor with a way to help themselves, thereby giving them a stake in the ongoing process of economic reform. By doing so, it generated support for the government at a critical time—if not for the adjustment program per se—among previously marginalized sectors. This support increased the feasibility of economic reform. Even if the ESF had instead focused its efforts on those who were directly affected by the adjustment program—the tin miners—it is unlikely that it could have eroded their entrenched opposition to the government's economic strategy. The rapid pace of adjustment coupled with the crash of world tin prices reduced the political power of their traditionally influential confederation. This implies not that those who are directly affected by adjustment do not merit compensation but that most efforts directed at those groups will have a marginal effect on the political sustainability of adjustment.[9] Pro-poor programs implemented during adjustment may at times create opportunities for building pro-reform coalitions among the poorest groups by enhancing their economic potential and political voice, and these are also important instruments for reducing poverty.

Peru

The Peruvian case unfortunately serves to demonstrate that programs designed to protect or benefit the poor, if carelessly implemented, can do more harm than good.[10] They often alienate the potential beneficiaries, as Peru's Program of Temporary Income Support demonstrates. The PAIT was a public works employment program, modeled on Chile's programs, which was implemented in Lima's shantytowns by the 1985–90 APRA government. The program provided sorely needed income support as well as some socially useful infrastructure. Yet it was implemented in an extremely top-down and partisan manner, with a great deal of clientelism in hiring as well as constant political manipulation of the workers. PAIT workers were often taken to political rallies to cheer for President Garcia, for example. The program's budget was also manipulated. Hiring was drastically increased before elections, but then jobs faded out quietly afterward. This system kept applicants in a constant state of uncertainty.[11] The perception that the program was used as a tool by the governing party ultimately undermined its public image. Most damaging, however, was the program's excessive centralism and top-down implementation, which led it to duplicate and undermine the efforts of local self-help groups that were critical to the survival of the poor. Its effects ran directly counter to the capacity building that is integral to poverty reduction.

Whatever marginal effects the PAIT program had on poverty alleviation were temporary, and the disruption caused to local organizations often had permanent effects. The case of Peru demonstrates the importance of having local groups participate in the programs that are designed to benefit them, as well as the damage that programs for the poor can cause if they are manipulated for partisan political purposes.

After the Garcia government debacle, the Fujimori government's attempt to implement programs for the poor also failed, largely because of the political context. Hyperinflation and extreme macroeconomic distortions left the government little choice but to implement a draconian stabilization and adjustment program in August 1990. In conjunction with the economic program, the government announced an emergency social fund to address the social costs of its austerity policies. Yet no program materialized until more than a year later, when, under pressure from external donors concerned about the social costs of adjustment, the government announced Foncodes: the National Fund for Social Compensation and Development. Two years later, the new fund still had not got fully off the ground. The primary reason was political: there was no presidential commitment to insulate the program from politics, as there was with the ESF. Indeed, the president insisted on naming the former secretary general of his political movement, who had little managerial experience, president of the fund, despite objections from donors. The weak administrative capacity and obvious political bent of Foncodes alienated many NGOs and community groups early on.

Another drawback is that the main architects of the social fund never perceived it as an integral part of the overall reform program. Thus the program has never been allocated sufficient priority—or resources in the domestic budget—to demonstrate the strong government commitment that is necessary to ensure its credibility and ultimately its success. Only in late 1992, in part because of pressure from donor agencies, did the president replace his political appointee with a manager from the private sector as head of Foncodes. Government spending on the program was also expected to double for 1993. Yet the government's commitment to the program remains marginal at best, and it will be difficult for it to overcome its image as a political tool and afterthought of the government.[12] Given the institutional autonomy of most social funds, they cannot operate without a high-level commitment to insulate them from politics *and* to guarantee them access to sufficient resources. No level of external support can substitute for a domestic political commitment. The Peruvian case is, unfortunately, a case in point.

Senegal

The two cases from Africa in the study, Senegal and Zambia, provide an interesting contrast in terms of the effects of political opening and the pace of reform on sustaining adjustment, reaching the poor, and building institutional capacity. In Senegal, adjustment has progressed at a rather slow pace for more than a decade, and the political system has remained a relatively stable—if limited—democracy. The first major attempt to compensate the losers from adjustment was the Délégation à l'Insertion, à la Réinsertion et à l'Emploi, set up in 1987. The DIRE, which was funded by U.S. AID, the World Bank, and the government of Senegal, provided civil servants who had retired voluntarily (*deflates*) and university graduates who would previously have gotten jobs in the civil service (*maitrisards*) with credits of up to US$50,000 to start their own businesses. Owing to the lack of training and follow-up, and to the prevalence of clientelistic criteria in the disbursement of loans, the DIRE had a very poor record, in terms of both repayment and the mortality of enterprises (32 percent). In addition, since the program's budget was administered through the public treasury, approximately US$3 million were lost or "filtered" in the process. The beneficiaries were a relatively privileged group, and the projects funded included bookstores and travel agencies in central Dakar. In short, an enormous amount of money for a country as poor as Senegal was squandered on relatively privileged groups.

Because of its poor record, the DIRE gradually faded out. Despite the program's original high visibility, its effects on the political sustainability of adjustment were minimal: the program's image was dominated by clientelism and the governing party limited its impact on any groups except its direct beneficiaries. Moreover, the program did not have any effect on poverty alleviation.

After a wave of civil unrest in February 1988, the government made another attempt to address the social costs of adjustment and set up the Agetip program in conjunction with the World Bank. Agetip was influenced by the success of the ESF and was also set up as an independent agency with a private sector director, in sharp contrast to the DIRE. Agetip responded to proposals from municipalities for labor-intensive infrastructure projects. In terms of efficiency and number of projects, Agetip has been remarkably successful and has even been recommended as a model for the reform of the Senegalese public sector.[13]

Yet Agetip, too, has been influenced by the political context in which it operates. There is no debate about reaching the poor and needy groups in Senegal, nor is there any kind of cooperative relationship between the government and the NGOs, which are the only organizations with extensive links to the poor. Agetip does not use poverty criteria for allocating its projects. Moreover, since the opposition boycotted the 1990 municipal elections, the only proposals that Agetip funds are those from mayors of the governing party. Although in some cases such proposals are directly related to poverty reduction, such as installing sewage and water facilities, in others they may be pet projects of the mayor, such as renovating the town hotel. On the other hand, the agency does employ primarily unskilled youth.

Because Agetip does not work with NGOs, it has very weak links to the poorest groups. There is a widespread popular perception that Agetip is "of the system" or is a tool of the governing party, and thus its effect on the political sustainability of adjustment—at least among those groups who are not of the governing party—has been limited. Its record on the poverty alleviation front is mixed: although it has provided a large number of temporary jobs and some sorely needed infrastructure in poor areas, the limited nature of beneficiary participation, particularly of the organizations that are most closely linked to the poor, has reduced its potential in terms of both project sustainability and capacity building.

In Senegal, the goal of poverty reduction—and indeed even any debate on poverty—has been subordinate to the interests of politically vocal groups within or linked to the state sector. The slow pace of reform has given these groups much more opportunity to "protect" their privileged positions within the system. The limited nature of political participation, meanwhile, has resulted in a suspicion of government-sponsored initiatives, limiting the potential impact of Agetip. It stands in sharp contrast to Bolivia's ESF, which, by working with a variety of political parties and NGOs was able to create support for adjustment—or at least goodwill toward the government implementing adjustment—among the sectors of society that had traditionally not had access to state benefits. In Senegal, it was the traditionally privileged groups that benefited the most from government efforts to address the social costs of adjustment.

Zambia

Zambia provides a sharp contrast to Senegal. Whereas adjustment in Zambia was postponed for years under the United National Independence Party (UNIP) government, and all kinds of state benefits were linked to party membership, the October 31, 1991, elections ushered in dramatic political change. Frederick Chiluba and the Movement for Multiparty Democracy (MMD), which campaigned on a pro-adjustment platform, took more than 75 percent of the vote. Upon taking office, the government began to implement a pro–free market economic strategy *and* publicly made reaching the poorest and most vulnerable groups a priority. Because of the enormous political changes, the influence of groups that had traditionally had privileged access to state resources was substantially reduced, and the government was thereby able to focus its efforts on the poorest. The sustainability of these changes will depend on the coherence of the MMD coalition, as well as on the extent to which previously marginalized groups can exercise an effective political voice.

Maize meal price policy is telling. The heavily subsidized price of maize—which consumed more than 15 percent of government revenue—had been the political bête noir for the Kaunda government, and repeated attempts to raise the price resulted in food riots and even a coup attempt in 1990. The coupon system, which was in theory expected to provide cheaper maize to poor groups, had become a tool of the UNIP party, while many of the poor were excluded from the system and had to pay three to four times the official price of maize on the black market. When the Chiluba government liberalized the price of maize in December 1991, keeping subsidies on roller meal—the coarse grind that only the poorest eat—there was no popular unrest. This was due in large part to the government's efforts to explain the measures to the public. Removing the subsidy also freed scarce public resources to allocate to the most vulnerable groups. In contrast, the Kaunda government usually announced measures overnight without explanation, which resulted in widespread protests. While under Kaunda entrenched interest groups with a stake in state subsidies had much more influence, the dramatic nature of political change in 1991, as well as the pace of reform measures, undermined the influence of such groups and made it possible to focus on the poor.

The Social Recovery Fund and Micro-Projects Unit programs in Zambia, which are funded by the World Bank and the European Community and are run out of the government's National Development Planning Office, are good examples of programs that reach the needy rather than the privileged. The SRF and the MPU, also influenced by the ESF, respond to proposals from community organizations, mostly for the renovation of existing infrastructure.[14] The programs require community contributions in cash or in labor. They have been successful in revitalizing the self-help spirit in many communities and in reaching remote areas long neglected by the state and are being expanded substantially under the Chiluba government.

By giving communities contact with and a stake in a government poverty alleviation program, the SRF and the MPU may enhance the political sustainability of economic reform and thereby create a basis of support among previously marginalized but numerically significant groups. In addition, the demand-based nature of the program inherently encourages such groups to exercise their political voice, something unprecedented in the Zambian context, where a one-party state dominated the system for several decades.

Poland

Poland presents a very different case that demonstrates the political constraints of reaching the poor and vulnerable.[15] In January 1990, soon after its inauguration, the first noncommunist government in Poland launched a dramatic, Bolivia-style stabilization and adjustment program. The program successfully stabilized hyperinflation. Yet political uncertainty soon stalled structural reforms, as several attempts to maintain a coherent government coalition in Parliament failed. Reforms such as privatization of the financially unviable state industrial conglomerates have been postponed because they are creating an unsustainable drain on the state budget. The longer such reforms are postponed, the greater the anxiety about their potential social costs, and the stronger the political opposition to adjustment, despite the absence of any viable alternative proposals.

The rapidly increasing budget deficit makes it difficult for the government to maintain the current social welfare system. Even before the collapse of public finances, the system, which is based on the concept of universal free access to all benefits, was known for its poor-quality services, unequal access, "informal" payments for services, and skewed incentives. Among other negative effects, the incentive structure promotes premature retirement among pensioners in the social security system, and excessive usage of specialized care and emergency and hospital services in the health system, which creates dramatic shortages. Government insolvency, coupled with the need to provide protection for the poor and unemployed, whose numbers will increase in the future, dictates an immediate revamping of the social welfare system.

Proposals being considered for reform of the health and social security systems in government circles would guarantee basic health care and social security insurance for those who needed them, while introducing private providers and the choice of services for those who could afford them. This plan would alleviate the financial burden on the government and enhance service quality by introducing competition. Concurrently, government resources would be targeted to provide a safety net for the increasing numbers of poor and unemployed. Unemployment before 1990 in Poland was "hidden," because excess workers were maintained on government and industrial payrolls. Open unemployment is now running at 12 percent, and in towns or regions that were dependent on insolvent state-owned enterprises it is as high as 30 percent. There is a clear need for programs that are more extensive than unemployment insurance for these regions. Poland is a classic case in which an extrasectoral effort, like a social fund or Chile-style public works program, would be an ideal mechanism to provide employment and infrastructure improvement, while giving impetus to the development of municipal government. Unfortunately, the political debate on the safety net lags far behind the proposals for reform, centering on emotional criticisms of government proposals rather than on any provision of realistic alternatives. This is a major impediment to progress of any kind.

Among the people there is widespread ignorance—and anxiety—about future social welfare because of the incoherent debate and the government's past failure to communicate or explain the ongoing reform process. Populist opposition movements have been quick to capitalize on this anxiety. By the summer of 1992, this anxiety and the lack of attention to the safety net issue led to a series of industrial strikes that virtually paralyzed the government and forced it to make the safety net issue a high priority. In September 1992 the government announced a social pact on the future of state enterprises that was to be negotiated with unions and the private sector. The government's new attempt to communicate its proposals to the public and to incorporate popular participation was a first step toward a realistic treatment of safety net and poverty issues in Poland.

The government also needs to find mechanisms for new forms of social assistance. Elected local governments were only recently constituted, but have been given primary responsibility for the provision of benefits to the poor and unemployed. Policymakers face a host of unresolved issues about the nature of benefits, their financing, who should be eligible for them, and their delivery. In the absence of progress, the appeal of both right- and left-wing strains of authoritarian populists is on the rise, fueled by latent fears about social welfare.[16] Rising poverty and the absence of an adequate safety net threaten to derail economic reform and jeopardize the democratic transition in Poland. Policymakers could clearly benefit from the lessons of Latin American experiences with social funds and public works programs.

Lessons for Future Efforts?

Several lessons emerge from the experiences of the countries examined in the preceding chapters. Safety net programs implemented during economic reform, such as social funds, can reduce poverty and have positive political effects on sustaining economic reform. They are also much less likely to arouse political opposition than are more obvious, long-term asset transfers, and governments clearly have policy concerns at a time when they are implementing many other "unpopular" policies.[17] Yet the success of such programs hinges, among other factors, on their operating in a transparent manner that incorporates the participation of the poor and thereby enhances their economic potential *and* political influence. The ability to perform in such a way on a large scale depends on available resources, institutional structure, and commitment from the highest levels to insulate the programs from partisan pressures, a commitment that existed in Bolivia but was clearly missing in Peru. Programs must be implemented as an integral part of the macroeconomic reform effort, so that successive governments will have a stake in their implementation, and so that beneficiaries have a stake in the ongoing process of economic transformation. These conditions are not always readily available. To a certain extent, the resources available and the political leadership in the case of Bolivia's ESF were the exception rather than the rule. Even then, the ESF was not able to reach the poorest; indications are that other demand-based programs such as Agetip (and the Pronasol program in Mexico, discussed in the appendix chapter) have not been able to either.[18] In some cases, such as Senegal, the authoritarian and clientelist nature of the party and local government structures serves as an additional constraint to the inherent difficulty that demand-based programs have in reaching the poorest sectors.

One gauge of a program's openness to various political actors is whether the allocation of funds correlates with electoral objectives. In the case of the PAIT program in Peru, the APRA party blatantly manipulated program enrollments for electoral reasons, dramatically increasing jobs offered in municipalities held by the opposition. Yet the strategy had only partial success in attracting votes, because the partisan manipulation of the program was obvious to much of the public. In the case of Bolivia's ESF, although actors at all different levels—from the governing party's presidential candidate to opposition party mayors—tried to reap electoral benefits from completed or planned ESF projects, there was no correlation between numbers of ESF projects and electoral results.[19] That was because the ESF allowed genuine participation from a variety of organizations and political parties. Thus municipal authorities or NGOs of the political opposition could take as much credit for ESF projects as the Nationalist Revolutionary Movement (MNR) government, even though the ESF was clearly affiliated with the MNR in the public vision, as is Mexico's Pronasol program with the Partido Revolucionario Institucional (PRI) (see the appendix).

There is no established link between democracy and reaching the poor, however. Even in democracies the poor are usually poor with respect to political voice as well as to resources. Ironically, of the cases covered here, the Pinochet regime had the most success in targeting the poorest, precisely because it did not have to answer to the more vocal middle sectors that a democratic regime would have to contend with.[20] However, a broader view of poverty reduction, in which the poor contribute to their own solutions, might place less value on the ability to target the poorest of the poor than on the program's ability to incorporate the participation of disadvantaged groups, even if they are not the poorest ones. Many projects, such as new schools or health posts, also have indirect positive effects for poorer groups that did not participate in their design. And, as is mentioned earlier in this chapter, reaching the poorest of the poor may require a totally different set of policies from those needed to reach the rest of the poor. Needless to say, targeting can entail high costs in time and resources.[21] In this light, the success or failure of demand-based programs seems to hinge more on their ability to generate autonomous grass-roots participation than on their reaching the poorest among the poor.

Institutional autonomy and the positioning of safety net programs are a concern in many countries. On the one hand, autonomy allows for rapid, transparent action that bypasses public sector bureaucratic procedures—which are often costly and time consuming—and directly channels benefits to the poor. A case in point is the DIRE in Senegal, which incurred a "loss" of US$3 million to the public sector. On the other hand, the longevity of extra-institutional safety net programs is uncertain, since neither their budgets nor their operating procedures have any permanent guarantees. To the extent that such programs are considered short-term measures during periods of adjustment or recovery, institutional autonomy is less of a concern. To the extent that they are considered longer-term complements to social sector policies, it is usually necessary to establish institutional links. Other programs have a hybrid nature: Agetip in Senegal is a semipublic corporation that is managed as a private sector firm. The successor to the ESF in Bolivia, the Social Investment Fund, remains a separate, autonomous agency that responds to the president but has new formalized links with the sectoral ministries. Chile's FOSIS is run out of the planning ministry.[22]

Institutional development plays a key role in determining the appropriate kind of program. Chile and Costa Rica, for example, both had a tradition of efficient public social sectors and strong pro-poor political parties; these institutions could provide the basis for implementing safety net policies through existing public institutions. In Bolivia, by contrast, such institutions were notoriously weak, and the only means to launch a wide-scale effort with relative speed was to bypass them altogether.

Political context also makes an enormous difference in the possibilities for redirecting resources to the poor. Dramatic political change, as in Zambia, or swift implementation of stabilization and adjustment, as in Bolivia, provides unique opportunities for doing so. Severe crises expand the pool of potential winners from reform.[23] Less open political systems and stalled economic reform, as in Senegal, give entrenched interest groups greater opportunities to protect their positions. The budget cutting that stabilization and adjustment usually require is far more difficult in contexts where patron-client ties serve as important bases of political support.[24] In Senegal, economic change was less sudden than in either Bolivia or Zambia and political opening far less straightforward, limiting the potential of programs that in theory were genuinely demand based. In Senegal, extensive political change seems unlikely in the near future, and thus programs will be limited by the lack of genuine party competition, particularly at the local level. In such instances it may well be necessary to provide some benefits to nonpoor or relatively privileged groups in order to make the allocation of some resources to the poor more salable politically. Strengthening the voice of popular sector groups may help, although it is unlikely to do so in entrenched authoritarian or one-party systems.[25] Increasing the political voice of the poor may also help to sustain changes in resource allocation in their direction. A note of caution is necessary, however. Although the reallocation of resources to temporary programs such as social funds is more politically palatable than is the permanent redistribution of assets such as land, temporary transfers are easier to reverse and thus may be more difficult to sustain for a prolonged period.[26]

The ability of governments to communicate their reform policies has an important impact on how they are received politically, as the cases of Peru and Zambia demonstrate. This same ability to communicate may facilitate the redirecting of resources to the poor. That was clearly true in Zambia; the contrasting situation in Poland demonstrates how the failure to communicate can result in political stalemate and, in the case of the safety net issue, lead to heightened popular anxiety.

The origins of many programs can be traced to the political context in which adjustment is implemented. Senegal's Agetip originated in the context of major civil unrest in protest to the social costs of adjustment in the aftermath of the February elections; Chile's employment programs were set up because the Pinochet government feared the public protest over unprecedented unemployment rates; and the Polish government finally began to act on the safety net issues because of the political challenge posed by the widespread strikes related to the social costs of economic reform. This context often plays a large role in determining what kind of program is set up and who benefits.

In addition to the political context, the *nature* of pro-poor programs is a factor in determining their political as well as antipoverty impact. Demand-based programs that require community contributions or participation are effective at creating the sustainable kinds of projects that are key to alleviating poverty, particularly if they become self-sustaining community initiatives or if they enhance local institutional capacity. At the same time, centrally implemented public works schemes may be better at providing rapid, mass-scale relief of the social costs of adjustment and at targeting the poorest groups. Public works schemes are a good short-term mechanism, but must also be supplemented with productivity-enhancing policies, such as credit, training, or community development, if they are to have longer-term effects.[27]

Note, too, that safety net programs cannot be expected to substitute for basic service provision or to make lasting changes in asset distribution or ownership structures. Neither can they make up for major adjustment-related trends in real wages or sectoral spending. At best, they are useful complements to the activities of weak sectoral ministries, and at the same time they can provide short-term income or employment; they cannot substitute for long-run economic growth. Yet social funds *can* make revolutionary changes at the local institutional level by allowing previously marginalized groups—such as NGOs or neighborhood organizations—to participate in safety net activities, by cooperating with the state in the design or delivery of social services by providing more effective channels for demand-making. And by investing in areas such as education and health infrastructure and encouraging organization and participation by beneficiaries, such funds make longer-term contributions to human capital formation.[28]

Ultimately, safety nets or other such initiatives cannot substitute for a broader central-level commitment to poverty alleviation, and their organizations cannot take the place of functioning line ministries. Perhaps more important, a central-level commitment is needed to allow actors of all political bents to participate. Without such commitments, the impact of such programs will be limited.

Implications for Policymakers

Many of the conclusions in this volume point to the constraints that political context, resource endowments, and the extent and nature of poverty place on policymakers. At the same time, they point to the political opportunities that can be created by dramatic economic reform and to some of the ways in which policymakers can take advantage of those opportunities.

One lesson is clear: policymakers must move quickly whenever opportunities arise, whether for macroeconomic reform or for safety net and social sector reform. In addition, safety net programs must be presented as integral parts of reform programs. Doing so will enhance their political impact, because the public will associate them with the overall reform program. It will also enhance their sustainability and visibility, because policymakers (and, where relevant, donors) will link their stake in the safety net program with that in the reform program.

Communication is clearly important to the popular acceptance of reforms and is also a cost-effective and noncontroversial policy measure. And to build new coalitions in support of economic reform and of the reallocation of public social welfare resources, it will be necessary, among other things, to inform the public about the potential benefits of change.

Another clear lesson is that a nonpartisan or private sector management approach tends to increase the efficiency and political potential of safety nets. Policymakers in almost all contexts can choose to rely on private sector managers rather than politicians for program management.

In addition, when the government or public sector institutions are largely discredited, placing the program outside the traditional public sector institutional framework makes it far more likely to establish a credible public image. There are clear examples that policymakers can use to determine what the appropriate links might be between short-term safety net programs and permanent public sector institutions. Bolivia and Chile provide useful contrasts: Bolivia, which has notoriously inefficient sectoral ministries, opted for a totally autonomous safety net program; Chile, which has relatively efficient public sector institutions, ran its employment programs out of the public sector and now has its social fund in the planning ministry.

When possible, a demand-based approach, combined with the participation of local institutions and nongovernmental organizations, tends to make programs more sustainable and gives beneficiaries a sense that they have a stake in the process of reform. In some cases, however, the urgency or scale of the employment situation, for example, may call for a central-level public works approach, at least in the short term. Again, past experience gives policymakers tangible examples on which to base their approach.

If investments in safety nets are to yield long-term results, they must also be part of broader strategies for social reform. Policymakers must actively seek to establish such links. When such reforms are politically or financially implausible, safety net efforts can still contribute to longer-term institutional reform. These contributions can be made at the local level. In Bolivia, for example, the ESF was able to enhance the longer-term capacity of local institutions and nongovernmental organizations. When the reform of public sector institutions is more plausible in the short term, such as Chile, safety net programs can have important effects on the process, by introducing the concepts of transparency, targeting, and demand-based approaches into public sector operations.

Since many of the effects of safety nets and compensation are as yet uncertain, experimentation will be unavoidable at times. In all cases, however, some simple concepts can be relied on to guide these efforts: the advantages of demand-based resource allocation and local participation, good communication with the public, private sector approaches to management, and the need to link safety net efforts with the overall reform program. All these ideas can contribute to the better implementation of safety nets and other compensatory efforts.

Conclusion

Social safety net programs implemented during economic reform can
have positive effects on political sustainability and poverty reduction, but
their ability to do so depends on the kind of program that is implemented,
on the one hand, and the political and institutional context, on the other.
Demand-based programs, for example, are most effective at simultaneously reducing poverty and attaining political sustainability. Through
their emphasis on autonomous beneficiary participation, such programs
enhance the political voice of the poor as well as their economic potential.
Centrally implemented public works programs, however, are better suited
for rapid, mass-scale targeting of the poorest sectors. In a more developed institutional context like Chile's or Costa Rica's, implementation is
facilitated by the use of existing public sector institutions. In the less
developed or inefficient institutional context that is more typical of countries undergoing a market transition, programs may initially have to be
autonomous from the public sector to achieve sufficient efficiency, scale,
and visibility. Political context and the pace and nature of economic
change are also important variables. Furthermore, government communication with the public is vital to generating political support for change.
Doing that will make it easier to introduce new approaches to social
welfare policy, through safety net policies in the short term and institutional reform in the longer term.

The safety net programs that are best suited to alleviating poverty and
ensuring sustainability are demand-based social funds. To be effective,
they require a degree of political openness as well as autonomy from
partisan or clientelistic influence groups. When the government is less
open, different kinds of programs may be appropriate. When the government is extremely vulnerable to the influence of pressure groups, the
extension of compensatory benefits to nonpoor but influential "losers"
may be a prerequisite—for sustainability reasons—to allocating some
resources to the poor, who will suffer the most if reform is abandoned.

Demand-based social funds are a particularly useful way to allow
community organizations, NGOs, and other grass-roots groups to participate in the small-scale initiatives that are usually out of the domain of
sectoral ministries but are key to self-sustaining development at the local
level, and therefore to poverty reduction. The demonstration effects of
community groups and NGOs organizing to present proposals to social
funds—and obtaining rapid and tangible results—are important to pro-

moting self-help methods of reducing poverty *and* to giving a new political voice and stake in the reform process to previously marginalized groups. This process can have significant effects on the political sustainability of economic reform. Such programs can also play a new role in helping remote or marginalized communities make contact with the formidable bureaucratic structures that characterize the public sectors of most developing countries. And finally, because they are government-linked institutions that introduce the concepts of efficiency, transparency, demand-based allocation, and subcontract-based implementation to the provision of social services, such safety net programs can serve as a basis for more general public sector reform.

Ultimately, the degree of representation and genuine popular participation that particular governments are willing to allow will be the factor that determines how well safety net programs can promote local institutional development and increase the political voice of the poor, and therefore the political sustainability of economic reform more generally. In the same manner, the programs' ability to reduce poverty will inevitably depend on the government's willingness to make them function efficiently and transparently, *and* on the broader context for poverty reduction, such as resource endowments. In order to succeed, the programs must be linked to a viable process of economic reform. Safety net programs such as social funds cannot take the place of viable sectoral policies in health and education, for example. They are designed to be important *complements* to mainstream services, whose objectives are to develop institutions, improve infrastructure, and increase people's income. In addition, they operate within a fixed economic parameter: to a large extent their ability to help reduce poverty over the long term hinges on the renewal of growth after adjustment and therefore on sound macroeconomic management.

Those who favor combating poverty through structural changes or the redistribution of ownership and assets will be disappointed in safety net programs such as social funds. Proponents of orthodox reform, meanwhile, could see the political sustainability of their efforts advanced considerably if they encouraged the poor to become new actors in the reform process through participatory safety net programs.

Appendix to Table 8-1

Argentina[a]

1. Under Alfonsín: Programa Alimentario Nacional (PAN)
   - Primary target: poor families—pregnant women and children
   - Targeted goals soon expanded to ameliorating eating habits, teaching mothers to use resources efficiently, encouraging breast feeding, and improving medical control during pregnancy and birth
   - Still essentially remained food packet program
   - No significant means to determine "need" but appears to have been reasonably well targeted; reached some but not all in need
   - Relatively centralized program

2. Under Menem: Bono Nacional Solidario de Emergencia
   - Used funds (created through 0.05–2.00 percent tax on revenues in 1988 of most affluent business firms) to issue bonds that served as payment for food in shops and supermarkets
   - Targeted to the poor
   - Allowed choice of food items as opposed to PAN food packets (PAN administration did, however, remain intact)
   - More decentralized administrative system: bonds were to be handed out at the local level by committees of program

3. Both programs have since been terminated (end of 1990)

4. Government: democracy

Costa Rica

1. Measures implemented during crisis, 1981–82[b]
   - Lower utility rates charged to slum dwellers
   - Credit lines established for the urban informal sector
   - Nutrition and preventive health programs maintained in the face of increased food prices

2. 1970s program[c]
   - Temporary emergency food packets program with substantial foreign assistance)

- Expansion of other employment and social programs

3. Government: democracy

El Salvador[d]

1. Social Investment Fund (FIS)
   - Success attributed to limited objectives; private sector–oriented management; government's commitment to keep fund out of politics; population's receptiveness to reconstruction efforts after civil war
   - Economic area aims: generation of employment; support for production; impetus for small-scale private enterprise
   - Social area aims: provide public health and education infrastructure, with preference to pregnant and lactating mothers, children; also priority to categories of municipalities (were poor and site of conflict during the civil war; are poor; located in areas of conflict; all others)
   - Still have difficulty reaching poorest communities

2. Government: democracy

Guinea[e]

1. Compensatory programs created to accompany adjustment begun in 1985
   - Public sector employees received allowances for transportation and food
   - New unemployed continue to receive nominal salaries and some being retrained
   - Infrastructure schemes have been created and private sector credit expanded to create jobs in the capital
   - Social development support project being prepared, with income-generating and social assistance schemes for the poor

2. Also participation in the Social Dimensions of Adjustment Project (SDAP)

3. Government: 1984–90: comité militaire de redressement national; end of 1992: multiparty legislative elections = movement toward full democracy

Guinea-Bissau[f]

1. 1987 adjustment program launched—social programs to accompany under title of Social Investment Recovery Project (SIRP):
   - Rice being subsidized for low-income public sector employees following price increases (with World Food Program assistance)
   - Health and education services to protect vulnerable groups to be provided through World Bank credits
   - Social and Infrastructure Relief Project being prepared to assist low-income, unemployed, and underemployed rural and urban workers
   - Efforts being made to explain to the population the reason for the reforms and the need for short-term sacrifice

2. Also in SDAP

3. Government: semidemocracy during reforms (dominant party = PAIGC party); by end of 1991, move to multiparty system

Guyana[g]

1. Social Impact Amelioration Program (SIMAP)
   - Envisioned as a two-year program (1989–91) consisting of four components: cash or food-for-work provided for employment generation projects (infrastructure works); income supplement for old-age pensioners; road rehabilitation; and technical and vocational training
   - Strategy focused on development from a community perspective

2. Government: authoritarian under Hoyte; December 1992 held presidential elections resulting in election of new president from different party

Jamaica[h]

1. Initial protection effort has proved unsuccessful owing to constrained resources and the fact that the target groups constitute about half the population
   - The Food Aid Program: targets school children, pregnant and lactating mothers, infants, the elderly, and the very poor

2. Newest social reform initiative: Social Well-Being Program
   - Proposed projects in health, nutrition, education, employment for external financing
   - Investment and adjustment reform Social Sector Development Project being financed by the government and the World Bank

3. Government: head = British monarch whose local representative, the governor-general, is appointed on recommendation of the prime minister

   Legislature = bicameral Parliament

Korea[i]

1. Adjustment program introduced in late 1980 included social measures to protect the poor
   - Medical assistance and health insurance to low-income groups
   - Temporary public works programs for the new unemployed
   - Income transfers to those unable to work
   - Increased expenditures on education and housing

2. Government: democracy—February 1981 ushered in the Fifth Republic with the election of President Chun

Morocco

1. Measures cited by Zimmerman[j]
   - Proposed elimination of across-the-board subsidies being accomplished by targeted compensatory programs for low-income urban and landless rural poor
   - Income transfer programs through food-for-work, school meals, and maternal and infant feeding programs
   - Reduction of expenditures on higher education to occur (see note below): emphasis to be given to equitable access to education and completion of the nine-year basic education program with fuller rural and female participation
   - Health and population services to target rural areas but resources for these sectors need to be increased
   - Vocational training being expanded to provide skilled labor where it is in shortage

2. Nelson commentary on 1988 flour reform[k]
   • Reform removed subsidy for high-quality flour and altered arrangements for subsidizing coarser flour
   • Reform had the effect of removing subsidy from the wealthy rather than targeting it to the poor (in contrast to Zimmerman's view that flour would be targeted to the poorer areas)

3. Government: modified constitutional monarchy
   • Executive: king who appoints prime minister (king is quite strong)
   • Legislature: Chamber of Representatives

4. Note: this higher education enrollment reduction lasted only one year; the next year, under political pressure, the enrollment jumped by 25 percent

Philippines[l]

1. Compensatory program not meant to continue long term
   • Immunization, nutrition, crop diversification, food-for-work programs implemented with support of UNICEF, World Food Program, United Nations Development Program, International Labor Office, and Oxfam
   • Particularly hard hit group: blacks

2. World Bank poverty program loan was being considered at time of writing to address reforms in one or more areas: land and other asset distribution, family planning, employment generation

3. Government: democracy—Marcos bows to pressure and leaves for Hawaii on the same day that Aquino is sworn into office, February 25, 1986

Spain[m]

1. Compensatory programs targeted largely toward labor
   • Unemployed workers affected by industrial reconversion program were, under certain conditions, given rights to three years of unemployment subsidy

- Workers over 55 years who lost jobs were given benefits indefinitely
- Job training and education programs expanded to target first-time job seekers
- Regions where restructuring took place named Zones of Urgent Re-Industrialization and their new and old enterprises given tax deductions, investment subsidies, and other assistance to expand employment

2. Government: democracy (with king)—death of Franco ushers in formation of democratic government, November 25, 1975

Thailand[n]

1. Compensation involved transfers to those adversely affected by reform measures, especially devaluation
   - Abolition of import surcharges
   - Temporary price controls on items like cement
   - Reduction of bank lending rates
   - Promise not to raise oil prices
   - Pledge of 3 billion bahts to military
   - Modest increase in minimum wage
   - Mandatory transfers of exchange profits from commercial banks to compensate those hurt by devaluation

2. Involved modest, general spending to weaken political pressures for stimulation that would have generated even more serious inflation

3. Rural funds were *maintained* (but not increased)

4. General combination of sequencing and positive incentives for trade reform operated as an indirect but highly effective form of compensation

5. Government: democracy from 1980 until February 23, 1991, military coup, which placed National Peacekeeping Council in power (king still there as a figurehead)

Turkey[o]

1. Essentially concentrated on housing program and development of infrastructure
   - Mechanism for extending property ownership to middle- and lower-income groups was sale of revenue-share certificates

Venezuela[p]

1. Social Development Project: financed by World Bank and Inter-American Development Bank
   - Financial and technical backing: US$3.8 billion
   - To cover period 1992–96
   - Major program compenents: maternal-child assistance covering nutrition, day-care, health (Programa de Asistencia Materno-Infantil, Beca Alimentaria, Hogares de Cuidado Diario); direct food subsidies; education (emphasis, primary and secondary levels and includes infrastructure work); rehabilitation of basic services (water, hospitals); and basic health programs

2. Above project represents shift from poverty reduction efforts of 1974–89, which focused on general food subsidies

3. 1989: introduction of economic reform program; adjustment sustained

4. Government: democracy

---

a. Georges Midré, "Bread or Solidarity? Argentine Social Policies, 1983–90," *Journal of Latin American Studies*. vol. 24 (May 1992), pp. 343–75.

b. Elaine Zimmerman, *Adjustment Programs and Social Welfare*, World Bank Discussion Papers (Washington, 1992), annex 2, p. 29.

c. Joan Nelson, "Poverty, Equity, and the Politics of Adjustment," in Stephen Haggard and Robert Kaufman, eds., *The Politics of Economic Adjustment* (Princeton University Press, 1992), pp. 222–61.

d. Carol Graham, "The Social Investment Fund in El Salvador: Poverty Alleviation in a Polarized Polity," Brookings, December 1992.

e. Zimmerman, *Adjustment Programs*, annex 2, p. 30.

f. Ibid., pp. 30–31.

g. George K. Dans, *Dimensions of Social Welfare and Social Policy in Guyana* (Georgetown: University of Guyana, 1990).

h. Zimmerman, *Adjustment Programs*, annex 2, p. 31.

i. Ibid., p. 31.

j. Ibid., p. x.

k. Nelson, "Poverty, Equity, and the Politics of Adjustment."

l. Zimmerman, *Adjustment Programs*, annex 2, pp. 32–33.

m. Nancy Bermeo and José A. Garcia Duran, "The Political Economy of Structural Adjustment in New Democracies: The Case of Spain," prepared for World Bank Project on Political Economy of Structural Adjustment in New Democracies, Washington, August 1992.

n. Richard Doner and Anek Laothamatas, "The Political Economy of Structural Adjustment in Thailand," World Bank Project on Political Economy of Structural Adjustment in New Democracies, Washington, June 1992.

o. Ziya Önis and Steven Webb, "Political Economy of Policy Reforms in Turkey in the 1980s," September 1992.

p. Fax from Moises Naim; *Poverty Reduction Handbook* (Washington: World Bank, 1992); and Moises Naim and Manuela Tortora, "From Speeches to Institutions: Poverty in Venezuela and What to Do About It," Washington: Carnegie Endowment for International Peace.

Other Experiences with Safety Net Programs

AMONG the other important safety net experiences that merit some attention are those of the United States, Ghana, Mexico, El Salvador, and Guyana.

The United States

Perhaps one of the first experiences with public works employment programs took place in the United States at the time of the New Deal.[1] The Federal Emergency Relief Administration was created in 1933 to give money to the states for relief payments and for creating jobs. In 1935 it was expanded with the creation of the Works Progress Administration (WPA). Within months this program employed 3 million people, helped to build and upgrade 2,500 hospitals, 5,900 schools, 13,000 playgrounds, and 651,000 miles of road. The unemployment rate, meanwhile, fell from 25 percent in 1933 to 14 percent in 1937.[2]

The sponsors of the WPA believed that government expenditure on construction would provide socially needed infrastructure and at the same time stimulate the building industry directly and related industries indirectly. By increasing the number of people employed in the construction industry, the government expected to cause a ripple effect in national employment. The WPA funded approximately half the cost of projects, and the grantee funded the other half. Nonfederal WPA projects relied on local governments to administer and cover the costs of the projects. In addition, there were components within the WPA to provide income relief for college students from poor families. This component provided part-time work and focused on "socially useful" projects, as well as part-time works programs for needy young people between the ages of eighteen and twenty-four who were out of school. At first the administration of the programs was concentrated in Washington, but after two years a more decentralized approach was taken, and local field offices were set up.[3]

There were clearly limitations to the WPA's ability to address unemployment and poverty during the Depression. By focusing on the construction industry, for example, it limited the kind of workers that benefited, since construction jobs require a considerable amount of physical effort and skill. This constraint was apparently not overcome by the targeting of public works activities to twelve so-called critical areas, because there were a relatively small number of construction workers among the unemployed in those regions. Regardless, the programs did have a notable effect on the unemployment rate during the Depression. The unemployment rate then dropped down to 4.7 percent in 1942 as the economy, by now fully recovered from the Depression, mobilized for war.[4]

In sum, although the WPA was important to ameliorating the effects of the Depression and high unemployment in the 1930s—and provided necessary income supplements and socially useful infrastructure in addition—it was less effective at reaching beyond a relatively skilled portion of the work force, and probably did not reach the poorest or neediest groups. The programs specifically targeted at youth may have had a more direct effect on the poor. The programs probably did generate a fair amount of positive political goodwill for the Roosevelt administration by demonstrating that the government was concerned about the social costs of the Depression.

Ghana

Like Zambia, Ghana went from being one of the richest countries in Sub-Saharan Africa at independence to being one of the poorest. Between 1970 and 1982, real per capita income declined 30 percent; between 1975 and 1983, real minimum wages fell by 86 percent.[5] To the extent that the data are reliable, 35.93 percent of the Ghanaian population was poor in 1988, although the living standards of the so-called nonpoor, who spent more than 60 percent of their incomes on food, were hardly very good.[6] After taking power in a military coup in 1981, Flight Lieutenant Jerry Rawlings combined authoritarian populist political tactics with the implementation of an IMF- and World Bank–sanctioned economic reform program, the Economic Recovery Program (ERP). Gross domestic product registered a positive growth rate of 8.7 percent in 1984, 5.1 percent in 1985, and 5.3 percent in 1986.

The program, however, was not without social costs, which came on top of more than a decade of severe economic decline. The primary opponents of the ERP were student groups, who were negatively affected by cuts in education, and civil servants, who lost jobs in the reduction of notoriously inefficient parts of the public sector such as the Cocoa Marketing Board. Rural groups, meanwhile, benefited from devaluation and the virtual elimination of the marketing boards, which had kept prices for their products artificially low. The Ghanaian program was receiving international attention for its economic success in the mid-1980s, at the same time that the United Nations Children's Fund (UNICEF) released its highly influential study, *Adjustment with a Human Face*. At the same time, the political situation in Ghana was becoming increasingly difficult because urban opposition was on the rise. Thus the government conducted a highly publicized study of the effects of the reform program on vulnerable groups in Ghana in 1987, and in February 1988, with support from the World Bank and the IMF, launched the Program of Action to Mitigate the Social Costs of Adjustment (PAMSCAD), "the most ambitious program on the continent to alleviate the social costs of adjustment."[7]

The program was launched with US$85 million in donations from international agencies. Although it was originally intended to protect the most vulnerable groups, it suffered from too complex a design and too much influence from individual donors; it also fell prey to the government's political ambitions. This began with the timing of the program: the government hoped that it would help consolidate its support in the March 1988 elections.

The PAMSCAD had five major components: community initiative projects, employment generation projects, activities to help the redeployed, projects designed to meet the basic needs of vulnerable groups, and education.[8] Programs were supposed to have a strong poverty focus, high economic and social return, and ease and speed of implementation, and were not supposed to create macroeconomic distortions. The largest PAMSCAD projects were employment programs designed to create 40,000 jobs over a two-year period. These included public works projects, credit schemes for small-scale enterprises and farmers, projects for women and small-scale miners, and labor-intensive projects to rehabilitate school infrastructure. There was also a food-for-work program run by local nongovernmental organizations and implemented in the north of the country during the dry season, when food production was very low.

Despite the ambitious nature of the PAMSCAD—or perhaps because of it—and the substantial amounts of external support, the program fared quite poorly in implementation. "Indeed a program such as PAMSCAD, which requires literally hundreds of administrative systems in rural areas, is precisely the kind of program that a government in a country such as Ghana finds most difficult to implement."[9] The program's components were too widely dispersed. The projects were divided among nine sectors, and thirteen central agencies were responsible for their implementation. This required an organizational and administrative capacity at the national and local levels that just did not exist. Thus urban areas, where the government has the most administrative control, received the most programs. In addition, there were a great many problems in targeting beneficiaries: by attempting to target all vulnerable groups throughout Ghana, the mechanisms were neither specific nor accurate. Women, for example, benefited disproportionately; most projects were biased toward the urban poor and laid-off civil servants. And because the program focused on centrally oriented implementation, the relatively vibrant NGO community, which could have contributed to implementation and targeting, was not involved in a significant manner, with the exception of the food-for-work program. Even the most successful of the programs, the community initiative program, reflected this centralist tendency and priorities that were established "at the district level on the basis of nationally-determined criteria."[10]

Relations with donors were also difficult. Instead of sending all funds to one central channeling agency, individual donors gave to—and wanted to influence—specific components. The amounts projects received thus varied greatly, and too many donors concentrated on specific projects. Disbursements were also slow, with lag times of a year or more.

While the Rawlings government had political objectives in the implementation of the PAMSCAD, it seemed committed to poverty alleviation
as well as to economic reform. Yet the unwieldy administrative structure
and centralized bias of the program severely limited its potential to contribute to either the political sustainability of the reform program or to
poverty alleviation. The program may have temporarily relieved the opposition of some civil servants and other urban groups, but it was far less
successful at reaching previously marginalized groups of poor and incorporating their participation in the reform program in any sustainable way.
The record of the PAMSCAD points to the advantages of extra-institu-
tional and simply structured demand-based social funds.

Mexico

A program that is gaining increasing national and international attention is Mexico's National Solidarity Program (Pronasol). The program is
a Bolivia-style demand-based social fund, but it is being implemented on
a much larger scale.[11] The Emergency Social Fund channeled US$240
million in four years; Pronasol started with a budget of $680 million in
1989 and increased to a projected US$2.3 billion for 1992.[12] If adminis-
trative and infrastructure costs were waived,[13] the ESF would have spent
approximately US$50 a year on each of its 1.2 million beneficiaries. By
the same calculation, with its 1992 budget, Pronasol would spend US$135
on each of the 17 million people in extreme poverty in Mexico. Thus the
program's resource impact is even greater than the ESF's. Pronasol's
high visibility—it received prominent mention in the president's 1992
annual address to the nation—also suggests that it is having an impact
politically. Also as with the ESF, the effects of Pronasol's outreach to
groups that had rarely if ever received state attention in the past cannot
be underestimated.

The design of Pronasol was influenced by the ESF and other demand-
based social funds, but it was also a product of President Carlos Salinas's
own research,[14] as well as of previous government programs that relied
on community initiative in the form of manual labor and food supply.[15]
There are 64,000 Solidarity committees nationwide, which are elected
locally. In response to popular demands, the committees design projects
in collaboration with government staff. There are four program areas:
food support, which includes extensive support for ongoing targeted food

subsidy programs; production; social services; and infrastructure.[16] In addition to these activities, Pronasol has three programs aimed at increasing the earning potential of the poor: Solidarity funds for production provide credit to farmers in high-risk, low-yield activities; Solidarity funds for indigenous communities support ethnic groups involved in local development activities; and women in Solidarity provides credit to workshops and small industries run by women. Pronasol supports sectoral ministries by expanding the country's health and education facilities and scholarship and school feeding programs. Finally, Pronasol supports municipal development and provides infrastructure to poor communities through its municipal and regional funds.[17]

Because of the wide range and large number of programs, it is difficult to make a singular judgment of Pronasol. Moreover, it is difficult to separate what may be justified criticisms of the political system—a semi-authoritarian system that is in theory in the process of liberalizing—from those of the actual design or content of the program. Ultimately, Pronasol's success as a demand-based program hinges on the extent to which the government is committed to genuine political opening and to allowing individuals and organizations of all political bents to join.

Pronasol's record to date varies, depending on the local party power structure and the capacity of grass-roots and community organizations. In many regions the program has come into conflict with authoritarian party bosses at the local level, indicating that nontraditional actors have at least been able to benefit to some extent.[18] While the president has demonstrated a willingness to let Solidarity committees undermine local Partido Revolucionario Institucional authorities, he seems less willing to allow the committees to operate independently in municipalities controlled by the opposition.[19] The extent to which Pronasol is able to reach previously marginalized groups, and to serve as an alternative to the PRI by providing a channel "through which popular groups can express their demands," will determine if the program can have the kinds of effects on the economic potential and political voice of the poor that funds such as the ESF have had.[20]

Like many similar programs, Pronasol has been greatly influenced by the political context. In the 1988 elections, in the face of new mobilizing forces on the left, the PRI had the worst electoral showing of its history, and President Salinas took power amid widespread accusations of fraud. Although Salinas did not fear massive social unrest, as did the governments of Senegal, Chile, and Poland, for example, he was painfully aware of how unpopular the cutting of social services by the de la Madrid government had been. Pronasol was a gamble that reversing that trend would change popular perceptions of government legitimacy. The government increased Pronasol activity in several regions where the opposition was strong, such as in Michaocan, Nueva Laguna, and Morelos, and was able to reverse its electoral fortunes. Yet it is not clear whether the electoral results were influenced by the curbing of inflation and the renewal of economic growth or by Pronasol.

Whether the program can last, given its institutional autonomy and its close connection with the persona of Salinas, is another issue. The recent creation of Sedesol as an umbrella agency to coordinate and direct Pronasol activities indicates some government desire to institutionalize the program on a more permanent basis.

Pronasol has been criticized as a populist tool and as a means for President Salinas to build up his personal base of power.[21] The former criticism stems from the president's tactics, such as his very public usage of the proceeds from the privatization of the national airline to provide electricity to 500,000 homes in the poorest regions. "Populist" or not, this action combines clever salesmanship with the philosophy underlying orthodox economic reform: to get the state out of the productive field and into the service provision arena. To the extent that Pronasol is generating support for a new government approach to providing social services *and* for a new channel of communicating with both central and local governments, the program is contributing to poverty alleviation and institutional development. It is difficult to criticize the government for reaping the rewards of a good program, since governments attempt to do so in most countries. Yet wherever Pronasol is reinforcing traditional clientelistic structures controlled by the PRI, the program's potential to contribute to local capacity building is being severely curtailed. The building of local capacity through Pronasol in relation to that of the PRI may be a very effective means to undermine the party's authoritarian structure and monopoly control. This may contribute to the president's popularity. Yet, because Salinas cannot be reelected, it need not be a major issue.

El Salvador

The Fund for Social Investment of El Salvador (FIS) was inaugurated in a difficult economic context, but at a relatively opportune political moment.[22] The FIS was initiated soon after the 1989 election of President Alfredo Cristiani, in the context of an economic reform program. Owing to the country's poor macroeconomic performance and the high costs of its decade-long civil war, poverty increased by 3.7 percentage points from 1985 to 1990, and up to 42 percent of the population was considered to be in extreme poverty. The designers of the FIS also had the benefit of hindsight and had carefully examined the Bolivian experience. They concluded that institutional links—particularly with the line ministries—had been lacking in the ESF's operations. Thus FIS projects must adhere to sectoral priorities outlined by the ministries, and complement the activities of those ministries through the renovation of schools and health posts, for example. The director of the FIS, like that of the ESF, was a prominent entrepreneur with credibility in diverse political sectors, a difficult achievement in a country as politically divided as El Salvador. The director answers directly to the president of the nation. Also, with the benefit of hindsight, the FIS was able to develop good procedural and auditing mechanisms before launching its operations, and was able to hire a staff with strong technical and managerial skills. The FIS began operating in October 1990, with US$33 million from the Inter-American Development Bank and US$6 million from the government of El Salvador. Since then it has also been able to attract approximately US$12 million from other donors, and US$15.88 million has been provided as counterpart funds by beneficiaries and soliciting agencies. The high degree of beneficiary support for the program indicates widespread popular support for and participation in FIS projects, which will make them more sustainable in the long run. Like the ESF, it has kept administrative costs to approximately 5 percent of the total.

The social groups that are given priority by the FIS are pregnant mothers and children aged 1–5; nursing mothers and children 1–6; children 7–12; and then women in general and youth of both sexes. The FIS also rated municipalities in order of priority. The first consists of those that are poor and were the site of conflict during the civil war; the second, consists of those that are poor; the third consists of those located in the areas of conflict; and the last category is composed of all the rest.

From its inception until September 1992, the FIS approved 1,503 projects benefiting 1.4 million persons, at a total cost of US$30.6 million— quite an impressive implementation record. In a population of just over 5 million, this would mean some political as well as poverty alleviation effects. The FIS also has had a good record of working with NGOs and community groups: community groups account for 56 percent of FIS projects solicited and NGOs for 10 percent, while municipalities account for 11 percent and the central government and state agencies 23 percent.[23]

The FIS's outreach to community groups and NGOs contributes to its apolitical nature. Equally important, however, is the program management's firm commitment to transparency and political neutrality. It is telling that the harshest critics of the program are, ironically, members of the governing party who are frustrated with the extent to which the FIS is benefiting other political groups! Also important, as soon as the peace accords were signed, the FIS approached the Farabundo Frente Marti de Liberacion Nacional to offer its facilities. Since then the FIS has implemented a few projects in conjunction with the FMLN. This cooperation is critical to combating poverty in many of the former conflict zones, and progress hinges on overcoming years of mutual suspicion between the former guerrillas and the government. The fact that the FIS—a semiautonomous actor but clearly a government program—is providing outreach to the FMLN may be an important catalyst in the political consensus building necessary for national reconstruction, and at the same time may contribute to poverty alleviation in the former conflict zones.

Despite its setting of priorities and its department of promotion, the FIS, like the ESF, has had difficulty reaching the poorest communities, which receive a disproportionately low percentage of funds. As of late 1992 the highest-priority municipalities, for example, had received only 6.05 percent of total FIS funds allocated to municipalities. Morazan, the department with the highest poverty index, received 13.1 percent of the FIS funds that are in theory allocated to it, totaling 18 projects, while San Salvador, with the lowest index, received 86.1 percent of its "allocated" funds, totaling 103 projects.[24] The distribution of funds is more equitable in per capita terms, however, because San Salvador has a population of 1.4 million and received 14.55 million colones, while Morazan has 140,000 people and received 3.19 million colones.[25] This problem is exacerbated by the political context: many of the poorest regions are also those in which the civil war was most intense; as a result, it is difficult for FIS personnel to work there. The difficulty in reaching the poorest sectors seems inherent to demand-based funds and should receive more research and operational attention. The FIS has attempted to get around this problem by planning some program—rather than project-based activities—ranging from school feeding programs to the building of town markets—that are guided by government sectoral priorities and can be targeted to specific areas. The programs will still be subcontracted out, as are other FIS projects. In addition, the FIS is launching a special project in one of the zones most affected by the conflict, Chalatanegro.

There are, of course, some other problems with the FIS. Although it has been able to cooperate effectively with the education ministry, for personal or political reasons there has been virtually no cooperation with the health ministry, and thus there is a relative shortage of health projects: 55 percent of projects are in education, whereas only 3 percent are in health. A potential challenge was the elections in March 1994. Given El Salvador's divided political context, it was likely that the FIS came under unprecedented political pressure.

On balance, though, the achievements of the FIS to date are impressive and much needed, given the extent of poverty and the current process of reconstruction in El Salvador. The FIS has had success in attracting donor support and is likely to be extended beyond its initial four-year period of projected operations. The fund's ability to combine political neutrality, efficiency, and transparency with high visibility, as the ESF in Bolivia did, suggests some impact on the political sustainability of reform. The fund's built-in links to the line ministries, coupled with its extensive reach to NGOs and local governments, maximize its ability to enhance the institutional development that is vital to long-term poverty alleviation.

Guyana

The Social Impact Amelioration Program (SIMAP) in Guyana was implemented in the most difficult of circumstances and has quite a different record from that of the FIS. When Guyana gained its independence in the late 1960s, it was one of the wealthiest nations in Latin America. Its statistics now are comparable to those of Haiti, the poorest nation in the region. Per capita GDP in 1989 was at the same level as in 1968, an economic record that is reminiscent of that of another former British colony in the study, Zambia. Also like Zambia, Guyana stands out as a country with an extensive infrastructure (rural health posts, schools, and water pipes, for example), that is woefully ill equipped and that has not been maintained for years.[26] After twenty-eight years of the Peoples' National Congress (PNC) command economy and a one-party authoritarian system of government—similar to the Kaunda regime in Zambia—the Guyanese government launched a World Bank– and IMF-assisted adjustment program, the Economic Recovery Program. Yet Guyana is distinct from Zambia in that political change and economic change were not simultaneous. The first free elections in thirty years in Guyana were held two years after the introduction of economic reforms, in October 1991. Cheddi Jagan, a former Marxist turned free marketeer, was voted in to replace the People's National Congress (PNC) government of President Desmond Hoyte. The political context was also complicated by an ethnic division between blacks and Indians, with roughly one-third of the population in the former group and one-half in the latter.

This context had various implications for the implementation of a social fund. First, it is very difficult to identify, much less target, less privileged groups in Guyana, because of the absence of reliable statistics and because almost everyone is poor: the income of two average wage-earners combined is insufficient to feed a family. Many of the employed are poor in Guyana. There is hidden unemployment, on the one hand, and vast shortages of skilled personnel in the public sector due to low wage rates, on the other. This is directly related to the second issue: line ministries—and the public sector in general—are virtually dysfunctional, because managerial and administrative systems have broken down. In Bolivia, the vacuum left by nonfunctional line ministries was filled by an extensive NGO community that was particularly active in health and education. In contrast, in Guyana NGOs are extremely limited in both size and scope, because of thirty years of domination by a one-party system in which NGOs had no legal status. Finally, and also reminiscent of the situation in Zambia, community self-help initiative and organizational capacity have by and large broken down. Decades of grandiose promises without government follow-through and the dearth of resources and support for small-scale local initiatives have produced great suspicion of the state and fear of political manipulation at the community level.[27]

The SIMAP was initiated in 1990 with US$2.8 million from the Inter-American Development Bank and US$200,000 in counterpart funds from the Guyanese government. The program, a demand-based social fund that was influenced by the ESF, had two goals.[28] The first was to protect the poor and vulnerable from the effects of the adjustment program, and the second was to stimulate the productive capacity of NGOs, community organizations, local governments, and the private sector in Guyana. The fund supports three kinds of activities: infrastructure, social assistance, and vocational training, particularly for youth. In the absence of regional or occupational statistics, the most evidently vulnerable of the poor were identified as priorities: young children, pregnant and nursing mothers, and the elderly. In addition, projects that have a counterpart contribution, either in cash or in kind, are given priority. The SIMAP is run out of the Ministry of Culture and Social Development by a six-member board of directors, three of whom are from the government; the others are from the private sector, the NGO community, and the University of Guyana.

The choice for directorship of the program reflects Guyana's complex political context. Philip Chan, the chairman of the board of directors, was a long-time diplomat with close ties to the PNC government. With a Chinese surname, half-Indian lineage, and close ties to a black president, he is able to bridge important cultural divides. But his close ties to the government and his lack of managerial experience are evident in the program's rate of progress and, more important, in its failure to break with restrictive government wage policy. This makes it difficult to maintain skilled staff. Indeed, it may be the determining factor in the SIMAP's potential as a program. At least some degree of institutional autonomy and political insulation, coupled with a management approach modeled on that of the private sector, has been key to the success of social funds like Bolivia's, Zambia's, and El Salvador's. The PNC government was reluctant to give the SIMAP this autonomy, as is evidenced by its refusal to let the program diverge from the public sector salary scales. Thus the program has not been able to establish the image, and the reality, of an exceptional public sector institution that demonstrates a new means of operating.

It is too early to fairly evaluate the SIMAP, particularly in view of the difficult context in which it began and the unclear effects of recent elections. The problems it has had to date are not surprising. First, the shortage of skilled staff, coupled with a lack of available criteria for evaluation, has led to a serious backlog of projects requesting funding. Second, grass-roots organizations will have to work directly with the line ministries if the program is going to have any kind of substantive impact. Yet these ministries are exceptionally weak, with the result that it is difficult to make timely progress. Third, SIMAP's image was tainted by the poor record of an emergency cash benefits system that was implemented in 1989 under the same name. Finally, it is not clear how Chan will fare under the new government because of his close affiliation with the previous regime, or how that association will affect the program.

Initial indications are that the new government is willing to allow the program to have increased autonomy, which is a good sign, although its image and method of operating may already be too established to change.

At the same time, the SIMAP is implementing desperately needed initiatives ranging from nutrition programs and school feeding to the renovation of health centers and other infrastructure. Even if its operations are on a small scale, the demonstration effects may be significant in reinvigorating local self-help efforts. Continued donor support, conditional on progress on the development of an information system and the revamping of salary scales, should contribute to the program's potential. Given the difficult context, however, it is likely that the program's achievements, both politically and in poverty alleviation, will be limited, at least in the short term.

Notes

Chapter 1

1. See Joan M. Nelson, "The Political Economy of Stabilization: Commitment, Capacity, and Public Response," *World Development*, vol. 12, no. 10 (1984), pp. 983–1006.

2. Helena Ribe, "How Adjustment Programs Can Help the Poor: The World Bank's Experience," *World Bank Discussion Papers* 71 (Washington, D.C., 1990). In this and other pieces Ribe has pointed out opportunities that adjustment provides for policymakers to build into macroeconomic policy measures that favor the poor. I extend this point to the realm of political economy and posit that the nature and speed of economic and political changes are critical in determining the extent to which adjustment provides opportunities to redirect public resources to the poor.

3. I would like to thank Joan Nelson for discussing this point in detail with me.

4. Poverty clearly increased in much of the developing world in the 1980s, particularly in sub-Saharan Africa and in Latin America. In Latin America, for example, poverty increased and became more urban in nature, though basic indicators such as infant mortality and literacy continued to improve. In Africa, the poor fared worse, and there was little or no improvement in those indicators that Latin America was able to maintain or improve. In 1985, 22.4 percent of Latin America's population was below a poverty line of $1 a day; in 1990 this proportion had increased to 25.2 percent. In Africa, this proportion was 47.6 percent in 1985 and 47.8 percent in 1990. In South Asia, while the percentage of poor was greater (51.8 percent), the rate was reduced to 49.0 percent by 1990. In addition, the poverty gap, or the mean distance below the poverty line, was worse in Africa (18.1 percent for 1985 and 19.1 percent for 1990) than for South Asia (16.2 percent and 13.7 percent) or Latin America (8.7 percent and 10.3

293

percent). "Implementing the World Bank's Strategy to Reduce Poverty: Progress and Challenges" (Washington, D.C.: The World Bank, April 1993), p. 5. It is also difficult to compare poverty trends across countries and regions because of differences in measurement techniques and in definitions of the poverty line. The Economic Commission for Latin America produced estimates quite different from those of the World Bank. The commission estimated that 37 percent of all Latin America's households were poor in 1990 and that 17 percent were in indigence or extreme poverty, with 31 percent urban (as opposed to 26 percent in 1980) and 54 percent rural. Despite lower proportional rates, the total number of poor was greater in urban areas. See *Magnitud de la Pobreza en America Latina en los Anos Ochenta* (Santiago: Cepal, August 1991), p. 77; and Anthony B. Atkinson, "Comparing Poverty Rates Internationally: Lessons from Recent Studies in Developed Countries," *World Bank Economic Review*, vol. 5 (January 1991), pp. 3–21.

5. "Just as populism stands for the false drama that growth per capita can exceed productivity growth, the question as to whether the poor suffer from adjustment programs poses a misleading dilemma." Eliana A. Cardoso, "Inflation and Poverty," Working Paper 4006 (Washington, D.C.: National Bureau of Economics Research, March 1992), p. 10. Two very good examples, documented in separate chapters of this volume, are Peru and Zambia. Several cross-regional studies comparing adjusting and nonadjusting countries have found that the social costs tend to be higher in those countries that avoid adjustment. See, for example, Francois Bourguignon, Jaime de Melo, and Christian Morrisson, "Poverty and Income Distribution During Adjustment: Issues and Evidence from the OECD Project," *World Development*, vol. 19, no. 11 (1991), pp. 1485–1508.

6. Negative trends can register in less than one year. Macroeconomic crises explain short-run trends, as during recessions unskilled workers are the first to lose their jobs. Long-run variations tend to be explained by factors such as the labor market. Minimum wage legislation does not improve distribution meanwhile, at least in countries like Brazil and Peru, as it tends to act as a disincentive to hiring, placing more workers in the informal sector. Eliana A. Cardoso, "Cyclical Variations of Earnings Inequality in Brazil" (Tufts University, January 1993).

7. These three policy aspects are discussed in detail in Giovanni Andrea Cornia, Richard Jolly, and Frances Stewart, eds., *Adjustment with a Human Face: Protecting the Vulnerable and Promoting Growth* (Oxford: UNICEF/Clarendon Press, 1987). See also, Tony Addison and Lionel Demery, "The Economics of Poverty Alleviation Under Adjustment" (paper prepared for World Bank symposium on Poverty and Adjustment, Washington, D.C., 1988).

8. This point is noted by Stephan Haggard in "Markets, Poverty Alleviation, and Income Distribution: An Assessment of Neoliberal Claims," *Ethics and International Affairs*, vol. 5 (1991), pp. 175–96; and by S. M. Ravi Kanbur, "Measurement and Alleviation of Poverty: With an Application to the Effects of Macroeconomic Adjustment," IMF Working Paper (Washington, D.C.: 1988).

9. There is also a trade-off between investment in the current consumption and future human capital of the poor, which is particularly relevant with the fiscal constraints introduced by adjustment, and it is noted by Francois Bourguignon

in "Optimal Poverty Reduction, Adjustment, and Growth," *World Bank Economic Review*, vol. 5 (May 1991), pp. 315–38.

10. This point was noted by Michael Lipton in an address entitled "Economic Research on Poverty: Some Issues," International Food Policy Research Institute, Washington, D.C., February 10, 1993.

11. Indeed, countries with ideal macro and meso policies have no need for safety nets. Other countries may implement macro policies that exacerbate poverty and inequality unnecessarily, creating a greater need for safety nets than would otherwise exist. I would like to thank Frances Stewart for bringing this point to my attention.

12. Omotunde Johnson and Joanne Salop, "Distributional Aspects of Stabilization Programs in Developing Countries," IMF Discussion Papers, 1988.

13. These include Bolivia, Chile, Costa Rica, El Salvador, Guinea, Guinea-Bissau, Jamaica, Korea, Morocco, Spain, Thailand, and Turkey. For detail, see chapter 8 of this volume.

14. For a description of experiences, see PREALC, *Empleos de Emergencia* (Santiago, 1988).

15. In a study of twenty-five countries conducted by Stephan Haggard and Robert Kaufman, established democratic regimes performed as well as authoritarian regimes in implementing stable macroeconomic policies in the 1980s. Yet the results also suggest that new or reconstituted democracies have the most difficulty maintaining fiscal and monetary restraint. For detail see Stephan Haggard and Robert Kaufman "Economic Adjustment in New Democracies," in Joan M. Nelson, ed., *Fragile Coalitions: The Politics of Economic Adjustment* (Washington, D.C.: Overseas Development Council, 1989), pp. 57–77. A recent comparative study found that elections in Latin America enhance rather than hinder the initiation of orthodox reform policies. See Karen L. Remmer, "The Political Economy of Elections in Latin America, 1980–91," *American Political Science Review*, vol. 87 (June 1993), pp. 393–407.

16. This hypothesis is proven in numerous cases in a cross-regional study conducted for the World Bank by Stephan Haggard and Steven B. Webb entitled *Voting For Reform: Democracy, Political Liberalization, and Economic Adjustment* (Oxford: Oxford University Press for the World Bank, 1994). Even in fully democratic regimes, implementing economic reform may result in a concentration of power in the executive branch. Robert Bates noted this point while serving as a discussant at a conference on the "Political Economy of Economic Reform," Institute for International Economics, Washington, D.C., January 11–13, 1993. At the very least, it requires some independence for key institutions involved in economic policymaking, such as central banks. See, for example, Alex Cukierman, Steven B. Webb, and Bilin Neyapti, "Measuring the Independence of Central Banks and its Effect on Policy Outcomes," *World Bank Economic Review*, vol. 6 (September 1992), pp. 353–98. At the same time, too much insulation can lead to excessive concentration of decisionmaking in the executive branch, which ultimately undermines democracy: voters are allowed to vote every few years, but they are not necessarily given any choice over the policies followed. This point is raised by Adam Przeworski, *Democracy and the Market: Political and*

Economic Reforms in Eastern Europe and Latin America (Cambridge University Press, 1991).

17. Nelson, "The Political Economy of Stabilization," p. 983.

18. Przeworski, *Democracy and the Market*, pp. 179–80. Przeworski notes that when a gradual rather than a radical program is chosen, that program may be abandoned when confidence declines. A radical progam may be slowed but is less likely to be reversed.

19. See Joan M. Nelson, "Poverty, Equity, and the Politics of Adjustment," in Stephan Haggard and Robert R. Kaufman, eds., *The Politics of Economic Adjustment: International Constraints, Distributive Conflicts, and the State* (Princeton University Press, 1992); and Haggard and Webb, *Voting for Reform*.

20. In general, specific safety net programs or targeted measures to compensate specific groups are adopted rather than broader subsidies that are more likely to jeopardize the fiscal balance. See Haggard and Webb, *Voting for Reform*.

21. A relevant example here was "popular capitalism," the active advertising of workers' options to buy shares in the Chilean private pension system in the mid-1980s. While there were limits to this strategy as well as to the system that resulted, it did enhance the political "marketability" of privatization. See, for example, Peter Diamond, "Pension Reform in a Transition Economy: Notes on Poland and Chile" (paper presented to Conference on Transition in Eastern Europe, Cambridge, Mass., February 26–29, 1992), p. 23.

22. Nelson, "The Political Economy of Stabilization." Tolerance for inequality may vary among countries, although there is not necessarily a direct correlation between this tolerance and the distribution of income in a particular country. Seventy percent of Brazilians polled, for example, felt strongly that income distribution in Brazil needed to be improved. Przeworski, *Democracy and the Market*.

23. This is particularly notable in the case of Poland, where the absence of consensus on a safety net virtually paralyzed the political debate, resulting in the resignation of the Olschewski government in mid-1992 and the vote of no confidence for the Suchocka government in 1993. A cross-country analysis conducted by Robert Bates found that countries were far less likely to maintain or to adopt protectionist trade mechanisms if there were compensatory or worker relocation mechanisms in place. See Robert H. Bates and others, "Risk and Trade Regimes: Another Exploration," Working Paper 95 (Duke University Program in Political Economy, December 1989).

24. For details on the political dynamic in Poland and the 1993 elections, see Carol Graham, "Safety Nets and Market Transitions: What Poland Can Learn from Latin America," *Brookings Review*, Winter 1994, pp. 37–39.

25. Lawrence Salmen, "Institutional Dimensions of Poverty Reduction," WPS 411 (Washington, D.C.: The World Bank, Policy, Research, and External Affairs, Country Economics Department, May 1990), p. 19; and Lawrence Salmen, *Listen to the People: Participant-Observer Evaluation of Development Projects* (New York: Oxford University Press, 1987).

26. I would like to thank Alan Angell for raising this point.

27. Nelson, "Poverty, Equity, and the Politics of Adjustment." There is also a similar debate in developed countries. In the United States, for example, the most politically viable programs affecting the poor have been universal programs, such as social security, which have gradually developed a pro-poor focus, versus some targeted programs, which have been underfunded and have failed to generate sustained political support. See, for example, Theda Skocpol, "Universal Appeal: Politically Viable Policies to Combat Poverty," *Brookings Review*, vol. 9 (Summer 1991), pp. 28–33. This does not discount the viability of targeted programs, particularly when they are aimed at groups that no one can oppose politically or when they are relatively successful programs (for example, the Head Start Program in the United States); see Robert Greenstein's response in "Relieving Poverty: An Alternative View," *Brookings Review*, vol. 9 (Summer 1991), pp. 34–35. It is also important not to ignore the plight of the middle sectors, which may suffer a great deal during adjustment. See Nora Lustig, "Poverty and Income Distribution in Latin America in the 1980s: Selected Evidence and Alternatives" (report prepared for the Inter-American dialogue, June 1990).

28. Marc Lindenberg and Noel Ramirez, *Managing Adjustment in Developing Countries* (San Fransisco: ICS Press, 1989), pp. 12–13. And while these groups may protest in such a way as to make life difficult for governments, they actually have less capacity to derail the adjustment process than does the private sector, whose cooperation, beyond aquiescence, is integral to program success. See Joan M. Nelson, ed., *Economic Crisis and Policy Choice: The Politics of Adjustment in the Third World* (Princeton University Press, 1990).

29. See, for example, the chapters on Bolivia and Senegal in this volume. See also Barbara Nunberg, "Public Sector Pay and Employment Reform: A Review of World Bank Experience," World Bank Discussion Paper Series 68 (Washington, D.C., 1989).

30. Joan Nelson's comparative study of democracies implementing adjustment found that regimes tended to get reelected when people perceived things were going well economically. Nelson, "Poverty, Equity, and the Politics of Adjustment."

31. See, for example, Cornia, Jolly, and Stewart, *Adjustment with a Human Face*; and Bourguignon, "Optimal Poverty Reduction, Adjustment, and Growth."

32. David Sahn initially raised this point (in the African context) about donors and the poor political economy message given to recipient countries when social spending was not compensated with reductions on the domestic front, such as cuts in defense spending. Sahn, "Economic Reform in Africa: Are There Similarities with Latin America?" (paper presented to workshop on "Macroeconomic Crisis, Policy Reforms, and the Poor in Latin America," Cali, Colombia, October 1–4, 1991), p. 23.

33. There is a distinction between the structural poor, whose status is defined by time, and the poorest, which is a static definition distinguished by relative income levels. I would like to thank Steen Jorgensen for raising this point.

34. Lawrence Salmen, "Institutional Dimensions of Poverty Reduction," WPS 411 (Washington, D.C.: The World Bank, Policy, Research, and External Affairs, Country Economics Department, May 1990). See also Amartya Sen, "The Political Economy of Targeting," keynote speech at World Bank Conference on Public Expenditure and the Poor: Incidence and Targeting," Washington, D.C., June 17–19, 1992.

35. The political difficulties involved in laying off and compensating public sector workers are detailed in Nunberg, "Public Sector Pay and Employment Reform." See also chapter 4 in Alexandre Marc, Carol Graham, and Mark Schacter, "Social Action Programs and Social Funds: A Review of Design and Implementation in Sub-Saharan Africa," AFTHR Technical Note No. 9, The World Bank, Washington, D.C., December 1992.

36. Haggard, "Markets, Poverty Alleviation, and Income Distribution," p. 195.

37. This conclusion builds on the work of Atul Kohli on parties and reform and of Barbara Geddes on the role of competition as an incentive for reform. The importance of the party system is also noted by Haggard and Webb, *Voting For Reform*. For detail, see John Echeverri-Gent, "Public Participation and Poverty Alleviation: The Experience of Reform Communists in India's West Bengal," *World Development*, vol. 20, no. 10 (1992), pp. 1401–22.

38. Indeed, most programs for the poor fail not because of insufficient finances, but because of incapacity to absorb resources or other inputs. See, for example, Judith Tendler, "What Ever Happened to Poverty Alleviation" (paper presented to Inter-American Development Bank—U.S. AID—World Bank Conference on Support for Microenterprises, Washington, D.C., June 6–9, 1988); and Michael M. Cernea, "Nongovernmental Organizations and Local Development," *World Bank Discussion Papers* 40 (Washington, D.C., 1988).

39. See, for example, Echeverri-Gent, "Public Participation and Poverty Alleviation"; and Henry Bienen and others, "Decentralization in Nepal," *World Development*, vol. 18, no. 1 (1990), pp. 61–75.

40. Azizur Rahman Khan, *Structural Adjustment and Income Distribution: A Review of Issues and Experiences* (Geneva: International Labour Office, 1993). In it Khan established four such categories: efficiently egalitarian (Korea); efficiently inegalitarian (Chile); inefficiently egalitarian (China); and inefficiently inegalitarian (Indonesia, Peru).

41. While inflation seems to be less of a tax on the poor than the decline of real wages, hyperinflation, or inflations of more than 100 percent, has immediate and devasatating effects on the living standards of the poor, as spiraling food prices can become a life-and-death issue. See Cardoso, "Public Participation and Poverty Alleviation;" and Stephan Haggard, "Markets, Poverty Alleviation, and Income Distribution."

42. In Latin America, for example, while the poor may not have borne the brunt of adjustment, poverty increased notably during the adjustment process in the 1980s. See Nora Lustig, "Poverty and Income Distribution in Latin America in the 1980s: Selected Evidence and Policy Alternatives" (report prepared for the Inter-American Dialogue, Washington, D.C., June 1990). Cardoso notes that the

poorest suffer most with repeated and failed stabilization policies, as they have the least room to cope with radical measures. See Eliana Cardoso, "Cyclical Variations of Earnings Inequality in Brazil," Working Paper (Tufts University, January 1993).

43. For detail on this point, see Nelson, "Poverty, Equity, and the Politics of Adjustment;" and also Eliana Cardoso and Ann Hewledge, "Below the Line: Poverty in Latin America," *World Development*, vol. 20, no. 1 (1992), pp. 19–37.

44. For an excellent comparison across Latin America, see Samuel A. Morley, "Structural Adjustment and the Determinants of Poverty in Latin America" (paper presented to Brookings Institution Conference on Poverty and Inequality in Latin America, Washington, D.C., July 1992).

45. Michael Lipton, "The Poor and the Poorest: Some Interim Findings," World Bank Discussion Paper 25, 1988.

46. Sen's theory and its implications for antipoverty policy are discussed in Francois Bourguignon and Gary S. Fields, "Poverty Measures and Anti-Poverty Policy," Delta Working Paper 90-04 (Paris: Centre National de la Recherche Scientifique, École Normale Supérieure, École des Hautes Études en Sciences Sociales, February 1990).

47. Caution is necessary so that vulnerable groups are not bypassed by an excessive focus on targeting. Too much of a focus on avoiding leakage to noneligible groups (E-errors) can result in far more serious errors of failing to reach some of the most vulnerable (F-errors). This is discussed in detail in Giovanni Andrea Cornia and Frances Stewart, "Two Errors of Targeting" (paper presented to World Bank Conference on Public Expenditures and the Poor: Incidence and Targeting, Washington, D.C., June 17–19, 1992).

48. This point is raised by Nelson, "Poverty, Equity, and the Politics of Adjustment."

49. Przeworski, *Democracy and the Market*.

Chapter 2

1. A slightly modified version of this chapter appeared previously as "From Emergency Employment to Social Investment: Alleviating Poverty in Chile," *Brookings Occasional Papers*, November 1991 (Brookings).

2. Despite Chile's strong macroeconomic and social welfare indicators, popular perceptions of the economic model remained surprisingly negative, particularly among low-income sectors, at least through the late 1980s. To some extent these negative opinions can be attributed to poor understanding of economics, particularly among low-income sectors, a lack of understanding exacerbated by an authoritarian regime that did not attempt to educate the public about its economic reforms, a policy that led to unrealistically heightened popular expectations during the transition to democracy. For details on popular opinion of the economic model, see Pablo Halpern B. and Edgardo Bousquet V., "Opinion Publica y Politica Economica: Hacia Un Modelo de Formacion de Percepciones Economicas en Transicion Democratica," *Coleccion Estudios Cieplan* 33 (December 1991), pp. 123–45.

3. The principle of targeting the poorest was an integral part of the "Chicago boys" philosophy. Its main proponent was Miguel Kast. His students effectively implemented the policy through the creation of regional and municipal branches of the state planning agency, ODEPLAN. SERPLAC and SECPLAC were set up as regional and municipal branch offices, respectively. For details about Miguel Kast and the Fundacion Miguel Kast, which advocates his philosophy as the basis for policies in the *poblaciones*, see Margarita Chadwick and Cecilia Ledermann, "Centros Integrales de Desarrollo Comunitarion: Una Contribucion a las Estrategias de Desarrollo Social," in Marcela Jimenez, ed., *Municipios y Organizaciones Privadas* (Santiago: InterAmerican Foundation and Universidad Catolica de Chile, 1990), pp. 35–42. I would like to thank Philip O'Brien for bringing this point to my attention.

4. The infant mortality rate declined more rapidly during the period 1965 to 1973 than it had in the previous decade. It then experienced another acceleration after 1976. Given the extreme economic crisis of the late 1970s, as well as the concurrent decrease in per capita public social welfare expenditure, the improvement in the rate at the time needs further explanation. Raczynski identifies as the most important factor the traditional preference, which increased at this time, that the Chilean state health system gave to mother and child health. In addition, the period from 1964 to 1980 was one of relatively low population growth. The total population grew from 8.3 million to 11.1 million, but the population under age fifteen only grew from 3.2 million to 3.6 million. Dagmar Raczynski and Cesar Oyarzo, "Porque Cae La Tasa de Mortalidad Infantil en Chile en Los Anos 70?" Documento de Trabajo (Santiago: CIEPLAN, August 1981). According to Bravo, fluctuations in health indicators have a direct relation to short-term economic changes. Infant mortality is the health indicator most sensitive to changes in economic output and employment trends, with the employment rate having the strongest effects on fluctuations in the infant mortality rate. Jorge Bravo, "Fluctuaciones en la Economia, El Empleo y en los Indicadores de Salud: Chile 1960–1986," Working Paper 341 (Santiago: PREALC, February 1990).

5. This figure dropped markedly as economic growth increased by 1987. In 1985, one-third of the monetary income of the poorest income quintile depended on cash subsidies from the social network; in the next income quintile it was 13 percent of income. By 1987, these figures had declined to 21 percent and 6 percent respectively. Tim Campbell, George Peterson, and Jose Brakarz, "Decentralization and Local Government in LAC: National Strategies and Efficiency of Local Response to Decentralization in Chile," LATIE Regional Study (The World Bank, November 1990), chap. 4; and Dagmar Raczynski and Pilar Romaguera, "Chile: Poverty, Adjustment and Social Policies in the Eighties" (paper presented to the Brookings Institution/Inter-American Dialogue Conference on Poverty and Inequality in Latin America, Washington, D.C., July 16–17, 1992). See, for example, *World Development Report 1990: Poverty* (The World Bank, 1990), chap. 7; and Helena Ribe and Soniya Carvalho, "Adjustment and the Poor," *Finance and Development* (September 1990), pp. 15–17.

6. Interview with Manuel Marfan, vice minister of economics, Santiago, January 17, 1992. The Aylwin government's economic strategy and its success at

maintaining macroeconomic stability during and after the transition, in spite of the inflationary effects of substantial overheating of the economy by the Pinochet regime before the 1988 plebiscite, are detailed in Genaro Arriagada Herrera and Carol Graham, "Chile: The Maintenance of Adjustment and Macroeconomic Stability During Democratic Transition," in Stephan Haggard and Steven B. Webb, *Voting for Reform: Democracy, Political Liberalization, and Economic Adjustment* (The World Bank, 1994).

7. The education program was targeted at the 900 most disadvantaged schools in the country and then extended to an additional 400, reaching about 13 percent of the primary schools. It provided physical improvements, teacher training, and programs to involve parents, and it hired young people from the communities who had completed their education as auxiliary teachers. For details on the education reforms, see Emanuel de Kadt, "Poverty-Focused Policies: The Experience of Chile," Sussex, Institute of Development Studies, DPS 319, January 1993, p. 316. Details on the youth training program, which was extended to 100,000 young people, were obtained from the author's interviews with the head of the program, Juan Jose Rivas, Ministry of Labor, Santiago, January 21–22, 1992. The programs are also described in Arriagada Herrera and Graham, "Chile."

8. These include A. Torche, "Pobreza extrema y gasto social: deficiones y opciones de politica económica," in APSAL-ISUC, Aspectos metologicas de las politicas de desarrollo social (Santiago: Naciones Unidas-UNICEF, 1987); R. Mujica and A. Rojas, as cited in Pilar Vergara, *Politicas Hacia la Extreme Pobreza en Chile: 1973–1988* (Santiago: FLASCO, 1990); and Molly Pollack and Andras Uthoff, "Poverty and the Labor Market: Greater Santiago, 1969–85," in Gerry Rogers, ed., *Urban Poverty and the Labour Market: Access to Jobs and Incomes in Asian and Latin American Cities* (Geneva: ILO, 1989). See David E. Hojman, "Chile after Pinochet: Aylwin's Christian Democrat Economic Policies for the 1990s," *Bulletin of Latin American Research*, vol. 9, no. 1 (1990), pp. 25–47. There is also substantial debate over the measurement indexes used, with some studies relying on the government's source, the Ficha Cas, which is based on ownership of household essentials and durables; others use income, either inclusive or exclusive of government benefits; others consumption; and others minimum wage versus the cost of a basic basket of goods.

Extreme poverty was defined as having a monthly income under 20,000 pesos, which would not be enough to meet basic subsistence needs. Vergara, *Politicas Hacia La Extrema Pobreza*, p. 64. Using the Ficha Cas, the government's measure based on ownership of durables, extreme poverty was 21 percent in 1970, 14 percent in 1980, and 12 percent in 1990. This measure has been criticized, however, as it fails to include income as an indicator. Raczynski and Romaguera, "Chile: Poverty, Adjustment and Social Policies."

9. Nonindigent poor workers, meanwhile, are concentrated in construction and services. For detail see Molly Pollack and Andras Uthoff, "Pobreza y Empleo: Un Analisis del Periodo 1969–1987 en el Gran Santiago," Documento de Trabajo 348 (Santiago: PREALC, July 1990).

10. Chile's overall macroeconomic position vis-à-vis its neighbors also improved substantially after 1973, resulting in one of the strongest economies on

the continent. See, for example, Carol Graham, "The Enterprise for the America's Initiative: A Development Strategy for Latin America?" *Brookings Review*, vol. 9 (Fall 1991), pp. 22–27.

11. Vergara, *Politicas Hacia La Extrema Pobreza*, p. 44. In 1969 the poorest 10 percent of Chile's population had 1.3 percent of total income; by 1989 their relatively small share had dropped to 1.2 percent. During the same interval, the share of the wealthiest 10 percent increased from 39.0 percent to 41.6 percent. Programa de Economia del Trabajo, *Encuestas de Empleo* (Santiago: PET, 1990), p. 79. Comparative studies show that in countries where labor is the most important factor endowment, such as Taiwan, liberalization of the trade regime will actually improve income distribution, while in countries such as Chile, where the most important factor endowment is natural resources (copper), income distribution is likely to become more unequal with commercial opening. Ronald Fischer, "Efectos de Una Apertura Comercial Sobre La Distribucion del Ingresso: Teoria y Evidencia," *Coleccion Estudios Cieplan* 33 (December 1991), pp. 95–121. Chile's distribution is much worse than the average for OECD or East Asian nations; it is about average for Latin America. Mario Marcel and Andres Solimano, "Developmentalism, Socialism, and Free Market Reform: Three Decades of Income Distribution in Chile" (paper presented to Brookings Institution Conference on "The Chilean Economy: Policy Lessons and Challenges," Washington, D.C., April 22–23, 1993).

12. Ninety percent of increases in social security payments during this time went to the *asignaciones familiares* (family quotas) and pensions for the poorest. By 1982 total spending in this field remained at only 28 percent of its 1970 levels. Vergara, *Politicas Hacia La Extrema Pobreza*, p. 44.

13. A detailed description of the pre-Pinochet social welfare system is beyond the scope of this paper. A comprehensive description can be found in Jose Pablo Arellano, *Politicas Sociales y Desarrollo: Chile 1924–1984* (Santiago: CIEPLAN, 1985), p. 289.

14. Arellano, *Politicas Sociales*; and Tarsicio Castañeda, *Para Combatir La Pobreza: Politica Social y Descentralizacion en Chile Durante Los '80* (Santiago: Centro de Estudios Publicos, 1990). Informal sector or self-employed workers, along with agricultural laborers, composed the bulk of the poorest sectors of the population in 1974. This sector represented 45 percent of the economically active population, earned on average the equivalent of the minimum wage or less, and received just over 14 percent of total national income. The vast majority (three-quarters or more) of workers in agriculture and services were in this sector, while only slightly more than 40 percent of industrial workers were in this group. At the other end of the scale, approximately 9 percent of the population received more than 35 percent of national income. The largest strata of the economically active population (46 percent) earned the equivalent of between one and four times the minimum wage and received approximately 50 percent of national income. This group comprised primarily salaried employees—mostly in service industries—and manual industrial workers. Alejandro Foxley and Oscar Muñoz, "Income Redistribution, Economic Growth and Social Structure: The Case of Chile," *Oxford Bulletin of Economics and Statistics*, vol. 56 (February 1974), pp.

21–44. There is some debate over the extent to which the system was biased toward formal sector workers.

15. Foxley and Muñoz, "Income Redistribution," pp. 31, 39. The system had slightly regressive tax effects as well, because social security contributions were tax deductible, and the highest paid workers paid the highest tax rates. In addition, it acted as a disincentive to employment by increasing the cost of hiring additional laborers. Foxley and Munoz, "Income Redistribution." This phenomenon has occurred in other Latin American countries with large informal sectors that have introduced relatively advanced labor legislation, such as Peru in the mid-1970s.

16. Vergara, *Politicas Hacia La Extrema Pobreza*, pp. 23, 43; and Erik Haindl and others, *Gasto Social Efectivo* (Santiago: Universidad de Chile, 1989).

17. Castañeda, *Para Combatir La Pobreza*. For example, the Fondo Comun Municipal was established. All municipalities contributed to this fund, which distributed resources from rich to poor municipalities. This often provided poor municipalities with independent resources for the first time.

18. Dagmar Raczynski and Claudia Serrano, "Planificación Para El Desarrollo Local? La Experiencia en Algunos Municipios de Santiago," Documento de Trabajo 24 (Santiago: CIEPLAN, June 1988), pp. 37–62. See also Dagmar Raczynski, "Descentralización y Politicas Sociales: Lecciones de la Experiencia Chilena y Tareas Pendientes," *Coleccion Estudios Cieplan* 31 (March 1991), pp. 141–51.

19. In addition to the government's programs, there were many continuing nongovernment efforts, in particular some led by the Catholic Church and the related Vicaria de Solaridad. While these efforts were clearly important, they were by no means of a size and scope comparable to the government's. Mariana Schkolnik and Berta Teitelboim, *Pobreza y Desempleo en Poblaciones* (Santiago: PET, 1988).

20. Vergara, *Politicas Hacia La Extrema Pobreza*. The origins of PNAC actually go back as far as the 1930s.

21. Dagmar Raczynski, "Descentralización y Politicas Sociales." A similar point about targeting is also made by Giovanni Andrea Cornia and Frances Stewart in "Two Errors of Targeting" (paper presented to World Bank Conference on Public Expenditures and the Poor: Incidence and Targeting, Washington, D.C., June 17–19, 1992). Excessive targeting may raise a conflict between the goals of reducing poverty and respecting the dignity of the poor. See also Norman J. Ireland, "Stigma and Quality as Self-Selection Mechanisms" (paper presented to World Bank Conference on Public Expenditures and the Poor). Vergara, *Politicas Hacia La Extrema Pobreza*.

22. Vergara, *Politicas Hacia La Extrema Pobreza*.

23. Veragara, *Politicas Hacia La Extrema Pobreza*, p. 205. The Inter-American Development Bank financed the lots with services, as it has done in several countries. The point about resource generation is made in Campbell (1992).

24. Castañeda, *Para Combatir La Pobreza*. Joseph L. Scarpaci, *Primary Medical Care in Chile: Accessibility Under Military Rule* (Pittsburgh: University of

Pittsburgh Press, 1988), p. 138. The extent to which resources flowed to private systems was notable: the private Isapres, which take care of 11 percent of the population, receive more than 50 percent of obligatory health care contributions, while the public Fonasa takes care of more than 70 percent of the population and receives less than half these contributions. Raczynski and Romaguera, "Chile: Poverty, Adjustment and Social Policies," p. 27.

25. Castaneda, *Para Combatir La Pobreza*, p. 245. Under the private system, private firms collect payments, manage funds, and supervise distribution. For detail, see Eliana Cardoso and Ann Helwege, "Below the Line: Poverty in Latin America," *World Development*, vol. 20, no. 1, (1992), pp. 19–37; and Peter Diamond, "Pension Reform in a Transition Economy: Notes on Poland and Chile" (paper presented to National Bureau of Economic Research conference on Transition in Eastern Europe, Cambridge, February 26–29, 1992).

26. See, for example, Vergara, *Politicas Hacia La Extrema Pobreza*, pp. 24–25. Raczynski and Romaguera, "Chile: Poverty, Adjustment and Social Policies."

27. Barbara Stallings and Robert Kaufman, eds., *Debt and Democracy in Latin America* (Boulder: Westview, 1989).

28. This conclusion is based on the author's interviews in Santiago in November 1990 with central and municipal government officials who implemented the emergency employment programs; with people who participated in the programs; with community leaders in neighborhoods where the programs were implemented; and with several academics specializing in employment or poverty issues.

29. The programs were allocated over 5 billion pesos, or approximately US$20 million, in the government's 1987 social spending budget of 274 billion pesos. The bulk of social spending (249 billion pesos) went to pensions, and a total of 20 billion pesos went to all social programs other than employment. In relative terms, therefore, 5 billion pesos was quite significant. The relative amount spent on employment programs at their height, in 1983, was much greater, as the programs employed approximately three times as many people in 1983 as in 1987. Data obtained from SERPLAC Metropolitana, Intendencia de Santiago. In a study of four of Santiago's poorest municipalities, PEM and POJH resources accounted for 30–90 percent of the total. PREALC, *Empleos de Emergencia* (Santiago: OIT, 1988), p. 188; and Carol Graham, "Recent Experiences with Employment Programs in Chile, Bolivia, and Peru," Memorandum, Inter-American Dialogue, Washington, D.C., March 1990. Recent estimates of this figure are as high as 13 percent.

30. Interview with Jorge de la Fuente, former head of the Department of Development and Information, SERPLAC Metropolitana, Santiago, November 19, 1990.

31. Graham, "Recent Experiences with Employment Programs," p. 8; and Schkolnik and Teitelboim, *Pobreza y Desempleo en Poblaciones*.

32. Graham, "Recent Experiences with Employment Programs," p. 8.

33. Ibid., pp. 9–10.

34. PREALC, *Empleos de Emergencia*, pp. 148–52.

35. Graham, "Recent Experiences with Employment Programs," p. 10; and PREALC, *Empleos de Emergencia*.

36. SERPLAC Metropolitana, "Memoria Departamento de Empleo, 1982–1990" (Intendencia de Santiago, 1990).

37. SERPLAC Metropolitana, "Memoria Departamento de Empleo"; and PREALC, *Empleos de Emergencia*, p. 123.

38. In addition to the national training program, the Servicio Nacional de Capacitacion y Empleo (SENCE) was run out of the Ministry of Labor. SENCE administered a variety of scholarship programs in conjunction with the private sector from the late 1970s on. Most of SENCE's activities, however, were concentrated in large private-sector firms, because it was difficult for smaller firms to participate in the subsidization system, and the firms that presented proposals to SENCE tended to concentrate on training for executives and professionals. Thus the effect of SENCE on the poorest and least-skilled sector of the labor force was minimal, as was its coordination with the special employment programs. Cristian Echeverria, "El Estado y la Capacitacion en Chile," Documento de Trabajo (Santiago: SENCE, 1990).

39. Graham, "Recent Experiences with Employment Programs." See, for example, Carol Graham, "The APRA Government and the Urban Poor: The PAIT Programme in Lima's Pueblos Jovenes," *Journal of Latin American Studies*, vol. 23 (February 1991), pp. 91–130; and Peter Ward and Sylvia Chant, "Community Leadership and Self-Help Housing," *Progress in Planning*, vol. 27, pt. 2 (1987), pp. 77–100. Interview with Jorge de la Fuente.

40. Many countries, including Panama, Peru, and Bolivia, found it necessary to implement employment programs in the early and mid-1980s. A comparison of the programs is beyond the scope of this paper, but it is relevant to note that the Chilean programs stand out in terms of decentralized administration, scale, and effective targeting of the poorest and most needy workers. See, for example, PREALC, *Empleos de Emergencia*.

41. Patricio Meller, "Adjustment and Social Costs in Chile During the 1980s," *World Development*, vol. 19, no. 11 (1991), p. 1559.

42. Because such programs are designed to be temporary, it makes little sense to pay above-market wages. However, POJH and PEM wages clearly fell far short of meeting even minimum basic needs. PIMO and PEP had more realistic payment scales. If payment scales are too high, there is little incentive to leave the program. In Peru, where the PAIT program paid the minimum wage, only 16 percent of workers were actively looking for other jobs. In contrast, 63 percent of PEM workers were actively seeking alternative employment. Graham, "The APRA Government," p. 128. Jaime Ruiz-Tagle and Roberto Urmeneta, *Los Trabajadores del Programa del Empleo Minimo* (Santiago: PET, 1984), p. 5.

43. Interview with Jorge de la Fuente. This was confirmed by several of the author's interviews with program officials and critics alike. Interview with Roberto Urmeneta, PET, Santiago, November 22, 1990. Interview with Dagmar Raczynski, CIEPLAN, Santiago, November 22, 1990. Interview with Ivan Moreira Barros, mayor, La Cisterna, November 23, 1990. Interview with administrator of POJH in La Cisterna, November 23, 1990.

44. Patricia Politzer, *Miedo en Chile* (Santiago, 1985), p. 36.

45. Interview with Roberto Urmeneta. Urmeneta cited the example of workers on the PanAmerican highway who, although still resentful of the low wage levels, at least felt some satisfaction in participating in a project of national significance. Pollack and Uthoff, "Pobreza y Empleo," pp. 11–13.

46. Interview with Karen Lashman, World Bank, Washington, D.C., November 13, 1990. Productive use of labor and good quality control are key factors in helping special program workers get reabsorbed into the labor force. The costs of establishing special employment programs are approximately the same whether the program is productive or not. However, the main benefit to both workers and society from such programs is the productive input, both in training provided and in infrastructure created. Joost Martens and Blas Tomic, "Los Programas Especiales de Empleos: Algunas Lecciones de la Experiencia," Working Paper 225 (Santiago: PREALC, April 1983). Vergara, *Politicas Hacia La Extrema Pobreza*, p. 331.

47. Schkolnik and Teitelboim, *Probreza y Desempleo en Poblaciones*; and interview with Isabel Vial, INDA, Washington, D.C., December 3, 1990. Nongovernment sources usually provide a breakdown of employment figures that separates special employment programs from the overall figures. Interviews with Jaime Ruiz Tagle, director, PET, Santiago, November 16, 1990; and Tito Cordova, Vicaria Pastoral Obrero, and former POJH worker, Santiago, November 21, 1990.

48. This was confirmed by the author's interviews in November 1990 with former program workers, program officials, and community observers. It is also confirmed by the author's field research in Peru, where a similar program, PAIT, had similar effects on malefemale relationships.

49. Official employment statistics described those who work as little as one hour a day as "employed." Thus more critical examination of official figures shows that the underemployment rate is higher. Although there is a great deal of differentiation in income levels in the informal sector, one means to gauge this rate is the size of this sector, defined as urban self-employed workers and domestic servants. In 1976, 35.1 percent of the economically active population was underemployed. In 1981, this figure was 34.4 percent. An analogous figure for 1989—although not exactly the same—is that the informal sector in Santiago was 29.4 percent of the economically active population. And to date, poverty levels remain closely correlated with unemployment, as is noted in table 2-3. Interview with Mariana Schkolnik, MINEPLAN, Santiago, November 19, 1990; PET, *Encuesta de Empleo* (Santiago: PET, 1989); interview with Jorge de la Fuente; and Gonzalo Rivas, "El Desempeno Empleador de la Economia Chilena Bajo El Regimen Militar," *Coyuntura Economica*, no. 14 (April 1987), pp. 47–115.

50. Vergara, *Politicas Hacia La Extrema Pobreza*, p. 329.

51. Interview with Jaime Ruiz-Tagle. Interview with Pedro Emilio Perez, SENCE, and former head of employment programs for the Quinta Normal region, Santiago, November 23, 1990. Interview with Mariana Schkolnik. For details see Clarissa Hardy, *La Ciudad Escindida* (Santiago: PET, 1989), chap. 9. See Graham, "The APRA Government."

52. For experiences in Peru and Bolivia, see Graham, "The APRA Government"; and Carol Graham, "The Politics of Protecting the Poor during Adjust-

ment: Bolivia's Emergency Social Fund," *World Development*, vol. 20 (September 1992), pp. 1233–51.

53. Interview with Pedro Emilio Perez. Perez was forced to resign from his position in the program administration at this point.

54. Interview with Manuel Barrera, director, Center of Social Studies, Santiago, November 20, 1990.

55. The top 20 percent, meanwhile, increased by 4.7 percentage points during the Pinochet regime vis-à-vis the 1960–73 period. Under Aylwin, their share has declined by 0.5 percent. Marcel and Solimano, "Developmentalism, Socialism and Free Market Reform," p. 7.

56. *Economia y Trabajo en Chile: Informe Anual, 1990–1991* (Santiago: Programa de Economia del Trabajo, 1991). This was particularly important as the government had to curb expenditure markedly in the first year, because of both the inflationary effects of the Gulf crisis (and the resulting increase in the costs of oil) and the overheating of the economy by the Pinochet government in 1988. The overall increase in social expenditure of 10 percent a year, meanwhile, has had positive effects on all quintiles except the highest, which suggests that social expenditure benefits the middle and bottom quintiles vis-à-vis the top 20 percent. Marcel and Solimano, "Developmentalism, Socialism and Free Market Reform," pp. 19–21.

57. The reform of the labor code included the elimination of a clause that allowed arbitrary dismissal; ended the time limit on strikes; and facilitated the creation of unions and improved the system of financing for labor organizations. For detail on this reform, see Arriagada and Graham, "Chile: The Maintenance of Adjustment and Macroeconomic Stability." Real minimum wage, meanwhile, was raised by 44 percent from September 1989 to September 1990, while the cost of living of the poor went up 35.8 percent. Jaime Ruiz-Tagle, "El Gobierno Democratico y Los Ingresos de los Mas Pobres," *Mensaje* 395 (December 1990), p. 484.

58. The family allowance (Asignacion Familiar) was raised by 1,100 pesos for workers earning less than 5,000 pesos and 800 pesos for workers earning between 50,000 and 70,000; and frozen for workers earning more than that level. The family subsidy (Subsidio Unico Familiar), which benefits nonsalaried workers, was raised by 8 percent, from 750 to 1,100 pesos. Still, minimum wage remains at 31.8 percent of its 1974 level, and the Asignacion Familiar is at 27 percent of its 1974 level. Ruiz-Tagle, "El Gobierno Democratico," pp. 484–85.

59. Marcel and Solimano, "Developmentalism, Socialism and Free Market Reform," p. 23. As with all the data on poverty in Chile, there is some debate over these figures.

60. Nicolas Flaño, "El Fondo de Solidaridad e Inversion Social: En Que Estamos Pensando," *Coleccion Estudios Cieplan*, March 31, 1991, pp. 153–64.

61. Ibid. Raczynski and Romaguera, "Chile: Poverty, Adjustment and Social Policies."

62. Flaño, "El Fondo de Solidaridad e Inversion Social"; and interview with Flaño.

63. Jimenez, ed., *Municipios y Organizaciones Privadas*; and Echeverria, "El Estado y la Capacitacion en Chile." Examples are SENCE's training scholarship

program, which was implemented by private organizations after a process of public bidding, and the role played by CONIN—a private, nonprofit organization—in state nutrition policy.

64. In the municipal elections, the governing Concertacion coalition (of Christian Democrats and Socialists) received 53.25 percent vote; the right received 29.67 percent; the independent Union de Centro of Francisco Errazuriz received 8.10 percent; the Communists received 6.60 percent; and the rest was split among independents. Embassy of Chile, Washington, D.C., June 30, 1992.

65. The advisory board for FOSIS, composed of professionals and academics in the field, has been informally constituted but to date has not been called to meet. Interview with Dagmar Raczynski, FOSIS advisory board member, Santiago, November 22, 1990.

66. Interview with Clarissa Hardy.

67. See, for example, Arturo Valenzuela, *Political Power Brokers in Chile* (Duke University Press, 1977); and Jimenez, ed., *Municipios y Organizaciones Privadas*. Since the 1800s municipalities have been perceived as an agent of the central government more than anything else. The 1925 constitution and 1938 Popular Front government introduced a new kind of centralization based on state intervention and strong presidentialism. Under the Pinochet government, centralization was increased through authoritarianism and ideological control.

68. Three laws were the basis of this process: the Nueva Ley Organica Municipal 1289 of 1975, the Ley de Rentas Municipales 3063 of 1979, and Ley 3551 of 1981. Two important complementary laws were Ley 3000 of 1979 and Ley 1-3063 of 1980. Castañeda, *Para Combatir La Pobreza*. Without the Fondo Commun Municipal, the municipal tax base would be regressive, as it is based on property values, car registration, and medium and large-sized business establishments. I would like to thank Dagmar Raczynski for pointing this out to me.

69. Author's conversations with PEM and POJH administrators, the mayor of La Cisterna, and Dagmar Raczynski. Also Carlos Clavel and others, "Estudio Sobre Los Programas Especiales de Empleo," Universidad de Chile, Departamento de Economia, Santiago, 1990. Dagmar Raczynski and Claudia Serrano, "Administracion y Gestion Local: La Experiencia de Algunos Municipios en Santiago," *Colección Estudios Cieplan* 22 (December 1987), pp. 129–51. Nelson Herrera, "El Presupuesto Municipal: Estudio de Casos: La Florida, Penalolen, Macul, San Joaquin, Puente Alto," Cuadernos de Trabajo 29 (Santiago: Centro de Estudios Municipales, 1989), pp. 7–9.

70. Campbell and others, "Decentralization to Local Government," Executive Summary, p. 3.

71. Jimenez, ed., *Municipios y Organizaciones Privadas*.

72. Interview with Dagmar Raczynski. Raczynski and Serrano identify three types of mayors under the Pinochet regime: politicized (the ones with the strongest ties to the regime); technical-entrepreneurial (tending to be young and skilled); and bureaucratic (tending to be older and the most difficult to categorize). The first were more likely to use the programs for political proselytizing, and the second for community improvements. Raczynski and Serrano, "Planificacion Para El Desarrollo Local."

73. Raczynski and Serrano, "Planificacion Para El Desarrollo Local," p. 48.

74. Interviews with Junta Vecinal directors Leonor Romero in Maipu (November 21, 1990) and Maria Ines Bravo in Villa El Cobre (November 17, 1990). Bravo recounted how she and her fellow directors were harassed and violently assaulted by the supporters of the former appointed junta directors.

75. This is confirmed by the author's conversations with Junta Vecinal directors in Villa El Cobre and Maipu, as well as with municipal officials in La Cisterna.

76. Interviews with Pedro Emilio Perez, Dagmar Raczynski, Ivan Moreira Barros, and Jorge de la Fuente.

77. There are now 5,010 Juntas Vecinales in Chile, of which 1,000 are in Santiago. In the period 1984–87 alone, their number increased by 700.

78. During the first four years of their legal existence, there were 9,000 Centros de Madres. The number grew to as many as 20,000 under the Allende government. This changed dramatically with the Pinochet government, which organized all juntas into the CEMA-Chile (Centros de Madres) under the directorship of Mrs. Pinochet. Yet women still participated, albeit on a lesser scale, because of the financial benefits they garnered from joint workshops and the social benefits that came from communal interaction. In 1987 there were 6,387 Centros de Madres, approximately half of them in Santiago. Hardy, La Ciudad Escindida, pp. 174–77.

79. Foxley and Muñoz, "Income Redistribution," p. 38.

80. Interview with Señora Mercedes, Villa El Cobre, November 17, 1990. Interview with Maria Ines Bravo. Interview with Leonor Romero. Neither Señora Leonor nor any of her junta colleagues knew anything about FOSIS.

81. Interview with Humberto Nogueira, academic director, Participa, Santiago, January 21, 1992.

82. Hardy, La Ciudad Escindida, pp. 181–82.

83. Philip David Oxhorn, "Democratic Transitions and the Democratization of Civil Society: Chilean Shantytown Organizations under the Authoritarian Regime," Ph.D. dissertation, Harvard University, September 1989.

84. Luis Razeto and others, Las Organizaciones Economicas Populares 1973–1990 (Santiago: PET, 1990).

85. The one exception is the Communist party, which has, at various times, played an important organizational role in many poblaciones. Yet, given its proscription during the military years and its marginal position in the current government, its role in providing significant linkages to the state is limited.

86. Carol Graham, Peru's APRA: Parties, Politics, and the Elusive Quest for Democracy (Boulder: Lynne Rienner, 1992).

87. Raul Rivadeneira, Agresión Politica (La Paz: Editorial La Juventud, 1989).

88. Trade union leader quoted in Alan Angell, "Unions and Workers in Chile during the 1980s," in Paul W. Drake and Ivàn Jausie, eds., The Struggle for Democracy in Chile, 1982–1990 (University of Nebraska Press, 1991), p. 204.

89. James Petras, "The New Class Basis of Chilean Politics," New Left Review, vol. 172 (November–December 1988), pp. 67–82.

90. Interview with Dagmar Raczynski.

91. Interview with Maria Ines Bravo.

92. Ibid.

93. For detail, see Dagmar Raczynski, "Disminuyo La Extrema Pobreza entre Chile 1970–1982?" *Nota Tecnica* 90 (Cieplan, December 1986). The same households that are poor in income may not be poor in education or housing, for example.

Chapter 3

1. A slightly modified version of this chapter appeared as Carol Graham, "The Politics of Protecting the Poor during Adjustment: Bolivia's Emergency Social Fund," in *World Development*, vol. 20, no. 9 (1992), pp. 1233–51.

2. Aid and public works programs are often used for political patronage ends, even in advanced industrial democracies. For examples see Carol Graham, "The APRA Government and the Urban Poor: The PAIT Programme in Lima's Pueblos Jovenes," *Journal of Latin American Studies*, vol. 23, part 1 (February 1991), pp. 91–130; and Peter Ward and Sylvia Chant, "Community Leadership and Self-Help Housing," *Progress in Planning*, vol. 27, part 2 (1987).

3. Joan M. Nelson, ed., *Economic Crisis and Policy Choice: The Politics of Adjustment in the Third World* (Princeton University Press, 1990); and several conversations with the author on this issue, Washington, D.C., October 1990.

4. For a detailed account, see Laurence Whitehead, "Bolivia's Failed Democratization, 1977–1980," in Guillermo O'Donnel, Philippe Schmitter, and Lawrence Whitehead, *Transitions from Authoritarian Rule: Latin America* (Johns Hopkins University Press, 1986), pp. 49–71.

5. Raul Rivadeneira, *Agresión Politica* (La Paz: Editorial La Juventud, 1990), p. 37.

6. The economic plan that the MNR announced as Decree Law 21060 was purportedly more radical than that of the ADN. The MNR then broke the "Pacto" in February 1989, at the initiation of the 1989 electoral campaign. For details see Catherine M. Conaghan, James M. Malloy, and Luis Abugattas, "Business and the Boys: The Politics of Neoliberalism in the Central Andes," *Latin American Research Review*, vol. 25, no. 2 (1990); James Malloy, "Bolivia's Economic Crisis," *Current History*, vol. 86 (January 1987); and Rivadeneira, *Agresión Politica*.

7. Rivadeneira, *Agresión Politica*.

8. In the 1991 municipal elections, the Acuerdo Patriotico (ADN/MIR) garnered 31.5 percent of council seats, the MNR 23.3 percent, and Condepa 8.4 percent. "Fernandez's UCS Takes Second Place," *Latin American Weekly Report*, December 12, 1991; and "Porque Tambillo," *Presencia*, July 15, 1990.

9. Rivadeneira, *Agresión Politica*. While participation rates of 50 percent and lower are common for countries where voting is voluntary, such as the United States, they are extremely high for a country with mandatory voting such as Bolivia.

10. Rivadeneira, *Agresión Politica*. This alliance was particularly odd as Jaime Paz had been persecuted by Hugo Banzer during the latter's dictatorship in the 1970s.

11. The minister of health, President Paz's brother, was actually of the MIR.

12. Rivadeneira, *Agresión Politica*.

13. Fernando Campero, "Prudencio Desarrollo Institucional del FSE," in Virginia Ossio, ed., *Fondo Social de Emergencia: Seminario de Evaluación* (La Paz: Fondo Social de Emergencia, 1990), pp. 41–55.

14. As the institutional structure to provide social assistance was very weak, it was allotted only 25 percent of funds; productive support was the smallest program, receiving less than 10 percent of funds. Steen Jorgensen, "La Experiencia del Banco Mundial Con el FSE," in Ossio, ed., *Fondo Social de Emergencia*, pp. 69–72; and Katherine Marshall, "The Genesis and Early Debates," in Steen Jorgensen, Margaret Grosh, and Mark Schacter, eds., *Bolivia's Answer to Poverty, Economic Crisis, and Adjustment* (Washington, D.C.: The World Bank, 1992; and the Emergency Social Fund offices, La Paz).

15. Jorgensen, "La Experiencia del Banco Mundial Con el FSE"; and Jorgensen, Grosh, and Schacter, *Bolivia's Answer*. The ESF's major donors were, in order of importance, the World Bank, the Swiss government, the Dutch government, the Bolivian government, U.S. AID, the British government, and various others.

16. Administrative overhead costs were kept to a minimum of 3–5 percent throughout the program's operation. The fund used only 100 people to manage 1,000 projects, while the Agriculture Ministry used 1,000 people to administer 50 projects. Jorgensen, "La Experiencia del Banco Mundial Con el FSE;" and interview with Jorge Patiño, former second in command, ESF, La Paz, August 25, 1990.

17. Jorgensen, "La Experiencia del Banco Mundial Con el FSE."

18. InterAmerican Development Bank, *Economic and Social Progress in Latin America: 1989*, report (Washington, D.C.: 1989), p. 276. Total population in 1988 was 6,918,000, of which 50.4 percent was urban.

19. Campero, "Prudencio Desarrollo Institucional del FSE," p. 52. "It was better to have ten projects with one bad one than just three projects and nothing more."

20. John Newman, Steen Jorgensen, and Menno Pradhan, "Workers' Benefits from Bolivia's Emergency Social Fund," Living Standards Measurement Study, Working Paper 77 (Washington, D.C.: The World Bank, 1991). Employment programs in general are not suited to reaching laid-off public sector workers, but rather are a means for redistributing income to the poor and improving infrastructure at the same time.

21. For examples of the record of centrally implemented programs, see Carol Graham, "From Emergency Employment to Social Investment: Alleviating Poverty in Chile," *Brookings Occasional Papers* (November 1991); Carol Graham, "The APRA Government and the Urban Poor: The PAIT Programme in Lima's Pueblos Jovenes," *Journal of Latin American Studies*, vol. 23 (February 1991), pp. 91–130; and Peter Ward and Sylvia Chant, "Community Leadership and Self-Help Housing," *Progress in Planning*, vol. 27, part 2 (1987), pp. 77–100.

22. There was no mechanism other than wage levels—which were higher than those in the informal sector—to target the poorest workers. For detail see New-

man, Jorgensen, and Pradhan, "Workers' Benefits," p. 9; and Margaret Grosh, "How Well Did the ESF Work?" in Jorgensen, Grosh, and Schacter, eds., *Bolivia's Answer*. For a detailed beneficiary assessment, see "Proyecto de Evaluación e Investigación del FSE: Impacto Social" (La Paz: Fondo Social de Emergencia, 1988).

23. Newman, Jorgensen, and Pradhan, "Workers' Benefits." "Proyecto de Evaluación: Impacto Social" (1988). Thirty-six percent of the workers responded that they had not been organized before, and only 12 percent remained unionized. These numbers may not be completely accurate because workers are often reluctant to "confess" that they belong to a union. Of the 12 percent that were organized, most were former miners.

24. "Proyecto de Evaluación: Impacto Social." Different kinds of programs had different effects. Some, such as *autoconstrucción* (self-construction) programs provided housing structures with low-interest loans, relying on the beneficiaries to complete the interior and to solicit the state for services such as water and electricity. One drawback was that the program underestimated the opportunity costs of beneficiaries' time, and their incomes often fell as they tried to complete their homes. Progress was slow and uneven, and the program was thus suited to the better-off among the poor. Other programs, such as social assistance programs (school lunch programs and day care), differed in that they entailed a much higher level of community participation and a higher percentage of women—77 percent—than most infrastructure programs. Still, knowledge of the ESF's role remained low: 60.1 percent did not know what the ESF was.

25. "Proyecto de Evaluación: Impacto Social" (1988).

26. This conclusion is based on the author's interviews with a large number of ESF functionaries, including former and current directors, as well as interviews with a variety of soliciting agencies that dealt with the ESF throughout its tenure.

27. Fernando Romero, "Emergency Social Fund of Bolivia," paper presented to the World Bank Symposium on Poverty and Adjustment, Washington, D.C., April 11–13, 1988. Geraro Avila, former director of operations, Emergency Social Fund, interview, La Paz, August 25, 1990; Fernando Campero, former second in command, Emergency Social Fund, interview, La Paz, August 25, 1990; and Mauricio Balcazar, former director of promotion, Emergency Social Fund, interview, La Paz, August 25, 1990.

28. Interviews with ESF functionaries of all levels; press archives, Emergency Social Fund, La Paz, August 1990. Maria Elena Querehasu, former director of promotion, Emergency Social Fund, interview, La Paz, August 29, 1990; Geraro Avila, interview, August 25, 1990; and Jorge Patiño, interview, La Paz, August 16, 1990; Luis Alberto Valle, executive director, Emergency Social Fund, interview, La Paz, August 29, 1990.

29. Mauricio Balcazar, interview.

30. Geraro Avila, interview.

31. Mauricio Balcazar, interview. Balcazar says that the U.S. consulting firm Sawyer Miller advised the MNR campaign to use the ESF more than it did. Balcazar was the head of the MNR's rural campaign.

32. Maria Elena Querehasu, interview.

33. Geraro Avila, interview. Maria Angel del Ponce, director of information, Emergency Social Fund, interview, La Paz, August 20, 1990.

34. During the electoral phase an MNR senator and associate of Sanchez de Lozada requested an increase in the campesino fund, aimed at the highly politicized mining cooperatives. A great deal of pressure was applied, and an increase for Potosi cooperatives was approved, despite hesitation on the part of the director of the campesino fund and repayment problems that persist today. The new government has also put pressure on the ESF to approve more credit to the cooperatives. Eugen Finkel, director, Fondo Rotativo Para Cooperativas, Emergency Social Fund, interview, La Paz, August 20, 1990; also, Mauricio Balcazar, interview; and Maria Elena Querehasu, interview.

35. Rivadeneira, *Agresión Politica*.

36. For a detailed account of these advertising slots, see Rivadeneira, *Agresión Politica*, pp. 120–40.

37. Luis Vasquez, former mayor of El Alto and current congressional deputy for the MIR for La Paz, interview, La Paz, August 22, 1990. The National Electoral Court received complaints from parties of virtually every political bent that the ESF was used as a tool of the governing party. Yet as this use was limited to the posting of flags and signs, the court felt that there was no ground upon which to consider this a violation of electoral rules. Carlos Zubieta, justice, National Electoral Court, interview, La Paz, August 21, 1990.

38. Even opposition mayors agree that the MNRs attempts to use the ESF were largely limited to this electoral period. L. Vasquez, interview, August 22, 1990.

39. Mauricio Balcazar, interview.

40. Luis Vasquez, interview.

41. Mercado was also the ADN candidate for mayor of El Alto in 1987. Author's interviews with former and current directors, La Paz, August 1990.

42. Eugen Finkel, interview.

43. Former ESF official, interview, August 29, 1990. ESF official, interview, La Paz, August 27, 1990. Zone chiefs are not authorized to approve projects, but they do have a clear sense of what does and does not fall under the ESF's mandate.

44. Emergency Social Fund official, interview, La Paz, August 20, 1990. Luis Vasquez, interview.

45. "Reiterada Critica Mirista a Dirección del ex-FSE," *Presencia*, June 7, 1990.

46. Voters elect party representatives to a municipal council, which then chooses the mayor. This system has substantial drawbacks. In some cases where the race between two front runners was extremely close, the council could not decide on a candidate. The outcome was that either the former mayor remained in place, or the terms were split, with each of the two candidates serving one year.

47. See, for example, Arturo Valenzuela, *Political Brokers in Chile: Local Government in a Centralized Polity* (Duke University Press, 1977).

48. International Lending Agency official, interview, La Paz, August 16, 1990.

49. In polls taken throughout Peru, when people were given a choice of what they wanted most for their communities, the overwhelming answer was football fields. Schools were also high on the list in rural areas, where access is difficult. Sewer systems, while a recognized need, were rarely a first choice. Jaime Crosby, director, Programa de Apoyo Social, Fredemo Campaign, presentation, The World Bank, August 2, 1989; and author's interview, Lima, September 3, 1990. International Lending Agency official, interview, August 23, 1990. Jorge Patiño, interview.

50. These conclusions are based on interviews with Ana Maria Ruiz Antelo, La Paz, August 24, 1990, and with a number of ESF officials. Electoral results were obtained from the National Electoral Court, La Paz, August 1990.

51. Luis Vasquez, former MIR mayor of El Alto, interview, La Paz, August 22, 1990.

52. Maurio Aparicio Duarte, mayor of El Alto, interview, El Alto, August 22, 1990; and *Presencia*, August 24, 1990.

53. Mauricio Antezana Villegas, "Informe Final de la Evaluación Acerca del Impacto Social de los Proyectos del Fondo Social de Emergencia en la Ciudad de El Alto," CEDLA (Centro de Estudios para el Desarrollo Laboral y Aguario), La Paz, November 1989. These conclusions were confirmed by my own interviews with beneficiaries in El Alto, August 27, 1990.

54. M. E. Querehasu, interview, La Paz, August 29, 1990; Luis Vasquez, interview.

55. The Catholic Church is responsible for 18 percent of education services in Bolivia, for example. Julie Van Domelen, "Working with Non-governmental Organizations," in Jorgensen, Grosh, and Schacter, eds., *Bolivia's Answer*, p. 72.

56. Antonio Peres Velasco, "Experiencia con el FSE: Pasado y Perspectivas: Una Vision No Gubernamental," in Ossio, ed., *Fondo Social de Emergencia*, pp. 127–40.

57. Van Domelen, "Working with Non-governmental Organizations." In particular the San Gabriel Foundation and Save the Children.

58. GodoFredo Sandoval and others, "Impacto Institucional del FSE" (La Paz: Estudios y Proyectos Socio-Economicos, September 1989), p. 14.

59. Van Domelen, "Working with Non-governmental Organizations."

60. Reinata Claros, ESF functionary, interview, La Paz, August 20, 1990. Grassroots organizations, on the other hand, had the most coverage across sectors. Of the twenty-two categories of ESF activities, grassroots organizations had projects in all but one. Van Domelen, "Working with Non-governmental Organizations."

61. Van Domelen, "Working with Non-governmental Organizations." For 1988, ESF funds were only 4 percent of the NGO budget in the health sector, for example.

62. Sandoval, "Impacto Institucional del FSE."

63. Von Domelen, Working with Non-governmental Organizations."

64. Ibid. For example, the central government in 1990 reiterated the need to control the NGOs and give the state some input in the distribution of external resources to NGOs.

65. This is demonstrated quite clearly by the contentious relationship that the ESF had with the FENASONGS (the National Federations of NGOs involved in health care), Acción un Maestro Mas, and CEPROSI, on the one hand, and the very positive relationship that the ESF had with the CEMSE on the other. Relationships were most problematic when differences in ideology were coupled with lack of communication between the ESF and the NGOs. At times the ESF personnel were too hasty with their evaluations and not sympathetic enough to the problems that NGOs—particularly for inexperienced administrators in remote regions—faced in procuring resources or in keeping programs operating on a strict schedule. In addition, the ESF often failed to communicate to its soliciting agencies when it had fund shortages. Nevertheless, some NGOs retained ideological antagonisms toward the ESF and were quick to categorize ESF criticisms of technical flaws as politically based. These conclusions are based on my interviews with a variety of NGO leaders in La Paz—including Fernando Salas, director, AUMM (Accion un Maestro Mas), August 24, 1990; Dr. Vargas, director, CEPROSI, August 24, 1990; and Mauricio Backadit, director, SENPAS, August 22, 1990—and on Fernando Rocabado, "La Asociación de Organizaciones No Gubernamentales en Salud (ASONGS) y el FSE," in Ossio, ed., *Fondo Social de Emergencia*, pp. 121–26.

66. This is demonstrated by the cases of Accion un Maestro Mas (AUMM) and CEPROSI. AUMM was a religious-based education group whose ESF funding was cut halfway through a project, purportedly because AUMM was not fulfilling the technical agreements of its accord. While this may have been the case, AUMM noted that the evaluation was flawed: the evaluator even made mistakes about the location of the project. The responsible ESF evaluator refused to discuss the case with AUMM. AUMM attributed this "unjust" treatment to political reasons. AUMM is far to the left and staunchly in opposition to the government, an important factor in its own perception of the politics of the issue. This perception was increased by the authoritarian manner of the evaluators handling the issue. AUMM was left with a large amount of debt and felt discredited at the field level, which exacerbated the tension. Sources: Fernando Salas, director, AUMM, interview, La Paz, August 24, 1990. Unpublished documentation and correspondence between the ESF evaluator and AUMM; AUMM's appeal document. An analogous case was that of CEPROSI, a health group based in La Paz. For reasons similar to the AUMM case, CEPROSI's funding was cut off, and a deposit it had made at the ESF not returned. The group was left in financial straits and with projects under way that it could not finish. Source: Dr. Vargas, director, CEPROSI, interview, La Paz, August 24, 1990. Again, political criteria were cited as a possible cause of what was perceived to be an arbitrary decision.

67. Geraro Avila, former director of operations, Emergency Social Fund, interview, La Paz, August 25, 1990. The cash problem resulting from a delay in payments by the Argentines for Bolivian natural gas exports forced the ESF to dramatically slow its activities for several months in late 1988 and early 1989.

68. Fernando Salas, interview; Vargas/CEPROSI interview; Luis Moreno, official, U.S. AID, interview, La Paz, August 28, 1989.

69. Reinata Claros, interview; Julie Von Domelen, World Bank office, interview, La Paz, August 16, 1990.

70. In one such case, an AID official cited inefficiency resulting from party favoritism in ESF resource allocation. He noted that two ESF housing projects in Pucari costing $150,000 were next to two similar projects built by AID that cost $30,000. As the ESF was a highly resource-efficient agency, this sort of criticism was the exception rather than the rule. Nor was the claim that party favoritism was involved substantiated. However, the *perception* that politics was involved definitely affected this official's view of the ESF. Luis Moreno, interview.

71. Peres Velasco, "Experiencia con el FSE."

72. Ibid.

73. Constance Sepeda, "After the ESF: The Social Investment Fund as Successor," in Jorgensen, Grosh, and Schacter, eds., *Bolivia's Answer to Poverty*, pp. 101–05; Jorge Patiño, lecture, The World Bank, June 13, 1990; and "Inauguran actividades del Fondo de Inversion Social," *Ultima Hora*, August 25, 1990.

74. In Chile, for example, even harsh critics of the Pinochet government's mass employment programs note that the programs played a critical role in providing at least minimal employment for large numbers of people, thus preventing frustration and political opposition on a much wider scale than occurred throughout the long process of adjustment in that country. For detail see chapter 2 of this volume.

75. In one case cited, community members said that the assistance programs were an MNR plot to "adormecer la gente"—put people to sleep. "Proyecto de Evaluación e Investigación del FSE: Informe Final Sobre La Evaluación del Impacto Social, 1988" (La Paz Emergency Social Fund, 1988).

Chapter 4

1. In Bolivia, the Paz Estenssoro government implemented the highly visible and extensive Emergency Social Fund with extensive help from external sources of funds; in Spain the Gonzalez government negotiated the Moncloa Pact with the private sector and the unions; the Monge government in Costa Rica, aided by large amounts of U.S. resources, ameliorated the effects of its stabilization policies by increasing the legal minimum wage, public sector wages, and public sector employment. In Thailand in the mid-1980s under the Prem government, compensatory measures seem to have played an important role in making certain economic reforms, such as the 1984 devaluation, palatable. While fiscally conservative technocrats dampened any broad tendencies toward compensation, many measures, such as temporary price controls, were symbolically effective in compensating losers. The losers from devaluation, for example, received special compensatory transfers, such as the abolition of import surcharges, the reduction of bank lending rates, and a promise not to raise oil prices. Other measures, such as export incentives, provided positive, non-zero-sum incentives and signals for firms to move in new directions. Rural development funds, meanwhile, were maintained throughout the adjustment process. The Ozal government in Turkey, also aided by external resources, extended revenue share certificates as a mech-

anism for extending property ownership to middle and lower income groups, developed an extensive housing program, and extended basic amenities to many deprived parts of the country. For detail on the case of Costa Rica, see T. H. Gindling and Albert Berry, "The Performance of the Labor Market during Recession and Structural Adjustment: Costa Rica in the 1980's," *World Development*, vol. 20 (November 1992), pp. 1599–1616. For the case of Bolivia, see Carol Graham, "The Politics of Protecting the Poor during Adjustment: Bolivia's Emergency Social Fund," *World Development*, vol. 20 (September 1992). See Nancy Bermeo and Jose A. Garcia Duran on the case of Spain; Richard Doner and Anek Laothamatas on the case of Thailand; and Ziya Onis and Steven B. Webb on the case of Turkey in Stephan Haggard and Steven Webb, eds., *Voting For Reform: Democracy, Political Liberalization, and Economic Adjustment* (The World Bank, 1994).

2. Under the Pinochet regime in Chile, mass-scale employment programs were in place for more than ten years, at one point employing 13 percent of the labor force. These programs, coupled with extensive mother and child nutrition programs and other health and education services targeted at the poorest sectors, were integral to protecting the poor at a time of severe economic crisis. In Ghana the Program of Action to Mitigate the Social Costs of Adjustment (PAMSCAD), which was funded largely by external aid, was important politically, although there were substantial problems in the implementation of the program, with some components working quite well and others not getting off the ground at all. In the Philippines at least lip service was paid to the safety net issue through the creation of the National Economic Development Agency (NEDA) and the Department of Local Government and Community Development, as well as the Peoples's Livelihood Program of Imelda Marcos, which was launched with great fanfare in August 1981, but came to be seen as a vehicle for consolidating the Marcos's support at the community level. Government concern for the safety net issue, couched in broader development terms, was continued by the democratically elected Aquino government, and the Community Employment and Development Program grew out of NEDA. For detail on Chile, see chapter 2 of this volume; for Ghana, see chapter 7; and for the Philippines, see Stephan Haggard, "The Political Economy of the Philippine Debt Crisis," in Joan M. Nelson, ed., *Economic Crisis and Policy Choice: The Politics of Adjustment in the Third World* (Princeton University Press, 1990), pp. 215–56.

3. *Caretas*, February 18, 1993, p. 26.

4. Joan Nelson, in an evaluation of the record of voters with respect to the continuation of economic reform programs, noted the pivotal role that noneconomic issues, such as ethnic or political violence, can play. See Joan M Nelson, "Poverty, Equity, and the Politics of Adjustment," in Stephan Haggard and Robert R. Kaufman, eds., *The Politics of Economic Adjustment* (Princeton: Princeton University Press, 1992).

5. This was noted in a comparative study of several countries implementing adjustment. See Marc Lindenberg and Noel Ramirez, *Managing Adjustment in Developing Countries* (San Francisco: ICS Press, 1989).

6. For details on the so-called *auto-golpe*, see Carol Graham, "Economic Austerity and the Peruvian Crisis: The Social Cost of Autocracy," *SAIS Review*, vol. 13 (Winter-Spring 1993), pp. 45–60.

7. Garcia, for example, was forced to seek asylum in Colombia. Several other APRA leaders, like Agustin Mantilla, were imprisoned. See *Caretas*, various issues, April-June 1992.

8. This term was coined by Jose Matos Mar, *Desborde Popular y Crisis del Estado* (Lima: Instituto de Estudios Peruanos, 1984).

9. "Inflation in Latin America and the Caribbean in 1992," *Cepal News*, vol. 12 (February 1993), p. 3; and James Brooke, "Peru's Leader Clears a Path with Sharp Elbows," *New York Times*, February 22, 1993, p. A3.

10. After his election and before his inauguration, Fujimori traveled to New York and to Japan, where he met with international financial community and government officials. At that point it was made very clear to him that there would be no international support for Peru if it continued to adopt "heterodox" economic policies. Upon returning to Peru, he changed his team of advisors and apparently became a new—and fervent—convert to economic orthodoxy.

11. The issue of communication in the implementation of economic reforms is critical. Far less severe policies have sparked major public protests, such as those in Jamaica in the early 1980s and Venezuela in recent years. When governments fail to educate or forewarn the public about reform measures, public protest is far more likely. In Zambia, for example, the Kaunda government repeatedly decreed maize meal prices overnight, with no public explanation, and was met each time with riots and even a coup attempt in 1990. The successor government of Frederick Chiluba was able to quadruple the price of maize in December 1991 with virtually no popular reaction, in large part because it explained the necessity of the measures to the public.

12. That figure was equal to 1 percent of GDP. Author's interview with Arturo Woodman, president, Foncodes, Lima, January 22, 1993.

13. Cynthia McClintock, "Peru's Fujimori: A Caudillo Derails Democracy," *Current History*, vol. 92 (March 1993), p. 115.

14. See, for example, Luis Abugattas, "Recesion: Atrapados Sin Salida?", *Que Hacer*, no. 80 (November-December 1992), pp. 54–59.

15. See, for example, Beto Ortiz, "Programa de Emergencia Social: Con La Olla No Se Juega," *Caretas*, Febrero 17, 1992.

16. Cynthia McClintock, "Peru's Fujimori: A Caudillo Derails Democracy," *Current History*, March 1993, pp. 116–17.

17. Brooke, "Peru's Leader"; and *Caretas*, various issues.

18. This conclusion is drawn from the author's repeated interviews with residents of various shantytowns in Cantogrande, Lima, and with researchers from the Instituto de Investigacion Nutricional who conduct dietary surveys in various Lima shantytowns and have been closely following the effects of the economic shocks on the nutritional and health status of the poor.

19. This conclusion is based on the author's interviews with people from a variety of sectors—from the urban poor to businessmen—in Lima in January 1993.

20. *Caretas*, March 4, 1993, p. 13.

21. These electoral results must be considered with caution, as many of the major political parties, such as APRA and AP, boycotted them in protest of new electoral rules—and perhaps also in fear of poor projected electoral support. For detailed results, see *El Comercio*, November 23, 1992, and *Caretas*, November 30, 1992.

22. The government also changed rules for electoral registration just before elections, making it difficult for some smaller parties to register. Still, an OAS observer mission declared the elections free and fair.

23. Polls taken by Apoyo, S.A., one of the most reliable polling firms in Peru, cited by the president of Apoyo in a presentation to Washington Office on Latin America/George Washington University Conference on the Prospects for Peace and Democracy in Peru, Washington, D.C., April 28, 1993.

24. Francois Bourguignon, "Optimal Poverty Reduction, Adjustment, and Growth," *World Bank Economic Review*, vol. 5, no. 2 (1991), pp. 315–16.

25. See the chapter by Laurence Whitehead, "Democratization and Disinflation: A Comparative Approach," in Joan M. Nelson, ed., *Fragile Coalitions: The Politics of Economic Adjustment* (Washington, D.C.: Overseas Development Council, 1989), pp. 79–93.

26. Several economists have noted the efficiency costs that economies incur when there is too much poverty, particularly if the poverty level rises above a particular society's ability to tolerate it: the so-called instability threshold. See, for example, Rudiger Dornbusch, cited in Adolfo Figueroa, "Social Policy and Economic Adjustment in Peru" (paper presented to Brookings Institution/Inter-American Dialogue's Conference on "Poverty and Inequality in Latin America," Washington, D.C., July 16–17, 1992), p. 31.

27. Giovanni Cornia, Richard Jolly, and Frances Stewart, eds., *Adjustment with a Human Face: Protecting the Vulnerable and Promoting Growth* (Oxford: UNICEF/Clarendon Press, 1987), pp. 23, 116. For comparative reference, social expenditure was 17.3 percent of the government's budget in Chile in 1980, 18 percent in Costa Rica, and 25.3 percent in the United Kingdom. There are clearly discrepancies in the measurement of this figure, as well as major discrepancies in quality of services, particularly in countries where the public sector is as inefficient as Peru's and where the bulk of social expenditure goes to staffing the ministries. In per capita terms, social expenditure in Peru is quite low, at $57 per person per year in 1980 and $12 per person in 1990. For detail on comparative social expenditure between countries, see Carol Graham, "From Emergency Employment to Social Investment: Alleviating Poverty in Chile," *Brookings Occasional Papers*, November 1991.

28. In addition to Sendero Luminoso, there were other guerrilla or paramilitary groups in Peru, including the Castro-style Tupac Amaru Revolutionary Movement (MRTA), which surfaced in 1984, and the APRA-party linked Rodrigo Franco Command, which surfaced in 1987.

29. Figueroa, "Social Policy and Economic Adjustment in Peru"; and Paul Glewwe and Gillette Hall, "Poverty and Inequality During Unorthodox Adjustment: The Case of Peru, 1985–90," Living Standards Measurement Study, Working Paper 86 (Washington, D.C.: The World Bank, 1992).

30. Roberto Abusada, lecture presented at Washington Office on Latin America/George Washington University Conference on the Prospects for Peace and Democracy in Peru, Washington, D.C., April 28, 1993.

31. The figures are for the capital city, Lima, which is the only city for which time series data were available. Instituto Cuanto, *Ajuste y Economia Familiar, 1985–1990* (Lima: Cuanto, 1991), pp. 50–53. Historically poverty levels have been much higher in rural areas of the country than in Lima. Because of the shift in demography and the growth in the relative size of the urban population, however, the urban poor are at least as numerous as the rural poor, even if they are a smaller proportion of the total urban population.

32. Ibid., p. 30; and Glewwe and Hall, "Poverty and Inequality," p. 41.

33. The 54.7 percent figure is calculated with time series data for Lima only. As rural poverty tends to be more severe, this figure may be higher. On the other hand, the rural poor tend to be less directly affected by short-term macroeconomic changes, as they have access to self-supply of food. For details on the Lima data, see Glewwe and Hall, "Poverty and Inequality." The estimate of 7 million extreme poor comes from Javier Abugattas, "The Social Emergency Program," in Carlos Paredes and Jeffrey Sachs, ed., *Peru's Path to Recovery: A Plan for Stabilization and Growth* (Brookings, 1992), p. 146.

34. Glewwe and Hall, "Poverty and Inequality."

35. "La Recesion Va Por Dentro," *Caretas*, April 1, 1993, pp. 26–29.

36. The child mortality rate fell from 106 deaths per 1,000 children under five years of age to 78 deaths. Both infant and child mortality rates were worse for rural than for urban areas: the infant mortality rate in urban areas went from 55 to 40 per 1,000, while in rural areas it went from 103 to 78 per 1,000. The child mortality rate in urban areas went from 79 to 56 per 1,000, while the rural rate went from 152 to 112. In absolute terms, though, the rural population is much smaller, so the number of children actually dying is about the same in urban and rural regions. Government of Peru, Encuesta Nacional Demografica y de Salud Familiar (ENDIS), 1986 and 1990–91. Advice for this survey, which was carried out by the National Statistics Institute, was provided by Macrointernational Inc., and Prisma, a Lima-based NGO.

37. Studies of the diets of poor children in the peri-urban areas of Lima conducted in 1972–74 and 1979–80 found that diets changed in composition in the face of inflation and devaluation and removal of subsidies, shifting their reliance for a protein source from animal products to fish products, for example, but the children retained their relative weights and heights over time. This indicated that budgets were stretched, but not at the breaking point, and that the urban poor of Peru had a great deal of flexibility in their consumption habits. Hilary Creed Kanashiro and George G. Graham, "Changes Over Time in Food Intakes of a Migrated Population," in P. L. White and N. Selvey, eds., "Malnutrition: Determinants and Consequences," *Current Topics in Nutrition and Disease*, vol. 10, Proceedings of the Western Hemisphere Nutrition Congress VII, Miami Beach, Florida, August 7–11, 1983 (New York: Alan R. Liss, 1984), pp. 197–205.

38. The study "The Effects of Economic Crisis on Feeding Patterns and Infantile Malnutrition in Urban Populations in Peru" was conducted by Guillermo Lopez de Romana and Hilary Creed Kanashiro of the Instituto de Investigacion Nutricional (IIN) in 1991. The norm for Peru is moderate stunting with normal to excessive weight-for-height. Incidence of acute malnutrition was 2 percent in Piura, 1 percent in Cajamarca and Cusco, and 0 percent in Lima. Yet it is likely that conditions are worse in remote rural areas, many of which are not monitored at all. These areas already had the poorest nutritional conditions to begin with and were probably affected by climatic downturns (such as a drought) as well as by government economic policies. While the rural poor have access to self-supply of food, the price of other inputs, such as fertilizer, probably increased, while government credit to the agricultural sector dried up. A smaller-scale study by IIN found an increase in acute malnutrition in rural areas in Piura, where since 1984 the proportion of children with a deficit of weight for height had almost doubled, while the number with acute malnutrition had quadrupled.

Also, author's interview with Claudio Lanatta, Instituto de Investigacion Nutricional, Lima, January 21, 1993. IIN, with a team of national and international medical and sociological researchers and logistical support from Johns Hopkins University, has conducted continuing surveys of nutrition standards and dietary practices in the peri-urban areas of Lima for more than thirty years. The more complete IIN data are contradicted by less complete studies conducted by the NGO PRISMA, which found that in the Lima shantytown of San Juan de Miraflores the deaths of newborns and infants younger than five years increased between 1987 and 1989, while levels of height and weight among the surviving infants were well below normal standards. Abugattas, "The Social Emergency Program," p. 143. This may be explained in part by the fact that Peruvian children are on average smaller than standard FAO/WHO norms, as is noted above.

39. It is possible that when the purchasing power of a family diminishes, the percentage of the budget spent on food increases, but only up to a certain level, because the family has other obligations to meet, such as fuel and transportation. Beyond a certain point, which may be the 60 percent level, net food consumption is likely to decrease rather than to use a higher proportion of the household budget. Lopez de Romana and Creed Kanashiro, "The Effects of Economic Crisis."

40. In Lima, in quintile 5—the wealthiest—8.5 percent of households used food aid programs, while only 8.1 percent, 2.4 percent, and 7.6 percent of the *poorest* quintiles used food aid programs in Piura, Cajamarca, and Cusco respectively. Ibid.

41. For a breakdown of U.S. aid, see Carol Graham, "A New U.S. Policy for Peru: A Preventive Approach to Regional Instability," testimony before the Foreign Affairs Committee, Subcommittee on Western Hemispheric Affairs, U.S. House of Representatives, Washington, D.C., March 10, 1993.

42. Creed Kanashiro and Graham, "Changes Over Time."

43. See B. Adrianzen and G. Graham, "The High Costs of Being Poor," *Archives of Environmental Health*, vol. 28 (June 1974), pp. 312–15.

44. See, for example, Julio Cotler, "The Political Radicalization of Working Class Youth in Peru," *Cepal Review*, no. 29, August 1986. For detail on the voting behavior of the urban poor, see Carol Graham, *Peru's APRA: Parties, Politics, and the Elusive Quest for Democracy* (Boulder: Lynne Rienner, 1992), chapters 7 and 8.

45. The poor have the fewest mechanisms to protect their meager savings during hyperinflation, while the wealthy resort to capital flight, overnight deposits, and the like. The tax of inflation that is under triple digits is far less severe for the poor than that of hyperinflation. See Eliana A. Cardoso, "Inflation and Poverty," NBER Working Paper 4006 (Cambridge, Mass.: National Bureau of Economic Research, March 1992.

46. This section is based on my more detailed account of the APRA's policies toward the urban poor, "The APRA Government and the Urban Poor: The PAIT Programme in Lima's Pueblos Jovenes," *Journal of Latin American Studies*, vol. 23, part 1 (February 1991).

47. In the first round of 1990 elections in Lima's twelve poorest districts, Fujimori garnered 39.6 percent of the vote versus Vargas Llosa's 22.7 percent. This contrasts with national totals of 28.19 percent for Vargas Llosa and 24.32 percent for Fujimori. In San Juan de Lurigancho, one of Lima's largest and poorest districts, Fujimori got 40.7 percent in the first round and 62.74 percent in the second, as opposed to his national level of 56.53 percent. For a detailed account of the voting record of Peru's urban poor in the 1980s and 1990s, see Carol Graham, *Peru's APRA* (Boulder: Lynne Rienner, 1992), chapters 7 and 8.

48. Marfil Francke Ballre, "Weathering Economic Crisis: Urban Women's Response to Recession in Lima, Peru" (paper presented at the International Center for Research on Women, Conference on the Economic Crisis in Peru, Washington, D.C., Spring 1988).

49. This translates as, "APRA-AP kitchens easily appear and easily disappear." Stephen Burgess, "The Communal Kitchens of Lima: An Analysis of Women's Organizations in the Barriadas," unpublished M. Phil. thesis, Oxford University, 1986. See also "Reflexiones de Mujeres Organizadas y la Ley del PAD," Centro de Investigacion Social y Educacion Popular, Lima, December 1986.

50. The conclusions about these programs are based on the author's interviews with program officials at the national and local levels, as well as a survey of PAIT workers in the Lima shantytown of Huascar, conducted in January-March 1988. For specifics about Huascar and the sample population, see the appendix. The IDESI was another program that provided small-scale credits to groups of informal sector workers. The workers as a group had to guarantee the individual credits, a structure similar to that of the Grameen Bank in Bangladesh. The program had an extremely good repayment record (98 percent) and in general seems to have avoided politicization. Evidence of this was its continuation under the new government and its receipt of substantial funds from Foncodes when that agency finally got off the ground. Reporte de Informacion Para Uso Gerencial, Foncodes, Gerencia de Planeamiento, No. 022-92-GPI, 1993. In general, though, the IDESI neither reached the poorest of the poor nor had any significant effect

on informal organizations. Another program, the PROEM, allowed companies to hire workers on a temporary basis without adhering to the labor stability code. For details on these programs, see Graham, "The APRA Government."

51. Burgess, "The Communal Kitchens of Lima." Author's conversations with numerous PAIT/PAD officials, both in the San Juan de Lurigancho district and in the central Lima office, January-March 1988.

52. "Historia de un Tren y algunas Piscinas Sin Agua," *Oiga,* February 9, 1987. The author also conducted site visits to the Olympic pool in San Juan de Lurigancho, as well as to a government-built "high technology" institute, which towered above most of the buildings of the district but remained empty and nonfunctional.

53. Burgess, "The Communal Kitchens of Lima"; and "Reflexiones de Mujeres."

54. My translation. "Primer Conversatorio Sobre PAIT-PAD," Centro de. Estudios Alternativos, Centro de Investigacion Social y Educacion Popular, Lima, March 1987.

55. The budget for 1986 alone was $22 million, or 300 million intis in a total public investment budget of 20,000 million intis. Peri Peredes and Maria Elena Vigier, "Los Trabajadores del Programa Nacional de Apoyo de Ingreso Temporal en Lima Metropolitana," unpublished manuscript, OIT/INP, Lima, January 1986; and Susana C. Pinilla, "Politicas y Programas de Promocion del Empleo: El PAIT y el IDESI," in Heraclio Bonilla and Paul Drake, eds., *El APRA de la Ideologia a la Praxis* (Lima: March 1989), pp. 215–42.

56. Minimum wage was approximately U.S.$36 per month at the time the study was conducted. The figure of 500,000 is the number that the program had employed through mid-1988. After that the program functioned on a much smaller scale. For detail on the composition of the PAIT work force and how the program functioned, see Carol Graham, "Recent Experiences with Employment Programs in Chile, Bolivia, and Peru," memorandum prepared for the Inter-American Dialogue, Washington, D.C., March 1990.

57. My translation. "El Jefe de Estado Fundamento el Proyecto de Disolucion de Coopop," *El Comercio,* January 19, 1988.

58. Interview with Nicholas Houghton, International Labor Organization, Lima, February 12, 1988.

59. The high percentage of women working in the PAIT reflects the complex position that women have in low-income families in the developing world, where they often act as both principal wage earner and keeper of the home.

60. See, for example, Peredes and Vigier, "Los Trabajadores del Programa Nacional." Female-headed households also tend to be among the poorest households, and their representation was disproportionately high in the author's sample/survey of PAIT workers in the pueblo joven of Huascar, in Cantogrande. This survey was conducted in January-March 1988. From its inception to its fading out in January 1988, the PAIT employed 2,100 people, affecting 17.5 percent of all households. PAIT Program Directorate, San Juan de Lurigancho, March 1988. For details of this survey, see Carol Graham, "The APRA Government and the Urban Poor."

61. Interview with Mary Fukumoto, Instituto de Investigacion Nutricional/ Universidad Catolica, Lima, August 28, 1987.

62. "Primer Conversatorio Sobre PAIT-PAD"; and author's survey of PAIT workers in Huascar, Lima, January-March 1988.

63. *Oiga*, September 19, 1988, pp. 14–15.

64. For detail, see Carol Graham, "The APRA Government and the Urban Poor."

65. Interview with Nicholas Houghton, International Labor Organization, Lima, August 19, 1987.

66. Interview with Peri Peredes, ATEC/ADC, Lima, August 25, 1987. Peredes's assertions were confirmed by the author's conversations with PAIT officials, at both the central and the local levels, and by the author's survey of PAIT workers in Huascar of San Juan de Lurigancho, Lima.

67. Interview with Peredes.

68. Interview with Nicholas Houghton, August 19, 1987. The author's 1988 survey of the PAIT in Huascar confirms these assertions.

69. Cantogrande Health Survey Team of the Instituto de Investigacion Nutricional, group interview, Cantogrande, Lima, August 29, 1987.

70. Part of the reason for this placement was that the second vice president, Carlos Garcia y Garcia, an active evangelist, purportedly wanted control of the program.

71. Control of the budget remained in an agency that had been set up at the end of the Garcia government, the Programa de Compensacion Social, which was run out of the presidency.

72. Beto Ortiz, "Programa de Emergencia Social: Con La Olla No Se Juega," *Caretas*, February 17, 1992; and "Social Assistance Program in Peru," Ministry of Economy and Finance, National Fund for Compensation and Social Development, presentation to Consultative Group for Special Assistance in Peru, Paris, June 21–22, 1993, p. 31. Figueroa, "Social Policy and Economic Adjustment in Peru."

73. At this point, Jorge Garcia Pacheco became the head of the Social Emergency Program, while Vidal Bautista remained as director of the Programa de Compensacion Social.

74. Before Foncodes, Salgado had been president of the holdover program from the APRA government, the PAD, which, as mentioned earlier, was known for its paternalism and bureaucracy.

75. Author's conversations with representatives of a variety of NGOs that attempted to work with Foncodes, Lima, June 1992. The original 1991 budget for social emergency spending was $161 million, although much of that amount was never disbursed. "Social Assistance Program in Peru."

76. The 1992 budget for social emergency and poverty alleviation spending was $225 million; of this approximately $86.9 million were disbursed. "Social Assistance Program in Peru."

77. "Social Assistance Program in Peru," chapter 3.

78. Again, approximately half of that (or $204.5 million) was to go to Foncodes. The rest was to go to PRONAA (the national supplementary feeding

program), the Vaso de Leche (Glass of Milk), school feeding, and other programs. Spending on health and education were to increase to $194 million and $338 million respectively. "Social Assistance Program in Peru," p. 31.

79. Foncodes office, Lima, 1993; and interview with Arturo Woodman, president, Foncodes, Lima, January 22, 1993. Under Woodman, Foncodes was actually planning to hire advisors from the Mexican program.

80. Governments often face major resource constraints during adjustment when foreign borrowing is limited. Francois Bourguignon, "Optimal Poverty Reduction, Adjustment, and Growth," *World Bank Economic Review*, vol. 5 (May 1991), pp. 315–38.

81. These conclusions are drawn from the author's interviews in Lima in November 1990 with various Caritas officials, including Mario Rios, the general secretary; and with Jaime Crosby, codirector of the Social Assistance Program of the Fredemo campaign. For background on the Glass of Milk Program and the Communal Kitchens, see Graham, "The APRA Government and the Urban Poor"; and Roelfien Haak and Javier Diaz Albertini, eds., *Estrategias de Vida en el Sector Urbano Popular* (Lima: DESCO, 1987).

82. "Programa de Emergencia Social." Even then, the most vulnerable group, which is preschool children, was not necessarily receiving food, nor were the mothers of those children receiving necessary information to cope with their care and feeding in the context of the shock. Interviews with Guillermo Lopez de Romana, director, Instituto de Investigacion Nutricional, Lima, October 1991. For detail on the overall U.S. aid program to Peru, as well as food aid, see my testimony on U.S. Policy Towards Peru before the House Foreign Affairs Committee, Subcommittee on Western Hemispheric Affairs, March 10, 1993.

83. "Repulsa Total," *Caretas*, February 24, 1992.

84. See, for example, Carol Graham, "Sendero's Law in Peru's Shantytowns," *Wall Street Journal*, June 7, 1991, p. A13.

85. This conclusion is drawn from the author's interviews in the shantytowns of Huascar and Pamplona Alta in 1990 and 1991, as well as with members of NGOs that work in several of Lima's shantytowns.

86. Adequate employment is defined as working a normal (forty-eight-hour) work week and earning at least a minimum wage.

87. While an average of 107 Foncodes project agreements were signed each month from January to June 1992, the average was 412 in the July 1992 period. "Compensacion Social," *Proceso Economico*, Suplemento Especial, no. 118, March 1993. This was directly related to the timing of Woodman's hiring, a change that indicated the government's increased desire to take the program seriously.

Chapter 5

1. I would like to thank Fred Schaefer of UCLA for his helpful comments on this chapter; Peter Watson and Leslie Pean of the World Bank for their logistical support; and Magatte Wade of the Agetip, Mamadou Kane of U.S. AID, and Daouvda Diop of ABACED for their kind help in Senegal.

2. Samba Ka and Nicolas van de Walle, "The Political Economy of Adjustment in Senegal: 1980–1991," in Stephan Haggard and Steven B. Webb, *Voting For Reform: Democracy, Political Liberalization, and Economic Adjustment* (The World Bank, 1994).

3. This raises the question of whether it is better to lift the largest possible number of people at the margin of the poverty line above it, using a straight head-count measure of poverty, or to focus efforts on improving the lot of the poorest, even if the number of people below the poverty line remains the same. The Sen index, for example, combines the head-count ratio with the average income shortfall and the measure of inequality among them to determine the severity and the incidence of poverty. Sen's theory and its implications for anti-poverty policy are discussed in Francois Bourguignon and Gary S. Fields, "Poverty Measures and Anti-Poverty Policy," Delta Working Papers 90–04, February 1990.

4. Robert Nichols, regional representative for West Africa, OXFAM, interview, Dakar, October 29, 1991.

5. Larry Diamond, "Introduction: Roots of Failure, Seeds of Hope," in Larry Diamond, Juan Linz, and Seymour Martin Lipset, eds., *Democracy in Developing Countries: Volume II–Africa* (Boulder: Lynne Rienner, 1988). Diamond notes that the "semi-democracy" of Senegal is the best example of the liberalization of a one-party state in Africa. For a detailed description of differences between one-party regimes in Africa, see Ruth Berins Collier, *Regimes in Tropical Africa: Changing Forms of Supremacy, 1945–1975* (Berkeley: University of California Press, 1982).

6. Lucy E. Creevey, "Muslim Brotherhoods and Politics in Senegal in 1985," *Journal of Modern African Studies*, vol. 23, no. 4 (1985), pp. 715–21; and Christian Coulon, "Senegal: The Development and Fragility of Semidemocracy," in Diamond, Linz, and Lipset, eds., *Democracy in Developing Countries*, pp. 141–78. Donal B. Cruise O'Brien, "Le Contrat Social Senegalais – l'Epreuve," *Politique Africaine* 45 (Mars 1992), pp. 9–20. After the February 1988 elections, one Dakar resident was quoted as saying that he rather liked the opposition candidate but that he would vote for incumbent President Diouf because, after all, "that's what the marabout ordered." Franziska Oppmann, "Senegal: The Myth of Democracy," *Africa Report*, May-June 1988, p. 51. Creevey and Coulon agree with the role of the marabouts in determining voter behavior. The influence of the marabouts was also confirmed by the author's interviews with three groups of women (approximately fifteen each) in two poor urban areas in Dakar and one rural village approximately one hour outside Dakar, on October 26 and November 2, 1991.

7. Interview with Babacar Niang, secretary general of the Parti pour la Liberation du Peuple (PLP), in F. Ndiaye, M. Prinz, and A. Tine, eds., *Visages Publics du Senegal* (Paris: L'Harmattan, 1990), pp. 165–66. Creevey, "Muslim Brotherhoods and Politics"; and Chrisopher L. Delgado and Sidi Jammeh, "Structural Change in a Hostile Environment," in Christopher L. Delgado and Sidi Jammeh, eds., *The Political Economy of Senegal Under Structural Adjustment* (New York: Praeger, 1991), pp. 1–20.

8. Goran Hyden, *No Shortcuts to Progress: African Development Management in Comparative Perspective* (University of California Press, 1983), chapter 1, particularly pp. 8–22.

9. The largest union, the Confederation Nationale des Travailleurs du Senegal (CNTS), is affiliated with the PS, which has a limited degree of control over the union. In return the CNTS is guaranteed four seats in the National Assembly and now holds the vice-presidency. This guarantees it a certain amount of influence, but also links its fate to that of the governing party. Interview with Chinsou Jones, head of Political Section, U.S. Embassy, Dakar.

10. Ka and Van de Walle, "The Political Economy of Adjustment in Senegal."

11. Gerard Salem, "Crise Urbaine et Controle Social a Pikine: Bornes-Fontaines et Clientelisme," *Politique Africain* 45 (Mars 1992), pp. 21–38.

12. Ka and Van de Walle, "The Political Economy of Adjustment in Senegal." Other countries, such as Poland and Costa Rica, have used similar tactics to avoid rapidly increasing unemployment. The drawback of such a strategy, in addition to the wage bill, is that it generates a negative incentives system in the public sector.

13. Nicholas Roffe, director, Agence de Credit pour L'Enterprise Privée, interview, Dakar, October 24, 1991. Roffe, who runs one of the few credit agencies in Senegal with an impeccable repayment record, refuses to lend to religious leaders, citing their responsibility for "destroying the Banking system." The negative effects of clientelism on loan practices are also well demonstrated by the record of the DIRE, which is discussed in detail below.

14. It is estimated that for every salaried Senegalese worker there are up to ten dependents. This condition was noted by a variety of people interviewed, including Roffe and Jacques R. Delons, International Labour Organization advisor to the DIRE, interview, Dakar, October 22, 1991. For a detailed account, see Carolyn M. Somerville, "The Impact of the Reforms on the Urban Population: How the Dakarois View the Crisis," in Delgado and Jammeh, eds., *The Political Economy of Senegal,* pp. 151–74. This phenomenon is not unique to Senegal. For a detailed account of its effects region-wide, see Mamadou Dia, "Indigenous Management Practices: Lessons for Africa's Management in the 90s," The World Bank, February 10, 1992, p. 9.

15. This conclusion is also based on the author's interviews with more than forty politicians, NGO representatives, and independent observers, as well as approximately forty-five urban and rural poor women in Dakar and its environs in October-November 1991.

16. Abdoulaye Bathily, secretaire generale du Ligue Democratique/Mouvement pour le Parti du Travail, interview, Dakar, October 28, 1991. The LD/MPT was one of the main parties—along with the PDS and the PIT—that formed the Alliance Sopi in 1988. LD/MPT and Jef/Mouvement Revolutionnaire pour la Democratie Nouvell (AJ/MRDN) were the two opposition parties outside the government with the largest following after May 1990. Both were Marxist in theory, but rather eclectic and pragmatic in practice.

17. The author interviewed approximately forty-five women, two-thirds in group interviews in poor urban areas of Dakar (poor areas of Medina and Niarry

Tally), and one group of fifteen in a rural "peulh" village (Tivaouane Kaay Baax) one hour outside Dakar. Most of the women did not even know of or understand the changes at the center. Those who did said that even with the changes, nothing had changed, that the poor remained in the same situation, that the politicians were only interested in the middle class, and that "the price of rice was still going up." The rural women remarked that even at the local level political changes meant little to them, as they had little access to political manipulation, which was controlled by the men. These conclusions about the political views of the disaffected were confirmed by the author's interviews with several representatives of NGOs who work primarily with the poorest and most marginalized groups. These include Mazid Ndiaye, director, RADI, Dakar, October 28, 1991; Fatime Ndiaye, director, CONGAD, October 25, 1991; and Daouvda Diop, director, ABACED, Dakar, October 23 and November 1, 1991.

18. Diamond, "Roots of Failure," p. 19.

19. Elliot Berg and Associates, "Adjustment Postponed: Economic Policy Reform in Senegal in the 1980s, report prepared for U.S. AID/Dakar, Development Alternatives, Inc., Bethesda, Md., October 1990; Ka and Van de Walle, "The Political Economy of Adjustment in Senegal." At $100 per capita a year, Senegal receives four times as much donor aid per capita as the average for African nations.

20. Catherine Boone, "Politics under the Specter of Deindustrialization: Structural Adjustment' in Practice," in Delgado and Jammeh, eds., *The Political Economy of Senegal*, p. 147.

21. Ka and Van de Walle, "The Political Economy of Adjustment in Senegal"; and Katherine Marshall discussing the Ka and Van de Walle paper at a conference on "Voting for Reform: The Political Economy of Adjustment in New Democracies," The World Bank, Washington, D.C., May 4, 1992.

22. Somerville, "The Impact of the Reforms."

23. "Enquête Emploi, Sous Emploi, Chomage en Milieu Urbain," Avril-Mai 1991, Rapport Préliminaire, République du Senégal: Ministère de l'Économie, des Finances, et du Plan; Direction de la Prévision et de la Statistique; Primature; Commissariat General—l'Emploi; Projet PNUD/BIT. Approximately one-quarter of the population of 7 million lived in Dakar in 1987. The service sector composes 52 percent of GDP, most of which is government, while industry composes 27 percent and agriculture 10 percent. Delgado and Jammeh, "Structural Change."

24. An increase in unemployment usually results in more workers entering the informal sector. This, coupled with a decrease in formal sector demand, places a downward pressure on informal sector wages.

25. Franziska Oppmann, "Senegal: The Myth of Democracy?" *Africa Report*, May-June 1988, p. 50.

26. Extrait des Minutes du Greffe de la Cour Supreme: Elections Legislatives du Février 1988," *Le Soleil*, March 4, 1988.

27. Interview with Wade in Ndiaye and Prinz, *Visages Publics*; and Oppmann *Senegal*.

28. This entails a number of changes, including giving eighteen-year-olds the vote and instituting a system of proportional representation for the 50 percent of the vote that is not taken by the majority. Edward Malchik, political officer, U.S. Embassy, Dakar, interview, October 25, 1991.

29. Abdoulaye Wade, Ministre d'État, interview, Dakar, October 24, 1991.

30. Ka and Van de Walle, "The Political Economy of Adjustment in Senegal." "Commission Announces Parliamentary Election Results," FBIS-AFR-93 -093, May 17, 1993.

31. Tyjan Sylla, general secretary to the president, interview, Dakar, November 5, 1991.

32. *World Development Report*, 1991 (Washington, D.C.: The World Bank).

33. Pierre Landell-Mills and Brian Ngo, "Creating the Basis for Long-Term Growth," in Delgado and Jammeh, eds., *The Political Economy of Senegal*, pp. 204, 258.

34. Makhtar Diouf, "La Crise de L'Ajustement," *Politique Africaine* vol. 45 (Mars 1992), p. 79.

35. Philippe Egger, "Travaux Publics et Emploi Pour Les Jeunes Travailleurs Dans Une Economie Sous Ajustement: L'Expérience de l'Agetip au Senegal," Occasional Paper 2, International Labour Office, Geneva, 1992, particularly pp. 8–10.

36. Daouvda Diop, "Phenomène de la Pauvreté: Dakar et Banlieue," paper presented to Symposium National sur L'Emploi, Secteur Informel/Secteur Refuge, May 1991, particularly pp. 12–24.

37. "Enquête Emploi."

38. The lower figure is from Berg, "Adjustment Postponed," p. 135, and the higher from Sylla, interview. Sylla was the head of the DIRE before he joined the General Secretariat of the Presidency.

39. For example, author's interviews with Felipe Bas, legal secretary to the president, Dakar, October 22, 1991; and with Jacques Bugnicourt, director, ENDA, Dakar, October 27, 1991.

40. I am grateful to Habib Fettini of the World Bank for raising this issue.

41. For a detailed description of the voting behavior of the urban poor in developing countries, see Joan Nelson, *Access to Power: Politics and the Urban Poor in Developing Nations* (Princeton University Press, 1979). For the voting behavior of the urban poor in Brazil see Robert Gay, "Neighborhood Associations and Political Change in Rio de Janeiro," *Latin American Research Review*, vol. 25, no. 1 (1990), pp. 102–18; for Chile see Carol Graham, "From Emergency Employment to Social Investment: Alleviating Poverty in Chile," *Brookings Occasional Papers*, November 1991; and for Peru see Carol Graham, "The APRA Government and the Urban Poor: The PAIT Programme in Lima's Pueblos Jovenes," *Journal of Latin American Studies*, vol. 23, part 1 (February 1991).

42. Interviews were conducted in three areas, two Dakar neighborhoods: Niarry Tally and Medina, and one semirural village approximately forty-five minutes from Dakar, Tivaouane Kaay Baax on October 26 and November 2, 1991. The women in Tivaouane Kaay Baax in particular needed training, as they

made a living from the buying and selling of locally produced agricultural goods and textiles, but they were illiterate and did not know how to use numerical measures or to count money. The NGO representative with whom the author visited the town was providing a training course in how to save their earnings.

43. Niarry Tally woman, interview, October 26, 1991.

44. Author's interviews with three groups of forty-five poor urban and peri-urban women, Dakar, October 1991.

45. I have written on the politics of the urban poor in various countries. For details on Bolivia see "The Politics of Protecting the Poor During Adjustment: Bolivia's Emergency Social Fund," *World Development*, vol. 20 (September 1992); for Chile see "From Emergency Employment"; for Peru see "The APRA Government and the Urban Poor"; and for Zambia, see chapter 6 of this volume.

46. Jacques Bugnicourt, director, ENDA, interview, Dakar, October 27, 1991. Bugnicourt's assertions were confirmed by the author's visits to several public housing projects in Dakar.

47. Abdoul Aziz Dia, directeur general, Office National de Formation Profes-sional, interview, Dakar, October 29, 1991.

48. As a result, while ACEP has an excellent repayment ratio, it is clearly not reaching the poorest groups, and it lends a disproportionately low percentage of its funds to women. Eleven percent of ACEP's funds and 23 percent of its participants were women. Nicolas Roffe, director, ACEP, interview, Dakar, October 24, 1991.

49. These conclusions are based on the author's field research in each of the three countries. For details on the PAMSCAD, see chapter 8 of this volume.

50. This was confirmed by the author's interviews with forty-five women in three urban and peri-urban areas. This distrust was particularly strong in the peri-urban village, where political information, for example, was often kept from the women by the village men. Senegal is no exception to other developing countries in this respect. Political parties usually have weak links to the poorest groups. State presence among the poorest varies more, however. It is relevant to note that in the other African case in the study, Zambia, where the UNIP party penetrated almost all levels of government and society, the party's links to the poorest groups remained weak. For details on Chile, see Graham, "From Emer-gency Employment"; for Peru, see Graham, "The APRA Government"; for Bolivia, see Graham, "The Politics of Protecting the Poor"; and for Zambia, see chapter 6 of this volume.

51. As in many African countries, in the absence of adequate state provision of these services, NGOs and international agencies such as UNICEF play a major role in providing health and education services. While their efforts are invaluable and should be supported, they cannot provide the comprehensive sectoral cov-erage that is needed and that should be provided by the line ministries.

52. Berg, "Adjustment Postponed." Richard Jolly, "L'Enfant et l'Ajustement Structurel–Visage Humain," in Philippe Engelhard, ed., *Endettement et Envi-ronnement Africain: Au Dela de l'Ajustement* (Dakar: Environnement Africain—ENDA, 1989), pp. 295–309.

53. David Sahn, "Economic Reform in Africa: Are There Similarities with Latin America?" (paper presented to workshop on Macroeconomic Crisis, Policy Reforms, and the Poor in Latin America," Cali, Colombia, October 1–4, 1991), pp. 44–45. Sahn notes that the slower the pace of adjustment, the slower the pace of poverty alleviation.

54. The first program targeted at the maitrisards was actually set up as early as 1984. It was called "operation maitrisard," and it issued loans to create 200 enterprises, which in turn created 1,800 jobs. Few of the enterprises turned out to be viable in the long term, however. For detail see Diouf, "La Crise de l'Ajustement."

55. Giovanni di Cola, fonctionnaire chargé de programmes, Bureau International du Travail/Dakar, interview, Dakar, October 31, 1991.

56. The cost of creating a job in the modern sector is $50,000.

57. Eliana Karp-Toledo, "Les Fonds d'Emploi: Sont-ils Efficaces? Une Evaluacion Socio-Economique de la DIRE/FNE au Senegal," AFTSP Division, The World Bank, July 30, 1991.

58. This conclusion is based on the author's interviews with people who either worked with or had some connection to the DIRE, including Mamadou Kane, project design officer, U.S. AID/Senegal, Washington, July 31, 1991; David Schear, former director, U.S. AID/Senegal, Washington, September 4, 1991; Babacom Gueye, BIT advisor to the DIRE, Dakar, October 24, 1991; Jacques Delons, principal technical counselor, BIT/Senegal, Dakar, October 22, 1991; Tyjan Sylla, former director, DIRE, Dakar, November 5, 1991; and a number of representatives from the NGO community.

59. Karp-Toledo, "Les Fonds d'Emploi," p. 3; also see preceding note on projects visited by the author.

60. Karp-Toledo, "Les Fonds d'Emploi," p. 3.

61. Roffe, interview. The influence of the marabouts on the banking system was also cited as a factor.

62. Karp-Toledo, "Les Fonds d'Emploi," p. 15.

63. Delons, interview, October 22, 1991.

64. This conclusion is drawn from the author's visit to eight DIRE-funded projects in October 1991. These were a bookstore in a modern building in central Dakar; Africa Travel, a travel agency in a relatively wealthy part of Dakar (the loan recipient/director sat behind an oversized ebony desk); a small sewing shop run by a "deflate" in a relatively poor area; a bakery run by two maitrisards that was only half built and semifunctioning; the high technology chalk firm, Nippon Sen; a furniture factory on an industrial avenue next to several other furniture factories; and a sewing firm in a poor area that had started as a one-woman shop and now had ten employees and produced for export. Of the eight projects visited, only two were located in low-income areas. The financial sector, rather than the government, should be funding operations like travel agencies in wealthy Dakar districts.

65. Several of the women interviewed by the author in Medina had attempted to obtain loans from the DIRE and had one of the two responses noted above.

66. The failure of the DIRE seems to have been recognized even by the government, and it is currently being reorganized under a new name, the Comissariat Generale de l'Emploi, with the technical cooperation of the ILO. Among other things, it now is focusing on coordinating the efforts of all the different actors involved in employment and credit schemes, a much more suitable activity for a state agency than its previous role as a private bank lacking capacity and technical staff.

67. Karp-Toledo, "Les Fonds d'Emploi," p. 1.

68. Much of the section on the Agetip is drawn from extensive interviews in October 1991 in Dakar with Magatte Wade, the director of the Agetip, and his staff, in particular Abdourahmane Kholle, technical director; and Gnou Gaye, management director, as well as visits to several Agetip projects with Mr. Diarra, director of field projects. It also draws from conversations with the relevant people in the World Bank team involved with the Agetip, in particular Peter Watson and Leslie Pean. The author is grateful for the interest and time that these people gave to this research.

69. This complements experiences of similar projects in other countries, such as the EC's Micro-Projects Unit in Zambia, where clear and detailed procedures for project selection protect the program from political pressure to make politically "useful" projects that are inconsistent with the program's mandate.

70. A. N. Sindzingre, B. Sene, and K. Sow, "Republique du Senégal, Agence d'Execution des Travaux d'Interêt Public Contre le Sous-Emploie," Rapport d'Evaluation Provisoire, Banque Mondiale, Septembre 1991, pp. 13–15; and Republic of Senegal, Ministry of Planning and Cooperation, "A Program of Action for Youth Employment," submitted to the Special Donor's Conference on Youth and Unemployment in Senegal, March 1989.

71. Sindzingre, Sene, and Sow, "République du Senegal."

72. Magatte Wade, interviews, Dakar, October 1991.

73. Mme. Sowede, director, National Council for Negro Women/Senegal, interview, Dakar, October 25, 1991. This was the case of an Agetip-funded NCNW project in the rural village of Sandialon-Dieba, where the community members themselves came up with a rotation system for labor. The is not unusual for rural zones in Africa, where the tradition of communal cooperation is quite strong.

74. Author's following of the press coverage of the Agetip, and the Agetip's own press file. Press coverage was particularly notable in the government-owned newspaper, Le Soleil, as well as on television.

75. Magatte Wade, interview, Dakar, November 4, 1991.

76. A. Kholle, technical director, Agetip, interview, November 4, 1991.

77. For details on Bolivia, see Graham, "The Politics of Protecting the Poor"; for Zambia, chapter 6 of this volume; and for Peru, Carol Graham, "Economic Reform and the Peruvian Crisis: The Social Costs of Autocracy," SAIS Review, vol. 13 (Winter-Spring 1993), pp. 45–60; as well as the author's direct involvement with the InterAmerican Development Bank in attempting to set up Foncodes.

78. Berg, "Adjustment Postponed."

79. Joseph Roger de Benoist, "Perspectives du Senégal," Marches Tropicaux et Mediterranéens, vol. 47, no. 2371 (Avril 18, 1991), p. 1004.

80. A. Kholle, interview, Dakar, November 4, 1991.

81. Author's interviews with Medina women, Dakar, October 26, 1991.

82. Mandione Gueye, directeur de l'Aménagement du Territoire, interview, Dakar, October 29, 1991.

83. Agetip Management Team, interview, November 4, 1991. One potential drawback of Food for Work in urban areas is that it has at times attracted rural youth to the cities to participate in the programs. *Wad Fadjri*, several issues, July 1991.

84. Food for Work has also been successful at targeting the poorest and improving neighborhood sanitation conditions in other countries, such as Peru and Zambia. Food for Work also makes important contributions to food security for poor households, and there is no direct relation between food security at the household level and self-sufficiency at the national level. Stephen Devereux, "Managing the Welfare Effects of Stabilisation and Structural Adjustment Programmes on Vulnerable Groups: With Reference to Sub-Saharan Africa," Food Studies Group, Queen Elizabeth House, Oxford University, November 1987, p. 30.

85. The Rapport d'Evaluation (Sindzingre, Sene, and Sow, "République du Senégal") concurs in its recommendations for a labor profile and a more systematic way of allocating benefits among regions, citing the relatively dire need of many small and remote communities.

86. Delons, interview.

87. This is similar to the case of municipal governments in authoritarian regimes. For a detailed account of municipal government in Chile, see Dagmar Raczynski and Claudia Serrano, "Planificacion Para el Desarrollo Local 3: La Experiencia en Algunos Municipios de Santiago," Documento de Trabajo 24 (Santiago: CIEPLAN, June 1988); and Graham, "From Emergency Employment." For an account of municipal government in Zambia, see chapter 6.

88. Abdoulaye Wade, minister of state and secretary general of the PDS, interview, October 24, 1991; Abdoulaye Bathily, secretary general, LD/MPT, interview, October 28, 1991; and Ed Malchik, U.S. Embassy, Political Section, interview, October 25, 1991. All those interviewed cited the exclusion of community participation and dependence on the center. One good example of the extent of centralization is the mayor of Kinchane, who lives in Dakar during the week and only goes to Kinchane on the weekends; he travels in a chauffeur-driven Mercedes. This is hardly an image that seems in touch with local realities in a poor municipality. Thierno Birahim Ndao, mayor of Kinchane, interview, Dakar, October 31, 1991.

89. Robert Nichols, OXFAM/Senegal representative, interview, Dakar, November 29, 1991.

90. Abdoulaye Bathily, Abdoulaye Wade, Ed Malchik, interviews. The municipality of Dakar, for example, gave almost 35 million CFA to neighborhood associations in 1991 (3 million in 1990), and many neighborhood associations have become linked to the municipality through its "Coordination des associations et mouvements de jeunes de la communauté urbaine de Dakar (CAN-CUD)." Between 500 and 600 associations were expected to participate in a

clean-up drive initiated by CAMCUD in late 1991. I am grateful to Fred Schaefer of UCLA for pointing this out to me.

91. "Peulh" woman interviewed in Tivauoane Kaay Baax, a village approximately forty-five minutes outside Dakar, November 2, 1991.

92. Thierno Birahim Ndao, mayor of Kichane, interview, Dakar, October 31, 1991. The mayor had received Agetip funding for two projects, the reforestation of the town plaza and cold storage facilities for the market, and was waiting for a third, the renovation of the town's hotel.

93. For detail, see Carol Graham, "The Politics of Protecting the Poor Diring Adjustment: Bolivia's Emergency Social Fund," *World Development*, vol 20 (September 1992), pp. 1233–51.

94. Daouda Diop, director, Association des Bacheliers Chomeurs Pour l'Emploi et le Développement (ABACED), and secretary general, Forum des Organisations Volontaires Africaines de Développement du Senégal (FOVSEN), interviews, Dakar, October 23 and November 2, 1991; and Michael M. Cernea, "Nongovernmental Organizations and Local Development," World Bank Discussion Papers, no. 40, 1988.

95. One of the major problems that the ESF had when it disbursed too fast or had too little follow-up was lack of viability and maintenance of infrastructure. The Micro-Projects Unit in Zambia sought to avoid the tradition of allowing infrastructure provided freely by the state to deteriorate by requiring a 25 percent contribution—usually in labor from rural communities and in cash from urban communities—to all projects that it funded. The result has been community contribution not only to the Micro-Projects Unit projects, but also to other activities after the project was completed. See chapter 6.

96. Sindzingre, Sene, and Sow, "République du Senegal."

97. Republic of Senegal, "A Program of Action."

98. Robert Nichols, OXFAM/Senegal representative, interview, Dakar, October 29, 1991.

99. One of the most prominent NGO leaders in Senegal, Mazid Ndiaye, who is recognized internationally as well as nationally, has a history of troubled relations with the state because of his opposition to the government. He has been imprisoned in the past; recently the government refused to recognize his NGO, RADI, despite its leading role in the field of agricultural extension services. Nichols, interview; Mazid Ndiaye, RADI, interview, Dakar, October 28, 1991. Nevertheless, the government also sees the NGO community as a positive counterinfluence to the growth of Islamic fundamentalism. For detail, see Helmut K. Anheier, "Private Voluntary Organizations and Development in West Africa: Comparative Perspectives," in Estelle James, ed., *The Nonprofit Sector in International Perspective: Studies in Comparative Culture and Policy* (Oxford University Press, 1989). Magatte Wade, interview, November 4, 1991.

100. Interviews included Diop; M. Ndiaye; Abdoulaye Ndiaye, AID/Dakar, October 21, 1991; Fatime Ndiaye, director, CONGAD, October 23, 1991.

101. M. Ndiaye, interview. The NCNW, which implemented a project with the Agetip, also cited this approach as a problem, particularly at the field supervision level. Mme. Sowede, interview.

102. Mme. Sowede, interview; Agetip Management Team, interviews. Magatte Wade, interviews. Sindzingre, Sene, and Sow, "République du Senegal." NGO Official who participated in Agetip projects, interview, Dakar, October 1991.

103. Diop, interviews; and Bathily, interview.

104. The perception that the government is doing something to make the adjustment process less costly may not contribute to popular support for the adjustment process per se but can yield support for the government at a critical time, which may be key to sustaining adjustment. I would like to thank Joan Nelson for introducing me to the distinction between these two concepts.

105. M. Ndiaye, interview. This insight was also shared by Nicolas Roffe.

106. Sindzingre, Sene, and Sow, "République du Senegal."

107. Another means of Agetip expansion that is already under consideration is for the agency to act as a consultant to other countries that are in the process of setting up similar agencies. While this may prove extremely beneficial to neighboring countries, it may also result, because of limited staff size, in insufficient attention to the important role that the Agetip has to play in Senegal.

Chapter 6

1. The first attempted agreement with the IMF was as early as 1973, but the reform program was stopped in the face of opposition from the Mineworkers' Union in 1974.

2. One notable exception is the Microprojects Unit (MPU), which is under the auspices of the National Commission for Development Planning but is funded and supervised by the European Community and, since 1991, the World Bank. While the MPU is not a program designed to protect the poor nor to reach exclusively the poorest groups, its role in stimulating community participation in the improvement and maintenance of social welfare infrastructure is an extremely valuable one and an experience that should be incorporated into continuing efforts to alleviate poverty in Zambia. The MPU will be discussed in detail in a later section.

3. This also had important implications region-wide. Detailed accounts can be found in Michael Bratton, "Zambia Starts Over," *Journal of Democracy*, vol. 3 (April 1992), pp. 81–94; and Carol Graham, "Zambia's Democratic Transition: The Beginning of the End of the One-Party State in Africa?" *Brookings Review* (Spring 1992), pp. 40–41.

4. Ridgeway Liwena, "Mtonga Quits Unip," *Times of Zambia*, November 13, 1991; "2000 Desert UNIP in Chipata," *Zambia Daily Mail*, November 12, 1991, p. 11; and "UNIP Chiefs Split," *Zambia Daily Mail*, November 15, 1991, p. 1.

5. This conclusion is based on the author's following of the media and the press in Zambia in the immediate postelectoral period, as well as conversations with a variety of government officials and nongovernment observers, including the new finance minister, Emmanuel Kasonde, on November 15, 1991.

6. Ravi Gulhati, "Impasse in Zambia: The Economics and Politics of Reform," EDI Development Policy Case Series, Analytical Case Studies 2 (The World Bank, 1989), p. 48.

7. Policy decisions were often determined by "non-economic factors that affect economic decisions [and] impose social obligations on individuals that limit their interest and capacity to support public concerns outside the community." Goran Hyden, *No Shortcuts to Progress: African Development Management in Perspective* (University of California Press, 1983), chapter 1.

8. For a detailed discussion of this phenomenon, see Mark Schacter, "Institutional Impediments to Structural Adjustment Reforms in Developing Countries," The World Bank, March 1990; and Richard Sandbrook, "Hobbled Leviathans: Constraints on State Formation in Africa," *International Journal*, vol. 41 (Autumn 1986), pp. 707–33.

9. Gulhati, "Impasse in Zambia," p. 28.

10. This process is discussed in detail in Morris Szeftel, "Political Graft and the Spoils System in Zambia—the State as a Resource in Itself," *Review of African Political Economy*, no. 24 (May-August 1982), pp. 4–21; and Ian Scott, "Ideology, Party and the Co-operative Movement in Zambia," *Journal of Administration Overseas*, vol. 19 (October 1980), pp. 228–38.

11. Cherry Gertzel, ed. *The Dynamics of the One-Party State in Zambia* (Oxford: Manchester University Press, 1984).

12. Emmanuel Kasonde, former permanent secretary for economics, current minister of finance, interview, November 15, 1991. Kasonde said that he left the government at this point because "the government stopped listening."

13. A similar "decentralization" process occurred in Ghana under the Limman and the PNDC governments. The local government structure in Zambia is discussed in greater detail later in this chapter. For a comprehensive account of the decentralization process in Zambia in the 1970s, see Michael Bratton, *The Local Politics of Rural Development: Peasant and One-Party State in Zambia* (Hanover: University Press of New England, 1980).

14. Production in 1977, after more than ten years of heavy government lending to the cooperatives, remained concentrated in the hands of 300 white farmers, who produced 60 percent of the total yield. Scott, "Ideology, Party and the Co-operative Movement in Zambia," p. 231.

15. A UNIP cabinet member's statement is telling. "Without the Party the bank manager could not see you to negotiate an overdraft for anything." Szeftel, "Political Graft," p. 7. See Tina West, "The Politics of the Implementation of Structural Adjustment in Zambia, 1985–1987," in *The Politics of Economic Reform in Sub-Saharan Africa*, Final Report Prepared by the Center for Strategic and International Studies, Washington, D.C., March 1992, pp. 169–200.

16. For an account of UNIP control of market stalls, see Earl P. Scott, "Lusaka's Informal Sector in National Economic Development," *Journal of Developing Areas*, vol. 20 (October 1985). For an account of the private sector's relations with the UNIP, see Andrew A. Beveridge and Anthony R. Oberschall, *African Businessmen and Development in Zambia* (Princeton University Press, 1979), chapters 1 and 7.

17. The extent of wealth that the political elite derived from illegal exports—principally gemstones, ivory, and subsidized commodities—is still not fully known. West, "The Politics of the Implementation of Structural Adjustment"; and Venkatesh Seshamani, "Towards Structural Transformation with a Human Focus: The Economic Programmes and Policies of Zambia in the 1980's," *Innocenti Occasional Papers*, no. 7, (Florence: Spedale degli Innocenti, 1990).

18. Typically voters will choose whichever option seems likely to provide them with the services that they desperately need. Only when basic needs, such as legal title to land, water, and electricity, are met, do local politicians pay attention to issues of national concern. For examples of the voting behavior of the urban poor in Brazil, Peru, and Chile, see Robert Gay, "Neighborhood Associations and Political Change in Rio de Janeiro," *Latin American Research Review*, vol 25, no. 1 (1990); Carol Graham, "The APRA Government and the Urban Poor: The PAIT Programme in Lima's Pueblos Jovenes," *Journal of Latin American Studies*, vol. 23 (February 1991); and Carol Graham, "From Emergency Employment to Social Investment: Alleviating Poverty in Chile," *Brookings Occasional Papers*, November 1991.

19. Robert H. Bates, *Beyond the Miracle of the Market: The Political Economy of Agrarian Development in Kenya* (Cambridge University Press, 1989), p. 92.

20. One example that reflects this is that voter turnouts were higher in the 1978 elections than in 1973. While Kaunda ran unopposed in both elections, in 1978 the opposition decided that a stance of "active rejection" was preferable to a boycott of the elections, as they had urged in 1973. Voter turnouts were also higher because there were more concerted attempts at voter education, 600 new polls were opened, and the political atmosphere was heightened because of Zambia's role in Zimbabwe's struggle for independence. Gertzel, *The Dynamics of the One-Party State in Zambia*, chapter 2.

21. Ibid; and Gulhati, "Impasse in Zambia," p. 28. Both the UNIP and the MUZ supported equal pay scales for black and white workers.

22. Robert Bates, *Unions, Parties, and Political Development: A Study if Mineworkers in Zambia* (Yale University Press, 1971), chapter 7.

23. Szeftel, "Political Graft," p. 19.

24. Gulhati, "Impasse in Zambia," p. 28. A good example of the lack of party control over unions and of the loyalty of workers to unions and companies rather than to the party is the case of President Chiluba. Chiluba, the leader of the 300,000–member ZCTU from 1974 until 1991, was an active opponent of one-party rule. When he was detained by the government in the early 1980s, his employer, Atlas Copco, continued to send his salary to his family. After his release the government attempted to punish Atlas Copco for continuing to employ him by withholding foreign exchange from the company, yet the company refused to fire him. Chiluba recounted this story to the public during a visit to his former employer a few weeks after becoming president. Author's following of television coverage of the speech, Lusaka, November 15, 1991; and "UNIP Pressurised for My Sacking," *Zambia Daily Mail*, November 16, 1991, p. 1.

25. In the 1973 elections, for example, the "no" vote was much higher in mining constituencies and in urban areas where the UPP was able to undermine

UNIP support. The "no" vote was 11.2 percent in 1973 and 19.3 percent in 1978. Voter turnout was also low in 1978: 39.8 percent (versus a still low 45 percent for the 1990 elections). For detail, see Michael Bratton, "Zambia Starts Over," *Journal of Democracy*, vol. 3 (April 1992), pp. 81–94.

26. This point is noted by David Sahn in "Economic Reform in Africa: Are There Similarities with Latin America?" paper presented to workshop on Macroeconomic Crisis, Policy Reforms, and the Poor in Latin America," Cali, Colombia, October 1–4, 1991, p. 45.

27. Social Action Programme Document, 1991 Report, Lusaka; and Thomas M. Callaghy, "Lost Between State and Market: The Politics of Economic Adjustment in Ghana, Zambia, and Nigeria," in Joan M. Nelson, *Economic Crisis and Policy Choice: The Politics of Adjustment in the Third World* (Princeton University Press, 1990), p. 258. The rescinded 1973 agreement called for consumer subsidy removal, wage freezes, and export diversification. The 1978 agreement called for the elimination of arrears on external credit, a 10 percent devaluation of the kwacha, a halt to the expansion of domestic credit, a wage freeze, higher agricultural producer prices, and rationalized copper production. In 1980, a three-year Extended Fund Facility for SDR 800 million was signed with the IMF with the objective of comprehensive structural adjustment, including expenditure restraint, reform of monetary and fiscal policy, redirection of government spending from urban subsidies to agriculture, revamping of copper production, a review of exchange rate policy, and the elimination of debt arrears. The following series of agreements culminated in Kaunda's ill-fated May 1987 decision.

28. Author's interview with Emmanuel Kasonde, Lusaka, December 15, 1991.

29. "Death Toll Rises to 23 in Zambia," *Washington Post*, June 28, 1990.

30. Authors interviews with Dag Aarnes, senior programme officer, Norwegian Agency for Development Cooperation, Lusaka, November 11, 1991; and Torsten Wetterblad, senior economist, Swedish Development Cooperation Office, Lusaka, November 18, 1991.

31. Cadman Atta Mills, "Structural Adjustment in Sub-Saharan Africa," EDI Policy Seminar Report 18 (The World Bank, 1989), p. 6.

32. Finance Minister Kasonde, interview, Lusaka, November 15, 1991. One could argue that in other countries public understanding of measures and careful explanation for them has done a great deal to make them palatable. In Peru the August 1990 shock program, in which food prices went up by 500 percent and gasoline by 3,000 percent overnight, was carefully explained to the public in a two-hour address by the prime minister/finance minister. Not only were there no riots, but in the trimester after the shock, Prime Minister Juan Carlos Hurtado Miller was the most popular man in the country! For a detailed account, see Carol Graham, *Peru's APRA: Parties, Politics, and the Elusive Quest for Democracy* (Boulder: Lynne Rienner Publishers, 1992). Seshamani, "Towards Structural Transformation," pp. 55–57.

33. The maize meal issue is discussed in detail in the next section. A detailed account of the decisionmaking process that preceded the implementation of the

measures appears in West, "The Politics of the Implementation of Structural Adjustment," pp. 92–95. Not only did the government not research consumption patterns well—only the poorest of the poor were consuming roller meal, as the price differential before December 1986 was not that great and the quality difference was—but the government also failed to explain properly to either the millers or the public a rather complex new pricing system. In the millers' case, the into-mill price was raised on December 4, and only on December 9, the last day of the riots, did the government send a memo to the millers explaining the subsidy system and enclosing forms for registration. The registration process could hardly have been completed in less than a week, and the millers faced a minimum of a two-week delay if they produced and sold subsidized roller meal.

34. Gulhati, "Impasse in Zambia," pp. 50–51.

35. I would like to thank Joan Nelson for introducing me to this concept in a series of discussions. For details in specific countries, see Carol Graham, "The Politics of Protecting the Poor During Adjustment: Bolivia's Emergency Social Fund," *World Development*, vol. 20 (September 1992); and Carol Graham, "From Emergency Employment to Social Investment" (1991).

36. Atta Mills, "Structural Adjustment in Sub-Saharan Africa," p. 21.

37. Robin Hinson Jones, political officer, U.S. Embassy, interview, Lusaka, November 14, 1991. Hinson Jones points out that one reason that the MMD was able to succeed was that so many civil servants helped them with organization and access to information. UNIP's strategy of threatening to fire MMD supporters was, if anything, counterproductive.

38. "First Multiparty Elections Set in Zambia for End of October," *New York Times*, Sept 5, 1991, p. A8. John Battersby, "Zambia's Gutsy Independent Press Had Key Role in Election," *Christian Science Monitor*, November 8, 1991, p. 7. Several observers interviewed noted the increase in freedom in the past two years. Blatantly antigovernment newspapers such as the *Weekly Post* began to operate freely, and the highly public trial and sentencing to death for murder of Kaunda's son, for example, demonstrated the extent to which the judiciary had established its independence. Kaunda deserves credit for allowing this process to continue.

39. Eva Richards, UNICEF Advisor, interview, Lusaka, November 14, 1991. The crowd of thousands at President Chiluba's inauguration may have been the largest ever assembled at a public gathering in Zambia. Peter J. Henriot, election observer and pastor of St. Ignatius Parish, interview, Lusaka, November 19, 1991; and John Battersby, "Zambian Leader Sets New Course," *Christian Science Monitor*, November 7, 1991, p. 3.

40. Hinson-Jones, interview. Author's conversation with Mary Barton, MPU deputy director, Lusaka, November 1991. "UNIP Seeks to Oust Kaunda," *Weekly Post*, November 15–21, 1991, p. 1; "UNIP Chiefs Split," *Zambia Daily Mail*, November 15, 1991, p. 1; and "2000 Desert UNIP in Chipata," *Zambia Daily Mail*, November 12, 1991, p. 1. For a brief account of the Chilean transition, see Carol Graham, "Chile's Return to Democracy," *Brookings Review* (Spring 1990), pp. 39–41. In Zambia, the important role of Jimmy Carter's team in guaranteeing free elections was cited by many observers and the press throughout the author's

interviews. For example, Maffat Muza, MMD member, interview, November 7, 1991; Chisasa Mulenga, election observer and MPU staff member, November 15, 1991; and P. Henriot, election observer, November 19, 1991.

41. Movement for Multi-Party Democracy, *Manifesto* (Lusaka, 1991).

42. Mike Hall, "Kaunda Officials Accused of Big Copper Fraud," *Financial Times*, September 25, 1991. p. 4.

43. *UNIP: The Critical Choice* (Lusaka: Party Manifesto, 1991), p. 4.

44. Such an approach was echoed by key members of his team, such as the finance minister, who stressed that "the people voted you into power, they are the bosses, they have a right to be consulted." Kasonde interview.

45. *Weekly Post*, November 8–14 , 1991; "UNIP Abused State Funds," *Sunday Times of Zambia*, November 17, 1991, p. 1; "Work Hard, Cabinet Told," *Times of Zambia*, November 12, 1991, p. 3; and author's following of press and television coverage in the two-week period following the election in Lusaka. At the time of reinitiating trade, Chiluba said, "Zambia may not be the centre of the universe, but it is the centre of our universe."

46. "Work Hard, Cabinet Told," *Times of Zambia*, November 12, 1991, p. 3.

47. "UNIP Homes Stoned," *Times of Zambia*, November 11, 1991, p. 1; and "Evict UNIP Officials," *Times of Zambia*, November 11, 1991, p. 3.

48. "UNIP Crumbles," *Weekly Post*, November 15–21, 1991, p. 3. Not only were there mass UNIP defections, even in Eastern province, but there was an immediate move to attempt to oust Kaunda from power. It is difficult to imagine UNIP as any kind of coherent political force any time in the near future.

49. This is frighteningly reminiscent of the last few months of the APRA government in Peru, in which all kinds of unrealistic promises were made to labor unions, and at the same time, state sector workers were not paid for the last two months, leaving an enormous debt for an already indebted new government. For details see Graham, *Peru's APRA*.

50. Lester Gordon, Harvard Institute for International Development advisor to the Finance Ministry, interview, Lusaka, December 16, 1991.

51. "Bank of Zambia Fails to Cope with its Accounts," *Weekly Post*, November 8–14, 1991.

52. This is demonstrated by the contrasting cases of Peru, Zambia, and several eastern European countries on the one hand, and Senegal on the other. In Peru, for example, the strong mandate given to Alberto Fujimori in 1990 because he was from *outside* the established political system gave him a great deal of room to maneuver, allowing him to implement a draconian stabilization program (which he had actually campaigned against) with virtually no popular protest. The Chiluba government's liberalizing of the maize price without popular protest is also indicative. In both cases, people voted for political change and an end to prolonged processes of economic decline and were willing to bear some sacrifices to attain those objectives. In Senegal, in contrast, political competition remains limited to debate among a small elite and is dominated by the governing Parti Socialiste. Popular unrest in the face of adjustment measures is a protest against the political system as often as against the measures themselves, as the February 1988 riots indicated. For detail, see Graham, *Peru's APRA*, chapter 7; and the

chapter on Senegal (chapter 5) in this volume. Even some high-level UNIP officials argued the need to move forward quickly in implementing a free market strategy. Mr. Liswaniso, permanent secretary, interview, Lusaka, November 13, 1991.

53. There were even criticisms that Chiluba had "coopted" unions into supporting his adjustment program. Melinda Ham, "Zambia: One Year On," *Africa Report* (January-February 1993).

54. Britain forgave 60 percent of Zambia's debt following the election, while the United States made the forgiveness of $110 million in debt conditional on an agreement with the multilaterals, which followed shortly thereafter. In January 1992, the government worked out a deal with bilateral donors to pay the $50 million to the World Bank that had left it suspended from Bank operations. The deal allowed the Bank to resume Zambia's disbursements and to plan a new lending program. "Late Arrears Deal Precedes Preston's Zambia Trip," *World Bank Watch*, February 17, 1992; "UK To Cancel Zambia's Debt," *Zambia Daily Mail*, November 9, 1991, p. 1; and "US To Scrap $270 Million Debt," *Times of Zambia*, November 18, 1991, p. 1.

55. Chris Chitanda, "Loyalists Grab Key Cabinet Portfolios," *Weekly Post*, November 8–14 1991; and "Review Policy, Urges Ssiaz," *Sunday Times of Zambia*, November 10, 1991, p. 9. Five different factions were identified in the Chiluba cabinet. The first was the "Group of Seven" and included Defense Minister Benjamin Mwila and Foreign Affairs Minister Vernon Mwaanga. This group's influence stemmed from their financial strength and connections to the private sector. The second faction was the "unionists," led by Home Affairs Minister Newstead Zimba. Chiluba owed a great deal to Zimba and the labor movement, where he developed his leadership skills, and which gave him a platform from which to launch his political career. The third faction was the "Young Turks," led by Higher Education Minister Akashambatwa Mbikusita-Lewanika. This group has its origins in the Zambia Research Foundation, a University of Zambia-based pressure group that was key in promoting the formation of the MMD. Mbikusita and Derrick Chitala of this group were the organizers of the 1990 Garden House symposium on multiparty democracy that resulted in the founding of the MMD. Within the cabinet, this group claimed the most of the ministerial and deputy ministerial posts filled by educated young professionals. The fourth group was the "Veterans' Group," which was led by Finance Minister Kasonde. It was a Bembe-speaking group, whose regional strength lay in the north. Before the announcement of the ministerial posts, this group served as a kitchen cabinet and had been strongly opposed to the appointment of Levy Mwanawasa, a technocrat and outsider, as vice president. The fifth and least influential faction was the "partymen," which included Minister without Portfolio Godfrey Miyanda, the de facto number three in government; Dipak Patel, the MMD campaign manager; Guy Scott, the agriculture minister; Stan Kristofar, the information minister; and others with no strong interest group representation but who had joined the MMD to fight for democracy.

56. L. Gray Cowan, "Zambia Tests Democracy," *CSIS Africa Notes*, no. 141 (October 1992), p. 5. Risks also stem from the confidence factor: the legacy of

aborted adjustment programs in Zambia under Kaunda and the government's lukewarm commitment to the private sector. For years the government tolerated but was hardly supportive of the private sector. See Performance Audit Report, *Zambia*, Agricultural Rehabilitation Project, Report no. 11890 (Washington, D.C.: The World Bank, May 1993), p. xi.

57. Ham, "Zambia," p. 39.

58. Tony Hawkins, "Now Zambia Points Way to Fiscal Rectitude in Adversity," *Financial Times*, February 10, 1993, p. 7.

59. In February 1988, after the increase in the price of gasoline, urban rioting left 300 dead and the democratic government of Carlos Andres Perez far weaker than before. As with the maize price increases in Zambia, the Venezuelan public was not prepared for the price increases, and the measures were not explained.

60. David Sahn notes that while poverty in Latin America increased with adjustment, in most African countries it stayed at the same level but did not increase because most rural poor are at least relatively isolated from the market; Latin America is much more urban. Furthermore, in Africa donors often made up for the shortfall in finances for social expenditures, while in Latin America they did not. Sahn, "Economic Reform in Africa: Are There Similarities with Latin America?" (paper presented to workshop on Macroeconomic Crisis, Policy Reforms, and the Poor in Latin America, Cali, Colombia, October 1–4, 1991), p. 5. Judith Amri-Makheta, International Labor Organization, interview, November 18, 1991.

61. Sahn points to this as an Africa-wide problem of political economy, with donors funding social programs while governments continue to spend on military programs and the like. Politics entails making choices, and African governments should not be excused from the need to highlight priorities and to make choices among different public expenditure goals.

62. Kasonde interview. The minister noted that an increase in the price of maize meal could be complemented with a measure such as the abolition of school uniforms, one of the expenses that most concerned poor families.

63. Melinda Ham, "Zambia: Luring Investment," *Africa Report*, September/October 1992, p. 41.

64. "Zambia's Goal: Both Austerity and More Social Spending," *World Bank Watch*, February 24, 1992, p. 7.

65. "A Preliminary Report of the Effectiveness of the Coupon System," Prices and Incomes Commission, Lusaka, August 1990, p. 2. Maize-related subsidies as a share of the government budget reached their highest level in 1988 at 16.9 percent.

66. Interview with Patrick Mulenga, director of research, Prices and Incomes Commission, Lusaka, November 12, 1991.

67. Some estimates are as low as $290. "Staff Appraisal Report, Zambia: Social Recovery Project," Report 9471–ZA (The World Bank, May 21, 1991).

68. Richard Pearce, "Food Consumption and Adjustment in Zambia," Food Studies Group, Queen Elizabeth House, Oxford University, Working Paper 2, December 1990; and *UNICEF Annual Report: Zambia 1991*. Pearce uses Prices and Incomes Commission data to measure urban poverty. The 20 percent figure

for rural poverty is based on Prices and Incomes Commission data, while the 80 percent figure is based on a 1980 ILO study. Rural poverty is much harder to measure because of the importance of nonmonetary income in rural households.

69. Genevieve de Crombrugghe, Carlos Escribano, Ian Thurairatnam, "Evaluation of Microprojects Programmes Zambia Lome II and III" (report prepared for the Commission of the European Communities, November 1991), p. 11; and *UNICEF Annual Report: Zambia 1991* (UNICEF, Lusaka, Zambia, 1991, preliminary version).

70. "Hospital Labs Shut Down," *Zambia Daily Mail*, November 13, 1991, p. 5.

71. Ibid.; and UNICEF Annual Report: Zambia 1991.

72. The explanations for this are varied, and may be due in part to the severity of the strain of cholera. Yet because Peru had a higher incidence rate (more than 200,000 cases in a population of 22 million versus 11,000 cases in Zambia, with a population of just over 7 million) and has faced a similar decline in per capita income levels in the 1980s, some of the explanation clearly lies with far more efficient health services as well as government efforts at public awareness in Peru.

73. Examples of such corruption are detailed in the next section. It is relevant to note here, however, the extent to which UNIP plundered the public coffers in its last few months in power. The Chiluba government reported that more than 50 billion kwacha (100 kw = $1) were diverted from the public budget in UNIP's final year (a figure that is too high to be realistic) and that the administration was in the process of allocating itself 19 billion more when the November 1 transfer of power took place. In addition, many billions more remain unaccounted for, and probably always will, as UNIP officials shredded massive numbers of government documents before vacating government offices. "UNIP Abused State Funds," *Sunday Times of Zambia*, November 17, 1991, p. 1; and author's following of the press and other news media in Lusaka during the two weeks following the elections.

74. Zambia's percentage decline in terms of trade over 1974 (terms-of-trade index, 1974 = 100) was 45.8 from 1975 to 1979 and 63.8 from 1980 to 1986. Gulhati, "Impasse in Zambia," pp. 3–4.

75. *World Development Report* (The World Bank, 1980), p. 228. Morris Szeftel, "Political Graft and the Spoils System in Zambia—The State as a Resource in Itself," *Review of African Political Economy*, no. 24 (May-August 1982), pp. 4–21; and Prices and Incomes Commission, *Social Economic Bulletin*, vol. 1 (April 1991).

76. Even though there were a great many political appointees at the district level and district governors were political appointees, at the provincial level the staff tended to be "more or less" professional and to have less turnover. Benny Zulu, assistant coordinator, MicroProjects Unit, interview, Lusaka, November 12, 1991. Author's interview with Ian Hopwood, area representative, UNICEF, and Eva Richards, planning, monitoring, and evaluation advisor, UNICEF, Lusaka, November 16, 1991. This was confirmed by the author's visits to health posts approximately one hour out of Lusaka in Nyangwena in Zambia, and two villages approximately one hour out of Dakar in Senegal. While the post in

Zambia lacked beds and other supplies, it had a full-time staff, including a doctor. In Senegal, despite repeated requests to the government by the villagers, there was no health post, and the only school had been built by the villagers themselves.

77. Earl P. Scott, "Lusaka's Informal Sector in National Economic Development," *Journal of Developing Areas*, vol. 20 (October 1985), pp. 71–100; author's interview with Huntington Jere, director, Human Settlements of Zambia, Lusaka, November 14, 1991; and author's visits to several Lusaka "compounds" in contrast to visits to "bidon-villes" in Dakar and "pueblos jovenes" in Lima.

78. Ian Scott documents this phenomenon in the rural cooperatives, for example, in "Ideology, Party and the Co-operative Movement in Zambia," *Journal of Administration Overseas*, vol. 19 (October 1980), pp. 228–38. It is also well demonstrated by the current food coupon scheme, as documented in Pearce, "Food Consumption and Adjustment in Zambia"; and Prices and Incomes Commission, "A Preliminary Report of the Effectiveness of the Coupon System," Lusaka, August 1990; as well as by the author's interviews focusing on this issue in November 1991 with government officials and nongovernment organizations in Lusaka. Zambia is not unique in this phenomenon; the one-party system in neighboring Zaire has produced similar results.

79. One donor noted that when criticizing Zambia's poor economic management, it was important to recognize the extent to which it was sanctioned by large flows of international aid. Aarnes, interview, November 11, 1991. Of the six other southern African countries rated as very poor in the Southern African Development Coordination Conference (SADCC), for example, Zambia was the highest recipient of IDA funds for 1991, receiving nearly $300 million by the end of the fiscal year (June 30). "Zambia Tops IDA Loanees," *Zambia Daily Mail*, November 15, 1991, p. 4.

80. Stephan Devereaux, "Managing the Welfare Effects of Stabilisation and Structural Adjustment Programmes on Vulnerable Groups: With Reference to Sub-Saharan Africa," unpublished paper, Food Studies Group, Oxford University, November 1987, p. 22. This conclusion is based on the author's interviews with international agency representatives, local and international NGOs, and officials in government programs for the poor in Lusaka in November 1991. This includes representatives of UNICEF, the World Food Program, the EC's Micro-Projects Unit, the Social Action Program, the YWCA, the Catholic Secretariat, and World Vision.

81. Seshamani, "Towards Structural Transformation."

82. A common statement in Zambia is, "If you eat rice, you haven't eaten."

83. In Peru, for example, the poor regularly shift their consumption patterns among rice, wheat, and potatoes and, if their income increases, they will buy a better form of protein, such as milk. Conversely, when income decreases they seek less expensive alternatives of a good nutritional value. See, for example, Hilary Creed Kanashiro and George Graham, "Changes over Time in Food Intakes in a Migrant Population," in P. L. White, and N. Selvey, eds., *Malnutrition: Determinants and Consequences: Current Topics in Nutrition and Disease*, vol. 10 (1984), pp. 197–205. A recent study of the consumption patterns of the urban poor of Argentina is Patricia Aguirre, "The Impact of Crises on Low

Income Urban Households in Argentina: How the Very Poor Survive" (paper presented to workshop on "Macroeconomic Crisis, Policy Reforms, and the Poor in Latin America," organized by Cornell Food and Nutrition Policy Program and the Centro Internacional de Agricultura Tropical, Cali, Colombia, October 1–4, 1991).

84. These are the informal sector and household surveys conducted by the Prices and Incomes Commission and the priorities survey of the Central Statistics Office, which is funded by the World Bank as a part of the social action program. The informal sector survey covers 1,260 households in low-income areas of urban Lusaka and provides data on employment and income levels in both low-income formal sector households and informal sector households. The data are also broken down by gender. The household survey has usable data from 2,800 households throughout Zambia, in all provinces, and broken down into 48 percent urban and 52 percent rural to reflect the last census. It provides information on consumption patterns over the past five years. In 1985, when a pilot survey was conducted, households were spending an average of 50 percent of their incomes on food, and low-income households, 60 percent. Patrick Mulenga, interview. The priorities survey is a multisector indicator survey that will use an extensive, nationwide sample in urban and rural areas. The sample size is approximately 9,000, and the survey was conducted by the Central Statistics Office with funding from the World Bank. The data for these studies have been collected but not analyzed completely to date.

85. Child malnutrition increased from 20 percent in 1970 to 6 percent in 1980 and to 20 percent in 1992. "Zambia: Prospects for Sustainable Growth," Country Operations Division, preliminary version (The World Bank, March 1993), p. 23.

86. Gulhati, "Impasse in Zambia," p. 4; "Staff Appraisal Report: Zambia/ Social Recovery Project"; and Prices and Incomes Commission.

87. Republic of Zambia, Social Action Programme Document, April 1, 1990; Patrick Mulenga, interview; and Prices and Incomes Commission, *Social Economic Bulletin*, vol. 1 (April 1991). The PIC estimated that low-income households spent 60 percent of their income on food in 1985. Credible estimates are now as high as 70 percent given the deterioration that has occurred since. The figures on nutrition-related deaths are 1988 figures from the Ministry of Health that were made available to me by Ian Hopwood of UNICEF.

88. "Zambia: Prospects for Sustainable Growth," p. 17.

89. Of these, 67.4 percent were poor and 58 percent were extremely poor. The average for sub-Saharan Africa is 47 percent poor and 30 percent extremely poor. Ibid.

90. The line was defined in 1987 as the "money value of goods and services needed by a household to support a minimum standard of living," which obviously entails assumptions about nutrient intake and what nonfood items are essential that are bound to raise some element of controversy. An estimate is made for a family of two adults and four children and is based on the assumption that the household spends 60 percent of its income on food. Data were taken from the PIC's 1988 informal sector survey, and then prices were adjusted for inflation.

Richard Pearce, "Food Consumption and Adjustment in Zambia," Food Studies Group, Queen Elizabeth House, Oxford University, Working Paper 2, 1990.

91. "Zambia: Prospects for Sustainable Growth," p. 104.

92. Ibid., p. 101.

93. Pearce, "Food Consumption and Adjustment in Zambia." The 1988 figures were 500 kwacha a month as the poverty line and 250 a month as the abject poverty line. The 1990 figures are particularly low when one considers that the average salary for a domestic servant is 2,500 to 3,000 kwacha a month (many earn less), that while the official price for a 25–kilogram bag of maize is 215 kwacha (approximately two to three times that price on the black market, where many poor are forced to buy maize), and that a family of four requires approximately 75 kilograms a month (a rather high estimate). PIC estimated in 1991 that 9,000 kwacha a month would meet the needs of an average household; this amount is far in excess of what even the average government official or laborer earns. UNICEF/Zambia, Annual Report, 1991. Monthly wages of 1,000 kwacha a month are not uncommon; schoolteachers earn approximately 1,600 a month. Mike Soko, NCDP functionary, interview, Lusaka, November 12, 1991; and estimates by Ian Hopwood, UNICEF representative, Zambia.

94. Pearce, "Food Consumption and Adjustment in Zambia," pp. 7–8. These trends are confirmed by the recently updated informal sector survey issued by the Prices and Incomes Commission in August 1991.

95. Robert H. Bates and Paul Collier, "The Politics and Economics of Policy Reform in Zambia," Duke and Oxford universities, 1992, pp. 6–7.

96. Pearce, "Food Consumption and Adjustment in Zambia," p. 9.

97. UNICEF/Zambia, Annual Report, 1991.

98. Prices and Incomes Commission, *Social Economic Bulletin*, April 1, 1991; and Graham Eele, programme director, Food Studies Group, Oxford University, interview, Oxford, November 21, 1991.

99. Prices and Incomes Commission, *Social Economic Bulletin*, April 1, 1991, p. 35; see also Seshamani, "Towards Structural Transformation," pp. 12–13.

100. Judica Amri-Mahketa, International Labour Organization, interview, Lusaka, November 18, 1991.

101. Group interview with neighborhood women's group organized by the YWCA in the Desai compound, November 13, 1991; interview with George Muleta, urban informal sector worker, Lusaka, November 16, 1991; and interviews with rural health post workers and Clement Chilambwe, school headmaster in Nyangwena, November 15, 1991. The deterioration is clearly visible within the past ten years, and it is interesting to note the case of one woman who had a large number of children with a large age gap: her oldest children received a relatively high-quality education, while her youngest now attends a school where there are no desks and no books. Dag Aarnes, NORAD, interview, Lusaka, 11 November 1991.

102. Peter Henriot, St. Ignatius Parish, interview, Lusaka, November 19, 1991.

103. Dr. Getu, Director, World Vision, interview, Lusaka, November 11, 1991.

104. Mikhael Candotti, EC representative to the National Commission for Development Planning, interview, Lusaka, November 13, 1991.

105. Kasonde interview; and Lester Gordon, HIID advisor to the Ministry of Finance, interview, November 16, 1991.

106. *UNICEF Annual Report—Zambia, 1991* (preliminary report), Lusaka, November 1991, p. 6.

107. Sahn, "Economic Reform in Africa," p. 36.

108. Francois Bourgignon, "Optimal Poverty Reduction, Adjustment, and Growth," *World Bank Economic Review,* vol. 5 (May 1991), p. 316.

109. Frances Stewart, "Protecting the Poor During Adjustment in Latin America and the Caribbean in the 1980's: How Adequate Was the World Bank Response?" paper presented for a workshop on "Macroeconomic Crises, Policy Reform and the Poor in Latin America," organized by Cornell Food and Nutrition Policy Program in collaboration with Centro Internacional de Agricultura Tropical (CIAT), the Ford Foundation, and UNICEF, in Cali, Colombia, October 1–4, 1991; and minutes from meetings from UNICEF Regional Meeting for sub-Saharan Africa, Nairobi, Kenya, November 1991.

110. Graham Eele, Food Studies Group, Oxford University, interview, Oxford, November 21, 1991. For examples, see Joachim Von Braun, Tesfaye Teklu, Patrick Webb, "Labor-Intensive Public Works for Food Security: Experience in Africa," IFPRI Working Papers on Food Subsidies 6, July 1991. One of the most controversial elements seems to be where to set the wage rate, but it seems that the best is somewhere below going market rates, in order to target the poorest, but not so low as to be counterproductive to poverty alleviation goals. Food-for-work schemes are an excellent way to reach the poorest, although their administrative costs seem to be their main drawback. In addition, there seems to be no clear relation between food security at the household level and food security at the national level, so it is not clear that food for work is a drawback to national food self-sufficiency. Stephan Devereaux, "Managing the Welfare Effects of Stabilisation and Structural Adjustment Programmes on Vulnerable Groups: With Reference to Sub-Saharan Africa," Food Studies Group, Oxford University, November 1987, p. 26.

111. Providing food to women is also a far more effective way to reach children than is providing income to men in Zambia, as often the income is spent on alcohol before it reaches the children. This is also the case in many countries in Latin America as well as Africa. Interviews with Tony Mornemount, World Food Programme representative for Zambia, November 16, 1991; and Huntington Jere, director, HUZA, November 14, 1991, Lusaka.

112. West, "The Politics of the Implementation of Structural Adjustment."

113. Mornemount interview.

114. See, for example, Richard Pearce, "Food Consumption and Adjustment in Zambia," and Prices and Incomes Commission, "A Preliminary Report of the Effectiveness of the Coupon System," Lusaka, August 1990.

115. "Meal Exports Denied," *Times of Zambia*, November 8, 1991; and Mornemount interview.

116. "Fertilizer Mess Greets Guy Scott," *Weekly Post*, November 15–21, 1991, p. 13.

117. Mornemount, interview; and West, "The Politics of the Implementation of Structural Adjustment."

118. Several of the main fertilizer distributors had delayed imports of fertilizer from Europe in order to get kickbacks from companies in neighboring countries. Thus when the Chiluba government took over, there was a serious fertilizer shortage as well. "Fertilizer Mess Greets Guy Scott," *Weekly Post*, November 15–21, 1991, p. 13.

119. Fernando Fernholz, HIID Advisor to NCDP, interview, Lusaka, November 12, 1991.

120. Bates and Collier, "The Politics and Economics of Policy Reform in Zambia," p. 58. In 1991 it was estimated that many poor households spent up to 70 percent of their income on food, and maize was a staple commodity.

121. Pearce, "Food Consumption and Adjustment in Zambia," p. 11.

122. Diocese of Monze, Zambia, *Development Report, 1990*, p. 2.

123. While in 1986 the riots focused on the price of maize, by 1990 they reflected popular discontent with the party and the political system in addition. Bates and Collier, "The Politics and Economics of Policy Reform in Zambia," pp. 71–72.

124. Prices and Incomes Commission, "A Preliminary Report on the Effectiveness of the Coupon System," p. 9.

125. In the author's group interview with approximately twenty women in the Desai compound, there were several statements such as, "Of course normal people weren't in the party except when they forced you to join." Forced conscription refers to having to join in order to get a necessary license or slot at the marketplace.

126. Pearce, "Food Consumption and Adjustment in Zambia," p. 13; and Kasonde interview.

127. Pearce, "Food Consumption and Adjustment in Zambia," p. 15; and Wetteblad, interview. Nevertheless, the system did provide important income support for some urban households, as it provided the equivalent of 25 percent of monthly maize consumption. "Zambia: Prospects for Sustainable Growth," p. 98.

128. Pearce, "Food Consumption and Adjustment in Zambia." Keeping subsidies on donated maize alone might be the optimal policy, as it would have less effect on the prices of domestically produced maize.

129. Gordon, interview; and Eele, interview. One possible option to reduce the price increase is to sell unmilled maize and let people grind their own with hammer mills, which people do in several other African countries. The main drawback of this option is that it underestimates the opportunity costs of the poor's time, particularly the urban poor.

130. Mornemount, interview; and PIC Social Economic Bulletin, p. 11.

131. Social Action Programme, 1991 Report, Lusaka, November 1991; and "Republic of Zambia: Social Action Programme for 1990–93," presented to Consultative Group for Zambia, April 1990.

132. Bolivia's ESF was successful both in providing efficient, highly visible, and extensive social sector and income generating activities that benefited poor

groups and in avoiding partisan politics. Detailed accounts are found in S. Jorgensen, M. Grosh, and M. Schacter, *Bolivia's Answer to Poverty, Economic Crisis, and Adjustment* (The World Bank, 1992); and Carol Graham, "Protecting the Poor During Adjustment: Bolivia's Emergency Social Fund," *World Development*, vol. 20 (September 1992).

133. EC, UNDP, the World Bank, and Dutch programs are all continuing.

134. This concern was expressed by a variety of donors whom the author interviewed in November 1991 in Lusaka. These included UNICEF, the World Bank, the Swedes, and the Norwegians. The UNIP's political use of the SAP was noted not only by donors but also by NGOs, the MILD opposition, and several civil servants with whom the author had interviews.

135. Richard Delgano, SAP coordinator, interview, Lusaka, November 11, 1991.

136. SAP 1991 Report, p. 2.

137. Mr. Banda, National Commission for Development Planning functionary, Interview, Lusaka, November 12, 1991. Richard Delgano, SAP coordinator, interview, Lusaka, November 11, 1991.

138. Eva Richards, UNICEF, interview, Lusaka, November 14, 1991; and Peter Henriot, St. Ignatius Parish, interview, November 19, 1991.

139. National Commission for Development Planning official, interview, Lusaka, November 12, 1991.

140. Author's interviews with several NGOs and donors that were involved with the SAP including the YWCA/Zambia, World Vision, the Catholic Secretariat, UNICEF, the Swedish government, the Norwegian government, and the World Bank. Ann Sutherland, YWCA/Zambia, interview, Lusaka, November 8, 1991; and Dr. Getu, World Vision, interview, Lusaka, November 11, 1991.

141. Interviews with Anne Sutherland; Dr. Getu; and Eva Richards.

142. This includes the SAP coordinator and representatives of the ILO, of UNICEF, and of the several NGOs interviewed.

143. Daniel Lubinga, "Urban Self-Help Benefits Poor Women," *Africa Recovery*, November 1992, p. 11.

144. Interviews with Tony Mornemount; and Huntington Jere, director, HUZA, November 14, 1991.

145. Mornemount, interview.

146. Patrick Mulenga, interview.

147. UNICEF/Zambia, Annual Report, 1991; and Graham Eele, Food Studies Group, interview, Oxford, November 21, 1991.

148. Mr. Wetteblad, interview, November 18, 1991.

149. Finance Minister Kasonde, for example, cited the program as a high priority in a speech at the Carter Center. While Kasonde may have accorded the program high priority, other elements in the government, in which antistate and antiplanning sentiments prevailed, did not. "Democracy and Economic Recovery in Africa: Lessons from Zambia," Report of the Zambia Consultation, June 10–11, 1992, The Carter Center of Emory University, Atlanta, August 1992, pp. 16–28.

150. The World Bank (IDA) gave $20 million, the EC $15 million, the government of Zambia $9.1 million, and the government of Norway $2.2 million.

Social Recovery Project; Annual Implementation Report, AFGPH, January 1993 (The World Bank 1993), p. 3.

151. World Bank Staff Appraisal Report, May 1991, p. 16. The bulk of the IDA credit, with the exception of $4 million, was placed on hold during the UNIP government's noncompliance with the adjustment program and the halting of disbursements in September 1991. This changed when the new government cleared its arrears with the Bank.

152. Interview with MPU director, P. Lusaka, November 8, 1991.

153. Social Recovery Project, Annual Implementation Report, The World Bank, January 1993, p. 8.

154. MicroProjects Unit, National Commission for Development Planning, Project Evaluation Guide, April 19, 1991.

155. Jones, interview.

156. The author noted this when an obviously busy rural health post doctor, one hour out of Lusaka, was told that he needed Ministry of Health approval to request staff housing for his post. While this is designed for sustainability purposes, that the ministry would actually provide the staff, one could also imagine that the time and cost entailed to travel to the Lusaka ministry as well as to the district council and the likelihood of being attended promptly could be preclusive in many cases. A school headmistress also complained of the number of times that she had to visit the district council to get approval. Even the international NGOs cited the bureaucratic procedure entailed in soliciting support from the MPU. One can only hope that this barrier will be reduced with an increase of accountability at the local level. This was clearly the case of the Nyangwena health and education project that was visited.

157. This was confirmed by the author's November 1991 visits to Chelston Primary School in Lusaka and to Nyangwena rural health post and school, both communities that had MPU projects, but improvements were going on in conjunction with, but independent of, MPU funding. In the case of Chelsea School, PTA donations had made the building of a new classroom possible.

158. Social Recovery Project Annual Implementation Report, p. 7.

159. Crombrugghe, Escribano, and Thurairatnam, "Evaluation of Microprojects Programmes," p. 46.

160. Mel Jones, director, MicroProjects Unit, interview, November 12, 1991.

161. This conclusion comes from a beneficiary assessment of the projects conducted for the World Bank. Social Recovery Project Annual Implementation Report.

162. Jones, interview.

163. Mickhael Candotti, former MicroProjects Unit director, interview, Lusaka, November 13, 1991.

164. Candotti, interview.

165. Benny Zulu, assistant coordinator, MicroProjects Unit, interview, Lusaka, November 12, 1991.

166. Zulu, interview.

167. Ham, "Zambia: Luring Investment." See also Mercedes Sayagues, "Zambian Villagers Struggle with Drought," *Africa Recovery*, November 1992, pp. 10–11.

168. Michael Bratton, *The Local Politics of Rural Development: Peasant and Party-State in Zambia* (Hanover: University Press of New England, 1980), p. 269.

169. Gertzel, "Impasse in Zambia," chapter 2.

170. Bratton, *Local Politics of Rural Development*; and Muzeta, interview. While the chiefs did not have the same level of power as did, for example, the marabouts in Senegal, they did still enjoy more following than the party in most remote communities.

171. Bratton, *Local Politics of Rural Development*, p. 36. This system was a mix of the Tanzanian party-based control and the Kenyan colonial centralism.

172. A detailed account of this appears in Scott, "Lusaka's Informal Sector."

173. Bratton, Local Politics of Rural Development, p. 265.

174. Various people interviewed noted the vast difference in political awareness between urban and rural areas, including Mel Jones, MPU; Dr. Getu, World Vision; and Huntington Jere, HUZA.

175. Bratton, Local Politics of Rural Development, p. 51.

176. Huntington Jere, interview.

177. *UNIP: The Critical Choice*, and Movement for Multi-Party Democracy, Manifesto.

178. "MMD Leading in Most Areas," *FBIS*, Africa-92-232, December 2, 1992, p. 42.

179. Kasonde, interview.

180. Dr. Getu, interview; Jones, interview. Members of the MMD, introducing the local taxes issue during the campaign, noted a change of attitude when people were made aware that they could expect some kind of accountability and performance from their tax payments. Kasonde, interview. Interviews: Huntington Jere; Chisasa T. Mwanza, field operations officer, EC MicroProjects Unit, November 15, 1991.

181. Muzeta interview.

182. Graham Eele and Anne Sutherland, YWCA/Zambia, interviews. Robin Hinson-Jones, Political Counselor, U.S. Embassy, Lusaka, interview, November 14, 1991.

183. Susan Ulbaek, NGOs in Zambia and Their Role in Social Recovery," The World Bank, October 1990. Sutherland, interview.

184. UNICEF/Zambia, Annual Report, 1991, and interview with Ian Hopwood, UNICEF representative, Lusaka, November 16, 1991.

185. NGOs in Zambia are very important in sponsoring community-based initiatives in the social welfare arena as well as sustainable agrarian techniques such as crop rotation. Good examples are the activities of World Vision in basic service infrastructure and the Catholic Secretariat in rural development.

186. Hyden, *No Shortcuts to Progress*; and author's interviews with several NGOs as well as visits to their projects, Lusaka, November 1991.

187. Interviews, Ian Hopwood, Anne Sutherland.
188. Candotti, interview.

Chapter 7

1. Giovanni Andrea Cornia and Sandor Sipas, eds., *Children and the Transition to the Market Economy: Safety Nets and Social Policies in Central and Eastern Europe* (United Kingdom: UNICEF, 1991), p. xxiv.

2. For details on these results, in which the (former Communist) Democratic Left Alliance of Alexander Kwasniewski received approximately 20 percent of the vote; the Polish Peasants party 16 percent; the Labor Union 6.5 percent; and the Democratic Union of Hannah Suchocka less than 12 percent, see *Washington Post* (World News), September 20, 1993; and "Ex-Communists Get it Right with Wrong Message," *Financial Times*, September 16, 1993, p. 3.

3. Labor minister Jacek Kuron labeled this initial popular tolerance to dramatic economic changes the "psychological shock" period.

4. Simon Johnson and Marzena Kowalska, "The Transformation of Poland, 1989–91" (paper presented to World Bank Project on the Political Economy of Structural Adjustment in New Democracies, edited by Steven Webb and Stephan Haggard, May 1992, abstract).

5. This point was raised initially by David Sahn in reference to Africa, but it is relevant to several cases, including Senegal and Peru as well as Poland, in the author's continuing study on the politics of social safety nets during adjustment. A caveat is that too fast a pace of restructuring could generate a rapid increase in unemployment, which could "prove both socially and politically costly, most likely leading to a reversal of policy." Olivier Blanchard and others, *Reform in Eastern Europe* (MIT Press, 1991), p. 35.

6. Katarzyna Tymowska and Marian Wisniewski, "Social Security and Health Care in Poland," PPRG Discussion Papers, no. 16, Polish Policy Research Group, Warsaw University, 1991.

7. Jan Rutkowski, "Social Expenditures in Poland: Major Programs and Recent Trends," Socialist Economies Reform Unit, Research Paper Series 1, The World Bank, Washington, D.C., December 1991, p. 1.

8. For example, low public understanding of the market transition resulted in the popular perception that market-oriented social sector reforms merely meant having to pay for the same poor quality services that were previously free of charge. In other countries, such as Zambia and Peru, the government's ability to communicate and to sell its reforms has been a determining factor in the public's response to unpopular measures. In Zambia, better communication allowed the Chiluba government to implement with no social unrest the same measures that had caused riots and even a coup attempt under the Kaunda government. In Peru, Prime Minister Hurtado Miller's detailed explanation and selling of his August 1990 stabilization package allowed the implementation of dramatic market changes with virtually no social protest. For detail, see Carol Graham, "Economic Austerity and the Peruvian Crisis: The Social Cost of Autocracy," *SAIS Review*, vol. 13 (Winter-Spring 1993); and Carol Graham, "The Politics of Pov-

erty and Adjustment in Zambia: The Hour Has Come," World Bank Draft Discussion Paper, Social Dimensions of Adjustment Unit, undated.

9. Jan Winiecki, "The Polish Transition Programme: Underpinnings, Results, Interpretations," *Soviet Studies*, vol. 44, no. 5 (1992), pp. 809–35.

10. These points are noted by Nicholas Barr in "The Social Safety Net during Economic Transition: The Case of Poland," World Bank Internal Discussion Paper, Europe and Central Asia Region, Office of the Vice-President, January 1992; and by Tymowska and Wisniewski, "Social Security and Health Care in Poland."

11. Fully private schemes, given the low level of purchasing power of the general population and the underdeveloped nature of capital markets and the regulatory system in Poland, would be economically unviable and socially unacceptable. This is discussed in greater detail in the section on the reform of the pension system.

12. Edmund Wnuk-Lipinski, "Freedom or Equality: An Old Dilemma in a New Context," in Bob Deacon, ed., *Social Policy, Social Justice, and Citizenship in Eastern Europe* (Aldershot: Avebury, 1992). See also Branko Milanovic, *Liberalization and Entrepreneurship: Dynamics of Reform in Socialism and Capitalism* (Armonk, N.Y.: M. E. Sharpe, 1989), p. 74.

13. Interview with Edmund Wnuk-Lipinski, director, Institute of Political Studies, Polish Academy of Sciences, Warsaw, September 16, 1992. Wnuk-Lipinski's conclusions about the majority of the general public's expectations from the state were confirmed by several of the author's other interviews.

14. Wnuk-Lipinski, "Freedom or Equality," p. 13.

15. Barbara Heyns and Ireneusz Bialecki, "Solidarnosc: Reluctant Vanguard or Makeshift Coalition?" *American Political Science Review*, vol. 85 (June 1991), p. 354.

16. Johnson and Kowalska, "The Transformation of Poland, 1989–91," pp. 29–31.

17. Interview with Renia Gortart, professor of political science, Warsaw University, September 11, 1992.

18. Johnson and Kowalska, "The Transformation of Poland, 1989–91," pp. 20–23.

19. Jolanta Tanas, Draft Country Report for Poland, Department for Promotion of Entrepreneurship, Ministry of Industry and Trade, Warsaw, May 1992.

20. Johnson and Kowalska, "The Transformation of Poland, 1989–91," pp. 39–40.

21. Splits occurred as early as the May 1990 municipal elections, when in Lodz, for example, the Solidarity Citizens' Committee was split between a Christian nationalist branch and a liberal-democratic one. Krzysztof Jasiewicz, "From Solidarity to Fragmentation," *Journal of Democracy*, vol. 3, (April 1992), pp. 55–69.

22. Leszek Balcerowicz, "Political Economy of Economic Reform: Poland, 1989–92," address at Institute for International Economics Conference on the Political Economy of Reform, Washington, D.C., January 14–16, 1993.

23. Interview with Renia Gortart, September 11, 1992.

24. In addition, with the return to an authoritarian regime no longer a realistic threat, another of the bonds that had held Solidarity together no longer existed. See Krzysztof Jasiewicz, "Problems of Post-communism: From Solidarity to Fragmentation," *Journal of Democracy*, vol. 3, no. 2 (April 1992).

25. Jerzy Hauzner, "Macro-social Aspects of the Development of the System of Interest Representation," in Jerzy Hauzner, ed., *System of Interest Representation in Poland 1991* (Cracow Academy of Economics, 1991).

26. Interview with Jacek Michalowski, director, Senate Research Staff, Warsaw, September 17, 1992.

27. Interview with Renia Gortart.

28. Interview with Jacek Michalowski.

29. Some observers also noted that Suchocka's rare position in Polish politics as a female head of government was an advantage, as from the beginning it distinguished her government from the two previous ones. Michalowski interview.

30. Apparently many Solidarity members did not expect that the government would actually fall when they supported the protest vote. Jane Perlez, "Polish Prime Minister to Stay Until New Elections," *New York Times*, May 30, 1993, p. 11.

31. For details, see endnote 2 of this chapter.

32. Jasiewicz, "Problems of Post-communism," p. 67.

33. An example of this was the 1988 Prices and Incomes Operation. See Branko Milanovic, "Poland's Quest for Economic Stabilisation, 1988–91: Interaction of Political Economy and Economics," *Soviet Studies*, vol. 44, no. 3 (1992), pp. 511–30.

34. Zbigniew Dresler, "The Enterprise as a Field for the Conflict of Interests in the Process of Systemic Transformation," in Hauzner, ed., *System of Interest Representation in Poland 1991*.

35. As there is no established collective bargaining mechanism in Poland, strikes very quickly involve the government directly and become politicized.

36. Three major strikes of that summer demonstrate the kinds of demands that workers were making. In the strike at the Millet factory, workers were striking to support the restructuring of their enterprises and ended on a fairly positive tone. The summer 1992 strike in the Lublin copper mine mixed genuine wage grievances with political opportunism by some of the strikes supporters, such as the radical branch of Solidarity, Solidarity 80; the former communist union OPZZ; and the KPN. Wage demands were unreasonable, and the strike focused much more on political issues than on negotiable demands. A third strike, in a car factory recently purchased by Fiat, jeopardized a $2 billion investment by Fiat—Poland's largest auto manufacturer—in a depressed area in dire need of investment. Workers demanded the same wages as Italian workers, 10 percent of the car value, and insisted on raising the retail price of the cars. Again OPZZ, Solidarity 80, and the KPN were involved. Interview with Krystyna Milewska, liaison officer, World Bank Resident Mission, Warsaw, September 24, 1992; Louisa Vinton, "Polish Government Proposes Pact on State Firms," *Radio Free Europe Radio Liberty Research Report*, vol. 1, no. 42 (October 23, 1992), pp.

10–18; and Barry Newman, "Vital Signs Point to Poland's Recovery," *Wall Street Journal*, October 22, 1992.

37. The summer of 1992 was characterized not only by opposition-supported strikes in industrial areas, but by a series of road blockades and protests against foreign competition by the farmers movement, led by an extremist politician and former local Communist party aparatchnik named Lepert and his Suma Obrona (self-protection) union. Lepert led Polish farmers, in conjunction with French and German farmers, in protests against foreign competition and against the interference of external agencies such as the World Bank.

38. Interview with J. Michalowski.

39. Eighty percent of private enterprises paid taxes in the lowest tax bracket, for example, indicating underreporting of earnings. Unpublished document prepared by Krystof Hagemeyer, advisor to Minister Kuron and professor of economics, Warsaw University; also author's interviews with Krystof Hagemeyer, Warsaw, September 14 and 23, 1992.

40. Ibid. The concept of popular capitalism or "capitalismo popular" was used to sell privatization of the pension system in Chile.

41. Interviews with Krystof Hagemeyer.

42. "Suchocka, OPZZ on Enterprise Pact' Negotiations," *FBIS*, EEU 92–183, September 21, 1992, p. 25.

43. "Center Accord Sets Conditions for Partners", *FBIS*, EEU 92–186, September 24, 1992, p. 16.

44. Vinton, "Polish Government Proposes Pact on State Firms," p. 17.

45. By the end of October, the OPZZ and other unions had declared their readiness to sign an agreement with the government on issues such as the excessive wage tax and on financial restructuring of enterprises and banks, with OPZZ requesting a government pledge to consult unions on matters vital to the interests of employees. The government accepted most OPZZ demands, as well as Solidarity demands regarding collective labor agreements. In December the National Solidarity Committee accepted the pact, conditional on the government's using the legislative fast track for implementing the conclusions reached. "Breakthrough in State Enterprise Act Negotiations," *FBIS*, EEU 92–212; "State Enterprise Pact Initialed," *FBIS*, EEU 92–220, November 2, 1992; and "Solidarity Tentatively Accepts Enterprise Pact," *FBIS*, EEU 92–235, December 7, 1992.

46. Interview with Ewa Lewicka, deputy chairman, Mazowsze Region Branch of Solidarity, Warsaw, September 22, 1992.

47. Vinton, "Polish Government Proposes Pact on State Firms," p. 18.

48. The coal strikers attempted to emulate the 1980 strategy of Solidarity. The government's plans were not without a rationale, meanwhile, as Polish coal costs much more than does coal on the world market. Stephen Engelberg, "Coal Miners in Poland Strike Over Wages and Job Threats," *New York Times*, December 14, 1992, p. A6.

49. "Poland: Try Again," *Economist*, March 27, 1993; "Polish Parliament Rejects Bill to Privatize Industries," *New York Times*, March 19, 1993; and Chris-

topher Bobinski, "Warsaw Clear to Privatise 600 Ventures," *Financial Times*, May 2, 1993.

50. Previously they employed as much as 80 percent. Interview with Irena Topinska, September 10, 1992.

51. Hagemeyer interview, September 23, 1992.

52. Ewa Guewa-Lesny, University of Warsaw, interview, Washington, D.C., November 11, 1992.

53. Interview with Edmund Wnuk-Lipinski, September 16, 1992.

54. Interview with Helena Goralska, advisor to the finance minister and Sejm deputy, Warsaw, September 22, 1992.

55. "Hungary Fights Unrest With New Social Contract," *New York Times*, November 29, 1992, p. A8.

56. Interview with Renia Gortart, September 11, 1992.

57. Interview with Jacob Michalowski, September 17, 1992.

58. "Workers in Eastern Europe know there will be difficulties. They want to help in coming up with answers. And they do not want to be the only ones bearing the costs." In late 1991, approximately one-fourth of workers in state factories were proreform, approximately one-fourth were against reform, and the rest were undecided. Melvin Croan, ed., "Is Latin America the Future of Eastern Europe?" *Problems of Communism*, May-June 1992, p. 50.

59. A survey of seventy-five state-owned enterprises in Poland found that managers were typically the inspiration and moving force behind change in the enterprises, with workers councils playing at best a facilitating role. Brian Pinto, Marek Belka, and Stefan Krajewski, "Microeconomics of Transformation in Poland: A Survey of State Enterprise Responses," World Bank Resident Mission, Warsaw, June 1992.

60. Interviews in Warsaw with Irena Topinska, Warsaw University, September 10, 1992; Jacek Kochanowicz, September 10, 1992; and Edmund Wnuk-Lipinski, September 16, 1992.

61. Richard Rose and Christian Haerpfer, *New Democracies between State and Market: A Baseline Report of Public Opinion*, Studies in Public Policy 204 (Glasgow: University of Strathclyde, Centre for the Study of Public Policy, 1992).

62. Wnuk-Lipinski, interview.

63. People would simultaneously support one-person rule and democracy; or equated industrial policy with financial bailouts of state industries. Hauzner, "Macro-social Aspects of the Development of the System of Interest Representation." The majority of Polish youth, for example, understand Western values only in the narrow sense of the consumer culture and display a great deal of apathy and passivity toward the political system and political issues in general. Piotr Glinski, "Cooperation Between NGOs and the Government in Poland," paper presented to the Regional Environmental Center for Central and Eastern Europe and Institut fur Europaische Umwelpolitik E.V., Reze, Czechoslovakia, June 1992; and Piotr Glinski, "The Youth Circles of the Polish Greens in the Eighties," Yale University Conference on Youth Culture and Political Participation," Prague, Czechoslovakia, June 26–28, 1992.

64. Interview with Marian Wisniewski, former advisor to ZUS on Reform of the Social Security System and Dean, Department of Economics, Warsaw University, September 16, 1992.

65. Interview with Patrick LaCombe, labor attaché, U.S. Embassy, Warsaw, September 18, 1992.

66. Blaine Harden, "Poles Sour on Capitalism: Walesa Accuses West of Preying on Country," *Washington Post*, February 5, 1992.

67. Interview with Ewa Lewicka, September 22, 1992.

68. This reflects a lack of trust in formal organizations that has held over from the communist years. Interview with Patrick LaCombe, September 18, 1992.]

69. Solidarity also favors and is actively involved in attempting to sponsor the development of small business in regions that have structural unemployment problems. Again, while this is good for reform, it is hardly a typical union position.

70. Interview with Patrick Lacombe.

71. Interview with Jacek Kochanowicz, September 10, 1992.

72. Rose and Haerpfer, *New Democracies between State and Market*, p. 12.

73. Opportunities for the informal activities that are a primary coping mechanism are *inversely* related to prosperity in eastern Europe; that is, the poorest economies do not generate enough resources to provide additional demand outside the regular economy. Ibid.

74. While a university professor in Warsaw can probably easily find a job even if the university is closed down, a laid-off defense worker in eastern Poland has far fewer options. In addition, Polish society has definitely been affected by more than forty years of Communist party control of the government. Foreign executives, for example, cite the difficulty of finding local personnel willing to take any kind of responsibility. Another major problem they cited was the lack of personnel with financial training. Interview with Michael Plesch, director of personnel, IBM-Poland, Warsaw, September 17, 1992.

75. The 18-24 bracket is followed by the 25-34 bracket. "Aktywnosc Ekonomiczna Ludnosci Polski Sienpien 1992" (Warszawa: GUS [Polish Central Statistical Office], 1993).

76. Only 7 percent of eastern Europeans in general are willing to move to a new town to find employment; in part this is due to the housing bottleneck (discussed below). Rose and Haerpfer, *New Democracies between State and Market*.

77. The problem is particularly acute for young people with vocational training who cannot find jobs. These conclusions are confirmed by the author's interviews with directors of several social assistance offices (discussed in detail below), who note that while most of their clientele is from the traditionally "residual" poor, they are increasingly seeing young people aged twenty to thirty-five who have either lost their jobs or cannot find employment.

78. Interview with Jacek Kochanowicz.

79. In July 1990, eligibility was reduced to those who had worked 180 days in the past twelve months, and benefits were reduced to 70 percent of the previous

wage in the first three months, 60 percent for the next six months; and 40 percent after. The minimum benefit—95 percent of the minimum wage—was the only indexed benefit. In 1991, coverage was limited to twelve months and benefits reduced slightly further. Barr, "The Social Safety Net during Economic Transition," pp. 7–8.

80. Interview with Irena Topinska.

81. In the health-care system, there is no public access to waiting lists, making it all too easy for officials to accept bribes and shift the order of the list. Interview with Katarzyna Tymowska, September 15, 1992.

82. Miroslaw Ksiezopolski, "The Labor Market in Transition and the Growth of Poverty in Poland," *Labour and Society*, vol. 16, no. 2 (1991), p. 181.

83. The benefit is 8 percent of the average monthly wage allocated per child.

84. Interview with Ewa Lewicka, September 22, 1992. Even if a targeted system were politically viable, it would require the development of an administrative capacity. As an income tax was only introduced in January 1992, there is at present no central agency that has records of individual incomes.

85. Henryk Flakierski, "Social Policies in the 1980s in Poland: A Discussion of New Approaches," in Jan Adams, ed., *Economic Reforms and Welfare Systems in the USSR, Poland, and Hungary: Social Contract in Transformation* (New York: St. Martin's Press, 1991), pp. 85–109. For the pension system, for example, it is estimated that only 20 percent of workers earn the 120 percent of the average minimum wage that would place them in a suitable privatized category to contribute to rather than the state's minimum fund under a proposed new system. Interview with Marian Wisniewski.

86. Rutkowski, "Social Expenditures in Poland," p. 9.

87. Interviews with Irena Topinska, Marian Wisniewski.

88. Katarzyna Tymowska, "Health Financing and Health Care Reform in Poland," paper presented to International Conference on Macroeconomics and Health in Countries in Greatest Need," Geneva, WHO, June 24–26, 1992, p. 6. A three-tier system was eventually introduced for particular kinds of medicines ranging from essential drugs, which remained fully subsidized, to nonessential ones, whose prices were freed. One reason the proposal was so negatively received is that people saw the price increases as a sign that the situation in general was deteriorating. Hauzner, "Macro-social Aspects of the Development of the System of Interest Representation," p. 50.

89. Interview with Brian Pinto, World Bank Resident Mission, Warsaw, September 24, 1992. "Full employment was the last and almost only advantage' of real socialism' when compared with welfare state' capitalist economies." Ksiezopolski, "The Labor Market in Transition," p. 177.

90. Interview with Edmund Wnuk-Lipinski.

91. Interview with Helena Goralska.

92. Large numbers of concentrated unemployed with no foreseeable relief can threaten political stability. Unemployment relief that still left a large percentage of the population inactive would not be sufficient. For treatment of this issue in Chile, see Carol Graham, "From Emergency Employment to Social Investment: Alleviating Poverty in Chile," *Brookings Occasional Papers*, November 1991.

93. Blanchard and others, *Reform in Eastern Europe*, p. 90.

94. In December 1970, food price increases led to social unrest and a change in government authorities. In June 1976, labor unrest at the Radom and Ursus factories caused the government to reverse food price increases and at the same time increase the prices it paid to producers, creating an unsustainable budgetary strain. See Wlodzimierz Sekula, "The Effect of the Marketisation of Food Economy on Changes in the Expenditure and Consumption," *Zywiene Czlowieka I Metabolizm*, vol. 18, no. 4 (1991), p. 344.

95. This is documented in detail in Branko Milanovic, "Poverty in Poland, 1978–88," Policy, Research and External Affairs Working Papers, WPS 637 (Washington, D.C.: The World Bank, March 1991); and Branko Milanovic, "Poverty in Poland, Hungary, and Yugoslavia in the Years of Crisis, 1978–87," Country Economics Department, WPS 507, (The World Bank, September 1990), pp. 16–17. Brunon Gorecki, unpublished paper, Warsaw University, Faculty of Economics, 1992, p. 7.

96. These findings are from the 1989 Central Statistics Office Household Budget Survey. H indicators for the households with the highest education levels were at least ten times lower than the average. Tomasz Panek and Adam Szulc, "Income Distribution and Poverty: Theory and a Case Study of Poland in the Eighties: 1980–89" (Warsaw: Research Centre for Statistical and Economic Analysis of the Central Statistical Office and Polish Academy of Sciences, 1991).

97. This conclusion is drawn from the author's interviews with several directors of social assistance offices in and around Warsaw in September 1992 and from Irena Topinksa, "The Impact of Social Transfers on Income Distribution: Poland, 1989," Socialist Economies Reform Unit, Research Paper Series 2, The World Bank, December 1991. See also Ehtisham Ahmad, "Poverty, Inequality, and Public Policy in Transition Economies," in Pierre Pestieau, ed., *Public Finance in a World of Transition*, Supplement to vol. 47 of *Finances Publiques* (The Hague, 1992), pp. 94–106.

98. In 1987 the lowest quintile held 7.60 percent of the income, while in 1990 it held 6.659 percent. The highest quintile had 36.059 percent in 1987 and 38.814 percent in 1990. Inequality is highest among farmers; for other groups the Gini coefficients are lower but of the ranges registered in most market economies. Underreporting of incomes limits the accuracy of the data, meanwhile. Gorecki, unpublished paper; and Brunon Gorecki and others, "Country Paper: Poland 1992" (Warsaw University, Department of Economics, 1993).

99. Gillian Paull, "Poverty Alleviation and Social Safety Net Schemes for Economies in Transition," International Monetary Fund Research Department Working Paper 91/14 (Washington, D.C.: IMF, February 1991). Ahmad, "Poverty, Inequality, and Public Policy in Transition Economies." Barr, "The Social Safety Net during Economic Transition." A typical example of such a town is Szczytno, in south-central Poland. The three "dinosaurs" that were the basis of the town's economy, the Unima electric factory, the Flax Factory (formerly Lenpol), and the Olsztyn Furniture Factory, have all been liquidated or are laying off workers. Smaller factories that are dependent on their demand for their products, or at least on the purchasing power of their employees, have also been hurt. The town

unemployment office is registering 200-300 unemployed a month while getting twenty offers at most. Benefits such resources for loans to help the unemployed start small businesses are virtually nil. Eugeniusz Pudlis, "Small Town Unemployment: Szczytno on the Brink," *The Warsaw Voice*, September 20, 1992, p. B4.

100. In the past, rural-urban differences may have also been exaggerated by an overestimation of rural equivalence scales. Panek and Szulc, "Income Distribution and Poverty."

101. In 1991 the government could not meet the payment levels that were required by automatic indexation. Johnson and Kowalska, "The Transformation of Poland, 1989–91," p. 59

102. Sekula, "The Effect of the Marketisation of Food Economy," pp. 248, 250.

103. This anxiety has had negative effects at the family level, for example. Cornia and Sipas, eds., *Children and the Market*. Its negative role has even been noted by some of the most enthusiastic architects of the market transition. See, for example, Andrew Berg and Jeffrey Sachs, "Poland," *Economic Policy Review*, April 1992, pp. 117–73.

104. Ewa Guewa-Lesny, University of Warsaw, Department of Economics, interview, Washington, D.C., November 11, 1992. Milanovic, "Poverty in Poland." Panek and Szulc, "Income Distribution and Poverty." Topinska, interview.

105. Embassy official, interview, September 11, 1992.

106. Paull, "Poverty Alleviation and Social Safety Net Schemes."

107. The retail price of milk was six times less than the producer price. Sekula, "The Effect of the Marketisation of Food Economy," pp. 243–44.

108. A "typical" Western male requires 2,900 calories a day at the most, and Polish levels are well above this figure. Meat consumption in Poland is at about the same level as the United States, which has one of the highest per capita meat consumptions in the world. Johns Hopkins University, School of Public and International Health, Department of Human Nutrition, October 1992; and interviews with Stanislaw Berger, director, and Barbara Kowrygo and Theresa Palaszewska-Reindl, Warsaw Agricultural University, Warsaw, Institute of Human Nutrition, September 18, 1992.

109. Interview with Berger.

110. Cash social transfers, which comprise pensions, family allowances, sickness benefits, and other social transfers such as stipends, signified a high percentage of gross national income in most eastern European countries. In 1989 this figure was 22.1 percent for Poland; 13.3 percent for Yugoslavia; 25.4 percent for Czechoslovakia; 22.4 percent for Hungary; and 21.2 percent for Bulgaria. Branko Milanovic, "Cash Social Transfers, Direct Taxes, and Income Distribution in Late Socialism," *Journal of Comparative Economics*, vol. 18, 1994, forthcoming.

111. Rutkowski, "Social Expenditures in Poland," p. 30.

112. Topinksa, interview.

113. Of the 11 percent, 6 percent was spent on unemployment, 1.5 percent on

social assistance, and the rest—92.5 percent—was spent on social insurance. Barr, "The Social Safety Net during Transition," p. 6.

114. Ibid.; interview with Topinska.

115. Rutkowski, "Social Expenditures in Poland," p. 26.

116. Ibid., p. 27; and interview with Topinska.

117. Interview with Topinska (1992).

118. Rutkowski, "Social Expenditures in Poland," p. 32. This changed with the introduction of the Social Assistance Act, and expenditures on direct assistance increased to 9 percent of social insurance expenditure in 1991. Topinska, interview.

119. Wisniewski and Tymowska, "Social Security and Health Care in Poland," p. 1.

120. Ibid., p. 6; and interview with Topinska.

121. Wisniewski and Tymowska, "Social Security and Health Care in Poland," p. 7.

122. Wisniewski and Tymowska, "Social Security and Health Care in Poland," p. 5.

123. Rukowski, "Social Expenditures in Poland."

124. Wisniewski and Tymowska, "Social Security and Health Care in Poland," pp. 8–10.

125. Interview with Krystof Hagemeyer, September 14, 1992. Wisnieski and Tymowska, "Social Security and Health Care in Poland"; Johnson and Kowalska, "The Transformation of Poland, 1989–91"; and interview with Marian Wisniewski.

126. Wisniewski and Tymowska, "Social Security and Health Care in Poland," p. 10.

127. Interviews with Topinska and Barr. Aleksandra Wiktorow and Piotr Mierzewski, "Promise or Peril? Social Policy for Children During the Transition to the Market Economy in Poland?" in Cornia and Sipas, eds., *Children and the Transition to the Market Economy.*

128. Tymowska, "Health Financing," p. 3.

129. Wisniewski and Tymowska, "Social Security and Health Care in Poland," p. 17; and interview with Tymowska.

130. Tymowska, interview. When Tymowska, an economist, first began writing about the economics of health care reform about a decade ago, she received a series of criticisms, in particular from the Communist-controlled health care journal, about the nonhumanitarian nature of an economist who worked in the social sectors!

131. Topinska interview and Barr, "The Social Safety Net during Economic Transition."

132. Topinska interview.

133. Ksiezopolski, "The Labor Market in Transition," p. 186.

134. Details on the plan have not yet been released. *Sztandar Mlodych*, no. 182, (September 1992), p. 3.

135. Memorandum of the Government of Poland on Economic Policies, Warsaw, 1993, p. 10.

136. Barr, "The Social Safety Net during Economic Transition."

137. The eleven in the order they appear in the act are: poverty, orphanhood, homelessness, need of maternal care, unemployment, physical or mental handicap, chronic illness, poor in child-rearing and domestic management, especially in single-parent or large families, alcohol or drug dependency, difficulties in adaptation to life after imprisonment, and natural or ecological disaster. "Republic of Poland: Social Welfare Act of November 29, 1990," *Dziennik Ustaw* (Journal of Law of the Republic of Poland), no. 87, entry 506 of December 17, 1990.

138. Topinska interview.

139. This conclusion is based on the author's interviews with the directors of various social assistance offices in Warsaw and its environs in September 1992.

140. Barr, "The Social Safety Net during Economic Transition."

141. Topkinska interview. Peter Diamond, "Pension Reform in a Transition Economy: Notes on Poland and Chile," paper presented to National Bureau of Economic Research Conference on Transition in Eastern Europe, Cambridge, Mass., February 26–29, 1992, p. 4.

142. Interviews with K. Tymowska and K. Hagemeyer, both of whom are advisors to the Labor Ministry.

143. Frances Millard, "The Polish Parliamentary Elections of October 1991," *Soviet Studies*, vol. 44, no. 5 (1992), pp. 837–55; and Gorecki and others, "Country Paper: Poland 1992," p. 6.

144. Memorandum of the Government of Poland on Economic Policies, Warsaw, 1993, pp. 10–11.

145. When an additional 20 percent was added to all wages to compensate for the new state income taxes that were introduced in January 1992, employers were forced to pay 45 percent contributions on a payroll that automatically increased by 20 percent. Wisniewski interview.

146. Wisniewski interview. Nowhere is there a genuine pay-as-you-go system, as political decisions are made all the time about how to deal with differences in annual rates of flows. A defined benefits system, like that in use in the United States, is related to past earnings. A defined contribution system, like Chile's, is based on past taxes. The former is better for those who will be employed by the same company for a long period of time; the latter is better for labor mobility. Diamond, "Pension Reform in a Transition Economy," p. 12.

147. Ibid., p. 11.

148. The discussion over the reform of the pension system has, until now, been dominated by those with experience with European pension systems. In mid-1991, however, the head of the ZUS, Wojiech Topinski, and one of his advisors, Marian Wisniewski, traveled to Chile to look at their privatized pension scheme. Initially ignorance about Chile—including the fact that its tradition of social service delivery is much older than Poland's—was a barrier to even considering the Chilean example, not only among Poles but also among many advisors from international agencies. Since then, however, the proposals now being considered in the government are heavily influenced by the original Topinksi and Wisniewski proposal, and previous opponents now support its hybrid models. Wisniewski interview.

149. Diamond, "Pension Reform in a Transition Economy," p. 25. Wisniewski interview. Memorandum of the Government of Poland on Economic Policies, Warsaw, 1993, p. 9.

150. Tymowska, "Health Financing and Health Care Reform in Poland," pp. 11–12.

151. Wisniewski and Tymowska, "Social Security and Health Care in Poland," p. 25.

152. Tymowska interview; and Tymowska, "Health Financing and Health Care Reform in Poland."

153. Memorandum of the Government of Poland on Economic Policies, Warsaw, 1993.

154. Irena Herbst and Andrzej Bratkowski, "The Housing Memorial," Proposal for Reform presented to the Institute of Housing Economy, September 1992.

155. Memorandum of the Government of Poland on Economic Policies, Warsaw, 1993, p. 11.

156. For a description of this process in Chile, for example, see Graham, "From Emergency Employment to Social Investment." Kwasniewski's one concrete electoral promise was to increase expenditure on pensions. This hardly bodes well for the transfer to a targeted safety net system. Broader social sector reforms, meanwhile, are likely to fall victim to the polarized political debate.

157. Tadeusz Kudlacz, "Local Governments in the System of Interest Representation," in Jerzy Hauzner, ed., *System of Interest Representation in Poland, 1991* (Cracow: Cracow Academy of Economics, 1991).

158. Abstention was also high in the 1991 parliamentary elections: 56.8 percent. Johnson and Kowalska, "The Transformation of Poland," p. 75. This level is about the same as Britain's. I would like to thank Alan Angell for pointing this out to me.

159. Remy Prud'homme, "The Rise of Local Governments in Poland," Laboratoire d'Observation de l'Economie et des Institutions Locales (L'Oeil), Institut d'Urbanisme de Paris, Université de Paris, July 1990; and Interview with Marek Borowik, delegate, Standing Conference of Local and Regional Authorities of Europe, Warsaw, September 24, 1992.

160. Prud'homme, "The Rise of Local Governments in Poland," pp. 13–14.

161. Pinto, Belka, and Krajewski, "Microeconomics of Transformation in Poland," p. 25

162. Prud'homme, "The Rise of Local Governments in Poland," p. 16; and Michael E. Bell and Joanna Regulska, "Centralization versus Decentralization: The Case of Financing Autonomous Local Governments in Poland," in Pierre Pestieau, ed., *Public Finance in a World of Transition*, supplement to vol. 47, 1992, of *Finances Publiques* (The Hague, 1992), pp. 187–201.

163. Bell and Regulska, "Centralization versus Decentralization," p. 196.

164. Interview with Jan Jakub Wyganski, Klon Foundation and consultant, American Committee for Aid to Poland, Warsaw, September 14 and 17, 1992.

165. Wisniewski and Tymowska, "Social Security and Health Care in Poland," p. 26.

166. Interview with Krystof Hagemeyer, September 14, 1992.

167. Remy Prud'homme, "Regional Development Problems and Policies in Poland" (Paris: OECD, 1992).

168. Interviews with Berger, and others, Warsaw Agriculture University, September 18, 1992; and with Krystof Hagemeyer, September 14, 1992.

169. Interview with Wlodzimierz Grudzinski, president of the board, Bank for Socio-Economic Initiatives, Warsaw, September 22, 1992.

170. Apparently there was an attempt to split Warsaw into seven autonomous gminas, each with its own administrative, telephone, and transportation systems, an attempt that had to be reversed becauase of administrative complexity. Interview with Professor Theresa Palaszewska-Reindl, dean, Faculty of Home Economics, Warsaw Agriculture University, September 18, 1992.

171. Interview with Marek Borovik, September 24, 1992.

172. Hauzner, "Macro-social Aspects of the Development of the System of Interest Representation." This is confirmed by the author's interviews with directors of social assistance offices in their description of relations with gmina authorities.

173. Interview with George Metcalf, director of Warsaw office, Gemini Project and Development Alternatives International, Warsaw, September 14, 1992. Interview with Irena Ostrowska, director of the Social Assistance Office, Ochota Gmina, Warsaw, September 16, 1992. Interview with Piotr Glinski, Polish Academy of Sciences, Institute of Sociology and Philosophy, September 17, 1992; and Glinski, conference papers, 1992.

174. A study in Silesia found that Protestant gminas had much lower abstention rates in general, and that they were more than 50 percent in favor of Mazowiecki, while Catholics tended to vote for Walesa. Interview with Renia Gortart, Department of Political Science, Warsaw University, Warsaw, September 11, 1992; and Heyns and Bialecki, "Solidarnosc: Reluctant Vanguard or Makeshift Coalition?"

175. In less developed nations, where local governments are extremely dependent on the center, local authorities often act as power brokers for central authorities in a rather clientelistic system. See for example, Arturo Valenzuela, *Political Brokers in Chile: Local Government in a Centralized Polity* (Duke University Press, 1977); and Carol Graham, "The APRA Government and the Urban Poor: The PAIT Programme in Lima's Pueblos Jovenes," *Journal of Latin American Studies*, vol. 23, part 1 (February 1991).

176. Hauzner, "Macro-social Aspects of the Development of the System of Interest Representation."

177. Interview with J. J. Wyganski, September 14, 1992.

178. For detail, see Graham, "The APRA Government and the Urban Poor," p. 64

179. Interview with Marek Borovik, September 24, 1992.

180. There are several initiatives in place to sponsor the development of gmina capacity. The Foundation for Socio-Economic Initiatives (FISE) and its sister

banking and investment organizations, BISE and TISE, are autonomous but state-supported institutions that sponsor the development of initiatives at the local government and nongovernment level. While the latter two focus on business promotion, the FISE focuses on institutional development. FISE has seventeen centers around the nation, with 12,000 clients. Another institution, the Institute of Cities, specializes in giving legal advice to gminas involved in privatization activities. The institute is also proposing a legal reform that would develop the gmina system, which does not distinguish between small and large townships (Warsaw is the same administrative unit as is a small provincial town) into a municipal system, where municipalities based around larger metropolises would then redistribute resources to smaller towns. Areas that are particularly depressed and void of resources, meanwhile, would fall under federal responsibility. Interviews with Krystof Herbst, director, FISE, Warsaw, September 14, 1992, and with Andre Lubiatov, director, Institute of Cities, and Piotr Vronsky, Institute of Cities, Warsaw, September 15, 1992.

181. Interview with Patrick LaCombe, September 18, 1992.

182. On public works in Chile, see, for example, Carol Graham, "The Politics of Protecting the Poor During Adjustment: The Experience of Bolivia's Emergency Social Fund," *World Development*, September 1992; and Graham, "The APRA Government and the Urban Poor."

183. A description of the "Generation of 88"—the workers and students that supported the May/August 1988 protests—is telling: "They were the first generation in postwar Poland who were not contaminated by Stalinism through the experiences of their parents. They were also the first generation that did not consciously experience the shock of martial law. This is probably the first mentally sane (in a social sense) postwar generation in Poland, a generation that has not experienced defeat. Glinski, "The Youth Circles," p. 1.

184. Christine M. Sadowski, "Civil Society in Poland," paper presented to Hoover Institution/AID Project on Economy, Society and Democracy, Washington, D.C., May 15, 1992, p. 6.

185. Sadowski, p. 7.

186. Glinski, "Cooperation Between NGOs and the Government in Poland," p. 4.

187. Interview with Jan Jacob Wisniewski of Fundacion Klon, Warsaw.

188. Interviews with J. J. Wyganski and Piotr Glinski.

189. Interview with Irena Topinska.

190. The PRC charges 24,000 zlotys per hour per nurse, much of which goes to its own overhead; smaller NGOs charge approximately 18,000 per hour, most of it going to the nurse. Interview with J. J. Wyganski.

191. Ibid.

192. NGOs do have a strong advantage in the provision of some services, such as those for the homeless. Ibid.

193. An exception to this was the 1990 pre-electoral period, when citizen's committees were the basis for everything from community charity to political activities. The role of these committees seems to have diminished after the "war at the top" of Solidarity.

194. For example the case of Bolivia before the Emergency Social Fund. Graham, "The Politics of Protecting the Poor during Adjustment: Bolivia's Emergency Social Fund," *World Deveopment*, vol. 20 (September 1992), pp. 1233–51.

195. Interview with Irena Ostrowska, Social Assistance Office director, Ochota, Warsaw, September 16, 1992.

196. Barr, "The Social Safety Net during Economic Transition." Income per person is defined as the combined income of all family members within households, minus alimonies paid, and then divided by the number of people in the household.

197. Ibid.; and Ostrowska interview.

Chapter 8

1. An underlying assumption of this study is that the alternative to making painful but necessary adjustments in most countries would have resulted in more severe economic crises with worse implications for the poor, and that the resource constraints that those adjustment entailed required a new approach to protecting the poor. See Francois Bourguignon, Jaime de Melo, and Christian Morrisson, "Poverty and Income Distribution During Adjustment: Issues and Evidence from the OECD Project," *World Development*, vol. 19, no. 11 (1991), pp. 1485–1508. For a detailed description of the record of a government that prolonged the implementation of such adjustments by implementing a so-called heterodox economic strategy in Peru, see Carol Graham, *Peru's APRA: Parties, Politics, and the Elusive Quest for Democracy* (Boulder: Lynne Rienner, 1992). Data on the fate of the poorest sectors during that period are found in *Ajuste y Economia Familiar: 1985–1990* (Lima: Instituto Cuanto, 1991). Another good example is the case of Zambia, which is detailed in chapter 6 of this volume.

2. A caveat, which I would like to thank Frances Stewart for noting, is that several nondemocratic regimes such as Chile and Indonesia have some of the best records at implementing pro-poor policies. This is the case if pro-poor policies are narrowly defined as providing basic services, but not if they are more broadly defined as fostering the independent capacity building initiatives that are integral to long-term poverty reduction.

3. Even in authoritarian Chile, an active and very effective public relations campaign—in support of so-called "capitalismo popular"—was used to generate public support for the privatization of the social security system, which initially was an extremely controversial policy measure but now has relatively widespread support.

4. For a detailed account, see Carol Graham, "From Emergency Employment to Social Investment: Alleviating Poverty in Chile," *Brookings Occasional Papers*, November 1991.

5. In 1987, the programs allocated 5 billion pesos or approximately $20 million in the government's total social spending budget of 274 billion pesos and employed approximately 165,000 people. The ESF, meanwhile, had approximately

$240 million for its four years of operations and on average employed approximately 3,000, or 0.3 percent of the economically active population.

6. For more detail on this case, see Carol Graham, "The Politics of Protecting the Poor During Adjustment: Bolivia's Emergency Social Fund," *World Development*, vol. 20, no. 9, 1992; or Steen Jorgensen, Margaret Grosh, and Mark Schacter, eds., *Bolivia's Answer to Poverty, Economic Crisis, and Adjustment* (The World Bank, 1992).

7. The ESF's successor, the FIS, attempted to have more direct effects on the social sector ministries by requiring all its projects to go to the ministries before approval. If the ministries delayed for more than a week, however, they forfeited their right to have input on project decisions.

8. For detailed results by district, see Graham, "The Politics of Protecting the Poor during Adjustment."

9. Tin miners were granted relatively generous one-shot severance payments when they were laid off.

10. For a detailed account of this case, see Carol Graham, "The APRA Government and the Urban Poor: The PAIT Program in Lima's Pueblos Jovenes," *Journal of Latin American Studies*, vol. 23, part 1, February 1991.

11. For detail on enrollments and election results by district, Ibid., p. 113.

12. Since Arturo Woodman replaced Luce Salgado in June 1992, there has been a notable improvement in the program's management, and the program has begun to implement projects in all regions of the country. The budget of $75 million was expected to triple for 1993.

13. From its inception in 1990 to the end of 1991, the program implemented more than 100 projects and created over 11,000 temporary jobs.

14. The proposals must go through local governments to prevent duplication and to ensure that they are in line with local government priorities. To prevent bureaucratic lag, however, the proposals are simultaneously sent directly to the MPU. Thus, if a viable proposal seems to be unfairly held up or denied in the local government, the MPU is able to follow up on it.

15. The detailed version of this case is Carol Graham, "The Political Economy of Safety Nets During Market Transitions: The Case of Poland," Transition and Macro-Adjustment Unit, Country Economics Department, Research Paper 3 (Washington, D.C.: The World Bank, January 1993).

16. Edmund Wnuk-Lipinski, "Freedom or Equality: An Old Dilemma in a New Context," in Bob Deacon, ed., *Social Policy, Social Justice, and Citizenship in Eastern Europe* (Aldershot: Avebury, 1992).

17. This point has been raised by Joan Nelson in "Poverty, Equity, and the Politics of Adjustment," in Stephan Haggard and Robert R. Kaufman, *The Politics of Economic Adjustment* (Princeton: Princeton University Press, 1992); and by Stephan Haggard in "Markets, Poverty, Alleviation, and Income Distribution: An Assessment of Neoliberal Claims," *Ethics and International Affairs*, vol. 5, 1991.

18. Julio Moguel, "National Solidarity Program Fails to Help the Very Poor," *Voices of Mexico*, no.15 (October-December 1990), pp. 24–28.

19. For detail see Graham, "The Politics of Protecting the Poor during Adjustment."

20. Graham, "From Emergency Employment to Social Investment."

21. This raises a question that faces all policymakers attempting to reduce poverty: whether it is better to lift the largest possible number of people at the margin of the poverty line above it, using a straight head-count measure of poverty, or to focus efforts on improving the lot of the poorest, even if the number of people below the poverty line remains the same. Amartya Sen made a major contribution to the measurement of poverty by combining the head-count ratio with the average income shortfall of the poor and the measure of inequality among them (Gini coefficient). Sen's theory and its implications for anti-poverty policy are discussed in Francois Bourguignon and Gary S. Fields, "Poverty Measures and Anti-Poverty Policy," Delta Working Papers 90–04, February 1990.

22. In Mexico, the new establishment of Sedesol as an umbrella institution for Pronasol seems an attempt to provide the program with formalized links and to ensure its continuation after the departure of Salinas. Bulletin of the Instituto Nacional de Solidaridad, June 1992; and lecture by Marco Antonio Bernal Gutierrez, President, Instituto Nacional de Solidaridad, at Johns Hopkins University School of Advanced International Studies, Washington, D.C., October 15, 1992.

23. This point was noted by Stephan Haggard at a conference on "The Political Economy of Policy Reform," Institute for International Economics, Washington, D.C., January 11–13, 1993, now published in John Williamson, ed., *The Political Economy of Policy Reform* (Washington, D.C.: Institute for International Economics, 1994), pp. 467–71.

24. Nelson, "Poverty, Equity, and the Politics of Adjustment."

25. Ibid.

26. I would like to thank Frances Stewart for raising this point.

27. Frances Stewart, "Supporting Productive Employment Among Vulnerable Groups," in Giovanni Andrea Cornia, Richard Jolly, and Frances Stewart, *Adjustment with a Human Face* (Oxford: UNICEF/Clarendon Press, 1987), particularly pp. 197–201.

28. This point has been raised by Margaret E. Grosh in "What Should Social Funds Finance? Portfolio Mix, Targeting, and Efficiency Criteria," LATHR Working Paper 3, Human Resources Division, Latin America and Caribbean, The World Bank, December 1990.

Appendix

1. Public works employment programs were also used in Britain during the recession of the 1970s and early 1980s. For detail on these, see "Los Programas Especiales de Empleo en Gran Bretaña," PREALC, Documento de Trabajo 242 (Santiago, May 1984).

2. Steven Greenhouse, "Lessons Across Six Decades as Clinton Tries to Make Jobs," *New York Times*, November 24, 1992, pp. A1, A12.

3. For detail on these programs, see E. Jay Howensteine, "Public Works Programs After world War I," *Journal of Political Economy*, December 1943, pp.

523–37; Harold Ickes, "Public Works in the United States of America," *International Labour Review*, vol. 35 (June 1937), pp. 775–802; and Collis Stocking, "Public Employment Service: Functions and Operations," *Monthly Labor Review*, June 1948.

4. Greenhouse, "Lessons Across Six Decades." Under the Carter Administration, the Comprehensive Employment and Training Act (CETA), a federal jobs program created in 1973, was doubled to cover 725,000 people. This program, unlike the WPA, was directly targeted at the hard-core unemployed. The experience of the CETA showed that public service programs were more effective than public works spending to provide jobs for the unskilled unemployed. Yet the programs were also criticized for fraudulent and inefficient administration, as well as for contributing to the overheating and double-digit inflation of the late 1970s.

5. Thomas M. Callaghy, "Lost Between State and Market: The Politics of Economic Adjustment in Ghana, Zambia, and Nigeria," in Joan M. Nelson, ed., *Economic Crisis and Policy Choice: The Politics of Adjustment in the Third World* (Princeton University Press, 1990), p. 274.

6. This poverty line, based on the Living Standards Measurement Survey (LSMS) conducted by the World Bank in 1987–88, uses a poverty line of per capita consumption of less than two-thirds the average. It is relevant to note that the percentage of income spent on food was not that different for the poor (69.1 percent) and the nonpoor (66.1 percent). This may be due to the extreme nature of poverty: the phenomenon where the Engel curve has an inverse U-shape, and for the poor households the percentage share spent on food would actually increase with a growth in income. The nonpoor, meanwhile, can hardly be well off if they are spending more than 60 percent of their incomes on food. Poverty incidences in rural areas were eleven times greater than in the capital, Accra. E. Oti Boateng and others, "A Poverty Profile for Ghana, 1987–1988," *Journal of African Economies*, vol. 1, no. 1 (March 1992).

7. Jeffrey Herbst, "Economic Crisis and Reform in Ghana," unpublished paper, Washington, D.C., 1991, p. 147.

8. Republic of Ghana, Ghana: Programme of Actions to Mitigate the Social Costs of Adjustment" (Accra, November 1987), particularly pp. 11–19.

9. Herbst, p. 157.

10. "PAMSCAD Donor Review Mission Draft Report," The World Bank, Washington, D.C., 1991, p. 7.

11. For detail on Pronasol, see Carol Graham, "Mexico's Solidarity Program in Comparative Context: Demand-Based Poverty Alleviation Programs in Latin America, Africa, and Eastern Europe," in Wayne A. Cornelius, Ann L. Craig, and Jonathan Fox, eds., *Transforming State-Society Relations in Mexico: The National Solidarity Strategy* (University of California Press, 1994), pp. 309–27; and Denise Dresser, *Neopopulist Solutions to Neoliberal Problems: Mexico's National Solidarity Program*, Issue Brief No. 3, University of California at San Diego, Center for U.S.-Mexican Studies, 1991.

12. It is somewhat difficult to quantify Pronasol's budget accurately, as some money may have been diverted from what would previously have been social

sector spending. Dresser, *Neopopulist Solutions to Neoliberal Problems*, p. 5; and Tim Golden, "Mexico's Leader Cautiously Backs Some Big Changes," *New York Times*, November 2, 1992, p. A3.

13. Administrative costs were approximately 5 percent of the total in the case of the ESF.

14. The framework for the Pronasol program is detailed in his Ph.D. dissertation. For detail, see George Grayson, "Mexico's New Politics: Building Sewers, Reaping Votes," *Commonweal*, October 25, 1992, pp. 612–14.

15. Dresser, *Neopopulist Solutions to Neoliberal Problems*, p. 15. Community labor and programs to encourage children to go to school have been implemented in Mexico for decades, meanwhile. This is noted in Alan Knight, "Solidarity: Historical Continuities and Contemporary Implications," paper presented to Conference on Mexico's National Solidarity Program: A Preliminary Assessment, University of California at San Diego, February 1992.

16. Dresser, *Neopopulist Solutions to Neoliberal Problems*.

17. Ibid.

18. For detail on these relations, see Jonathan Fox, "The Difficult Transition from Clientelism to Citizenship, Lessons from Mexico," paper presented to UCSD workshop on "Mexico's Solidarity Program: A Preliminary Assessment," February 1992; and Ann Craig, "Solidarity: Deconstructing Discourse and Practice in the Politics of Concertation" (paper presented to UCSD Workshop, February 1992).

19. A case in point is the withholding of benefits from the tortivales program from forty-eight Mexico City municipalities where the opposition was particularly active. Dresser, *Neopopulist Solutions to Neoliberal Problems*. For detail see Fox, "The Difficult Transition"; and Ann Craig, "Solidarity."

20. Dresser, *Neopopulist Solutions to Neoliberal Problems*, p. 26.

21. For detail, Ibid.

22. For detail on the political situation and on the peace talks, see Terry Lynn Karl, "El Salvador's Negotiated Revolution," *Foreign Affairs*, vol. 71 (Spring 1992), pp. 147–64; and Enrique Baylora, "Salvaging El Salvador," *Journal of Democracy*, vol. 3 (April 1992), pp. 70–80.

23. Presentation by FIS Directorate, December 7, 1992.

24. Ibid.; "FIS: Memoria de Labores," Gobierno de El Salvador, San Salvador, 1992; and "Reporte de Avance 14 Del Programa del Fondo de Inversion Social de El Salvador, Agosto 1992.

25. In December 1992, the exchange rate was $1 = 8.91 colones.

26. For detail, see George K. Danns, *Dimensions of Social Welfare and Social Policy in Guyana* (Georgetown: University of Guyana, 1990).

27. "Guyana: Social Amelioration Programme," IDB-SIMAP Mission, Consultants' Report, January 1990, as discussed in internal InterAmerican Development Bank memorandum on Guyana, July 16, 1990.

28. Ibid. SIMAP staff actually traveled to Bolivia to visit the ESF in September 1989.

Index

371